Willy B.

Dedication

To Maude Nelson, Lizzie Murphy, Jackie Mitchell, Rose Gacioch, Edith Houghton, Babe Didrikson Zaharias, Toni Stone, Connie Morgan, Mamie "Peanut" Johnson, Ila Borders, and Justine Seigel.

Epigraph

"Nobody understands how hard it is to win and how much it hurts to lose." – Tony LaRussa.

Acknowledgments

Thanks to Denise, Leigh, Chris, and Casey, who braided Willy's pigtails before every game and told her to sing "The Star Spangled Banner" out loud at the World Series.

Willy B. Superstar:
Willy's Ballgame Continues
By Dennis N. Ricci

"I Can't Help Myself (Sugar Pie, Honey Bunch)" – Music and lyrics by Brian Holland, Lamont Dozier, and Eddie Holland, 1965.
"The Harder They Come" – Music and lyrics by Jimmy Cliff, 1972.
"Respect" – Music and lyrics by Otis Redding, 1965.

WILLY B. SUPERSTAR
Copyright © 2011 Dennis N. Ricci.
All rights reserved.

ISBN-13: 978-1535262545
ISBN-10: 1535262540

PROLOGUE

THERE'S NEVER BEEN A PITCHER LIKE WILLY BEAL BEFORE
By Samantha Khoury, Staff Writer
Sportsworld

There's never been a pitcher like Willy Beal before! This reporter arranged to meet Willy at her condo after the Alexandria Dukes' game with the Johnstown Flood. At this writing, Willy is the top pitcher in the Class AA Mid-Atlantic League with a 7-0 won-lost record and 0.86 ERA. The female ballplayer wore ragged denim jeans, beat-up sneakers with two differently colored socks on each foot, a long-sleeved men's white shirt unbuttoned over a powder blue tank-top, and matching headband, wristbands, and nail polish. Willy was quiet, still, and serene, barely moving a muscle, except for her mouth to speak. Soft and controlled, Willy spoke with studied composure.

WILLY BEAL: "I don't think it should be all that surprising if the first woman in the majors is a pitcher. I always thought of pitching as being kind of a *female* role in the game...Baseball is the only sport where the *defense* holds the ball. Pitching is such an active, aggressive form of defense that it seems like an offensive position, but it's still defensive. The pitcher carries the *seed* of the game in her hands." Willy cupped her hands as if holding a ball. "She brings forth the seed and *delivers* it into play." She extended her hands outward, before slowly drawing them back to her breast. "All *life* in the game stems from the pitcher's hand. The *fruit* of the game comes from the pitcher delivering her pitch and she *bears* the burden of winning or losing the game." Willy's fluid gesturing of arms and hands seemed as if she were performing an interpretive dance. "But, then again," Willy continued, "if you look at the pitcher-catcher relationship, it's the pitcher who plays the *masculine* role. The catcher is the *feminine* receptacle, superficially passive, openly waiting to *receive* the seed from the pitcher, but also the one who *protects* the pitcher, *nurtures* the pitcher, and stays at *home* to guard it by laying down her own body." Willy paused and smiled, her brown eyes open wide and sparkling as she said, "And they do it face to face!"

We came to the interview expecting to find a gum-chewing, fast-talking, slow-witted jockette and instead she elaborates psychosexual masculine-feminine metaphors about baseball. Willy easily shifted gears into Near Eastern and East Asian philosophy and mysticism.

WILLY BEAL: "I got into Buddhism, Zen mostly, and Taoism and Hinduism through yoga and meditation, which are part of my mental and physical regimen, just like aerobics and running a few miles. Buddhism is as much of a discipline and a philosophy as a theology."

SPORTSWORLD: "Aren't there many different branches of Buddhism and can't you combine elements of Buddhism with other religions?"

WILLY BEAL: "Of course, as the Dalai Lama says: 'Whatever you believe, believe it.'...I went on a retreat one summer. Buddha camp! But I found it took a level of devotion and self-denial I wasn't ready for."

When this reporter first introduced herself to Willy, she jabbered in double negatives and disjointed Stengelese syntax with her pals on the Dukes. Once our interview began, however, she articulated only carefully constructed phrases. *Who is the real Willy Beal?*

WILLY BEAL: "I think there are lots of fans who'll get a kick out of it if I get to play in the big leagues one day...Almost everybody has played baseball or softball and anybody who ever played ball has dreamed about playing in the majors. I'm somebody who wasn't supposed to make it. I'm just like most people and they're just like me!"

SPORTSWORLD: "Many of the players who've seen you in action never expected to see a woman ballplayer with so much physical strength, athleticism, and determination."

WILLY BEAL: "I see women like that every day...And not only athletes. In the supermarket, shopping at the discount stores, getting on the bus to go to work, and picking up their kids from school or daycare. We've raised a whole generation of smart girls and strong girls. Here we are!"

Willy's baseball pedigree comes from her grandfather, Rube Henry, a pitcher whose pro baseball career spanned over 30 years, playing with such all-time greats as Satchel Paige, Josh Gibson, Cool Papa Bell, Ted Williams, and Joe DiMaggio. Willy started playing tee-ball at age three and threw her first pitch at five. "Papp called it a ball," Willy recalled laughing. "He was a tough task-master." For the first 25 years of Willy's life Rube Henry was her teacher, coach, and biggest fan.

Less than a year ago, Willy was twenty-seven years old, living with her mother, and working part-time as an assistant track and softball coach. Her grandfather, Rube Henry, a former Negro Leaguer and Major Leaguer, had passed away two years earlier. An old friend of the family, Peter Jones calls to invite himself for a visit. Jones, himself the son of a pro ball player, is a veteran big leaguer, looking forward to making the transition from star player to manager. Willy throws batting practice to Jones in a schoolyard and confirms his expectation that her skills were as sharp as any big league pitcher he had ever faced, after which Jones invites Willy to join his winter league team in Venezuela.

Willy takes a leap of faith to go play ball for three months in Venezuela. Willy joins Peter and meets their winter league teammates on las Medias Blancas de Maracay, including other big leaguers, Mercurio Mercado, Memo Alvarez, Billy Velasco, and several young prospects from the Buffalo Wolves.

In her first pro game, Willy hurls a two-hitter and subsequently pitches three consecutive shutouts. After the winter season concludes, Maracay wins the league championship and Willy's 6-1 record earns her Pitcher of the Year honors. In the Caribbean Series, Willy pitches two games in three days and, despite a no-decision and a loss, attracts the attention of the fans, media, and scouts. With the stroke of a pen, Willy's right arm becomes the property of the New York Diamonds.

Willy joined the New York Diamonds at spring training in Florida. Willy meets the owner, manager Tom Vallery, and key players, especially second baseman Cal Bonham, pitcher Gil Douglas, pitcher Sandy Lee Danielson, outfielders Roy Burton and Andy Gilbert, shortstop Demeter Fortune, and pitcher Bruce ("Jake") Jacobson. Willy met reliever Steve ("Zinger") Filsinger and catcher Paul Cello, with whom Willy says she has become the closest of friends. In spring training camp, Willy comes under the tutelage of Rudy Judd, pitching coach, and Lew Shankleton, minor league pitching instructor, both of whom graded her as the best pitching prospect in the organization.

    Willy Mae Beal's first language–her mother tongue–is baseball. Its jargon comes naturally to her and she easily applies its truisms to the world at large. Willy is a tireless practitioner and student of the science of pitching. Even if this intelligent and flamboyant player fails to become Big League Baseball's first show girl, Willy Beal is special.

CHAPTER 1

At the midtown Manhattan corporate headquarters of the New York Diamonds, Tom Vallery peered at the washroom mirror, carefully checked his grey-speckled black curls, adjusted his wire-rimmed glasses, which never appeared before the cameras in the dugout or clubhouse, and inspected three tiny gashes caused by hastily shaving before breakfast rather than in the evening prior to going to work. Gathered with Sebastian Fabian in the posh conference room were the general manager, assistant general manager for player development, vice-president of player personnel, and minions from the advertising, promotions, media relations, and public relations departments, a strange combination of people to bring together to discuss a roster move. The manager pulled up a chair next to Harvey Wanamaker, the boss of the team's front office. Information packets were spread out on the table containing scouting reports, stat sheets, and photographs of Willy Beal. There also were reprints of Samantha Khoury's *Sportsworld* article.

"She's the next America's sweetheart?" guffawed the director of public relations. "She doesn't exactly make a fashion statement. Look at this...old tee shirt, tattered blue jeans, no- name brand sneakers, goofy hat."

"Let me see," said Kristin Tracy, vice-president of player personnel, as she thumbed through the glossies. "What are you talking about? She's adorable. Those big, beautiful eyes! That smile!"

"I thought she'd look more butch," said the Assistant GM, Alan Blaylock.

"She's a fruitcake, too," said the GM, Harvey Wanamaker.

"She hotdogs it on the field and the fans eat it up," said an ad man

"Did anyone see that news conference? She's a wise-cracker." said a promo man.

"Oh, you guys are wrong!" Kristin declared. "She's not a clown. The players say she's very sweet, not full of herself either."

Tom Vallery nodded seriously, "She's a little bit of a flake, but she's no dummy."

"Tom and Kristin are right," the owner told the others. "She has talent, brains, looks, and personality with a capital *P*. The showtime factor! She really could be America's new sweetheart. There are dollar signs in those sweet brown eyes. Megabucks!"

"If she can cut it," Tom said softly.

"Take a look at the numbers, Tom," said Fabian. "She blew the socks off the Mid-Atlantic, the top Double-A league."

Willy Beal's statistics with the Alexandria Dukes read: 7 games pitched, 63 innings pitched, 7 wins, 0 losses, 33 hits allowed, 6 runs allowed, 6 earned runs, 35 strikeouts, 13 bases on balls, 7 complete games, 2 shutouts, 0.86 earned run average, .149 opposition batting average.

"I thought we had a program of player development." Tom looked to Alan and Kristin, *the brains* in the room, before returning his attention to the owner, *the power*.

"Tom," thus spoke Fabian. "I'm not a stat wizard like you, but I do know big league teams routinely promote pitchers with won-lost records *under* .500 and

ERAs *over* 4.00. Her numbers aren't merely good, they're *huge*!"

"Why can't we move her up to Triple-A?" suggested Tom. "This is a big step. Give the kid a break. Give *me* a break."

"Will we have to screw up the starting rotation every twenty-eight days?" joked Harvey.

"Oh, please," Kristin groaned in disgust.

"Will she go on the DL for PMS or something?" the promo man speculated.

The ad man chimed in: "I heard she only wears a bra when she's on the ballfield."

"When she showed up on the first day of spring training, she said hello to the guys in the locker room, started peeling off her clothes and kept right on talking...buck naked!" informed the GM.

"You...are...an asshole!" Kristin hissed bitterly.

Harvey smiled smugly at Kristin and said, "Relax, I'm just joking." They glared at one another.

"I'm still not sure she's ready," Tom said to Fabian.

"The numbers are there, Tom," interrupted Alan, the youngest exec at the table. "You know as well as I do that the big gap between the majors and minors is for *hitters*. After seeing maybe one or two quality pitchers in a league, they come up to face three or four guys like that on every team. Hitters sink or swim. Pitchers stay level and float. Willy Beal is one of those quality pitchers, isn't she? You said yourself she has the tools."

"What I need is a lefty. Harvey, help me out here," said Tom.

"What you need is a starter, lefty *or* righty," Harvey replied. "You can't keep using Filsinger as a stopgap."

"True, I need him back in the pen. Brooks and Langevin will burn out by August unless Zinger can get back to middle relief," Tom told the GM, the man who tried to release Steve Filsinger at the close of the last campaign.

"You've used eleven different starting pitchers," Harvey continued. "We've called up and sent back seven Triple-A pitchers and we're only six weeks into the season."

"Tell me about it!" laughed Tom. "But Rudy and I want to see our pitchers excel at every level before we..."

"Tom," said Fabian as he leaned forward with hands folded on the tabletop. "I think Willy Beal can be an impact player."

Bingo! The man said the magic words: "impact player." *Discussion over! Not if, but when*, thought Tom.

"How soon?" the manager inquired.

"Harvey, get the paperwork going and call Alexandria. Kristin, I want you to make yourself available to Willy for whatever she needs. She might feel more comfortable dealing
with another woman."

She gave Fabian a two-finger salute without looking up while she read Sam's piece and exclaimed, "Did you guys read what she said about male and female roles of pitchers and catchers and the feminine nature of pitching?"

"The writer dreamed that stuff up," Harvey said dismissively. Then, to Tom's consternation, the owner and the general manager began to discuss the Diamonds' pitching rotation. "We have the USTV game of the week on Saturday and we'll be on Sportsnet Monday and Thursday," said the GM.

"We could start her this Monday and next Saturday, but we'll miss out on the network game," suggested Fabian. "So, it'll have to be Saturday and Thursday."

"I'd want her to go tomorrow or the next night against Philly," protested Tom. "Otherwise, I'll have to bump Jacobson or Danielson!"

"You can handle those two prima donnas," said Fabian, frowning thinly.

Tom Vallery fumed. For three years, the owner had lain down the ground rules and collected the playing pieces while Tom ran the ballclub with unqualified support from the top and unquestioned authority from his players. *Willy Beal arrives and Fabian now decides who pitches when!*

"As far as the lifestyle of the soon-to-be-rich-and-famous is concerned," said Alan Blaylock, "the private investigator's report shows a female athlete who cusses like a sailor, loves music and books, and lives like a monk...or, should I say, a nun?" Such reports were routine. There were indeed behaviors and vices that wouldn't be tolerated on America's Home Team, but some sins were worse than others and being an impact player cured almost all ills.

"We did some surveys and publicity in Alexandria," said the PR man. "Kids love her, women love her, and there are lots of men who think strong, athletic women are sexy as hell." Fabian, animated with enthusiasm, said, "It's a known advertising paradigm that men like to look at an attractive woman and *women* like to look at an attractive woman."

"Is that what this is all about?" asked Big League Baseball's highest paid manager.

"Baseball is show biz," responded the owner, "but she's the best pitching prospect to come out of the farm system since Danielson and Douglas."

"I'm not questioning her ability," Tom grumbled. "But only seven games in pro ball!"

The owner again addressed his manager with close scrutiny, "If she gets bombed, pull her out. If she flops, we'll send her back to the minors, but, if she clicks, you'll have the fourth starter you need to break the pennant race wide open." Fabian then cupped his folded hands behind his head and settled back in his soft, brown leather chair. "This isn't what I originally had planned for her, but she could be the biggest thing to hit the Big Apple since Broadway Joe, the Louisville Lip, or..." He got up from the table and walked past the framed, portrait-sized blowup of Colonel Jacob Ruppert and the Great Bambino on opening day in 1923. He dramatically pointed at the photograph. "She might be the biggest drawing card since the Big Guy himself."

However, as the VP of player personnel whispered to the assistant general manager, "None of the names he mentioned turned out to be easily manipulated or controlled by their promoters." Kristin Tracy suspected that neither was Willy Beal inclined to be anybody's puppet.

Willy Beal would be the most glittering jewel in the Diamonds' crown, a workhorse on the mound and a

show horse for the media. The first woman in the big leagues could even
become the best pitcher in baseball, but, for Fabian no less than Tom Vallery, the bottom line was that the Diamonds better be in first place by the Fourth of July and in the Series come October.

Tuesday morning, Willy buzzed around her condo in Alexandria trying to sort out what to pack up and bring to New York from that which could be shipped later. She looked in the mirror and wrinkled her nose, then flipped on the TV to watch *Wake Up, America!* and looked in a mirror. Her Alexandria Dukes publicity photo, with the "A" on the cap airbrushed out, was projected in the background as the morning news and fluff show's host babbled.

"If you're the sort of person who likes things to stay the same or wishes the world would return to the way it used to be in some idyllic time past, then go back to bed, pull the covers over your head, and forget about baseball...because, this morning, the New York Diamonds announced that pitcher Willy Beal is being called up from their Alexandria farm team to become the first woman in baseball history on a big league roster."

The female co-host bubbled forth a cliché: *"We've come a long way, baby."*

Then Willy heard her hunky male partner say, *"We hope to have a live telephone interview with Willy Beal, but we've been unable to reach her so far this morning."*

"What?" she puzzled, then remembered she forgot to recharge her cell phone before hitting the sack the night before. "Oh, shoot!" she cried as she picked the unused land-line phone off the floor, reinserted the modular plug, and dialed 1-212-555-1212.

"*What city please!*"

"The number for USTV in New York, the network, the studio..."

"*Thank you for calling UST&T! The number is...*"

Willy happily answered their simplistic "softball" questions and got a charge out of hearing her own voice echoing through the TV's speaker. She reached the Meadowlands at half past four after dropping off all her baggage except for a duffle bag and her carry-all at the Sheridan in Bergen Township. This afternoon in the middle of May was the hottest day of the year. The temperature read 93 degrees in northern New Jersey. "Add ten degrees in the city," said the cab driver, meaning Manhattan. Willy was damp and sweaty under her tee shirt, holey jeans, and floppy hat. Her braided 'do was falling out as she entered the stadium's service gate. A blubbery-lipped security guard barred her path.

"I'm Willy," she said with a giggle and a jaunty step.

"You're the fifth girl today that said she was you. One of 'em looked like a boy!" he responded, holding out his hand, rubbing his thumb against two fingers. "Let's see some ID, ma'am."

As Willy pawed through her carry-all to find her chunky leather wallet, she heard someone singing, "Wil-lay, Wil-lay, Wil-lay! Willy's goin' to the show. New York Diamonds!
Yessir, Willy's in the money now. Wil-lay, Wil-lay, Wil-lay!" She turned to see a street person clad in a beret,

plaid jacket, frayed slacks, and battered shoes. He was clapping and smiling behind wrap-around sun shades, carrying an open bottle of cheap wine. He continued to sing, "Wil-lay, Wil-lay, Wil-lay!" The security guard grunted after inspecting her Florida driver's license and watched her fumble to gather up her belongings.

"Never thought I'd see the day," he sighed.

Willy looked up at him, flashed the smile that already had been selected to grace next week's cover of *Sportsworld*, and said, "Me neither!"

She found Shelly Kravitz, the equipment manager, in the clubhouse, who presented her with a blue and gold cap, blue team blazer, white pinstriped home uniform, bluish pinstriped holiday uniform, grey road flannels, brand new and shiny black cleats, and two sets of socks and stirrups. She unfolded the home jersey and drank in the sight of BEAL 28 inscribed on the back. She gave Shelly a grateful hug and hustled to the locker room.

Paul Cello was on his way to the stadium to work with his not-ready-for-prime-time backup, a kid nicknamed Pigpen, who would learn to be a catcher from the master. His *sensei* was to teach him how to call a game, handle the pitchers, and handle their pitches, not to mention the birds and the bees, basic civility, and personal hygiene. Paul flipped on the radio in his vintage '65 pony car, a cherry red classic. The talk show star's voice rang out: *"Fabe's at it again. What's with the owners in this town anyway? A girl? Let's get real, please!"* Paul stabbed the channel selector with his middle finger. "Sit on this, asshole!" The catcher moved from left to right on the AM spectrum and found the shock jock's drive time competitor blowing full-tilt on the same subject. *"What's next? An all-girls team— the Colorado Rockettes? An all-gay team–the Staten Island Fairies?"* This time Paul punched out the radio with his fist. "Screw 'em all! You'll show 'em, Willy. We'll show 'em!"

Upon Willy's arrival in New York, all was not sublime for the team that Sebastian built. The Diamonds were in third place behind Atlanta and Florida with a record of 22-18, only a half game ahead of fourth-place Philadelphia. The theme among the Big Town's sports columnists was to put the blame on the ace pitcher, Bruce Jacobson. Dale Goodwyn wrote in the *Daily Mail*: "The man with the golden arm is headed for 20 losses instead of 20 wins. At $5 million in pay, Jake is a one-armed bandit making off with $250,000 for each loss, if my method of calculation suits your fancy." While the batting averages of Fortune and Bonham were respectively converging on the .300 mark, Burton was leading the league in homers, runs batted in, total bases, and slugging percentage. Gilbert was right on Roy's heels in run production, but also led the league in strikeouts, and Demeter Fortune, who had never fanned more than thirty times in any season, already had twenty-four strikeouts, almost all coming on called third strikes. Yet, Demmy was faring much better than Jake with the fans and wags. In fact, his two simultaneous streaks were the talk of the town: he had hit safely in 21 straight games and fielded errorlessly at shortstop for 40. In another week, he would be halfway to the record streaks of DiMaggio and Ripken. *Stay tuned, folks!*

Apart from Cal Bonham's courting of Demmy, neither Jacobson nor Fortune had done much of a job of winning friends in the clubhouse or press room. Perhaps not surprisingly, the two narcissuperstars–a genus of homo athleticus identified by Brad Lucas of the *Journal*–openly disliked each other as well. Behind the scenes, Fabian was being bad-mouthed by the "weak sisters" and "have-nots" as well as the win-or-lose moneymakers in Big League Baseball. Fabian's team had ruffled the feathers of his fellow roosting owners with the contract deals given Jake and Demmy, which raised the bar for bargaining with everyone else's players, making a mockery of the luxury tax on payroll and the top-secret salary cap.

After Monday's night game, Samantha Khoury dragged Brad Lucas up to one of the hot food bistros in the Meadowlands sports complex. He wanted to go to the Stage Door Deli in
Manhattan to exchange insulting remarks with the servers, but she was too hungry to tolerate the driving time. "So, how come Fabian turns out to be the one to bring a woman to the majors?" Sam asked Brad. "He's no liberal. That's for sure."

Brad carefully pointed the ketchup dispenser at his plateful of fries and squeezed. Sam watched him rub the tip over the crest of the piled slices of potato and deposit the thick, red sauce over them. He pronged his fork into the pile, but brought his mouth all the way down to the dish to snatch the first mouthful of hot and steamy delight. "All Fabian wanted to do was find out if she could really pitch, give her a year of seasoning in the minors, and bring her up for a one-game media event at the end of the season," Brad said, deftly chewing and breathing between phrases.

"Like Charley Finley did with Satchel Paige and Ted Turner with Jim Bouton?"

"Exactly," he said, slurping his ginger ale, sucking in an ice cube, swirling it inside his mouth, and then shooting it back into the glass. "Especially if the D's were out of the pennant race in September, he'd need a diversion to pacify the angry multitude."

"Bread and circuses!" she said, lifting her tuna melt on whole wheat toast. She closed her eyes and touched her tongue to a tiny droplet of mayo oozing from a corner. She licked it gently with a little hum in her throat and opened her eyes to meet Brad's. He smiled as she pressed the sandwich between her fingers and rolled her tongue along the edges of the bread, turning at each corner, smearing tuna, cheese, and white mayonnaise on her lips.

"But," said Brad, gently touching the red slice of tomato after lifting the top of the bun from his burger. "Right off the bat in spring training, Vallery, Judd, and Shankleton let the big boss know she was a lot better than they thought she'd be. That changed the whole picture," he said, placing his finger beneath the leaf of lettuce shrouding the moist, warm juicy piece of beef awaiting his passion. He quickly reassembled the burger and bun, hoisted it to his mouth, and tore his teeth into it with a vengeance.

"She was white hot in Alexandria," said Sam, her eyes sparkling as she watched Brad push deeper and deeper into the flame-broiled slab of meat. "And Jake and Filsinger haven't
been getting the job done up here," she added, never breaking her gaze upon Brad's sensuous feeding.

"Willy and Fabian are made for each other," he declared after swallowing, wiping his mouth, and catching his wind. "It's like Colonel Ruppert and the

Babe, or, maybe, Colonel Tom Parker and the King. Ha! Except, I think Ms. Willy is smarter than either one of those boys were. She's created her persona and she knows exactly what she's doing. She's written the script. Let's see how it plays."

Sam took three little nips at her sandwich, and then cast her eye on the long slice of kosher dill resting on her plate. Her tongue rolling suggestively, Sam made sure Brad was watching as she scooped the pickle and raised it to her lips. Before snapping the first crunch, she licked it up and down, twirled it in her mouth, glided the edges of her front teeth ever so lightly over it, and sucked its rich salty taste. "She's physically mature, but..." Sam said of Willy. "She might even be the prototypical superwoman of the twenty-first century...yoga, aerobics, and baseball! I'm wondering about her sexual maturity, though."

"You see virginal innocence? The message that I'm getting is *sexual intimidation*. Strikeouts are *ritual castration*. Very large athletic men are scared shitless of her," laughed Brad, still observing Sam's mouth caressing the pickle.

"She's celibate from what I can gather. I guess I'm focused on Willy the woman more than Willy the player," said Sam. The pickled dill was spent but for the stem dangling limply from its gnawed stump. "I think she's very shy and vulnerable. She's awfully bright, though."

"Oh, come on, Sam!" taunted Brad. "She's a bloody genius. A clever, calculating, manipulative...She's got her act together and she's ready to play it to the hilt, couched in that smiley face with pigtails routine," he said.

"Oh, you're so wrong about her," shouted Sam, noticing the sweat glistening on Brad's forehead, herself feeling wetness in the nooks and crannies beneath her clothing. "You mind if I have one?" said Sam, laying her finger alongside Brad's little dish of fries and raising her brow in query.

"I suppose you understand her better than I because she's a woman," Brad said as he pinched a french fry between his fingers and held it for Sam to bite.

"A little, maybe," she told him, holding out her tongue. He placed the soggy but still warm fry onto it, letting his finger brush the pimply pink texture of the moist tip. She closed her eyes and sniffed the aroma of the hamburger on his hands.

"She *is* a good pitcher, I grant you that," said Brad, sipping his soda with glistening eyes.

"Everybody knows that already, Brad." She slurped her own drink and giggled as she caught him following a trickle escaping the corner of her mouth.

"I can't figure out yet whether she looks good on the mound because she's sexy, or she looks sexy on the mound because she's good," Brad said to Sam, his voice lush and hushed in contrast with the bustle and clanging of plates, glasses, and silverware around them.

"So, if she winked her eye at you, the slant of your column would change overnight, so to speak. A little change of editorial position..." Her laughter carried across the table to Brad's ears as Sam's fingers danced inside her handbag, retrieving her billfold.

"Do you think she's gay?" he asked, reaching for Sam's wrist to stop her from waving a credit card at the server.

"Who can say? She won't let on a thing about her private life." Sam wiggled her butt against the cushion of her seat and smiled, "Of course, you know I'd do anything for a story, Brad."

Brad Lucas looked at Sam expectantly and asked, "You ready?"

"For sure," said Sam, swilling the last drop from her drinking glass and chomping a mouthful of crushed ice.

Brad jiggled his keys in one hand and tossed some bills onto the table with the other, asking her, "My car or yours?"

The much ballyhooed new recruit's arrival in the Diamonds' clubhouse was anything but low-key. She greeted Big Gil, Sandy Lee, Larry, Cal, and Rudy, each joyful hug and kiss being longer and warmer in turn, interrupted by a howl of "Oh, jeez, the tall girl is back!" from Zinger. Willy held him around the neck, the two of them chattering like magpies, as she swung to and fro in midair.

Because she was a rookie, Willy was assigned a back-row, far-corner locker with the coaches and cigarette smokers, two groups of marginal social status. She was put between Zinger on one side and pitching coach Rudy Judd on the other–a situation as comfortable as being cushioned by two fluffy pillows.

Tom Vallery viewed Willy's reception with detached interest, never having observed anything so closely resembling togetherness in this particular clubhouse. When Paul Cello arrived, as if on cue, it was time to talk shop.

"I don't know what I'm supposed to do," she asked him almost meekly.

"Relax," he replied gently. "You're not penciled in to start 'til the weekend. Just sit out in the pen and cheer like hell."

"Tom's gonna let me start?" Willy asked.

"What do ya think you're here for, babe?" Paul said, amused, but not surprised at her naiveté. "Tom and Rudy want ya to get your feet wet in relief first, but the front office is breathin' down Tom's neck to put ya on television on Saturday."

"You're shittin' me!" she sang out, digging her fingers into his arm.

"Like I said," he laughed. "Relax!"

Cal Bonham took pause to note the intimate tone of Willy and Paul's chat. He also noted the way in which the pitcher and catcher tilted their heads toward one another as they sat
face to face with Willy jiggling her foot the whole time. Zinger whispered in Cal's ear, "They have what you call rapport, I suppose."

"Yeah, I'll say," quipped Cal. Zinger shrugged his shoulders.

The presence of Harvey, Alan, and Kristin, on hand to dog the footsteps of Fabian's hot new piece of merchandise, was good for a few laughs among the Diamonds. "Bean-counter alert! Call stadium security. Quick!"

After polite hellos from this or that resident star, Tom introduced Willy to the Millennium Channel's broadcasting team, Jeff McCarty and Cameron Hammersmith. On the air, the Diamonds' play-by-play duet seemed to be the standard ex-jock and real announcer combo. Jeff, the former catcher, was the analyst, or "color man," and Cam played the role of the "real" announcer, when, in fact, he was a monster slugger in his playing days, but he had been broadcasting long and well enough to be accepted as a pro. Jeff, however, often provided comic relief and was prone to outrageous statements. Once, Jeff called bat day in the Bronx "one of the most frightening moments in all of sports." Jeff was popular, but was thought to be a shill for Sebastian Fabian. Jeff's unassailable baseball expertise was too often tainted by the team's interests. Jeff didn't shy away from criticizing a Diamond over the air, but, whenever he did so, he was likely grinding the owner's axe.

CHAPTER 2

The attendance for tonight's game with Philly Town was counted at 37,000. The bookkeeping brigade at Fab Co. was in for hellfire from the boss in the morning for not pushing group sales with weeknight discounts or throwing blocks of freebies to local advertisers for giveaways. Given the impulse to win it all this season, repeating as the champions of baseball next season was secondary to the proven theorem that the biggest years at the gate follow championship seasons. To poll four million next year, the long-term prize desired by Sebastian Fabian, required at least three million fans through the turnstiles this year. Thus, Fabian demanded a minimum of 40,000 to attend any game.

"Thirty-five thousand is a sellout in Boston. It's half empty here," said he. "I never want to see Gilbert and Burton home runs bouncing off folded-up seats in the grandstand on the highlight films. Are we all clear on this?"

Awestruck, Willy smiled without uttering a word in the New York Diamonds' dugout through the national anthem and an uneventful first inning, after which she walked across the playing field with Zinger, fellow rookie pitcher Todd Strickland, backup catcher Pigpen, and Hank "Handy Man" Froelichs to the bullpen. Set-up reliever Tim Langevin would stroll out to the pen in the fourth inning and Larry Brooks, as is customary for a big league closer, would join them in the seventh. Handy Man held the title of bullpen coach, but this was Zinger's domain and the king continued to reside in the pen between starts. Now Willy's promotion to the big club was expected to result in his permanent return "home" to the pen. As they approached the bullpen door together, Willy heard her name called and saw hands waving at her. She chirped, "Hey, what's up?" and waved both arms in return. Zinger disapproved. "You can't get too chummy with the bleacher creatures," he said, dragging her by a red, white, and blue ribboned pigtail over to the pen's wooden bench and pointing for her to sit.

    The game moved sluggishly through the sixth inning with the score, New York 1 Philadelphia 0. Willy's feet hadn't yet touched the ground and she was unable to concentrate
her attention on the workmanship of Gil Douglas. Larry came into the bullpen to say, "Big Gil ain't got it tonight."

    "His asthma's flarin' up," said Handy Man.

    "His fastball ain't poppin'," added Larry. "He's throwin' all breakin' stuff."

    "If he gets in trouble, Tom'll be quick with the hook," said Tim.

    "We better get ready to get ready," said Zinger, the most senior firefighter of the crew. In the top of the seventh, Gil walked the first batter on four. "That's my cue," Zinger announced.

    Two singles and a pop fly loaded the bases with one out. Tim started throwing alongside Zinger as another base hit scored two. Exit Douglas and enter Filsinger. His first pitch was hit for a double and two more scored. Strick nearly jumped out of his pants when Handy Man told him to warm up with Tim. Zinger's second pitch was knocked through the infield for another hit and Tom went from dugout to mound, gesturing with his left hand. Tim took over with runners on second and third, trailing 4-1. The Philly swingers greeted the southpaw with two quick hits and it was 6-1.

The manager's nightmare unfolded: the starter falters too early; the middle reliever fails to hold; and, instead of going to the closer, the manager starts working backward through the bullpen. Tom was at the mound once more and Willy got up to throw as Strick prepared to go into the game, but the manager signaled for the righty, not the other lefty, and Handy Man Hank pointed a bulbous thumb at the woman from Old Saint Pete. Willy stood paralyzed, gawking at the bullpen coach, feeling dizzy and euphoric as Larry called to her, "Get your booty out on the floor, lady. This is it!" Willy's nervous tension dissipated as she wrapped her jacket over her right shoulder, adjusted her cap, and dashed onto the turf with legs kicking high and braided pigtails dancing in her wake. She felt the flow of blood, the surge of adrenaline, and the quickening of her pulse within, but she barely heard the loudest ovation since the D's took the field for their home opener back in April. It began before the announcement of her name over the public address system and drowned it out.

Tom and Paul stood together as Willy reached the center of the diamond. Both men were laughing. "This one's shot to hell, wouldn't you say?" said the skipper.

"Sounds like we're winnin' six to one in October instead of losin' six to one in May," clucked the catcher.

Impervious to the thundering noise in her honor, Willy moved her eyes from one to the other, asking, "Huh? What do you mean?"

Tom shook his head with a chuckle and tossed Willy the ball. As she rubbed it between her hands, the ballgirl tugged at Willy's sleeve to remove her jacket.

She was still too numb to smile at Paul as he ran through the signals with his back shielding his hands from the runners on first and second.

"One fastball, two slider, three curve, a fist is a pitchout. A pinky wiggle is a pickoff and, if I wiggle my forefinger, it's a change-up. For you, that's the cutter. If I don't sign, that means same pitch, different location. Otherwise, you select the delivery, since I don't have enough fingers for five pitches."

"Five?" Willy asked.

"Yeah," answered Paul. "Rudy wants ya to throw the screwgie. That's five pitches."

"I'll shake you off every time you call it."

"Okay," he easily agreed. "The only thing to look for is if the real signal is the first, second, or third of the set I'll be flashin'. If the first is one, or the second is two, or the third is three, that's it. Got it?"

"Yeah!" she responded, finally smiling.

"Ya sure?"

"Of course," said Willy, fluttering her eyes. "It's a pattern. Willy's no dummy, remember?"

"No, babe, ya sure aren't," Paul said softly. Then he raised his voice to ask, "So, who're we playin', what's the score, and who's up?"

Willy wagged her head and shuffled her feet, accounting, "Philly's up six-one, two on, one out, and the number six spot's coming to bat...Frankie Martel, third baseman."

Paul pulled his mask over his face and smiled through the wires. "Now, let's get to it." After she whipped half a dozen warm-up pitches, the home plate umpire, Big Jack Finigan, motioned for Martel to step into the batter's box. Willy did a little walkabout around the mound, had a few words with the ball, twirled it in her hand, and repeatedly kicked her right heel against the rubber.

"This is my spot!" she yelled.

Up in the broadcast booth, Jeff McCarty said, "It looks like our newest addition is a little bit of a hot dog out there."

"I think that goes without saying," said Cam Hammersmith.

Willy took the sign from her catcher, drew her hands together at her waist, and watched Martel call time to tie his shoe. *Here we go again!* Willy told herself: *You know they always let the batter call time when he's standing in, so he can bail out and not get nailed. He's trying to rattle the rook.* Martel resumed his stance after methodically knotting his laces and Willy stepped back onto the rubber, turned her head toward each base runner, and looked into the plate before delivering a sidearm fastball. The batter whirled and called time again as Willy released the ball. Big Jack waved his arms signaling "no pitch." Willy thought: *They never let the batter call time and bail out when the pitcher's into the stretch and ready to release the ball.* Paul stood upright, jabbered at Finigan and Martel, and tossed the ball back to Willy. Frankie rubbed his neck, took a few deep breaths, and scratched his crotch. *I've come too far for this bullshit!* Another sidearm fastball nearly singed Martel's eyebrows as he scarcely spun out of the way in time to avoid being plunked. The ump made no gesture–ball one. Paul settled into his crouch and called for a curveball. Willy set to throw, drew back her arm for the overhand delivery, pumped her front leg, and saw Finigan wave his arms, push past Paul, shove Martel away, and point an accusing finger at the woman on the mound.

"Now what?" she said aloud.

"Balk!" the umpire called out.

The two Quaker City runners ambled to second and third and Paul went to talk to his pitcher. "We got ourselves a situation here," he said. "Big Jack's got a bug up his ass about ya. He goes, 'Why's that *cunt* have to show up in my game?' So, we gotta work through it some way or other."

"He said that about me?" yelped Willy, bouncing up and down, trying to peer over at Finigan, but Paul kept shifting to block him from her view.

"Settle down!" commanded Paul. "Ya gotta come to a complete stop between your wind-up and stretch. Ya know that! Stand still for five minutes and pitch from the stretch position if ya hafta...but remember this is just a mop-up for the team and a tune-up for you." Willy listened, nodded her head, and kicked little divots in the dirt with her spikes. "If Big Jack tries to cheat ya, I'll do the arguin'. *You*," he said as he touched his pointer finger to the topmost button on her jersey, "just act like a lady and pitch like a man!"

Martel chased an outside fastball for strike one, and then looped an inside curveball into center field. Roy Burton plucked it from the air on the run and fired past the cut-off, directly to Paul at home on one bounce, stopping the Phil on third from tagging up to score. Willy's first pitch to the next batter was smacked toward the hole at short. Demeter Fortune caught the ball bare-handed and sailed it to Thor Andreason covering first, all in one motion, ending the forty-five-minute inning.

Cam told the Millennium Channel viewers: "Good hustle by Fortune and a pretty piece of pitching by Willy Beal, but, after six and a half, the Diamonds are down, six to one."

Willy ran to Fortune, reaching for a high five. "Nice play, Demmy! Yeah!"

"It's only a game, Willy," he responded, slapping lightly.

"Saying baseball is just a game is like saying music is just noise," she said, as they ran off together.

The ninth spot was due to bat in the home half of the inning. Willy was trying to decide whose wood to borrow when she saw Joe Manlius at the bat rack. She looked to Tom, who
indicated with a downward fanning of his palms for Willy to sit down.

"You're taking me out? I'm not gonna get to bat?" she shouted. There came a slap on her behind and a yank by the arm from Paul. "Whoa!" she yelped.

"Put a lid on it!" he said. Tom was beyond earshot, but Paul nevertheless whispered, "Don't stand there bitchin' at him. He's just doin' his job."

"Whatever happened to free speech?" Willy asked defiantly.

"It's like you're tryin' to get tough or show him up or somethin'. Take your beef to him later in private."

"Oh, my bad!" said Willy. "Should I apologize?"

"Wouldn't hurt," he replied. Then Paul sat back with his arms folded and laughed loudly. "Why're ya sittin' here?"

"What?" she questioned him, slightly pouty.

"This is where ya hit the showers," said Paul. "Do I hafta explain everythin' to ya?"

Willy playfully tucked the tip of her tongue in the corner of her mouth and said, "Maybe not everything!" Then she grabbed her blazer and glove and left the bench.

Willy ran back to the locker room and quickly showered and changed into her raggedy jeans and a plain white tee shirt. She had intended to blow-dry her hair and watch the rest of the game with Zinger and Tim in the clubhouse, Gil having gone home to recuperate. She was curious to see how Strick would do in the last two innings and she realized that tonight's hopelessly lost game was not at all meaningless to her. Ugly or not, it was her first and so she
headed back to the dugout with her wet hair tucked under her D's hat. She took a seat next to Benny Marquez, the utility man, who was thoroughly amused by Willy's intense interest in watching Thor tap a meek grounder back to the box to cap the eighth inning.

The general manager surprised Willy when he rushed into the dugout from the runway. "Where the hell have you been?" he groused. "USTV News called. They want you to go on live at 11:30!"

"Who, me?" she asked, astonished.

"Who do you think?" Harvey snapped sharply. "You better get a move on. They're sending a cab to pick you up. It'll take too much time to get to Rocky Center, so they want to do it from your motel room. The news crew is already there waiting for you."

Willy gazed down at her tee shirt and patted her damp hair. "Aaah!" she screamed, bolted from the bench, jostled Harvey as she passed, and scampered down the runway. "If the cab comes, tell him to wait," she sang over her shoulder to the GM.

"You've only got twenty minutes," he warned.

Willy sought Zinger in the clubhouse and found him ravaging corned beef on a bulky roll. "Is Michelle in the stadium?" she asked.

"No, Willy," he answered, uprighting himself in the chair which had been propped on its back legs against a wall "Why?"

"I gotta go on the late-night news and I'm a disaster area. Look at this here!" she exclaimed, waving her hand-clutched shirttail, then pulling off her cap and spinning her crinkled, drippy curls. "I need some serious help."

Zinger's laugh boomed. "Looks like snakes growing out of your head. Ha! Medusa!"

"Oh, that's just fine," smirked Willy. "That'll be my nickname–Willy 'Medusa' Beal."

As Zinger fell into hysterics, Willy dashed away to find Harvey Wanamaker again.

"Is Kristin Tracy at the park tonight?" she asked him breathlessly.

"No, she doesn't come to watch a game unless Fabian orders her to," the GM said.

"Shoot!" Willy pounded her balled fists against her thighs.

"What's the matter with you? You've got to get going, Willy." Harvey seemed as riled up as she was.

Zinger appeared in the clubhouse doorway. "Can I help?" he asked with sincerity.

"You wanna do up my hair for me?" she pursed testily.

"I have enough trouble combing my own," he replied, fingering his short, thin thatch.

"Willy," said Tim from within the clubhouse. "Samantha Khoury's in the press room."

"All right!" shouted Willy and she ran off once more.

"The girl's hyper," the GM said to Zinger.

"She ought to be," sighed the veteran reliever. "Heck! Nobody ever interviewed me after two-thirds of an inning."

Sam Khoury was leaning on the edge of her chair, munching on a powdered donut while listening to two local wags being lectured about some inconsequential subject by Brad Lucas. Willy called to her from across the press room. Sam looked up and said, "What's the deal?" and in the process spilled half-chewed donut crumbs onto her skirted lap.

"Come on over here." Willy waved frantically at the opposite end of the room.

"Nice outfit, Willy!" teased Sam. "Is it new?"

"Shush!" moaned Willy. "I need your help. They want me on the network news tonight."

"I know," nodded Sam. "We heard. You haven't much time, you know."

"I've got nothing to wear...My hair's soaking wet..." Sam had laughed, but was surprised when she focused on Willy's wide, teary, and desperate eyes. Visibly trembling, Willy clasped Sam's hands, bit down on her lower lip, and hissed, "I'm scared, Sam. I can't do it by myself. Please come with me. Please!"

Sam responded more warmly than Willy expected, smiling and wrapping a dangling strand of Willy's hair around her finger. "Let's go do it, pal."

"The cab's at the service gate, Willy!" Harvey wailed.

Willy asked Sam, "What should I wear? I don't have anything except jeans and sweatshirts."

The two women stopped walking and looked at each other. "I got it!" Sam snapped her fingers. "Go grab a clean uniform from your locker."

"Great idea!" Willy's eyes flashed with pleasure.

"Goddamn, Willy, hurry up!" Harvey bellowed.

"Button it, Wanamker!" retorted Sam. "She's coming."

"What're you, her press agent?" he asked impatiently.

"Not a bad idea," Sam said wistfully.

Willy returned with a set of Diamond pinstripes flung over her shoulder. "What do you think about pink ribbons in my hair?"

"Super!" said Sam, nodding excitedly.

"Judas H. Christmas!" the Diamonds' general manager hollered in anguish. "It's twenty past eleven. Get going!"

The Cambodian cabbie whisked them on and off one exit of the Garden State Parkway as Sam tugged and snarled a brush through Willy's unruly locks. She clutched a hank and said desperately, "Your hair's like so different from mine."

"You don't say!" Willy pretended disbelief, and then told Sam, "Just part it down the middle and brush it all out to the sides. I'll pull it and you tie it on each side. Then we'll brush out each piggy-tailer. Got it?"

"Got it!" said Sam, before burying her nose in a handful of Willy's hair. "What kind of shampoo do you use?" she asked.

"Natural herbal cocoa butter and banana," said Willy.

"Can I try it?" asked Sam, furiously stroking the stiff plastic brush through Willy's hair.

"No problem," answered Willy. "Ouch! Watch it, Sam!"

"Sorry, pal!"

The cabbie laughed convulsively at the scene reflected in his rearview mirror as he motored to the front of the Sheridan, where a white USTV van with a rooftop satellite dish was parked. Willy panicked. "I left my wallet and keys back at the stadium."

Sam thought Willy was ready to start crying. "Chill out, pal! I'll pay this guy and the geek at the front desk will let us into your room. The news crew's in there, right?"

Willy closed her eyes and inhaled deeply, fluttering her hands in the air. *Don't lose it, Willy!* Sam threw a wad of money onto the front seat and lunged out of the cab as Willy opened her eyes to see the smiling driver holding a small notepad and a pen. Sam implored Willy to hurry as she signed her first autograph as a *bona fide* big leaguer, affectionately patting the cabbie's hand while scribbling her signature. A hefty, bearded man, wearing a windbreaker with the network logo, barked "She's here!" into a walkie-talkie and literally pushed Willy through the door, into the elevator, and down the hallway to her rented room with Sam stumbling behind them. "Ninety seconds to air" was all he spoke.

Marc Bergeron, the remote site director, awaited Willy and told her to sit in a chair in front of the curtained balcony window. Trim, slim, and slight of build, Willy thought that Marc had a good body for an infielder. He said, "We're on in one minute," as he knelt at her feet. He pointed behind him and to either side. "We have two monitors. One shows the anchor in the studio. The other shows what's actually on the air. Don't look at the monitors. Look at Jacques."

A massively muscled brother with shaven head and gold earring was poised at the edge of the bed, hoisting a minicam on his shoulder. Jacques kept one eye on the lens as he winked with his other and said, "Smile, pretty lady!"

"How do I know when I'm on?" asked Willy, now shaking from head to toe.

"I'll cue you with a nod and the cut-throat sign," Marc answered while deftly hooking a little cordless microphone to the front of her shirt. "I'll be right behind Jacques on the bed," he added, handing her a tiny earpiece. "Listen through these. The monitor's on a thirty-second delay from the satellite relay."

Marc watched with sheer amazement as Willy shut her eyes, inhaled, held it, exhaled, muttered something that sounded like "Jesus Krishna," then completely stilled her body, and reopened her eyes with a face of pure serenity. He tugged at the plug in his ear, whispering, "Here we go...three, two, one...," as Sam caught Willy's eye for an instant and pumped her fist.

The anchor's familiar face came on the full-color screen to Willy's left. The audio commenced: *"My name is Foster Castel, and this is 'Newsline'..."* Trumpets sounded the theme. The picture zoomed to the starry night background behind the anchor's desk with the sound of crowd noises underlying his voice, this time prerecorded: *"It's been said that the great thing about baseball is its timelessness, that it is essentially the same game passed on from generation to generation...despite social and political upheaval, economic crises, and war... enduring for the better part of two centuries. It is a game that gauges time by its own measures of outs and innings instead of minutes and seconds, and the playing field includes the architecture around it...And yet, with its constancy and timelessness, in the middle of an otherwise ordinary baseball season, suddenly, something happens which never happened before...Tonight, at the Meadowlands in East Rutherford, New Jersey..."*

Willy watched the monitor show her own image in distant miniature, gliding over the outfield turf under the stadium's artificial daylight. Her pigtails bobbed around her head as the PA blared: "Now pitching for the Diamonds, number twenty-eight, Willy Beal." She was astonished at the vociferous cheering that greeted her entrance.

"Our guest this evening is New York Diamonds' pitcher, Willy Beal."

Willy smiled, snuck a peek at the monitor, and laughed at herself.

"Also joining us from our Los Angeles affiliate is Doctor Elizabeth Harding-Hebb, a professor of women's studies and the author of *Whither Feminism?: The Pseudo-Masculine Mystique.*" Doctor Lizzie Hard-Head, as Willy mischievously memorized her name, appeared rather more glamorous than scholarly with puffy hair fresh from the beauty salon and gaudy jewelry aglitter. "We'll be back after these messages."

Marc figuratively slashed his throat and said, "Rest easy, Willy. It's a two-minute commercial break."

Willy shifted uncomfortably and crowed, "I'm sweating like a pig!" Then she tightened her lips, crossed her legs, and daintily folded her hands in her lap, saying, "Excuse me," in a demur voice.

On camera, two minutes later, Willy shared a split screen with Foster Castle, who opened: "Willy Beal, you made history tonight. You're the first woman ever to play big league baseball. How do you feel?"

"I feel fine, thanks. How about you? How do you feel, Foster?" responded Willy, perfectly composed, her smile gleaming.

"Perhaps, I should rephrase the question."

"Go right ahead, Foster," Willy said in a cheery voice.

In a stage whisper, the remote site director told Sam that Castle was amused. "He never laughs this early in the program, except to ridicule a really dumb guest. I think he likes her already."

"Let me put it this way," said the anchor. "Why Willy Beal? Are you a singularly unique phenomenon, one of a kind? Or are you the tip of the iceberg...the first of a whole generation of female athletes poised to break through the heretofore exclusively male domain of professional baseball?"

Willy shifted her weight in the chair, cupped her chin in the palm of her hand with her forefinger alongside her nose, and said, "I could think about that question for a week and still not come up with an answer...It's a good question, though, Foster."

"Thank you," the anchor chuckled.

She's playing with Castle and he's eating it up! an interested viewer said to himself.

"It's not like I went to play youth baseball or high school and college softball thinking I was the best player out there, whether it was all girls on the field or I was the only girl on the field."

The anchor's boyish face, familiar to viewer's worldwide, curled the slightest of grins, signaling a fully loaded question: "But how is it that you've been able to fulfill a dream...which I venture to say, most of us have entertained at some point in our lives...to play in the majors, something no other woman has ever been able to do? What makes you special, Willy Beal?"

"I'm nothing special,"Willy answered with ease. "I'm taller than the average woman, but I can't think of a single aspect of pitching where that makes any difference...but maybe it helped me to get noticed." When Willy laughed, Castle laughed as well, and then she cut him off. "Seriously, there's always been a definite preference for taller players and a prejudice against shorter players, even though baseball's not a game of physical size and strength. It's a game of coordination, agility, and brains." She paused to tap her temple for the camera, and then said, "I think it's a matter of expectations. There are millions of girls in this world playing softball, but baseball scouts don't see those skills as transferable to baseball and I really don't understand why. It's the same game! No one expected to see a woman in the bigs, but now here I am. Still, I can't tell you how my particular case affects the chances of other women. I can only speak for myself."

She's having no trouble doing that. She's amazing! the interested viewer thought aloud.

"I've studied the game's history and I know many women came before me who played pro baseball mostly against men or on men's teams...Maude Nelson, Lizzie Murphy, Jackie Mitchell, Edith Houghton, Toni Stone, and Ila Borders...They all could've made it in the bigs, if given a chance, maybe, but that didn't happen."

"Your grandfather was a professional baseball player. Do you think you're the product of heredity or your environment?"

"I don't know," she warbled after a fleeting silence. "I keep saying 'I don't know' every time you ask a question, don't I?" Following that slight diversion, Willy continued. "My grandfather, Ruben Henry, had something to do with *both* my heredity and my environment. I'd say equally...but I've been lucky, too."

"In what way?"

"I have to give some credit to Peter Jones."

"Of the Buffalo Wolves," queried Castle. "He's a long-time friend of yours. Am I correct?"

"That's right. It was Peter who offered me the chance to play winter ball with his team in Venezuela. Everything just kind of took off from there."

"That's to his credit, being something of a mentor to your career."

"Yeah," Willy said cheerfully. "I guess you could say Peter's my mentor."

"But why do you say you're lucky?" Castle asked.

"I've heard so many stories about good players having a bad day or making a bad play when the scouts are watching. I've tried out for teams and didn't make it. The coaches *looked* at me, but they didn't *see* me. Most athletes go through that. I was fortunate that I played well last winter and this spring in the minors and that my teammates won while I was pitching."

"Do you think Sebastian Fabian, owner of the Diamonds, deserves some special credit?"

"Not especially, no," Willy answered without hesitation.

That's fine with me, Willy, said the viewer. *I don't expect you to kiss up to me.*

"Why not?" Castle countered.

"I love the Diamonds, all my teammates. I love the coaches I worked with in spring training, Rudy Judd and Lew Shankleton, my manager, Tom Vallery, of course. It might've been a historic event tonight, like you said, but for me this is only the beginning. The owner is just like a lot of other baseball men over the years...Branch Rickey, Bill Veeck, Rube Foster, and John McGraw... who'd do anything to win, even if they had to change the world to do it."

The owner was impressed: *Willy, did you just line me up with that pantheon of giants? Or did you put me in my place, in their shadow, at their feet? Aren't you clever? Riddles in the subtext!*

At the second commercial break, Willy slumped in her chair, frantically fanning her face with her hands. "Whew!" Marc came to her and knelt again, rather like a corner man ready to coach, prepare, and patch up his fighter between rounds. "Did I just make a complete fool of myself in front of a million people or what?" she worried.

"More like ten million..." said Marc.

"You were great, pal!" said Sam.

"You were," Marc said while lightly stroking the back of her hand. "Castle thinks you're a doll...er, uh...I mean, that's good."

"I know what you mean, Marc." Willy smiled shyly and, for the second time tonight, she held hands with a perfect stranger.

The next eight-minute segment of *"Newsline"* began with Elizabeth Harding-Hebb lecturing, "I think

the question from a woman's viewpoint is misaddressed, Foster. It's not 'Why
Willy Beal?' but 'Why is Willy Beal the first and *only* woman in Big League Baseball?' What we have here is a woman, who, typically for her generation, has reaped the benefits of the women's movement, but doesn't advertise herself as a feminist. It's another disturbing example of a woman defining her success in a strictly male role. Her legitimacy, if you will, seems to be based on the statements of her male proponents to the effect that Ms. Beal is just as big, just as strong, just as aggressive as her male counterparts. Hence, this particular woman is acceptable to the male power structure of professional sports because she's unlike other women. What's most disturbing is that she is apparently willing to allow herself to be glamorized–as something of a hood ornament for her team's owner–and she has not been forthcoming about issues of interest to women, particularly minority women, not even in the very restrictive sense of identifying the barriers that still exist to greater participation of women in organized sports, an issue which she is obviously uniquely qualified to speak to."

    Sam grabbed Marc's arm and shouted, "What the hell is she trying to do? She's just reciting her own agenda, riding Willy's coattails onto national television to promote her friggin' book."

    Willy hissed, "Will you shush, Sam? I wanna hear what this woman is saying."

    Marc raised a finger to his lips. "Psst! Shhh! We're going back on live."

In the studio, Foster Castle, with a wry grin, told the viewers, "A little voice in my ear is telling me that Willy Beal may want a chance to respond."

"Best believe I may!" blurted Willy. She winced when she heard her comment echo through the monitor.

Lizzie Hard-Head interrupted, "I'd like to conclude my remarks first...There is no indication that Willy Beal's popularity will translate into bettering the status of women of all ages in sports at all levels and, if such is the case, then her appearance is a fluke with no significant impact on women in this country."

Willy heaved a sigh and carefully kept her gaze trained on Jacques's minicam eye as she took Marc's prompt. "First off, I don't appreciate being called a hood ornament and those comments about my being acceptable because of what you're saying are my masculine characteristics as a pitcher simply proves that I'm not a fluke. You don't need to be two hundred pounds of muscle-bound beefcake or have testosterone overload to throw a big league fastball."

Lizzie jumped back into the fray, chiming, "You have a particular obligation as a role model to other women of color..."

"I don't see as I need to be lectured about issues facing women of color," said Willy, "and I don't see myself as a hero or a role model, at least not yet. You have to earn that...but, if what I'm doing is important to people, I think that it's not limited to women only, or female athletes only..." Willy flashed her winning smile and sang triumphantly, "As far as feminism goes, I define it as the ability to make choices and it's plain to see I've chosen to follow a path that a woman hasn't been expected to take. *So, of course, I'm a feminist,* but my personal views on this or that issue aren't really important..."

Off camera, Foster Castle peered admiringly at the woman in the monitor. A jazz aficionado himself, Castle compared Willy's words to the music of Miles Davis: unique, abstract, and totally unexpected.

However, Lizzie wasn't finished, but before she and Willy could go at it again, Castle intervened. "One could belabor the point further, but I think Ms. Beal has already addressed it." Then, Lizzie's voice softened, "Please don't misunderstand me. In fact, Willy Beal, you *are* special, despite what you say, and you've opened an unprecedented window of opportunity."

"Like I said, Professor. It's only the beginning." Willy strategically interjected.

"Please, Willy, call me Liz," said Professor Harding-Hebb with a lilt in her voice. "I've never been to a baseball game in my life, but I'll be in the front row cheering for you on my next trip east."

Nice move, Willy. You know how to give stage and take it back.

"On that note," the anchor signaled, "our program will continue in a moment."

After the cameras cut away, Marc said to Willy, "She came after you, but you won her over. Nice work, Willy!"

Then Willy startled as Castle's voice came directly into her earphone. "Willy, we're pulling the plug on the good professor for the final segment. We want to go with you alone. Can you wing it for eight minutes?"

"Yeah, sure, okay," she stammered.

At his penthouse overlooking Central Park West, Sebastian Fabian swung his legs out of the white satin sheets, which were being pulled and untucked by the latest inductee of his personal Playmate of the Night Club. She grunted, rolled onto her back, and snored with her mouth opened. He tucked his feet under a pillow and propped his head on his hands in front of the TV at the foot of the bed. Sebastian much preferred watching the real woman on the screen.

On camera once again, Castle said, "Before we continue with Willy Beal of the New York Diamonds, I'd like to inform our audience that we extended invitations to Sebastian Fabian and the Commissioner of Big League Baseball, Hamilton Fisher, to join our program tonight, both of whom respectfully declined due to previous commitments."

Actually, the Commish is the one with previous commitments. I told Castle that this is Willy's moment to shine.

"I do want to clarify a few things said earlier...if that's all right, Foster," Willy said in a small voice.

"Go right ahead," said Foster as they resumed on-air.

"We could talk about how the performance gap between men and women has narrowed in a lot of different sports, or how differences in size and strength have been getting smaller and smaller." Willy's eyes strayed to the monitor and she carefully gestured to say, "Like I said before, I think it's a matter of perceptions and expectations. *I'll see it when I believe it!*..And I didn't misspeak, Foster. Maybe I've opened people's eyes to see the world differently. *See me and believe it.*"

Marc leaned to whisper to Sam, "Did she rehearse this?"

"Improvisation," Sam snorted. "Twenty-eight years in the making."

"So," baseball's first female star continued. "I believe that we have to pay homage to all those that came before us, and my own family history is so wrapped up in the history of the game that I don't know where one ends and the other starts. No one goes out on the stage alone, whether she's an athlete or not, or a role model to millions of people or just a few. We all bring something with us, and take something while we're here, and we have an obligation to put something back."

Stage whispering as before, Marc moved his mouth closer to Sam's ear. "Castle's just beaming at her face on the screen."

"Have you set any personal goals for yourself?" asked the anchor.

"Well, I pitched in one inning of one game tonight. I'm just one player on the New York Diamonds, trying to keep my spot on the team and help us win a pennant. Right now, I'm thinking about playing and winning some ballgames." Tilting her head and smiling broadly, Willy's voice sang out, *"To play's the thing. The game's the thing."*

"If you can paraphrase Shakespeare, I can paraphrase Spike Lee," said Castle, in a contrived attempt at urban vernacular, *"Willy's got game!"*

"You got it, Foster," she giggled happily.

"I don't believe it," Marc softly told Sam. "She roped him into a private two-way conversation on the air. Nobody does that."

You played off Castle like a pro, Willy! thus complimented the viewer who was the owner.

"We'll return with a brief word about tomorrow's edition of *'Newsline'* after these messages," concluded Foster Castle with professional finality. He was indeed quite taken with Willy. More importantly, however, Castle knew that this woman was about to take center stage and he scooped the other network news organizations as well as USTV's elephantine sports division.

Life is good. Welcome to Electronic Medialand, Willy Beal!

Meanwhile, Sebastian Fabian reconsidered rousing his lifelike centerfold for another go-round, but he kept the lights off and his eyes closed. Someone else's face was the object of his passion tonight.

CHAPTER 3

The pressing piece of business for the Commissioner of Big League Baseball, Inc. was a midnight summons to Jack Finigan to his Madison Avenue office with chief umpire Ken Crenshaw and the league president, Sherman Long, in touch via conference call.

"Are you there, Sherm?" Hamilton Fisher said into the speakerphone as Big Jack sat in stiff, silent, and cross-eyed formality. "Don't fall asleep on me, Sherm," the Commissioner said with more sarcasm than humor.

There came a rattling cough and throat clearing. "Yeah, Ham, I'm here. You did get me out of bed," said Long with another coughing spasm. "Give me a minute."

"Sure, fine," agreed Fisher, who next said, "Ken, Jack, Sherm, here's how it is. Willy Beal makes her first BLB appearance and the man behind the plate lets the batter screw around, calling time on her when she's ready to pitch, and then goes and slaps her with a balk."

"Now, Mr. Commissioner..." Big Jack started to say.

"No more bullshit!" the Commissioner shouted, visibly shocking the veteran umpire. "You all know what I'm talking about. I'm not about to allow anyone to create the impression that Big League Baseball is a reactionary institution populated by sexist dinosaurs who can't stand to see a woman playing a man's game. If she mouths off, decks somebody, or throws a spitball, give her the thumb like anybody else, but no more bullshit! The balk call tonight was borderline at best."

"Did she complain to you about me?" asked Big Jack, looking falsely incredulous.

"No, I've not spoken with her," Fisher replied. "Tom Vallery called me." The name alone commanded enough respect to bring any further debate to closure. "I don't know whether
she's just the *first* woman, or if she'll go down in history as the *only* woman, but she's here and it looks like she's here to stay. If there's another incident involving Willy Beal and an umpire, I'll hang your carcass out to dry, Ken. It's on your head to enforce discipline and fairness," the Commish added, addressing the chief ump.

The league president, fully awake by this time, said, "Willy Beal's acceptance is one issue where the fans, the media, the players, *and the owners* are all on the same side."

Indeed, Hamilton Fisher took the opportunity earlier in the evening to canvass the owners and co-owners in both leagues, two of whom were women, first to assure them that there was no "hidden agenda" to put a quota of women on each team's roster, and second to warn the barons of the ballgame that they better be prepared to respond to questions about scouting, recruiting, and developing female talent. However, in light of Willy Beal's arrival, the only negativity to emerge from the ranks of ownership was directed at Sebastian Fabian and the Diamonds–most vocally from the Chicago and Buffalo franchises–for circumventing the amateur draft process in signing Willy. The Commissioner understood that professional baseball was, first and foremost, a profit-making business. An attorney by trade, Ham Fisher already set his legal staff onto the task of bolstering Fabian's position, although the

Commish personally believed that BLB should have held a lottery-style draft to determine which teams had the right to bid for her. Nevertheless, Mr. Commissioner was more of a caretaker than a czar, and supporting the "done deal" was the sole prudent course. As the electronic sounder on his digital watch indicated one a.m., the Commissioner sat at his personal computer to e-mail messages of congratulation to Willy Beal and Sebastian Fabian–the owner he most admired professionally and detested personally. The Great American Game's share of the public's sports dollar suffered for five years before fully recovering from the cataclysmic strike and lockout of the 1990s and fan loyalty took another direct hit with the next decade's steroid revelations. The pastime's savior, avatar, and guardian angel is Willy Mae Beal. Fisher knew well that the majority of the fans cheering in big league stadia were women and children and Fabian had found them the perfect hero.

At dawn's breaking, while reading last night's box score and three versions of the game's description in the *Daily Mail, Journal,* and *Today USA*, Willy knew exactly what she had done as she read the pitchers' line. After the three veterans failed to retire more than one batter in the seventh, Willy Beal walked into her first big league game and shut down the visiting side for the night. On Wednesday, Sandy Lee lost his first of the season as Fightin' Philly took its third in a row and dropped the Diamonds into a third-place tie with the Florida Fish.

Before the week's fourth game, Willy visited the wives' room. She enjoyed entering the spouses' sanctuary, where the conversation seemed to be more concerned with hair than baseball: "Can you see my roots?"..."Which ones? The grey or the black?"..."Do you think my hair looks good this short? I didn't like the way he cut it last time. Too choppy!" There was also talk of food: "We went to this fabulous place."..."I adore French onion soup, but every time I get it, I spend the rest of the night on the john." There was talk of kids as well: "Our youngest has a learning disability. Thor did, too, but it wasn't recognized years ago." Alas, baseball was a constant–a job that often came home with hubby, sometimes to find a bad day at work replayed on television and in newspapers and constantly contested to submerge a spouse's plans, schemes, needs, and dreams.

Willy listened, enjoyed breathing in the atmosphere, and was accepted into it with natural ease. Leota Douglas called out, "When you get married, Willy, will your main man come in here and hang with the girls or strut around the clubhouse with the guys?"

Keith Whalen hadn't gone out of his way to be chummy with his female teammate, but Joy Whalen exhausted herself in fawning over Willy. "I think what you're doing is just fantastic," said Joy in her flat midwestern accent. "I'd like us to get together and chat one of these days."

"Okay, thanks," Willy said politely. "That'd be nice."

"I'd like to talk to you about my personal savior," said Joy, a lady with a mission. "I see the light of the Lord in your eyes."

Observing that Willy was cornered, Michelle Filsinger joined them and said, "Hi, Willy! Hi, Joy! How are we girls tonight?" As Michelle grinned at Willy, Joy abruptly announced that her face needed fixing. "Works like a charm," giggled Michelle, snapping her fingers.

"The Jewish broad comes over and *The Word* clams right up."

As Saturday's probable starter, Willy would ride the Diamonds' bench on Thursday night. Masked, padded, and ready to backstop the game's first pitch from Jake, Paul ducked his head under the dugout roof and told Willy, "Grab a clipboard and pens from my locker so you can get a book on the hitters for when we go down to Philly in a couple months."

Willy jumped. "You got it, partner!" She went to the locker room and pulled open the chain-link door that bore the sign: 18–CELLO–PLAY ME. The clipboard on the top shelf held in its teeth a packet of 3X5 cards. A slip of paper, written in Paul's surprisingly graceful script, taped to the clipboard read: "Take notes on anything that catches your eye and keep the card in your pocket when you pitch." Willy smiled at the photos of wife Lorraine, daughters Jessica, Ashley and Megan, Campy, Yogi, and Johnny Bench pasted all over the inside of the cubicle and closed the door. "That says it all about Paul."

Thursday's game against Quaker City, a winner spun by Jake, was to be the Diamonds' last with Eastern Division rivals for almost a month. The next twenty-eight games would be the "make-or-break" stretch for the D's to move into first place, and they would have to do it at the expense of Central and Western clubs, including two home-and-away sets with first-place and second-place teams. Jacobson was superb, carrying a one-hitter into the seventh inning, and the Diamonds led 2-0 on back-to-back homers by Fortune and Gilbert. In contrast to Sandy Lee, who came off the mound full of talk and enthusiasm, Jake retreated to a corner of solitude in the dugout between innings. When Jake gave up a hit and a walk with one out in the seventh, he left the dugout and wrote out a prepared statement for the postgame press confabulation.

In the D's locker room, Zinger was toweling off his pits when a petite, bespectacled woman asked, "Can you tell me where to find Willy Beal?" She stood, roughly eye level with his belly.

He looked down at her to say, "You just keep walking around until you see a six-foot- two-inch *shiksa* with no tits whatsoever, and..."

"Zinger!" came Willy's voice. "What're you saying? Why're you calling me a 'chick'?"

Zinger's voice boomed with laughter. "I said *shiksa*, not 'chick'!"

Willy, carefully wrapped by a towel across her shoulders and waist with another one turbanlike on her head, said, "He really is just about the sweetest person in the world...sarcastic, though...Now, uh, who're you?"

"I'm Melanie Rogovin. I'm with *He, She, & We* magazine," she replied. "We want to do a feature article on you."

"Wouldn't you be more comfortable if we met someplace else?"

Melanie said no and she and Willy talked quietly for several minutes. The questions were simplistic, but Willy answered politely, feeling a shade motherly toward the painfully shy and inexperienced reporter. After the interview concluded, Willy dressed in her street clothes, clipped her Running Mate to a belt loop, and headed out of the locker room, listening to saxophonist Candy Dulfer through her ear buds. She felt nature's call and detoured at the stalls. She kept the buds plugged into her ears while unbuckling her belt and didn't hear someone approaching. Willy saw two sneaker-shod feet underneath the slide-locked metal door. *Rumble! Thump! Kick! Grunt!* A set of fingers grabbed at the top of the door and a D's cap over a bushy black head of hair slowly came into view, as did a hand holding a miniature camera-phone and a flash of light.

"You've gotta be kidding me!"

"What in the hell's goin' on?" Willy heard Sandy Lee's voice and that of Larry Brooks: "Leave Willy alone, you!" She swung open the door, still zipping her pants and tucking her shirttail, to find Sandy Lee, Larry, and Big Gil holding the stalker by the waist, arms, and legs as he kicked and squirmed. Someone called out, "Security's on their way!" and the wanna-be paparazzo moaned in anguish as Zinger snatched his camera-phone, flung it into the toilet, and kicked the flusher with his big foot.

"How do these whack jobs get in here?" someone wondered.

"The same way the groupies do?" came a response.

Willy was pleasantly surprised when she read Melanie Rogovin's article in *He, She & We*. Wrote Melanie: "Add her spirituality and intellectualism to her athleticism and musician's soul and you have the complex package that is Willy Mae Beal."

Earlier in the day, Willy received a frantic call from Art Ridzik. "How're you doing, Uncle Artie?" she happily greeted him.

"Cripes, Willy!" Art sounded frazzled. "My phone's ringing off the hook. I've got people who want you to make appearances, endorsements, investments, everything!"

"Chill out, Artie!" laughed Willy. "I gotta find a place to live, move out of my condo in Alexandria, buy me a car...Take care of Willy first."

"Ever since you said you were hooked on diet soda, I've heard from the American Cola Company, Cola King, Bubble-Up...They all want you to do a commercial."

"You're kidding me!" she exclaimed.

"Just stay put," directed Artie. "I'll be over there in fifteen minutes."

"I'm hungry," Willy said meekly.

"I'll bring lunch." *Click!*

Artie arrived with a gourmet-to-go pasta primavera salad plate for his client, but Willy's appetite was choked by the smell of salami, ham, and hard-boiled egg in her agent's antipasto. "First things first!" snorted Artie. Then he snatched a forkful of meat, cheese, and lettuce into his mouth and reached for his attaché case. "Here's a power of attorney. It gives me the right to sign contracts for you, open bank accounts, get you a personal loan..."

"What for?" Willy asked incredulously.

"You'll need money for things, Willy." His words were muffled by chewing. "This way, we have the cash for deposits on a house or an apartment, furniture, new clothes, whatever you want. We'll put the rest into an IRA and money market accounts. So, your paycheck will go to paying off the loan. Oh, yeah, I stopped by the stadium on my way here. There was a check waiting for you." He handed it to her. "Endorse it. I'll use it to open up an account at First City. Then we'll set you up with automatic deposit and electronic banking. We ought to get a small savings account at a bank in Jersey, too."

Willy's eyes bugged out as she read her net pay. She hadn't given a thought to the fact that her salary increased exponentially overnight to the major league minimum of $300,000 plus the $50,000 personal service stipend.

"I need your signature for a joint account and applications for debit cards, credit cards, and the personal loan. I've also got papers for setting you and me up as a partnership for tax purposes. Do you have life insurance? We should make a will, too."

Willy spun her head, closed her eyes, pulled at her pigtails, and screamed, "Aaah!"

"Am I going too fast for you, honey?"

"Better believe it, Uncle Artie!"

"Just sign your name. I'll take care of everything. Trust me," Artie said. "Do you know where you want to live?"

"The City," she crooned dreamily. "I heard Chelsea and Soho are the cool places."

"Lofts go for about thirty grand, Willy."

"That's not bad," she replied.

"That's thirty grand a month!" he informed sternly.

"Oh," she sighed. "Don't forget about my wheels. I've got one all picked out," she began to say.

"You didn't put any money down, did you?" he said, panicky.

"Just window shopping," she laughed. "I checked out an XYZ car in Alexandria, the new solar hybrid. Willy's gotta go green."

Artie chuckled. "I know a fella at a Nimoco dealership in Paramus. We should do a lease deal."

Willy shook her head with amusement. "Why do I have to own an apartment and lease a car?" Adding after a thoughtful moment, "But let's do the will and life insurance...to take care of Mama if something should happen."

Artie nodded, then quacked, "You can bet Fabian's already insured your life *and your arm* for at least a couple million bucks with Lords of London, same as Danielson, Douglas, and Jacobson, with himself as beneficiary." Willy felt ill at ease with both Artie's adversarial attitude toward the team she loved and the fact that he never once mentioned *baseball*. Nonetheless, she sent off her agent, lawyer, and business partner with a fond hug and kiss.

A small stack of mail and the first trickle of fan letters by fax and e-mail awaited Willy at the stadium less than forty-eight hours after her appearance on "*Newsline*." The next day, the post office deposited two cinched sacks of cards and letters for Willy at the Sheridan. The Diamonds would be hitting the road to Cincinnati for the weekend and Zinger invited Willy home for brunch with Michelle and their children. When he arrived at Willy's motel room to pick her up, she was sitting spread-eagled on the floor with a pile of fan mail and fan faxes in her lap. She had been ripping open envelopes and reading all morning, but was barely halfway through the two bags full, with torn and folded sheets of paper scattered about.

Willy laughed. "This one says I'm an angel sent from heaven and that one says I'm a demon straight from hell." Willy showed Zinger a few specimens from the throw-away pile.

"Some real sickies out there, huh?"

She wagged her head. "They don't bother me none. I can spot the bad ones right away. The hate words jump off the page. I just toss 'em." Overwhelmingly, however, with differing levels of erudition and grammar, the fan mail essentially expressed the same idea: the world was falling in love with a girl named Willy. She clutched a handful to her breast and beamed at
Zinger. "Isn't it unbelievable?"

Before brunching at the Filsingers', Willy played with twelve-year-old Stephanie and ten-year-old Mikey in the downstairs family room. Each of them held a stack of baseball cards with dozens more strewn around them. Turning over one and reading the back, Adam squealed, "My dad made three hundred and sixty-four errors!"

"Let me see that," Willy demanded gently, taking the card from him and pointing with her long, elegant finger. "That's not the word 'error.' It's ERA," she said.

"It means earned run average, you little dork," Stephanie said to her younger brother.

Sidling up to the boy, Willy explained, "An ERA of 3.64 means if your dad pitches nine
innings, the other guys usually get about three and a half runs, which is okay if the Diamonds score four or five. Right?"

"Not if we only get one or two runs," said Stephanie.

"But he's mostly always been a relief pitcher," said Willy with Zinger's son and daughter listening attentively. "See, his career totals are 115 wins and 132 saves."

"Daddy's good," said Stephanie. "I hate it when people boo at him."

"Your dad's the best, Steph," said Willy.

At the table, the siblings squabbled and kept asking why there was no meat, Michelle and Zinger argued about a $75 bill to tune up a lawnmower that he never used, and Willy heard Michelle say, "we haven't made up our mind," in the singular, and knew she meant exactly what she said. Afterward, Michelle dismissed the kids to help Zinger pack for the road trip as a pretext to talk alone with Willy. Michelle piled dirty dishes, silverware, and cookware on the counter and declared, "I'd have to have a maid if I worked full time. There's much too much to do with Zinger away on the road half the year. The kids have gymnastics, karate, dancing, soccer, baseball, softball, girl scouts, cub scouts...Stephanie takes a computer class on Saturdays. Who has time to do stupid housework? Who has time to work? Not me! Most couples need two incomes. We're lucky that Steve's had a good, long career."

"It seems to me you're lucky *period*!" said Willy. "I really love Zinger–as a friend, I mean."

"He thinks the world of you." Michelle smiled, blowing a mouthful of smoke after lighting a cigarette. "You're teaching Steve something. There's still too much crap in the world preventing men and women from just being friends, but truly friends. It's a gift."

Willy reached for Michelle's hand to hold and murmured, "Hey, I'm getting two friends out of the deal."

CHAPTER 4

The Diamonds and an entourage of camp followers–about thirty wags, a dozen of Fabian's people, and a few spouses with preschool-aged kids–winged to pro baseball's first city late Friday afternoon. Since the team chartered its own plane, the players were spared quick getaways after night games to catch the next available commercial flight during road trips.

The team from New York City touched down in Cincy with time for only a brief respite before setting out to the stadium. Some of the players, including Paul, had rental cars waiting for them at the airport. In fact, the Diamonds' catcher had a rent-a-wreck lined up in advance for every stop on the road through the first of October. Zinger and Willy rode to the stadium with Paul, arriving about fifteen minutes before Tom's pregame meeting. On their way down to the hotel's parking garage, her two buddies detoured into the men's room, leaving Willy to be accosted by a pack of polite, but insistent, autograph hounds.

Paul and Zinger emerged from the washroom. "Don't ya ever wash your hands?" Paul asked.

"I make it a point not to piss on my fingers," Zinger replied. They pushed their way toward Willy and rescued her from the thrill-seekers. "Get a life, will ya?"

Standing shoulder-to-shoulder on either side of her, each with a hand clamped on one of her arms, they might have been bodyguards but for their wisecracking as they led her into the gift shop. Willy remained between them like a cuffed prisoner while Zinger bought a pack of

Turks. When Paul unfolded his wallet at the cash register as well, she gasped, "Oh, no! Not you, too!"

"Nah, I quit smokin' years ago," said Paul, as he laid down a dollar bill for a package of baseball cards.

"You're just a big kid, huh?" Willy said affectionately.

"Aw, shit, I got myself. What a waste!"

"I hate that they don't put gum in the package anymore," Willy complained.

"I got some Wazoos with comics in my pocket," Paul said, carefully unwrapping and placing the powdery pink slab into her palm.

"I like the stringy stuff that comes in a pouch like chewing tobacco," said Zinger.

Willy made a sour face. "It's too thin. No flavor! You need a whole, big handful to blow a proper bubble."

On the car ride, Zinger said, "Stephanie and little Mikey holler at me. I'd like to stop. Michelle's smoking doesn't help either."

"Don't blame her," scolded Willy. "If you stopped, maybe she could, too."

"Can we lighten up, kids?" Paul asked pleasantly.

Tom Vallery shuffled his pitching rotation by calling up Jay Phillips from Jacksonville after being knocked out of the box in the first inning earlier in the week. Todd Strickland was demoted on paper, but never departed and was recalled the very next day. Willy sat next to Rudy Judd, supposedly watching him chart Jay's pitches and taking notes on Cincy's hitters, but, instead, she focused on her young southpaw teammate and his opposite number, Wayne Cahill.

After Jay pitched six strong innings, he tired and threw "water balloons," as Rudy described them, and loaded the bases. Tom put Tim Langevin into the game. For the third time in a row, the Diamonds' reliever let inherited baserunners score, blowing the lead and allowing Cincy to tie the game before he retired the side. However, Tim would "vulcher" the win, as the D's came back with two runs off Cahill in the eighth and Larry Brooks threw two hitless innings to notch the save.

The players returned to the hotel after the game, fending off the star chasers, get-a-lifers, and groupies swarming the lobby. "Time for bed, chilluns," said Sandy Lee Danielson, his arm draped around a heavily made-up woman with sleepy eyes, barely out of her teens.

Zinger brushed aside a youngster holding a pen and baseball cards.

"They're not even real card collectors," he spoke to Willy's disappointed eyes. "They're runners for dealers. They get guys to autograph the cards, then they resell 'em for twenty-five bucks apiece."

"One kid tried to get me to autograph a batch of thirty cards while I was sittin' on the crapper," said Andy Gilbert.

"Hey, Lee Roy!" a brassy teenager called to Roy Burton, as he waited by the elevator with his wife, Lizann.

"My name's Leroi," he said with studied decorum.

The teen, wearing white denim slacks covered with multicolored ink marks, bent over and offered her plump buttocks to Roy, waving an uncapped felt-tipped pan and looking up at him backward with her head between her knees and her hair mopping the floor. "Please, sign my pants!" she begged.

"I don't sign clothing," Roy said softly as he followed his mortified spouse through the elevator doors.

Upstairs, Willy was bent on crawling between the sheets, watching a little tube, and getting a good night's sleep for Saturday's game. Before she could shed her clothes, Paul appeared at her door, carrying loose-leaf binders and a large, flat, white box with steam emanating from it. "I brought eats," he announced. "We got work to do, babe."

"You know I don't eat pizza," she complained.

Dropping the binders onto the bed, Paul lifted the lid and unveiled his glorious feast. "It's all-natural, whole wheat pizza," he explained happily. "A veggie special with double cheese, skim-milk mozzarella! Behold!"

"You just pigged out in the clubhouse an hour ago, Paul," said Willy, daintily plucking a mushroom from a glob of molten cheese.

"Empty calories!" said Paul with tongue in cheek.

Willy carefully balanced a wedge-shaped slice in her hand and puckered her lips to blow away the steam before carrying it to her mouth. She closed her eyes as her teeth sank into the spongy, thick cheese. She nibbled one, two, three bites and drew back the slice with an elongated string of mozzarella trailing through the air. Paul's eyes were locked in a stare when she opened hers. "You like watching me chew with cheese hanging off my lip?"

"Everything ya do is so elegant," Paul said admiringly.

"Oh, hush up!" Willy dismissed him with a smirk and wave of her hand, but felt a little tingle as she scooped her piece of pizza and nipped off another bit, not quite as gracefully this time. Her mouth full, Willy's eyelids drew closed and she hummed sweetly while chewing. "It is good," she said.

"See?" Paul said, and resumed tearing and gnashing his own piece. Then he cracked open the books. As he began to talk his way through the Big Red Machine's batting order, Willy eyeballed the batting, pitching, and fielding charts, the computer printouts of statistics, and thumbnail scouting reports. "Ya don't need to worry much about the defensive charts, but the batters' charts are real important."

She looked at the stenciled baseball diamond with patterns of green and red lines fanning out to represent the range and frequency with which a batter hits flies and grounders and where they go. She fretted a moment and said, "I think it'll almost be easier tomorrow than it was in Double-A, partner."

"How so?"

"Except for a few rookies, I know all these guys, and I have a pretty good idea of what kind of hitters they are and what they can and can't do. In the minors, the hitters were all strangers."

Paul nodded. "Sure, but there's a wild-card factor up here."

"What's that?" she asked.

He leaned toward her and tapped his finger on her knee. "You, babe! There's always an element of luck when a new pitcher faces a team for the first time. Like, we know Rod Weams is a good bad-ball hitter, but that doesn't mean we fastball him over the plate unless we think he can get the sweet part of the bat on your slider. We don't know if McAllister can handle your slider or if ya can beat him with your fastball. We have to find out all that stuff."

Paul let his hand rest on her leg as he spoke. Willy wished he hadn't done it, but hoped he wouldn't take it away. After three hours of stats, charts, and Paul's nonstop jawboning, Willy exclaimed, "This is hard work!"

"Life is hard work," Paul said in reply, his eyes twinkling. "But it's really a simple game...pitcher pitches, batter bats, three strikes and you're out."

"Ri-i-ight," Willy laughed.

Nine hours later, Willy shooed away wags barking questions while she threw her twenty warm-up pitches to Paul alongside Rudy. *Pop! Click! Flash!* "Smile for the cameras, Willy!" said the paparazzi. From behind a see-through plastic screen overlooking the field, a nationwide television audience heard: "Welcome to USTV's Game of the Week...This is Zack Traynor. Rob DaSilva and I will be bringing you the play-by-play, along with color commentary from Dave Warren. Today's game from pro baseball's birthplace in Cincinnati, Ohio, is between two third-place teams, but, as I'm sure all of our viewers know, the baseball world is abuzz about this young woman..." The screen showed Willy methodically winding up and throwing in the Diamonds' bullpen. "Willy Beal, making her first big league start for the New York Diamonds!"

"There's no question that the curiosity factor is high this afternoon," said the voice of Rob DaSilva, "but Willy Beal has steered clear of the media to concentrate on preparing for today's game, almost to the point that one might wonder whether she's fully aware of all the attention on her."

Dave Warren said, "There's definitely a protective circle around her, made up of some of her teammates and Diamond manager, Tom Vallery. His words are to leave her alone and let her pitch."

"And what sort of a pitcher are we likely to see today?" DaSilva asked Traynor, a former major leaguer turned announcer.

"The scouting reports say that Willy Beal has a deadly slider that's effective against both left- and right-handed batters, a fair curveball, and a live, hopping fastball. She has excellent control, moderate velocity, and she uses sidearm, overhand, and three-quarter overhand deliveries, making it tough for hitters to read what pitch is coming. She seems to be a combination of finesse and power pitching. It remains to be seen how well she can do with those tools in the Senior Circuit."

DaSilva told the viewers, "We'll begin to find out in a few moments."

Cincy put runners in scoring position against Willy, but failed to bring home a run as she ended both the first and second innings with strikeouts. The Diamonds scored one in the second and two in the third on doubles by Keith Whalen and Cal Bonham. In the bottom of the third, with two outs, a buggywhip fastball came down the middle of the plate to Cincy's catcher, Chad Boswell, and he hit it into the right field seats for a home run. It was the first gopher ball that Willy had served up since the winter league playoffs. Paul scurried out to her as Boswell rounded the bases. Willy was muttering and jamming the rubber with her toe.

"Forget it, babe! It's nothin'!" said Paul.

Willy sighed, bit her lip, and hissed, "I'm okay, Paul." She wouldn't look him in the eye and he went back to his stand behind the plate. Willy set down the next six Redlegs in order until the fifth frame, when right fielder Rod Weams jumped on a hanging outside curve for a second homer, making the score New York 3 Cincinnati 2. This time, Willy kicked up a huge, billowing cloud of red clay from the mound, and she even followed Weams part of the way around the bases, howling at him: "You got lucky, Rodney!"

Willy's antics drew laughter and sympathetic applause from the crowd. When Weams touched home plate, he said to Paul, "She's kinda hyper, isn't she?"

"Sure is! Better duck next time up," Paul replied. He trotted toward Willy to settle her down. "Nice show ya put on for the people, babe. Finished now?" She nodded, still not making eye contact. "Good! Listen, ya ended the first and second and started the fourth and fifth with strikeouts. We nailed two guys in a row on three pitches...fastball in, breakin' ball away, and fastball in. Then Weams read what was comin' and jumped on the breakin' ball."

"I know what we've been doing, Paul," Willy said testily.

"Uh-huh," he smiled, "and so do they. We gotta break the pattern. The next guy's a lefty. Let's go up-and-in and down-and-in with the slider. If he hits it, he won't be able to pull it." Then Paul said, "Ya made two little mistakes and got burned. Welcome to the majors, Willy!"

Willy pitched out of the inning with a soft fly ball and opened the sixth in identical fashion. Cincy's first baseman and clean-up batter, Jason McAllister, worked Willy through seven pitches and drew a base on balls. The runner should have been erased by a tailor-made double-play ball that was hit a few feet to the left of second base, but Cal, after taking the flip from Demmy, leaped high to evade the sliding Jason and his off-balance throw arrived too late at first base. The new batter was right-hand-hitting Jose Roman. Paul signaled for a screwball, but Willy shook him off. She nodded at his sign for a curveball and got a called strike. Then Paul gave no sign, meaning that he wanted her to throw the same pitch again. She dropped her arm to submarine and spun the pitch past Roman's swing, but it deflected off Paul's mitt and rolled to the backstop. The runner on first easily took second as the scoreboard flashed "PB" for a passed ball.

"A mix-up on the signs," Rob DaSilva told the USTV audience.

Paul stormed to the mound in a rage. "Don't you ever, ever cross me up like that again!" Paul was livid. "Throwin' underhand made it curve like a slider instead of droppin' like a curve."

Willy kept her eyes trained on the ground as she said, "Sorry, partner."

"Hey, look at me," he commanded. She raised her eyes without lifting her head and saw her catcher smiling. "Shit happens!" he said. "Now, I can't get Jake to throw his fastball out of the strike zone with two strikes...Make me happy, okay?"

"Okay!" Willy tried to go up-and-in with an overhand, offspeed fastball, but Roman muscled it inside the bag at first base, past Thor's outstretched glove hand, for an extra-base hit, driving home the tying run from second. Cal came over to visit Willy at the mound to tell her to keep the ball low and inside to the next batter and the result was a quick ground ball to shortstop for the third out.

The story of Willy at the bat was a one-liner: "Three hacks and you're out!" After being fanned in the top of the second, Willy hung her head and shuffled back to the D's dugout, dragging her bat behind her. The unwritten players' code of honor dictates that the failed performer be given his or her space. Thus, no one commented, nor did anyone sit beside Willy, fuming on the bench. When Willy went to bat a second time, in the fifth, catcher Chad Boswell warbled, "How's the humble pie taste, hot shot?"

Willy tucked the bat between her legs, tugged at her pigtails to free them out from under her helmet, shoveled some dirt with her hands, rubbed them together, gripped the bat's handle, and rolled it between her palms. Without casting her gaze upon him, she said, "Boz, if you say one more word about my hitting, I'll bean you in the on-deck circle next inning."

"I thought you had a sense of humor."

"This isn't funny."

The umpire yelled, "*Stee-riike!*" The pitch had come to the plate while Willy's head was turned to talk to the Boz Man.

"Ha! I thought you were too sharp to fall for a cheap trick like that." As Boz tossed the ball back to his pitcher, he taunted, "Wrong-oh!"

"I like a dude who can admit when he's wrong," said Willy, keeping her eyes directed toward the pitcher's mound. Two hacks later, Willy limply returned to the

D's bench. Once again her mates gave Willy her space, but not for long.

Cal called to her, "Good eye, kid! You held off swinging at the first pitch. Shows you're learning patience, discipline."

"I had help from the catcher," she snickered.

After Willy retired the side in order in the seventh, Rob DaSilva made his pronouncement, "We have a tie game through seven this afternoon in the Queen City and right now I'd have to say the most impressive thing is the way Willy Beal continues to throw strikes, without being overpowering, to keep her New York D's in this ballgame."

Zack Traynor added, "It's hard to believe it's her first start in the majors."

"She's been here before." In a nursing home far from the stadium, a frail, withered hand pointed shakily at the TV screen in the recreation room. The clean-cut young attendant gave the elderly woman a perplexed look. "That's what the old folks used to say when a child would be too smart, too wise, too good at what she could do...She's been here before." The Ghanaian immigrant smiled at the elder's foolishness of superstition and resumed watching his favorite athlete perform.

Cincy's lead-off batter, Weams, who hit the second home run off Willy, popped up to third on a sidearm fastball to end the inning. Willy trotted off the field to unexpectedly warm applause from the out-of-town fans. Feeling good about having put Weams away, Willy lingered on the dugout steps and waited for Paul. "That was easy," he said.

The pitcher's spot was due to bat second in the top of the eighth, but, before Willy could pull a bat from the rack, Tom crooked his finger at her. "Benny's going to bat for you," he said.

"You're not pulling me out, are you?"

The manager smiled and said, "You pitched well. Let the bullpen try and win it."

"The game's tied. I'm not even tired," she insisted.

"Cello, is she tired?" Tom asked coyly.

Paul replied to Tom, but trained his view on Willy. "She threw ten pitches last inning. Six of 'em were outta the strike zone. She's down to high school velocity. She's tired."

"Paul?" she moaned in dismay.

"Hey, lady," Tom chided. "Are you going to bust my chops every time I take you out of a game?"

Willy looked down at her shoes, saying, "I expect so."

Tom smiled, but Paul shook his head. With a disgruntled look on her face, Willy sauntered toward her battery mate and slumped next to him on the bench.

"Do I hafta tell ya to hit the showers again?" he joked.

"After a hundred pitches, I'm probably not the sweetest young thing you've ever been next to..."

"A hundred and seven...Sure ya are."

"But this is still my game. I can't watch the rest of it in the clubhouse," said Willy.

Bending to unstrap his shin guards, Paul laughed, "I wouldn't go in there if I were you either, babe."

"What do you mean?"

"Will ya get a clue?" he boomed. "There are wags from every paper, magazine, and TV station in the country waitin' to talk to ya after the game."

Willy threw back her head and stretched her legs to say, "Well, my adoring public can wait. I'm staying right here." Keith already lined a single to right center and he moved to second on Benny's slow roller to third. "I could've done that," grumbled the poorest hitting pitcher in the world. Then, Cal struck out and Demmy lined out to third, ending the inning along with Willy's chances for a win in her first outing as a starter.

"Stop your cussing!" Willy swatted Paul's hatless head, but gently so, as he fumbled with his no-sooner-off-than-on-again shin pads. "Rudy said he just left 'em on when he got old," she teased, "even when he was on deck." Paul stuck out his tongue and she popped a gum bubble at him. "Is Tom putting Larry in?" she asked him.

"No," he answered. "Zinger's gonna pitch. Never bring your closer into a tie game in the eighth inning. There's no leeway if the game's tied. If it stays tied, he stays for three or four innings instead of three or four outs. Most closers throw hard. If a breakin' ball hangs or a straight fastball comes over the middle of the plate–boom! We lose."

Steve Filsinger, veteran of five hundred relief appearances, induced the first batter in the eighth to hit a routine grounder to Demmy at short. With Paul and the other Diamonds back on the field, Willy headed for the showers. By the time she dressed and popped open a can of diet cola, Zinger gave the Cincinnatians a double, an RBI single, another double for a second run, and the D's were down, 5-3, going into the top of the ninth. A downcast Zinger dragged himself into the locker room. "I'm sorry, Willy. I blew your first game. I feel like crap."

"You're gonna take the loss, not me," Willy said.

"But still," he whined, "you pitched too good for us to get beat."

Willy went to Zinger with her hands held out to him. "Listen," she told him, "I'm not gonna die 'cause we lost one game."

"I'm just a little depressed," he said glumly.

Five o'clock lightning failed to materialize from the bat of Andy Gilbert as he grounded out to second. As soon as the game ended, Tom Vallery searched for Willy in the clubhouse.

"Willy, I think I should go into the press room with you."

"That's fine with me, Tom."

Then he said, "Please, if I squeeze your arm or kick you underneath the table, just shut up, whether you're answering a question or being asked one."

"Okay," laughed Willy. "Why?"

"It's amateur night in there. Off-the-wall questions might throw you for a loop. The regular sports beat reporters are waiting to talk to the usual suspects– Cal, Roy, Andy, Keith, and Paul...and especially Zinger."

"Poor Zinger," Willy lamented.

"He'll be all right," Tom chuckled. "They'll ask him what went wrong and he'll say, 'I stunk up the place.' That's all. He's an old pro"

Tom and Willy left the clubhouse and headed down the corridor to the packed and noisy press room. Contrary to his usual postgame accouterment, Tom kept his cap on and his glasses off. Tom took hold of Willy's arm and ushered her through the doorway. The move was obviously something he would never have done with a male player, but the gesture came naturally to someone who had been escorting women for all of his adult life.

Willy accepted it comfortably, fully expecting Tom to pull out her chair before being seated at the conference table, which was already set up with microphones and sundry recording and broadcasting equipment. The assault of shouted questions, probing hand-held and boom mics, video cameras, and flash bulbs was instantaneous. Willy thought that she couldn't have made her way from the front to the back of the room without Tom pulling her by the arm and, as she soon noticed, the D's general manager pushing her from behind.

The tired and worn locker room question came up first. "Why does everybody ask me about the locker room?" Willy responded cheerfully. "What do you think's going on in there anyway?"

There was laughter as Tom added, "The New York Diamonds are a Big League Baseball team, not a bunch of schoolboys. We don't need to make special rules or otherwise tell a group of twenty-five adults how to behave while showering and changing clothes."

Willy set out for her run the next morning from the hotel at quarter past five. She stopped short at the newspaper boxes in front when she saw *Today USA*'s headline: "Introducing Willy B. Superstar" on the front page, not in the sports section! The caption read: "New York
Bullpen Wastes Stellar Debut Performance."

Willy had no change in her sweatpants' pocket. So, she returned to the lobby and walked to the front desk. She asked the clerk, "Can I borrow a dollar to buy a paper? I'll pay you back later. I'm in room 409."

The desk clerk, who had been at his stand since the night before, said, "Never mind that," producing a copy from behind the counter. "Take it, but on one condition."

"What might that be?" she asked, pretending to be suspicious.

The man pulled a pen from the inside pocket of his suit coat and gave Willy a charmingly sly grin. "Sign it and give it back to me."

She took the pen and scrawled "Willy Beal slept here" across the front-page picture.

On the road, Paul would find his way to Willy's hotel room to say hello and return two or three hours hence with Zinger or Cal to ride to the ballpark. On the eve of a scheduled start, Paul came to Willy's room for a long night's work with the charts, stats, and scouting reports, even if it was after midnight following a ballgame. Willy anticipated Paul's visits, making sure she showered, fixed her hair, and put on fresh streetwear before he came by. His timing was unpredictable, but he never failed to show. She also began to dread homestands because of the absence of his visits. Paul was full of advice and philosophy. "Don't bean anybody. It's horseshit and somebody can get hurt that way. Don't knock the umps in front of the wags. They're people, too. Nobody likes to look bad. Besides, they can get even. Every beef should be a fresh start, not a continuation of the last argument."

"You do a lot of compromising," said Willy, smiling.

"Yeah? Well, listen. Out on the field we got you pitchers, who think the whole game revolves around you. The hitters think it belongs to them, the manager thinks it's all his, and the umps think it's theirs. The catcher is the position where all those lines intersect."

"Like alternative realities," quipped Willy.

"Uh-huh," said Paul. "The catcher is the center...the hub of the wheel...and he's got to keep it turnin'."

"So, you guys are the same as everybody else. You think the whole game revolves around you, too."

"Sure," Paul said glibly, "but it does!"

On the road meant another town and another press conference: "Do you consider yourself the female Jackie Robinson?"

"No," she chirped curtly. "He played second base. I'm a pitcher."

"You've broken the gender barrier just as he broke the color barrier. Surely, you see the parallels," the interrogator persisted.

"Well, of course, I do, but we live in a different world today. I know the history of the kind of stuff Jackie Robinson and Larry Doby and men like my grandfather had to put up with. I'll never disrespect that. I also know about how Judge Landis voided Jackie Mitchell's contract because she was a woman and Toni Stone's teammates told her to go home and bake biscuits … but I haven't had to overcome those kinds of obstacles."

"Willy, you've been criticized in some quarters for being more accessible to white fans than black fans."

"That's not a question." Willy turned to point across the room. "Next!"

"Why won't you respond?"

Willy stared with the eyes of cold fury. "Like I said, it's not a question!"

Sebastian Fabian watched a video replay of Willy's most recent session with the media. He said,

"When she pitches, they love her. When she laughs, they love her. When she cries, they love her ... And when she gets mad, they love her." Present in the room were Alan Blaylock and Kristin Tracy, currently Fabian's two favorite young middle managers in the baseball operation. Fabian declared, "Life is good. Willy puts asses in the seats." He walked to his desk and picked up a letter. "The lefty-loosey liberals think she belongs to them. The right-wing loonies think she's theirs ... The pink hats love her. Joe Six Pack loves her. The ghettos, barrios, and suburbs love her. Little kids follow her like the Pied Piper. Teenage girls want to *be* her and teenage boys want to *do* her. People are starting to call the team Willy and the Diamonds. It sounds like a rock band. Ha!" Fabian winked at Kristin. "It defies logic!" Then Fabian fancied aloud, "She's done half her job already. We've made quota on season tickets. We're sold out except for the cheap seats. We're selling out in small-market towns on the road. TV ratings are the highest in years. Ad rates are up. Revenue is up. Everybody's making money...Now, she has to get the other half of her job done...as a pitcher."

"He's obsessed with her," Kristin said to Alan. "He's completely distracted from the team."

"No, he's not," Alan replied. "Harvey says he's using Willy to get his hands into the dugout. Vallery's steamed because Mr. Fabian's calling the shots. When Willy pitches, it's his call, not Tom's. He dictates the rotation and Jake is really bent out of shape. We have three nationally televised games in a week and Willy's starting two of them."

CHAPTER 5

As a counterpoint to Willy's four-hit, three-run quality appearance on Saturday, Sandy Lee was tagged for seven hits and six runs in four and a third innings on Sunday, giving up
round-trippers to McAllister and Roman. Zinger put out the fire in the fifth, but Tim took over the mound for the next inning and served up another gopher ball to McAllister and the Diamonds went down, 7-1.

The team moved on to San Diego to open a three-game set on Memorial Day. If the Diamonds could bounce back from jet lag–playing a Monday afternoon game after deplaning at midnight–they had an opportunity to feast on a last-place ballclub. The road stop in San Diego marked a homecoming for Demeter Fortune, whose hitting streak ended Sunday at twenty-five games. Had it not been for Dale Goodwyn's declaration that Demeter Fortune was the best-hitting shortstop since A-Rod, Ernie Banks, and Honus Wagner, Demmy wouldn't have had the foggiest notion who Ernie and Honus were. Yet, seeking to emulate his well-respected teammate, Cal Bonham, Demmy donned the frock of a baseball traditionalist to rag the local press corps at his former place of business. "It's great to play in a city with so much baseball tradition. The Big Town is full of the history of the sport–not like here!" The local media played and replayed Demmy's poorly-thought-out remarks and when he walked from the on-deck circle in the first inning, San Diego transformed into Flatbush for one glorious moment as the boos rained upon his head.

During the home team's batting practice, Willy strolled over to Leo Cortez, San Diego's manager, to introduce herself. Leo listened with great interest as Willy told him how impressed she was with his dedication to using baseball to help children, as told to her by all-time great Yo-Yo Fuentes in San Juan. Leo furrowed his brow and screwed up his face, saying, "Let's keep that little story between you and me. Okay, Willy?" Willy was uncomprehending. Cortez shook his head and laughed, "If our GM ever got wind that our top Latin American scout was havin' dinner with you *the night before* you signed with the Diamonds, he'd fire the poor bastard. Hall of Fame Yo-Yo or no Hall of Fame Yo-Yo!"

Afterwards, Willy noticed that Gil Douglas left the sidelines after finishing his pregame warm-up, but he didn't appear to be in the dugout or on the field with the game about to get underway. Willy went back to the locker room to grab the clipboard and note cards that Paul now regularly left for her, although she doubted that she would ever pause during a game to read her notes like a crib sheet before pitching to a batter. Willy trotted through the locker room doorway, her spikes playing the concrete like a tap number, past the stalls, where she saw a pair of size fourteen cleated soles jutting out from under one of the clamped-shut doors, accompanied by the sound of retching, coughing, heaving, spitting, and a sob. Willy paused to absorb a tidbit from the secret life of heroes and hurried away before she intruded upon Big Gil's dignity.

The Diamonds beat the host team once, twice, thrice. Now, the D's in second place, ahead of the Floridians and within a game and a half of the Atlantans, filed onto the airport bound bus and spent a sleepless night in flight to San Francisco. Some of the guys decided to find a fancy restaurant at noontime. Willy initially begged off, determined not to eat, since she would be pitching that evening. The game was scheduled for a six o'clock start to hit prime time east of the Rockies, as USTV cancelled its rerun of the week to carry "*Willy II*" after the corporate eyeballs boggled at the overnight ratings for "*Willy I*" in Cincinnati. Willy was forcibly abducted from her hotel room by Cal and Zinger and whisked away to "the best seafood place on Fisherman's Wharf." She stomped her feet in protest when they came to get her, but was wearing a frilly blouse, new jeans, earrings, and her going-out shoes. In the back of the restaurant, seated around a row of tables pushed together, the visiting ballplayers ate, drank, and made merry, with Willy using the tines of her fork to keep Zinger's thieving fingers off her baked stuffed mushrooms and zucchini sticks.

"Of all the eatin' places in this here town," declared Sandy Lee. "Lookie who's here!"

From his seat at an adjacent table came San Francisco's all-star first baseman, Tony Ortega. His deep, accented voice cut through the room. "Hey, Daniels!" big Tony bellowed.

Sandy Lee tilted his head and looked up. "It's Daniel-*son*, ya big dumb ass!"

"Yeah, *Danielsonofabitch*!" Ortega clamped his large hands on Sandy Lee's shoulders and shook him playfully.

Cal said, "Tony, have you met Willy?"

Tony set the Rebel free and offered his hand across the table to Willy. "We heard all winter about la

Macha. Everybody knows Macha is coming," he smiled warmly, leaned over Sandy Lee's shoulder, and pulled Willy's extended hand to his lips and blew a kiss onto it. "It's a pleasure to meet you, Willy Macha."

"Ooh!" She wiggled in her chair and her dangling earrings danced around her head. "The pleasure's mine, Tony Ortega."

"Knock it off and drink your carrot juice," said Paul. Willy stuck out her tongue at the catcher, and then returned her gaze to Ortega's broad, smiling face.

Veteran southpaw Cliff Allyn was on the mound for the Golden Gate Titans. Cliff was what one would call "ruggedly handsome," meaning not cute. He wore his stringy black locks
long in back–in style, out of style, then in and out again. He had a thick moustache, giving him a look that might do well in western movies, although he would make a better rustler than a sheriff, Willy concluded. Cliff had gone through a ten-year career cycle of gradually becoming one of the league's top hurlers, fortunately developing his split-fingered fastball before back and shoulder problems forced him to abandon hard throwing. He also was reputed to throw the slimiest of spitballs, but, of course, he denied it. "That's against the rules, or so I've been told," he flatly stated, time and again.

The media hype and hoopla was much more in evidence tonight as compared to Saturday with Willy holding court for the wags before the game and after. For the Bay Area media, Willy Beal was tonight's special guest star, but the top billing in San Francisco baseball was reserved for the local team's manager, Charlie Novak. Whereas Tom Vallery was said to be a manager's manager, Novak was a player's manager–at any rate, in the eyes of those who responded to his dugout brand of "tough love" and the few he deemed worthy of playing for him. There were more than occasional punches thrown in the clubhouse, but the players who played hard or well enough to stay out of his doghouse knew Charlie would back them up–no matter what. The enigma was that his better players–flashy Donnie Ross, gentlemanly Eric Jackson, jovial Tony Ortega, laconic Cliff Allyn, chronically overweight Bruce McElroy, modestly unassuming Greg Ruggieri, and pseudo-intellectual Gary Steele–albeit in their contrasting ways, were generally antithetical to Novak's tough-guy style.

The home plate umpire was Rochemont Guilford. Monty was the biggest ump in baseball. At well over 300 pounds, he was, as Paul said, "the biggest hot dog with relish" in the game. His third-strike and out-at-the-plate calls were more entertaining than the action on the field. Before her first pitch of the game, Monty said to Willy, "Give them sons-of-bitches some hell, lady blue."

With one away in the top of the first, Demmy expertly drew a walk, but he was erased by a hard-hit double-play ball off the bat of Andy, and Allyn returned to the dugout unscathed. Willy put down the Frisco Gigantics, one-two-three, in the bottom of the first. Allyn brought the fans to their feet by throwing six straight strikes past Roy and Thor, and Willy set down the side in order once more in the second. Paul had told Willy, "The key to beatin' Frisco is keepin' Donnie off base and keepin' the ball away from the big guns, Tony and Eric." A couple of close, inside pitches to the San Francisco hitters helped Willy establish control of the plate and she was breezing through skipper Novak's batting order as she went up to bat in the Diamonds' third. Willy stared unblinkingly into Cliff's grizzly sneer as he fired a high, hard one. The fastball appeared as a flash of white homing straight for Willy's eyes. She went *splat*! with her face in the dirt, feet kicking, and bat waving in midair.

"There's no double standard for Willy Beal about retaliation for close pitches...at least, as far as Cliff Allyn and his manager, Charlie Novak, are concerned," Rob DaSilva announced to his USTV audience.

"But the New York Diamonds may be another story," said Zack Traynor. "Everyone is up and standing in the Diamonds' dugout." As Willy slowly lifted herself from the ground and
brushed off her soiled jersey, Zack said, "Tom Vallery is yelling something to home plate umpire Monty Guilford."

"But don't expect Tom to get any satisfaction from Guilford. The crew chief saw Willy Beal's brushbacks of Ortega and Jackson earlier," Rob opined.

On the other side of the partitioned broadcast booth, Cam Hammersmith told the Millennium Channel viewers, "Paul Cello and pitching coach Rudy Judd are on the top step with Vallery."

"It almost looks as if Rudy is holding Cello in check," said Jeff McCarty, "and Novak's got his crew on their feet in the home dugout."

Back on the network side, Rob explained, "This crowd has grown awfully quiet...We are, I'd venture to say, a pitch away from an old-fashioned, bench-clearing brawl."

"Or a beaning," Zack whispered with his hand covering the microphone.

Willy's knees were rubbery and trembling wracked her body such that the bat held in her right hand whipped around in small concentric circles as she planted her feet in the box. The sweat poured from beneath her plastic batting helmet. She hummed a guttural note from deep within her throat, loud enough for catcher Gary Steele to hear, her mantra invoking the names of Tony Conigliaro and Ray Chapman. She edged her front foot beyond the partially obliterated chalk line of the batter's box to within a hair's breadth of touching the white slab in black outline. With bat held upright, she crouched at the waist and, in the fashion of the great William Howard Mays, brought her head directly over the plate. Her eyes riveted onto Cliff Allyn's expressionless glare. "Come on with it!" she snarled through her teeth.

San Francisco's skipper folded his arms and uttered, "I don't freakin' believe it."

USTV's DaSilva's monotone raised in pitch a bit. "Willy Beal defiantly challenging the southpaw after the apparent knockdown...Crowding the plate..."

"Sonofagun!" exclaimed Millennium Channel's Hammersmith.

Allyn heaved a soft lob a good three feet outside. Willy stepped away from the plate and Steele deliberately walked behind her, brushing his mitt against her backside. "Chill out! He made his point." He walked in front of her and tossed the ball back to Allyn. "So did you. It's over with!" Steele walked back behind the plate and stooped into his crouch. "You're one gutsy ballplayer, Willy." She just smiled without replying and readied herself for Allyn's next pitch. Three hacks later, Willy returned to the Diamonds' bench, fanned again.

Welcome to the National Baseball League, where the pitchers have to bat!

Willy led off the bottom of the third by walking third baseman Andre Harris. A well executed bunt and a throwing error by Keith Whalen put runners on first and third with one out. Willy looked hard and long at Ross, batting from the left side. The five-feet-seven base-stealing virtuoso held his bat parallel to the ground and crouched so low that he seemed to be sitting in a chair, reducing his already minuscule strike zone to a laser-thin line. Paul signaled for a slider. Willy shook him off, but he called for it again. He wasn't worried about a walk in this situation, but rather a fly ball for a hit or simply deep enough to score Harris from third. The slider was the bait if indeed Ross was swinging for the outfield. He was and he lofted a foul pop toward the first base side. Paul stormed out from behind the plate, tossing his mask over his shoulder and shoving aside the great hulking umpire. The catcher waved away Thor, who had come running from first base, and lunged onto the dugout roof to grab the out, nearly tumbling backward into the Golden State team's den were it not for a gracious supporting arm from pilot Novak. Willy stood out on the mound, swinging her arms in an exaggerated clapping gesture, followed by a two-fingers-in-the-mouth whistle and a flamboyant thumbs-down aimed at the next batter, Vic Wilson. The USTV cameras even caught Ross smiling at Willy's act as he descended into his dugout. With the D's infield playing in for a twin-killing or play at the plate, the G's second sacker lined an offspeed fastball between Keith and Demmy for a base hit, and San Francisco tallied the first run of the game. In the Diamonds' half of the sixth, right fielder Dino DeSantis rapped the first base hit off the venerable Allyn, but was forced at second by Keith's grounder to shortstop. Applause and scattered chants of *"Wil-lee! Wil-lee!"* came from the nonpartisan crowd as Willy went to bat. The nationwide television viewers saw the tall, slender, pig-tailed woman bend deeply at the waist and knees into a sitting position with her bat held straight out from her right shoulder.

"Willy Beal taking a page from the Donnie Ross book of hitting..." Rob DaSilva announced.

Zack Traynor added, "It makes sense for her to try to cut down that big target she gives. With three whiffs in three times at bat, she might as well try anything."

Rob called the action: "The infield is in, looking for a sacrifice bunt...Here's the pitch...swung on...a hard grounder to Harris at third. He goes to second for one, and...no play at first!"

"Vic Wilson, very wisely, holding on to the ball," said Zack. "Willy Beal flew like the wind down the line to first base, fast enough to have beaten out an infield hit, but it goes down as a groundout force play."

On the other side of the glass partition, Cam's voice raised in excitement, as he intoned,
"With the score San Francisco one, New York nothing, there are two out and–for the first time in big league history–there's a *woman* on base!"

The USTV director, Russ Heman, ordered a split-screen view of Cal Bonham batting and the former schoolgirl track star's long-strided lead off first, but Willy's anticipated flight to second base, or beyond, ended in anticlimax as Cal flew out to Eric Jackson in shallow center. As the two teams changed sides between innings, the whiz kid of USTV Sports directed two cameras to be permanently trained on Willy while she pitched, one for a full body shot, the other for a facial close-up. "The number three camera can follow the ball," Russ said. "She's goofing around one minute and on fire the next. She's better than the damn game!" Ten minutes hence, the entire network crew in the broadcast booth erupted with laughter while monitoring the New York affiliate's "teaser" being sent home via satellite, during a sixty-second break for local station identification. Dave Warren, the highest-paid TV personality in the Big Apple, wearing a pink carnation in his lapel, matching the ribbons tying Willy's pigtails, put on a ballsy matchbook cover school of announcing voice to say, "Can a woman pitch in the big leagues?" After a dumb-faced pause, he shouted, "That, ladies and gents, may go down as the *stupidest* question in baseball history...*Guess who* has a one-hitter going into the seventh inning in the city by the bay!" He paused again, still not a hint of a smile, and quacked, "Film at eleven!"

"For those of you just tuning in to tonight's USTV telecast," said the voice of DaSilva, "we have quite a pitchers' duel between the veteran Cliff Allyn and the rookie Willy Beal, with San Francisco leading one-nothing. The Diamonds have one out and a runner on third, here in the top of the seventh. Fortune led off with a double...only the second hit of the game surrendered by the left-hander, Allyn...and he moved to third when Gilbert grounded out to shortstop. Burton, the switch-hitter batting right-handed steps in...He leads all of baseball in home runs with fourteen, but he's been struck out swinging twice tonight by Allyn...A foul straight back for strike one."

Zack commented, "Cliff Allyn is working exclusively with the split-finger fastball to Burton."

"Here's the oh-one pitch...Swing and a miss, strike two," DaSilva called.

Said Zack: "He went after a high, inside pitch...An offspeed fastball sailing up, not the split-finger, which breaks down like a screwball...Expect Allyn to go to that same spot again."

Said Rob: "The oh-two pitch...A long, long drive to left center field...Gone! The fabled Candlestick wind carries Roy Burton's fifteenth homer of the year out of the park and puts the New York Diamonds on top, two-to-one."

Down in the dugout, Roy received his mates' glad-handing with a disgruntled look on his face. "I didn't really hit the ball well," he said.

Cal crowed from a corner seat on the bench, "You knocked the sucker into the mother lovin' bay, Leroi!"

"I oughtta know when I hit the ball well, and I didn't," he retorted. "I can't hit Cliff worth shit no more." No one addressed the point any further with Mr. Burton.

Minutes later, shortstop Miller Drake jumped on a sidearm fastball for a long hit, going into third base standing up, successfully challenging Andy's arm from left field. After Willy retired the next two batters, Novak lifted Allyn for a pinch-hitter, who snaked a "seeing-eye" single between Cal and Thor on the right side of the infield, good for sending home the game-tying run. Next, Donnie smashed a liner past Cal for another hit. With the hometowners cheering and clapping for a rally, Willy ignored Donnie's ambling two-step lead toward second, knowing that even baseball's prince of thieves would hesitate to challenge Paul's still lethal throwing arm with two outs. She blew an overhand fastball past Wilson for an inning-killing strikeout and ran off the field to a spontaneous round of applause from the Bay Area fans. Standing atop the dugout steps, Willy doffed her cap and waved to the 45,000 assembled and gave them a shake of the pigtails.

Willy's aplomb was unfortunately premature. In the eighth, Eric Jackson–probably the Golden State Clippers' best all-around player–doubled with one out. Willy whiffed Steele–to the obvious delight of her battery mate–but gave up a single by Drake, allowing Jackson to scamper homeward with the game-leading run. Willy didn't need to turn around to know that Tim and Zinger were up and warming in the Diamonds' bullpen. When Monty called ball four on Harris, Willy's fourth walk of the night, she expected to see Tom walking on the field. Instead, Rudy lumbered toward her, motioning for Paul to join them at the mound.

"Are you tired, honey?"

"I don't get tired, Rudy. They're just catching up with me, I guess."

"For the moment!" chimed Paul. "No bullshit, Rudy. She hasn't lost a thing."

"Good!" the pitching coach said to the catcher. "Tom wants to keep her in for one more at-bat, so he can see what Novak's gonna do with the pitcher's spot up after this next guy."

"She can blow this clown away with sliders," Paul said.

Rudy concurred, and gave Willy a wink before returning to the dugout. Then Willy motioned with her forefinger to Harris on first and, with a little dancing step, did likewise to Drake on second. She shouted, "Might as well sit down, guys! You're not going anywhere!"

Willy's first slider broke in, the second one broke away, and the third broke in, as Rob declared, "That's strikeout number three for Willy Beal...pitching out of a jam for the second consecutive inning...but the boys and the girl from New York City trail, three to two."

Meanwhile, the soft, fluffy serves of an aged and obese knuckleballer, Bruce McElroy, blanked the Diamonds in the eighth and ninth, sealing Willy's first defeat of the season.

Rob DaSilva came down from the broadcasters' cloister and entered the visitors' dugout via the back way before Willy had a chance to escape into the clubhouse sanctuary. Despite wearing the losing pitcher's tag, she was USTV's player of the game.

DaSilva was a journalist at heart and by training; he worked as an announcer for three reasons: money, money, and money! Rob, already under criticism for blatantly cheerleading for the female phenom, zeroed in on the third inning. "What was going through your mind when Allyn knocked you down?"

With a momentary pause, Willy shook her head and sighed loudly, almost melodically. "I can't even remember it," she said.

DaSilva laughed, but he did so with on-the-air control. "He threw a fastball at your head and you hit the dirt, fearing for your life, it seemed."

Willy deployed a theatrical laugh of her own as she dismissed the notion of a brushback or knockdown. "Sometimes a pitch slips out of the pitcher's fingers. I'm sure that's what happened. I might've overreacted." Rob smiled, acknowledging that she was not about to engage the question.

The postgame wrap-up on the Millennium Channel was understandably more partisan. Cam said, "Willy Beal's first big league win is turning out to be elusive indeed. She spun a four-hitter last Saturday and a six-hitter in tonight's ballgame, netting her one no-decision and one loss. There's no way she can keep pitching like that without bringing home some wins."

"You're absolutely right, Cam," said his booth mate, Jeff. "But, for the moment, she's oh and one and the D's drop another half game back of idle Atlanta."

The next night, Sandy Lee beat San Francisco 4-2 on a five-hitter, outdoing the combined efforts of righty starter Winston Dixon and lefty reliever Greg Ruggieri. The Diamonds took three out of four from Novak's crew over the weekend. Showcased on the game of the week, Jake started out pitching like the best southpaw in the majors, only to go into the fifth inning looking like the faceless server in a home run derby. However, Tim returned to his old form and pitched four perfect, hitless, runless frames for a 6-5 victory and Big Gil won a shutout in Sunday's "rubber game." Since the Atlanta Tomahawk-Choppers were swept three straight in Colorado and the Florida Fishies dropped two of three against Arizona, the New York Diamonds boarded the "red-eye" charter from the Left Coast to New York as the first-place team in the Eastern Division by a margin of a game and a half.

There was an evening to rest, relax, and repack before catching the overnight flight for home at midnight. At the hotel, Zinger rapped on Willy's door, weighted down by two grocery bags. "What's all this!" she asked happily, stepping aside to let him enter.

"Sunday night supper in New Rochelle," Zinger declared. "Take-out Chinese!" He unpacked the bags full of plastic and cardboard containers. "This is the place to go for Chinese food. They even have take-out and fast-food Japanese, too. I always hit this sushi place at Embarcadero when we're in Frisco."

"Sam Khoury told me San Franciscans never call it Frisco," said Willy, opening, sniffing, and sampling the items being laid out on her bed and nightstand.

"I got your veggies for you," he said, quite pleased with himself. "And I got spring rolls. The stuff inside is shredded, not chopped up like egg rolls." Willy nodded as he kept on talking. "Do you want tea?"

Willy smiled and reached for the plastic cup of tea. "This is so sweet, Zinger, but you don't have to take care of me like this all the time."

"What, you shouldn't eat?" After eating his fill, Zinger uncapped a silver butane lighter and ignited a cigarette, forming a billowing cloud around his head. "You can really pack it away, Willy. You ate twice as much as me."

"Damn, Zinger!" She made a sour face, her mouth closed and chewing as she waved away the smoke. "You know what smoke-free hotel means? Anyway," she said, crunching a mouthful of noodles, "it's that lighter of yours...smells like poison gas. Why not get one of those little Flic lighters?"

"This was a graduation gift from my father," Zinger said, proudly puffing on his unfiltered Turk. My old man was not too pleased about me becoming a ballplayer. A nice Jewish boy is supposed to go to college, be a doctor, lawyer, businessman, but not a professional athlete."

Willy studied him closely. "Isn't there a cultural belief about not putting your body at risk?" she asked. "After a while, though, didn't he accept it?"

Zinger nodded. "What the hell! It was his own fault. He was a big fan. That's what got me started. He just didn't expect me to be that good, or to get as far as I did."

"I don't see how you can perform on the field, smoking the way you do," Willy said.

"I don't need any more guilt. I've got a Yiddish mother to give me all the guilt I need," he said, adding, "She's seventy-two and still kicking ass."

"Does she smoke?"

"No," he said contritely.

"Gotcha!" Willy laughed, pointing her finger at him.

Zinger dreamily for a moment, then said, "I love the movies...Especially old ones!"

Willy gave him an expectant look, then asked, "Who played three different characters based on Josh Gibson?"

Zinger paused between chews to answer, "James Earle Jones."

Willy tried another name: "Jimmy Pearsall?"

"Anthony Perkins."

Willy shot back, "Monty Stratton?"

"Jimmy Stewart."

"Dutch Holland?"

"Jimmy Stewart again!"

"His wife?"

"June Allison, both times!"

"Dizzy Dean, Pete Alexander, and Satchel Paige?"

"Dan Dailey, Ronald Reagan, and Lou Gossett, Jr."

Then Willy threw Zinger a curve, "Who played Babe Ruth...?"

"William Bendix and John Goodman."

"...in *Pride of the Yankees*?"

"Himself!"

Willy dangled her open palm. "Don't leave me hanging here." He slapped her five.

"My favorite actor is Rod Steiger," Zinger told Willy. "One time I saw an old interview with him on some talk show and he said his latest film was a story about heroes...*real heroes*...which he said were ordinary people who had the guts to get out of bed in the morning."

"That's what it's really all about, isn't it?" said Willy, scraping up the last bit of cabbage from her spring roll and carrying it on a plastic fork into her mouth.

CHAPTER 6

A day of R&R back home in the Jersey suburbs, before opening a three-game set with the Tinseltown Trolley-Dodgers, turned into a frenetic whirl of apartment hunting in Manhattan with Art Ridzik and a broker whose name Willy couldn't remember.

Artie gave Willy a quick tour of his new office suite in Long Island City. It was small, but everything, including the desk-top computers and photocopiers, smelled new. "Did you buy all this stuff with my money, Uncle Artie?"

"We haven't made much of anything yet, Willy." Art looked stunned, truly wounded by Willy's question in jest. "Actually, I'm renting this suite with an option to buy. It's an office condo, but everything here–all the furniture–is rented."

"I was just kidding," said Willy, smiling and patting his arm.

"But you know something?" Art said. "Don't be surprised if some of the promotion and advertising deals pay good money up front and the big-name national brands could bring in more in residuals than you make in salary from the Diamonds."

"Yeah, right!" she scoffed. Willy pulled up a chair at Art's desk to attack the piles of file folders and correspondence, the result of his wheeling and dealing. She studied his face and asked, "How come you and your wife split up after thirty years together?"

It was a touchy subject. "People change." Willy shrugged, not satisfied with the reason and unhappy that he was withholding information about himself, especially since she was treating Art as "almost family." "We've got plenty of stuff to do today," he said, getting down to business. "Maybe we'll go to Paramus and write up the lease for your car tomorrow morning."

"Don't forget about my present for Mama," Willy said. She planned to give her mother a more austere and practical Nimoco sedan.

"We can have my guy put in an order through a dealership in the Old Saint Pete area...Oh, my friend, the mortgage broker, can shop around different banks to get us a good rate for your brownstone unit."

"Whatever you say, Uncle Artie."

"You should plan on getting with me, say, every Monday, unless you're on the road, so we can stay on top of your personal appearances."

"No appearances on days when I'm scheduled to pitch! I'll stress out," said Willy.

"How am I supposed to figure that out?" Art snapped. "I've heard from community groups, churches, synagogues, temples, mosques, youth baseball and softball leagues, public
schools, private schools, parochial schools, Yeshiva schools, fraternities, sororities, student groups, parent groups, teachers' associations, and women's groups...Maybe you should steer
clear of them. No politics, you said."

"I'll talk baseball," she chuckled.

"I think the deal with ReVerse looks good. It's a merchandising natural for you."

"I'm not a pair of designer sneakers, Artie!" she protested. "ReVerse running shoes are way overpriced."

Art ignored her comment. "We should do the deal with American Cola right away. They want to get you into the studio to tape a commercial ASAP."

"That sounds good. It is the brand I drink," she mumbled.

"This could be real big!" Artie grinned as he opened another manila folder.

Willy saw the corporate logo and yelled, "Get real, Artie! I'm not about to do any ads for fast-food burgers. No way!"

"Oh, come on, Willy. Their people know you're a veggo. They want you for their public service activities."

Willy was adamant. "Lose that folder, Uncle Artie!"

Art said unhappily, "Okie-dokie, we'll put the burgers on the back burner."

"Thank you," Willy said with a dainty smile.

"Now we have the interviews and talk shows...Let's see what we've got...*Lifetime, He, She & We* magazine, *Ebonette*, and *Sportsworld*, of course. Did they call you about the cover story?"

"I talk to Sam Khoury a lot," Willy replied.

"She's kind of a snotty little..."

"Don't say it!" Willy warned. "She's my pal."

"There's USTV, Sportsnet, and public TV wants to do a piece on you. No money, though!... *'The Goodnight Show'* wants you. *'After Midnight'* wants you. The producer of *'Live from New York'* wants you to be the guest host on Saturday night."

"You're kidding me!" she hummed, bouncing on her chair. Then she shook her head and said, "Maybe after the season's over!"

"Oh, yeah, I almost forgot about the *Playmate* interview."

"I don't believe you, Artie!" declared Willy.

"They don't want you to pose for the centerfold, Willy!"

"I don't see any harm in that, really. The naked human body is natural perfection. I'm not ashamed of my body, you know!"

"What?" Art was aghast. "It doesn't exactly fit the image we're promoting, for crying out loud."

Willy suppressed a laugh. "Chill, Artie. I'm kidding...but, anyway, the answer's no." Art grunted and talked about merchandising toys, computer games, clothing, baseball equipment, and cosmetics. "I don't even wear makeup, except sometimes lip gloss."

"You're turning down all the best deals," Art complained. "This is the chance of a lifetime, sweetheart. Money makes the world go round, Willy. You might as well get your share."

"It's not about money," she sighed and smiled sadly.

"Fine," he said patronizingly. "Be practical, then. The average career lasts five years. You're twenty-eight. We have to strike while the iron is hot...And another thing–I expect we'll be ready to hit up Fabian to renegotiate your contract soon."

Willy said warily, "The guys say it's a bad idea to get into a contract hassle during the season."

"We're not going to watch Fabian make millions off you while he pays you spit for three years 'til you qualify for salary arbitration."

Dave Warren of USTV Sports interviewed Willy in front of her locker before the next home game. As

they talked, Willy carefully slid one arm and then the other out of the sleeve holes of her sweatshirt, kept it wrapped around her as far as her elbows, took an already buttoned team jersey, wiggled her wrists into it, and let it drape her front as she pulled the sweatshirt off and the jersey on in a single motion, revealing only a glimpse of her flat tummy while she
smoothed and tucked her shirt.

"No cheap thrills in this locker room!" quipped the TV wag.

At game's end, Willy, partially shielded inside her locker, watched as Demeter Fortune, in full-color flesh tone, emerged from the shower and snapped his towel at any teammate's rump that crossed his path. After Demmy's adolescent reign of terror quieted down, Willy lifted her foot to step into a pair of undies. *Smack!* The silent assassin's tightly spun terrycloth saber whipped across one cheek and then– *Smack!* –likewise for the other. *"Touche a la tush!"* Demmy laughed with glee as Willy, stunned and speechless, rubbed the injured spot. "You're one of the guys, right?"

"Yeah, that's right," she fake-cried, still rubbing, too indignant to laugh.

The Diamonds' shortstop wore a conceited grin as he turned the corner to the next row of lockers, only to reappear a moment later and say, "Cute glutes!"

"Shush!" she howled, grabbing an available sneaker and heaving it at him as he ducked around the corner again. Willy smiled to herself as she dressed. Something had triggered Demmy to say, "Let's be friends!" by way of a slap on the rump. To Willy it was well worth the sting.

Willy anxiously anticipated the next game she was to pitch, but the embarrassment of having to bat caused stomach aches, pangs of fear, and nausea. Although everyone was generous with advice, Willy sought out Demmy. Watching him was a clinic in itself.

"Can I throw to you?"

"No, let Handy Man do it. Stand here and talk to me."

Demmy first used a short left-handed swing, imitating Cal's "chicken-wing" flapping, and then did the same from the right side. He followed with a level line-drive stroke before swinging up to pull the ball toward the outfield fences.

"The whole idea of swinging through with the bottom hand and pulling off the top hand is because the bottom hand does all the work. A right-handed hitter is working with his left arm as the strong arm and vice versa. That's why there are so many right-handers who learn to bat left-handed. You get the advantage of being closer to first base and more power from the left side." Demmy talked about and demonstrated Hank's and Babe's wrist-flicking, swinging lefty and righty, respectively. He went on to imitate Joe D., pointing the bat at the pitcher like a rifle, and Stan the Man, who twisted and coiled himself like a snake in the batter's box. Willy told Demmy that Turkey Stearnes batted from an almost identically unorthodox stance in the 1920s and '30s. "Ted Williams said there was no such thing as a true level swing because the pitch is coming down from the elevation of the pitcher's mound," he said. "You're really hitting the ball into the ground." Demmy paused to drill a pitch from the bullpen coach. "Sadaharu Oh cut the ball in half, like he was wielding a samurai sword, and he kept his weight off the front foot by lifting it up in the air, like a flamingo." Demmy completed the demonstration by dangling his left foot with knee fully bent, striding out only as his bat cut through the next toss from Handy Man, driving the ball at least four hundred feet straight-away. Willy suspected that Demeter Fortune couldn't date the Immortals on a time line, but he was nevertheless a repository of their legacy to the game, a keeper of the flame in his own right.

    Meanwhile, Sebastian Fabian met with the Fab Co. marketing staff at his midtown digs. "The ratings on Saturday afternoon and Thursday night came in at the highest year-to-date numbers for the network and each time slot," reported Fab Co.'s director of marketing. "Look at the demographics. We drew the hard-core baseball junkies and couch potatoes, all age groups." he added.

    "We can add wrinkle cream and acne medicine as well as erectile dysfunction meds to the list of advertisers," remarked a thoroughly pleased Sebastian Fabian.

    "That's correct, Mr. Fabian. She's media dynamite!" said the advertising director.

    "She's media gold!" said the owner, not to be outdone in the hyperbole department. "Let's up the ad rate for thirty-second and sixty-second spots on the Millennium Channel games right away," said the owner.

    "What about the team promo?" asked the Diamonds' head honcho of public relations.

    "Roll out the Willy tee shirts!" Fabian decreed.

    "Do we go with the tee shirt design we tested in Alexandria?"

Fabian wrinkled his brow and turned up his nose. "The cartoon caricature of Willy was too cutesy. Screen a photo of her face...Let's order them in pink, blue, and white...Set the price at $19.95 at the stadium."

"We'll put in a rush order for 50,000," said the PR maven.

Back in the comfort of her motel hideaway, Willy meditated, napped, and read a short novel by the Japanese author Mishima, a recommendation from her e-mail pen pal, a pitcher named Hideki Saito. At quarter past eleven, she flipped the channel selector to catch Dave Warren's sports report.

"In the American League East, everyone's asking if the Buffalo Wolves are for real. Believe it, ladies and gents! The Wolves are one game under five hundred, but they're in second place, trailing Baltimore by just two games. With the Bronx Bombers and Toronto in a tailspin and Boston carrying the best-paid disabled list in baseball, Buffalo could be this year's Cinderella team and the biggest reason is the comeback of Peter Jones...Let's go to the video tape. Tonight at the stadium in the Bronx, third inning, one aboard, and goodbye! Into the upper deck in right center field..."

Curled up under the covers, Willy bolted upright and shouted, "Go, Peter! Yes!" as P.J.'s video image plastered the ball out of sight.

"Then, in the fifth, he does it again. A solo shot...this time, almost over the roof...That's Reggie's and Mickey's territory!"

"All right! Woo!" Willy was clapping and bouncing on the bed, cheering on her friend from afar.

"Let's take another look in slow-mo," Warren said, and the head shot of P.J. on the screen showed his eyes fluttering as he set himself at the plate, then widening as he "saw" the ball and strode into the pitch. Willy made a mental note that not all big hits are pitchers' "mistakes." Peter simply saw his pitch and yanked it.

Warren's voice wore on: "Peter Jones now has nine home runs on the year and he's tied with his teammate, Toby Clay, for the league lead in RBI at thirty-two. At the end of last season, LA was trying to give this guy away. You mean to tell me that a New York City team can't use a guy like him? What's up with that, ladies and gents?"

Regrettably, she missed the chance to hook up with P.J., since the Wolves returned to their upstate home after Monday's game in the city. She tried Peter and Charlene's new number in Buffalo and got their voice mail. An hour later, Peter rang back.

"Peter 'Home Run' Jones," she greeted him.

"Hey, cuz," he sang cheerfully. "You caught my night on the town?"

"Are you and Toby Clay in a tater collecting contest or what?"

P.J. laughed heartily. "Yeah, we'll see if the old man can keep up with the kid. You've made a pretty big splash yourself, Willy."

Charlene's voice came through crisply over the old-school land line: "Is that Willy? You're wasting minutes talking silliness, Peter. Let me have a turn."

"Hi, Char!" Charlene and Willy proceeded to talk more silliness for a full half hour before she had to head to work at the Meadowlands. The Jersey coliseum was a modernesque, symmetrical horseshoe built for football and adapted for baseball. More than 75,000 fans packed the stadium for Willy's first start at home. The media blitz was relentless for forty-eight hours as radio and television stations ran contests for free tickets to the show being billed as *"Willy Brings Her Act Home to the Big Apple."* Notables from Albany, Trenton, and the Great White Way smiled with the owner as the flashbulbs popped and live-action minicams rolled. The beautiful people preened in their luxury sky boxes and chants of *"Wil-lee!"*, *"Beat LA!"*, and *"Let's go Dees!"* resounded from the sporting Mecca west of the city, even before batting practice was underway. Willy avoided the madness by lying low and sneaking into the stadium with Paul two hours before the gates opened. She suited up while he gorged himself on donuts and potato chips in the clubhouse. Willy did some stretching and wind sprints as the grounds crew dumped and raked bags of red clay around the rectangular islands in the turf. Ready for a breather, Willy climbed over the fence and followed the accessway to the concessions arcade beneath the stands. A concessionaire with a "Ras Tafari–Lion of Judah" sweatshirt and dreadlocks flowing from beneath his Diamonds' cap was filling and setting up tall plastic cups of cola and singing to his portable music player, blasting from under the counter.

"Real reggae!" exclaimed Willy, as she leaned over the countertop, brought her face close to his, and sang with him eyeball-to-eyeball in harmony:

"As sure as the sun will shine,
I'm gonna get my share of what's mine,
'Cause the harder they come, the harder they fall, one and all.
Oh-oh, the harder they come, the harder they fall, one and a-a-all..."

Paul came running toward them, shouting, "I've been lookin' all over for ya!" He took hold of Willy's arm and pulled her away. "Ya can commune with the common people some other time. We got work to do, babe."

"Shame on you, Paul!" she said, stumbling to keep in step with him.

"Hey, I'm commoner than anybody," he said, as they headed out to the field, adding, "Nice voice, babe! Would ya sing somethin' for me some time?"

"Anytime!"

"Throw for a few minutes so I can see what kinda stuff ya got tonight," said Paul.

Willy stood at the pitching rubber in the Diamonds' bullpen and waited for Paul to settle into his crouch. Instead, he went down to his knees and sat on the ground. "Why are you more than sixty and a half feet away from me?"

"To get a better angle," said Paul. "So throw already!" Willy delivered the first of her practice pitches to him. "Good, babe!...The fastball's poppin'...Now sliders...Over the top first...Good!...Now go sidearm...Good! Three-quarter sidearm...Okay!" Paul held onto her twentieth practice toss and stood. "Let's stop before ya start workin' too hard," he said as she came toward him.

"Well?" she asked, cocking her head to one side.

Paul winked. "I think you're gonna be lookin' real good tonight, babe."

Willy knew full well that Paul Cello's praise meant far less than her performance against LA in the game about to begin. Nonetheless, she felt a rush of excitation as she said "thanks" in a voice scarcely above a whisper.

For Willy to recount the game as anything short of pure magic would be to deny the way in which the crowd, her teammates, and her pitching coalesced. *"Wil-lee!, Wil-lee!, Wil-lee!"* LA's shortstop, Shawn Dawes, powdered Willy's first pitch toward "no man's land" in left center field, but Demeter Fortune streaked across the infield to knock it down and fired the ball to Thor Andreason for a dazzling first out of the game. *"Wil-lee, Wil-lee! Beat LA! Beat LA!"* LA's second-spot hitter, Kal Davis, safely beat out a drag bunt for a hit, but, as he attempted to swipe second, Paul fired a rocketlike throw to Cal Bonham for out number two. *"Wil-lee, Wil-lee! Let's go Dees!"* Each play was greeted by a joyous leap from the woman on the mound and a deafening cheer of approval from the Meadowlands' faithful. When LA's first sacker, Quinn Burgess, hit a high pop to Keith Whalen at third, Willy's sprinting exit from the playing field ignited a chanting, standing ovation. *"Wil-lee, Wil-lee, Wil-lee!"*

"It's only 8:15," declared Cameron Hammersmith, voice of the New York Diamonds on the Millennium Channel, "and this joint is jumping like an outdoor rock concert at midnight!"

In the dugout, Rudy Judd handed Willy a towel and asked how she felt. Willy patted her cheeks and the back of her neck and smiled radiantly. "I feel like an angel that just started to fly."

The starting pitcher in LA blue was lefty Corky Calderon, author of the season's first no-hitter. The Diamonds' home turf was an artificially carpeted canyon, "the dead-ball zone," as Andy Gilbert called it, but tonight it became a hitter's paradise. The switch-hitters, Burton and Fortune, boomeranged two of Corky's fastballs for home runs in the second and third. Demmy drove an opposite-field foul-pole dinger and Roy sent a tape-measure blast out of the ballpark–allegedly smashing a window in the Brendan Byrne Arena on the other side of the complex, a baseball "big fish" story. It was that kind of night.

Willy was touched for three hits in the first three innings, but opened the fourth frame with a full-count strikeout of Burgess, followed by three straight strikes on down-and-in sliders to LA's football-to-baseball cross dresser, Kirk Tatum. Back in the second inning, Paul signaled Willy to throw him a fastball on Big Tate's first time at bat and last season's home run champ slapped a single through the infield. Paul cautiously called for nothing but breaking balls to the number-five hitter, Gordy Gustafson. "He's a catcher. He don't hit too much, except when it counts." Gus took a free pass on four balls. Paul again kept Willy throwing curves and sliders to Darryl Harris, the center fielder, who found a low outside curveball to his liking and knocked it back through the middle for a hit. With runners on first and second and two outs, the Diamonds' pitcher and catcher conferred. "I'm messin' with your rhythm, huh?"

"No," said Willy, smiling. "They are."

"Listen," said Paul. "Let's go up the ladder on this next guy. He's a stiff. Three fastballs on the inside corner...at the knees, at the thighs, and at the waist. He'll fall like a tree."

"What was that you told me about the best hitter in the league being the one at the plate?"

"That was some other guy," snorted Paul. "He ain't him."

Three pitches later, the crowd was chanting Willy's name once more as she ran from the mound with her right fist reaching skyward. "Like Lady Liberty holding the eternal flame!" declared telecaster Jeff McCarty.

"In the middle of the fourth," said his partner, Cam. "It's the Diamonds two, LA nothing...Oh, what a night!"

Willy and Paul went to sit at different spots on the bench after the fifth ended. Paul leaned forward with his cap and mask off, but his chest protector and knee pads left on, mindlessly munching a handful of sunflower seeds. Willy walked to the cooler and tapped a cupful of water, all the while eyeing her battery mate, who, still not looking at her, sighed in response to some unspoken woe. Willy carefully raised the paper cup above her shoulder and chucked it at his head.

"Direct hit!" The entire Diamond bench applauded.

Paul yelped, "Jeez! Who the...? What the...?" as the water dripped through his unkept black curls and onto his forehead.

Willy, bobbing with joy, said, "We just zipped 'em one-two-three, and you've got nothing to say about it?"

Paul, wiping his face with his sleeve, said softly, "What's to say? Your pitchin' tonight is one of the best pieces of work I've seen all year, babe."

"Thanks, partner," she said and returned to where she had been seated. A moment passed and Paul joined her. They sat together, sharing handfuls of seeds and pistachios until the Diamonds' half of the inning was over.

With one away in the sixth, Burgess dropped a clean single into center for LA's fifth and final hit of the ballgame. The PA system rang out: "Batting for Los Angeles, number thirty-three, Kirk Tatum, left field." The boos resounded, amid calls of "Where's your shoulder pads, taterhead?" Paul, humming the Notre Dame fight song to unnerve the moonlighting footballer, stooped behind the plate and made no pretense of flashing signals. Willy knew what to do and she swept away Big Tate with three hard breaking sliders, exactly as she had done before.

In the Diamond dugout, the usually unflappable manager exclaimed, "Flipping incredible!" As Willy retired the side on Gustafson's short fly to left, Tom thought, *Paul's the maestro and she's the soloist, playing her instrument to perfection under his direction. They couldn't be more in sync if they were reading each other's minds.* As Tom's team went down in order in the bottom of the sixth, an idea resonated in his imagination: *Every year we've been "one player away," but this year I have a fourth starter as good as the front three and no one expected her to be here.* As Willy set down the team once known as the Brooklyn Bridegrooms in order in the top of the seventh, for the first time since spring training, Tom contemplated his postseason bonus check.

Willy went to bat for the third time in the game in the home half of the seventh. She had hit a slow roller back to the pitcher in the third and grounded out again on a bouncer to third in the fourth. "At least you're not always strikin' out anymore," Cal encouraged. Three hard ones from Calderon sent her back to the bench, struck out and fuming.

The refrain of *"Wil-lee, Wil-lee!"* echoed with every pitch as Willy put away the last eleven LA batters in succession, capping the eighth and ninth innings with third-out strikeouts. The wildly cheering throng watched the best team in baseball exchange high fives, low fives, and sky fives with the young phenom who just earned her first big league victory on a five-hit shutout. Willy skipped out to center field and raised her arms as if to embrace the multitude. She bowed deeply from the waist and blew a kiss. With her picture projected on the closed-circuit video screen above the electronic scoreboard, Willy pointed between her breasts, crisscrossed her arms, and pointed her finger to 75,000 souls as one: *"I...love...you."*

"She's givin' me the chills, man!" Sandy Lee told Big Gil.

"Can you believe this?" Cal asked Demmy.

"Like nothin' I've ever seen!" Roy said to Andy.

In the next twenty-four hours, a film clip of the scene aired on every commercial television and cable outlet across the United States and Canada. The banner of *Today USA* read:
"Willy B. Superstar Debuts on Broadway–It's a Hit!"
Sebastian Fabian, from his luxury sky box overlooking the playing field, watched baseball's prima ballerina take her bow. The owner of the Diamonds was laughing so hard tears spilled from his eyes. His happiness bordered on dementia. "Willymania!" he announced, trying to catch his breath between hysterical bursts of laughter. To his amazement, one of his entrepreneurial schemes came

together bigger, better, and more swiftly than he dared to anticipate.

When the clubhouse doors were unlatched after game's end, wags in motion sought out
players of various degrees of articulation for sound bites and printable quotes. *Sportsworld*'s Sam Khoury shocked Willy and most others present by grabbing and kissing the star of the show. "You were so excellent tonight, pal."

"Hey, Khoury!" Dino DeSantis called with lips puckered and arms open wide. "How about me? I got two hits off Corky." Sam wiggled her middle finger at the rookie right fielder.

Dale Goodwyn said to Brad Lucas, "I think there's one reporter who's lost her objectivity. Wouldn't you say?"

"My friend," Brad told Dale. "They'll grab something to eat, sit and gab later, text and tweet each other, meet downtown to shop tomorrow...Sam acts like the groupie, but she's the one on top of the hottest story in town."

CHAPTER 7

Half an hour before the Diamonds' next game, Willy wandered the field, mingling with the guys watching and taking batting practice, when Cal introduced her to Quinn Burgess and Shawn Dawes, two of the LA blue butts she kicked the previous evening. They chatted until Shawn looked over to the sidelines and pointed at a noisy crowd of children calling for Willy.

"Look, look, look!" she exclaimed, cupping her hands over her mouth, as she ran to the front row of seats on the first base side, near the Diamonds' dugout. Crammed into the walkway and hanging over the guardrail was a rainbow of little girls' faces, a hundred variations on herself, wearing Diamond caps, Willy B. tee shirts, and pigtails or braids. There were corn rows, dreadlocks, and string braids; long, fluffy blonde and frizzy strawberry curls; short, straw-colored toe-heads and waist-length, wispy corn silk, and silken raven-haired; crimped, permed, and relaxed; thick, full-bodied brunettes and spiky redheads. The faces were chubby, cheeky, and gaunt; freckled, bronze, pale, tan, amber, and ebony; toothy and full-lipped or thin-lipped and trembling; wide-eyed, blue-eyed, brown-eyed, hazel-eyed, and almond-eyed. All were yelling, waving, jiggling, and reaching for Willy.

A tall woman with poker-straight grey hair squeezed through the squirming and squealing gaggle. She was dressed in white shirt, blue shorts, D's hat, and sneakers, and introduced herself as Sister Mary Francis. "We're from the junior softball association in Jersey City. All the girls come from Our Lady of the Assumption church and the Malcolm X elementary school," sister said.

"I don't believe this!" Willy was feeling giddy and light-headed to the point of tears. She leaned over the rail and submerged as much of her head and upper body into the crowd of little girls as she could. She wanted to touch, hug, and kiss every joyous one of them. They smelled and tasted deliciously of bubblegum, soda, and pure youth. Cell-phone cameras flashed and video cameras rolled as electronic and print wags picked up the scene.

"Every team wants to call themselves the Diamonds or the Willys," said the broadly smiling sister. "You're their special hero, Miss Beal."

Willy felt a rush of emotion and struggled to keep her legs from wobbling when she finally forced herself to leave them, gasping "I love you!" and waving as she ducked into the dugout.

Willy's made-for-TV persona and the symbolism of Willy B. Superstar resonated like an omnidirectional magnetic web: uptown and in the lush green hilly 'burbs of North Jersey, Westchester, Long Island, and Connecticut; downtown and in the 'hoods of Newark, Bed-Stuy, the South Bronx, and the village of Harlem. Willy Beal was a mosaic of funk, rock, and jazz; a piano concerto and a rappin' rhyme; street chic, yuppie trendy, Madison Avenue slick, and blue-collar bootstraps.

The Diamonds and San Francisco split the first two games as Big Gil won on Friday and Jake lost to Allyn on Saturday. Virgin Islander Winston Dixon would pair off with Willy for the finale, a rare Sunday night affair, scheduled to give the Millennium Channel a prime-time monopoly. Tom called a team meeting and workout in the afternoon prior to Friday's game. Awaiting Willy at her locker was a message from the owner to meet him at Gracie Mansion in the city at 10:00 a.m. Saturday morning. Willy heard that Fabian worked at his stadium office during weekdays when the team was home, and so she went upstairs to the labyrinthian corporate fortress, discretely tucked away from players, fans, and the media. The offices were small and compact, but dripping with opulent appointments and furnishings, from the soft, fluffy carpeting to the artwork adorning the walls.

"Is he in?"

Fabian's secretary sneered a plastic smile, and said, "Yes, but he's tied up in a meeting. He isn't expecting you, is he?"

"Just call him and tell him I'm here," Willy said firmly, as her eyes darted about, absorbing the atmosphere of the king's anteroom. The executive secretary pushed a button and waited for a return buzz.

"Yes, Trish?"

"Mr. Fabian, Willy Beal is here to see you...Yes, now," said Trish, narrowing her eyes to glance at Willy.

"Well, then, send her in!"

Trish waved her palm toward the door. It opened and Sebastian Fabian emerged behind two gawking, youngish men. "Sorry, I have to kick you fellows out. Harvey will call you later." They tried to be cool, but they had just been given an abrupt lesson in corporate priorities. "Welcome, Willy," Fabian said, extending his hand as she came through the doorway.

"This is like the great hall of the King of Diamonds," she declared, laughing at her own joke.

"Ha! If I'm the King, you're the Ace of Diamonds," Fabian bellowed as he sat in his leather swivel chair and swung his legs behind his clutter-free desk.

"Don't let Big Gil and Sandy Lee hear you say that," said Willy feeling at a disadvantage while standing before the seated owner. "Can I grab a chair?"

"What can I do for you, Willy?" Fabian was surprised and amused as she pulled a chair alongside his, behind the desk.

"It's about your note, asking me to meet you at Gracie Mansion tomorrow morning, Sebastian." She deliberately established their conversation on a first-name basis.

"The mayor has invited representatives from all of the city's sports teams to a ten o'clock brunch. The governor will be there, too..."

"Which one, New York or New Jersey?"

"New York," he replied. "We'll have to stroke the other one next week. Politics! I've also asked Bonham, Fortune, Burton, and Gilbert to come, but the competition has gone and resurrected two of their living legends to upstage us." Sebastian Fabian smiled and said, "So, I need you, Willy."

"But I have a previous commitment," she said. "I'm going to a pee-wee baseball tournament in Queens...I don't like celebrities who break promises."

With a trace of a smile, Fabian studied her face, and said, "Why don't you send your buddy, Filsinger? Kids love him. He's a big teddy bear." Willy was hesitant. Then she said, "I'll send some of my people with boxes of tee shirts and posters."

Willy leaned into him, close enough to smell his designer-label cologne, and proposed, "I'll come...if and only if you donate 200 replica uniforms, from caps to stirrups, picking up the licensing fee to BLB, Inc."

"Oh, is that all?" As Fabian pretended to be testy, he moved still closer to her.

She pulled back from him a bit. "Outfit the program coordinators with computers and software for registrations, health records, and stats."

"Computers? Sure," he responded genuinely, thoroughly fascinated with his brightest star. "Well?" Fabian asked with an open-hands gesture.

"I'll be there," Willy sang, deliberately giving him a sampler of her singing voice, and pranced out the door. "See you later, Sebastian."

Alma Henry Beal returned home from church services a little after ten on Sunday night, feeling melancholy, recalling how her eight-year-old daughter would sing in the car all the way home from church, some twenty years ago. Alma turned on her TV set to relax before bedtime. The movie of the week was a who-done-it. She tuned in at the station break.

"This sports update is brought to you by the American Cola Company...And now from USTV in New York, here's Dave Warren."

"It was just like old-timers' day at Pilot Field in Buffalo this afternoon as forty-year-old Brian Robbins won his 300th big league game, with thirty-five-year-old catcher Jed Guerin behind the plate. The comeback kid, Peter Jones, a spry thirty-eight, by the way, cracked a three-run home run in the fourth, as the Wolves beat Central-leading Kansas City, four-zip ... Meanwhile, at the Meadowlands in New Jersey, *You Know Who* has a perfect game going into the fifth inning." Dave Warren flashed a Cheshire-cat grin with Willy's picture smiling in the background and said, "Stay tuned, ladies and gents!"

Alma covered her face and gasped, "Oh, sweet Jesus! My little girl!" Then she switched to the Millennium Channel and said a little prayer of thanks for not cancelling cable service when Willy moved out of the house.

Another 75,000 screaming banshees turned out for the rubber game of the set with the Bay City Rollers. Two out, top of the fifth, no score, and Willy had put away fourteen batters in a row when Paul Cello called time and came to the mound. "Look at the scoreboard," he said from behind the grill of his face mask. Willy knew there was nothing but goose eggs on the board for the San Franciscans and she was halfway through the required minimum of twenty-seven outs. "I can't take the pressure, babe," he said as her eyes widened in disbelief. "How about if we hang a slow curve to the next guy? A nice, clean, harmless little hit! The
world's not ready for this. Let the next girl do it or wait 'til next year." Willy's face was expressionless as she read Paul's lips and he sounded out the unspeakable "no-hitter."

"Oh, damn you, Paul Cello! Why'd you have to say that?" She kicked dirt onto his feet.

"No-hitter, perfect game, no-hitter!" he squawked in the face of timeless superstition.

"Ooh!" she exclaimed, prancing in front of him and spitting on the ground.

"Something seems to be going on out there, fans," announced Cam.

"A somewhat animated discussion between pitcher and catcher, I'd say. There goes pitching coach Rudy Judd out to the mound," commented Jeff.

Rudy lumbered at a pace slower than a jog, but full-tilt for the former catcher, up to the decidedly inharmonious battery. "What's goin' on with the both of you?"

Willy held her arms stiffly at her side and screeched, "He said 'no-hitter' to me! Right out loud...on purpose!"

With hands on hips, Rudy's powerful legs–which had driven 242 home runs and backstopped 1,403 big league games–stomped the ground and threw up more dirt onto Paul's black shoes. "Why'd you have to jinx her that way? The poor kid!"

"She's wound up too tight," Paul said with thorough composure. "She's been thinkin' about it. She's readin' tomorrow mornin's paper...Willy does the perfect number! She's gonna blow it...and the game."

"Maybe he's right, sweetheart," Rudy said kindly. "Sometimes your want-to gets in the way of your can-do."

Willy kept her eyes looking downward. "Why don't the two of you get out of my face and let me pitch, please?"

Paul and Rudy went their separate ways.

The hitter, Miller Drake, dropped a soft line drive into short right field for a base hit. The full-to-overflowing crowd sighed in disappointment, and then forced a halt to play to give the Diamond pitcher a two-minute ovation.

Paul slowly rose from his crouching position to mutter, "I was only kiddin', Willy. I was just tryin' to loosen ya up." She was too far away to hear, but she riveted her eyes to his for a few seconds and turned away.

At first base, Drake said to Thor, "Do you know what just happened?" Thor nodded, paused to lift his cap to fluff his new topknot from the Men's Club for Hair, and kicked the bag. With a snort, Drake said, "It's a good thing he didn't tell her to bean me."

"No doubt about it!" Thor looked toward Willy, who was setting to take Paul's sign for the first pitch to a new batter. "If Paul told her to," Thor unsmilingly made the sign of the cross and blew Drake a kiss.

At USTV's broadcasting headquarters in Rockefeller Center, Dave Warren checked the line scores from the day's output of games and proofread the copy for his sports report due to
air in twelve minutes. Warren loved his job and hated to work. He greatly preferred doing his
shtick for the six and eleven o'clock newscasts rather than going out of the studio to cover anything, especially a ballgame at night. Cathy Stafford, his producer, brought him a folder of old newspaper clippings. "I dug through some old clip files for 'today in history' type fillers," she said. "The dates are July second, 1933 and 1963, Dave. Carl Hubbell beat St. Louis in seventeen innings, 1-0, at the Polo Grounds. Then, thirty years to the day, Juan Marichal and Warren Spahn go sixteen innings at Candlestick, and Marichal wins it, 1-0."

"Are we talking numerology or astrology here?" said Warren, unconsciously stroking his thick, dyed-brown pompadour.

"Well, the dates aren't perfect," Cathy told her boss. "It's June second and it's been over fifty years, but the same franchise, two pitchers and a double-shutout, on a Sunday..."

"Yeah, but nobody keeps their starters into extra innings anymore," laughed Warren.

"Vallery's not the only manager in the bigs who'll leave a pitcher in for extra innings. He's done it with Douglas and Danielson. If a game's tied, low scoring, and a low pitch count...I think Dixon's near 100 pitches, but Willy's only thrown 78 pitches in eight innings."

"What's happening now?" asked Warren.

"They're in the bottom of the eighth," answered Cathy, who went directly from a summer internship to a full-time job with media star Warren last autumn.

"Get the Millennium Channel on the monitor so that I can see the game," said Warren, who was pushing USTV-New York's vice president and general manager to promote Cathy to assistant sports director before somebody stole her from them. "I'm throwing out the first four minutes of copy. I'll wing it. I just hope Vallery doesn't pull Willy out."

At that very moment, Willy knelt on deck, still hitless in ten trips to the plate. She had continued to use the low-crouching stance, imitating Donnie Ross, and in her head she saw a drag bunt down the first base line, but the sign from Silvio Romero, coaching at first base, said to swing away. Willy watched second baseman Drake throw out Keith on a ground ball and strode up to the right-hand-side batter's box. Willy gripped the bat's handle with an inch separating her hands so that she could quickly slide her top hand up the barrel and square to bunt. Feeling awkward after passing up the first pitch for a called strike, Willy drew back her bat still farther, keeping it parallel to the ground, but this time closed her hands together. As pitcher Dixon went into his stretch, Cam described the action: "There's a picture perfect drag bunt...Ortega charges in...Dixon goes over to cover...catcher Steele scoops it...No throw! No play! Willy B.'s safe at first."

"She literally tore down the line like a shot," said Jeff McCarty.

"I think people have been forgetting that this young woman was an all-state sprinter just a few years back," said Cam.

"Will she steal?" asked Jeff as the camera showed Willy walking a lead off first.

"If the green light is on, Tom Vallery should have his head examined for risking injury to his newest star pitcher." The audience heard the co-announcer, Cam, but Jeff heard the words of the would-be replacement manager.

Sebastian Fabian habitually began his work week late Sunday evening in his corporate war room, ready for the opening of the Tokyo stock exchange. Fabian pressed the button for sound as Dave Warren's face appeared on one of the six video screens in Fab Co.'s main office.

"Is this spooky or what? Thirty years to the day after Carl Hubbell shut out the Redbirds for seventeen innings in Manhattan, Juan Marichal shut out the Milwaukee Bees for sixteen innings in Frisco, outdueling Warren Spahn. On this very night, Willy Beal, pitching for the current New York Senior Circuit team against Hubbell's and Marichal's former team at the Meadowlands, is shutting out the Gigantics in the top of the ninth, on her way into extra innings. Is it fate, karma, kismet? Is it the sword in the stone, baseball's Excalibur, to be pulled by the hand of the best pitcher in a generation?" The chuckles of the weekend news anchor came over the air as Warren said, "Let's go to the video tape...Second inning, Vic Wilson batting, and look at that slider drop. Swish! He's history...Where did this woman come from? Pitching in her backyard since she got out of college! Give me a break, ladies and gents. Somebody should've signed her up ten years ago."

Fabian picked up the phone and dialed his secretary's home number. "Sorry to bother you so late, Trish," he apologized, although she had a multiline telephone, computer terminal, and fax machine in her basement office. Such calls were hardly unusual. "Ring Neal Cox. He's the CEO of Sportsnet's parent company. I want tonight's game coast to coast. It's still prime time in the Pacific and Mountain zones. Tell him they can pipe into our audio and video by satellite link. I'll call the president of USTV Sports myself to see if they'll simulcast it, too. All for free! We'll waive the local blackout. Call me to close the loop in five minutes." *Click!* Fabian circled his desk after punching up Arnie Rutledge's private line in Darien, Connecticut, then switching to speaker phone and putting the receiver down on the desk set. "Arnie, it's Sebastian Fabian."

"No, no, no! You bought the network. We're all to be shot at dawn or fired at nine. Is that it?"

"I wish, Arnie," joked the man with the resources to buy and sell off the pieces of all four major broadcasting systems. "You own more stock in that money-loser than anyone. You'd stay on, I assure you. I couldn't afford to buy you out."

"So, what can I do for you, Mr. Fabian?"

"Would the locals east of the Mississippi mind pre-empting the usual fare of infomercials and sit-com reruns to carry some all-night baseball?"

"You're serious, aren't you! What's the deal? No strings?"

Fabian taunted, "Let's try some word association. I say Willy Beal and you come in your pants."

"I do see big ratings numbers and happy advertisers," Rutledge replied. "Let's talk turkey. Give the radio network all weekend Diamond games during the summer."

"Done!" said Fabian. "How about announcers for tonight?"

"DaSilva stayed in town to tape his radio show. I'll get him on his pager at the stadium," said Arnie.

"He can get cozy in the booth with Cam and Jeff," chortled Fabian. "The countdown is ten minutes to simulcast."

"It's a pleasure doing business with you, Mr. Fabian."

The owner of the Diamonds then called Tom in the dugout on his cellular phone. "Don't take her out until somebody scores...Yes, I'm serious...Of course, don't let her get beat up...If there are runners on base and threatening to score? No, ten million fans holding their eyes opened with toothpicks do not want to watch Brooks or Langevin, Tom! Let her pitch her way out of the jam. It'll be better than a movie!...No, it won't kill her. I don't care how many pitches she's thrown. You kept her on the mound this long, didn't you?"

Tom rolled his eyes and twitched his neck. He said not a word, but thought: "Willy Beal comes to town and allows Fabian to stick his ass into *my* game."

The firm timbre of Rob DaSilva's voice emanated from the TV's speakers: "Welcome to our USTV viewers from around the country, joining those of you watching on cable via Sportsnet and the Millennium Channel. I'm Rob DaSilva along with Cameron Hammersmith and Jeff McCarty, the radio and television voices of the New York Diamonds...Jeff?"

"Thank you, Rob. As we get ready to go to the top of the tenth inning, what we have is a classic duel between New York's Willy Beal and San Francisco's Winston Dixon locked in a double-shutout...Cam?"

Said Cam, "The big bopper, Tony Ortega, takes a slider on the outside corner for strike one..."

Said Rob, "Through nine innings, opposing twirler Dixon has given up three hits and two walks while striking out seven, including Andy Gilbert, a two-time victim."

Said Cam, "Ortega takes strike two on a slider hitting the inside corner..."

Said Rob, "In the meantime, Willy Beal carried a no-hitter into the fifth and a one-hitter into the ninth. Both hits came with two outs, and each was followed by a routine fly to end the inning..."

"There's a sidearm fastball, low and away," said Jeff. "Her top-seamer clocked at eighty-eight. A one-two count on Ortega..."

"Incredibly, Willy's thrown only ninety pitches," Rob said.

"She looks fresh as a daisy out there, too," Jeff said.

"She's walked no one tonight, and fanned four," Rob said.

"Make that five!" proclaimed Cam. "Ortega chases a sidearm slider cutting into the inside corner of the plate. He was just plain fooled on that one."

Jeff announced, "That's the routine Willy B. used to fan LA's Kirk Tatum–another powerful lefty swinger–the other night, except this time she sneaked in an offspeed fastball,
which gave Tony something to think about. A decoy!"

"She's also used that low-and-away slider to whiff a right-handed hitter, Vic Wilson, twice, as well as the man at the plate, Eric Jackson," said Rob.

"Jackson came into tonight's game with a .329 batting average, third best in the league," said Jeff. "He's oh-for-three tonight against the Grand Dame of the Meadowlands."

"The home plate ump calls time," said Jeff. "This capacity crowd is still thundering Willy's name after she racked up that kay against Ortega."

The television cameras showed Willy at the mound and on the stadium's video screen, elevating her arms in a calming gesture–a soft, fluttering motion–then raising her finger to her lips. She turned and repeated the performance art in sign language, facing the opposite way.

Rob DaSilva cupped his hand over the mike and whispered into Cam's ear, "Fabian owns the Diamonds, but she owns the fans. This is not to be believed."

Eric hit a line drive into the glove of Roy and Steele quit running halfway to first base as Cal grabbed a turf-buoyed grounder and flipped the ball to Thor, covering the bag, for the out.

"At the end of nine and a half innings of play, it's San Francisco nothing and New York nothing," said Cam.

"As the clock tolls midnight, Eastern Daylight Savings Time, only a handful of fans have made any effort to leave the stadium," said Rob.

Darnell Greene, one of Willy's recently recalled minor league teammates, pinch-hit for DeSantis in the seventh and opened the Diamonds' tenth by drawing a base on balls. With Thor batting, Darnell caught Dixon and Steele napping and easily stole second base. Thor grounded to short, Paul flew out to left, and Tom sent Benny to hit for Keith. Benny sliced a single up the middle, putting runners on first and third with two outs. Willy was scheduled to bat. As she walked from the on-deck circle to the batter's box, she looked over her shoulder toward the dugout and wondered why Tom wasn't calling her back in favor of a pinch-hitter. Willy, unaware of all the attention centered on tonight's game, stepped in to bat left-handed once again. Sil flashed the "bunt" sign. Out of the corner of her eye, Willy saw Darnell streak from third base, as she dragged the bunt toward first. She did a little sidestep to avoid kicking the ball–a rulebook out–and thereby lost a fraction of a second, enough for Winnie's toss to reach the back-peddling Ortega in time to put her out. Winnie's quick reflexes in fielding the ball had more to do with squelching the play than Willy's hesitating step. As for Tom, he would be skewered for a royal roasting in tomorrow's papers for calling a suicide squeeze with two outs.

Next inning, thousands of hoarse-voiced Willymaniacs gave out a collective groan as Andre Harris hit a fast skipping triple. Next up was a bench-warmer, who laid down a perfect bunt and Harris crossed the plate to score on the successful squeeze. Now trailing 1-0, a deflated Willy committed the cardinal sin of walking the opposing pitcher, Dixon. Novak, playing tit-for-tat with Tom, seemed bent on keeping his starter in the game to the bitter end.

The theme of the night must be "Pitch 'til you drop!" thought Willy.

Ross failed to beat out an infield grounder to end the inning. A standing-O, *"Wil-lee, Wil-lee!"* and *"Let's go Dees!"* accompanied Willy's trot to the dugout. However, she noted with more interest that the double-play duo, Cal and Demmy, usually two cool cukes, departed the field with the vilest of curses on their lips. Demmy howled, "No way are we gonna lose this game!"

Cal picked up the bat that gave him oh-for-four on the night and splintered it against the dugout's concrete sidewall. He selected another Louisville Betsy and walked placidly up the steps to take his stand at the plate. Cal hit Winnie's first pitch between Ortega's and Wilson's converging gloves for a single. Demmy smashed Winnie's next pitch to deep left center, well past the reach of Ross and Jackson. By the time the ball was retrieved and relayed, the two fastest male Diamonds were sliding across the plate and into the bag at third, respectively. The game was tied, 1-1, and the potential winning run stood ninety feet from the plate. Demeter Fortune smiled as he saw Willy jumping, waving, and clapping under the dugout roof. He paused to sample the joyful noise of the fans, but knew they cheered for her, not him. She was the most fascinating of women, and he realized that never before tonight had he burned to win a game for anyone other than himself.

Andy swung away and flew out to Ross in left, but not deeply enough for Demmy to tag up and score. Roy flicked a hard grounder to Drake at short, who looked to the plate–but Demmy held at third–and threw to first for the easy out. Darnell went to bat, fouling off two and nodding at four to draw his second free pass. Novak approached. Dixon was finished. The left-handed relief ace of the Bay Area Bombers, Greg Ruggieri, got the call to face Thor, but Tom beckoned. The Diamonds' field pilot, playing the percentages, sent for right-handed Joe Manlius to bat for Thor. Joe crushed Greg's first serve into the soft hands of Drake, who stepped on second for the force out.

"So, we go to the twelfth inning," announced Cam, the former home run king. "The game's tied, 1-1."

"And yes!" said Jeff, the ex-all-star catcher, "Willy Beal is still on the mound."

Willy put the lid on the twelfth stanza by fanning the greatly talented Eric Jackson. This time, she sailed a cross-seam fastball past his bat when he was looking for a slider. Ruggieri walked Paul to start the bottom of the twelfth, then served up a double to Benny. There were runners on second and third with none out. Yet again, Tom let Willy bat, although she would have elected to pinch hit to go for the win. *"Wil-lee! Wil-lee! Wil-lee!"* Willy stroked Rags' one-and-one pitch in the air to left for an out. *Let's go Dees!"*

With the Meadowlanders clamoring for a fatal blow, Ruggieri whiffed Cal and Demmy, one after the other. Drake singled off Willy in the thirteenth, but Harris hit a tailor-made double-play ball to Demmy, sending the battle-weary Diamonds to bat once more. Rags Ruggieri retired the New Yorkers, three up and three down, and Willy scampered out for her fourteenth inning of pitching at 1:30 a.m.

"You can talk about a second wind and a third wind," Rob told millions of droopy-eyed viewers, "but Willy B.'s still throwing eighty percent strikes."

Jeff added, "She's right on the money with her control. If anything, she seems to have gotten stronger."

Willy gained two quick strikes on Steele, but then fell behind, three balls and two strikes. She tossed a buggywhip fastball over the plate and the world-class catcher pulled it down the left field line, hitting the "foul" or "fair" pole for a homer. Absent her usual theatrics, the crowd greeted the insulting blow with silence and watched their hero go to work on the next batter. A pinch-hitter for the pitcher's spot and lead-off batter Ross became Willy's seventh and eighth strikeout victims. She secreted Papp's Heater and showed it in anger. The radar gun feeding the pitch speed display on the scoreboard clicked off three digits in front of the decimal point for the first time all night, reading 101.0 on the two-strike pitch to Ross. "Where the hell did that come from?" Paul wondered. After Wilson bounced to Benny at third, Cam declared, "Trailing two-to-one, the Diamonds go to the bottom of the fourteenth, looking for lighting to strike one more time."

Knuckleball artist McElroy came in to clinch the save for the Jolly Green Guys. His first flutterball caromed off the bat of Joe for a single and his second butterfly was clubbed by Paul to Drake for a 6-4-3 double-play. As many of the downcast attendees headed for the exits, Benny smashed a low liner that bounced off the third base bag, beyond Harris's reach. The single was Benny's third straight hit since entering the game. Willy sat still and silently on the D's bench. She watched Tom motion for Jon "Pigpen" Pantagones to bat for the pitcher with two outs and the tying run at first. Benny ran to second with the pitch and Pigpen lofted a 450-foot fly ball to center. Eric Jackson raised his arms and caressed the ball between his gloved and bare hands.

Rob laid his head on the desk in the broadcast booth and pulled the microphone to his lips. His eyes were shut tightly as he said, "Just in time for the late news on the West Coast and sign-off on the East Coast, this game between two of the league's divisional leaders is over." He paused momentarily, allowing "dead air" to roll from sea to shining sea, and then went on: "Willy Mae Beal came to work last night and turned in the finest pitching performance by anyone this season. She's going home this morning the losing pitcher...Our thanks to the Millennium Channel and Sportsnet...For Cam Hammersmith and Jeff McCarty, this is Rob DaSilva, USTV Sports."

The last thing Willy wanted to do was hold a press conference at two o'clock in the morning. Even Dave Warren was reportedly sighted in the press room. She stood under the shower's spraying nozzle for a half-minute, dressed in shorts and a sweatshirt, and wrapped her hair in a black silk scarf. Her body was clean, but her face was worn and drawn as she went to meet the waggery.

"Do you realize that you have the best earned run average in the league?" asked Dale Goodwyn. After four games started, Willy had one win and two losses with an ERA of 1.86.

"That's nice, but I'd rather have had a win tonight."

CHAPTER 8

One result of Willy's spectacular showing and the Diamonds moving into first place was that Brad Lucas became even more insufferable. Brad devoted most of his ink to bemoaning Willy's theatrics, crowd-baiting, and other antics. A quieter, more modest Willy better suited his taste. Likewise, he preferred an overpaid bunch of losers badgered by an overbearing owner to the finely tuned machine that Fabe's ball club became. The Diamonds' charter flew cross-country Monday morning for a three-game stand in Los Angeles. Luckily, the first game would be on Tuesday, giving "Lady and the Cramps," Brad's latest nickname, a desperately needed night off after the five-hour marathon.

A voice message from Sebastian Fabian preceded Willy at the Sheridan Wilshire when the Diamonds arrived there mid-afternoon, Monday. "It's about the Golden Guild Awards reception tonight. I want you to join me," he said. "Be ready at seven sharp."

"What am I supposed to do?"

"Nothing," answered the owner. "Just come with me. Have fun. It's great publicity. Think of the people you'll meet. All in one place! Willy, you're not just another ballplayer. You've got star quality. You're box office...like they are."

"Me?" She was amazed.

"That's great!" he crowed, as his laughter reverberated over the phone. "That innocence is part of your charm."

Willy had unconsciously lain down on the bed with her arm resting across her forehead, caressing the phone with her other hand. She asked, "Then, are you asking me out on a date?" She crossed her legs, jiggling her right foot to a silent rhythm inside her head.

"Yes, you could put it that way."

"Aren't you still married?"

"I'm divorced," he replied. "Three times!"

"I don't know if this is such a good idea, Sebastian."

"It's like you said, a date...not a proposal...not a proposition...just a date."

"Okay!" she sighed deeply. "You say you think it'll be fun?"

"You bet," said Fabian. "What's more, you and I belong there. We're the Ace and the King of Diamonds, the stars of the team."

"I won't tell the other guys you said that."

"The limo will be out front at seven."

With less than three hours before the limousine was to pick her up, Willy asked Paul to drive her somewhere–*anywhere*–to buy a dress. "Rodeo Drive in Beverly Hills," she decided.

"That's a real place? I thought it was made-up, like Hollywood," jibed Paul, exaggerating his rough and tumble blue collar accent.

"You better get going," said Zinger, who was relaxing in front of the tube with a bag of corn chips and store-bought onion dip. "They're rolling out the red carpet already."

"Paul, please don't drive like a maniac," Willy implored even before they got into the car. Changing lanes in congested downtown traffic, leaning on the horn, and flipping the bird to fellow motorists was known as "pulling a Cello" among the New York Diamonds.

Frazzled but unscathed, they arrived at a very chic specialty shop. Willy waved her hand and turned up her nose at rack after rack. "Oh, this is good," she exclaimed at last. "It looks like an Indian or Asian print." She held it in front of her for Paul to view. He just shrugged.

"It's Indonesian, ma'am," said the salesperson, heady from the scent of a quick, off-the-rack sale.

"I can wear ivory and seashell stuff with it," she said to Paul's vacant eyes. "Jewelry, partner," she teased. "You know, earrings, necklaces, bracelets...tongue rings..."

"I didn't think you owned any bling-bling." In front of the register, Paul said, "That's gotta be way over the limit on your Gold Card." She handed her charge card to the cashier as Paul ogled the price tag. "You'll need a contract extension to pay for this."

Willy leaned her head to his ear and whispered, "Didn't Lorraine teach you anything? I'll dry clean it and bring it back tomorrow. I'll say it didn't fit."

As Willy signed the slip and the salesperson wrapped, Paul cleared his throat and said conspiratorially, "Isn't that some kinda bad karma in your Zen and Tao stuff?" Willy playfully punched his muscled arm. Then she rubbed the spot as if to cure it.

Back at the hotel, Willy spied Gil Douglas about to lower his huge frame into an elevator as she and Paul came through the swinging glass doors.

"Yo, Big Gil!" she called, creating a stir in the crowded lobby.

"Is that *her*?" a woman asked excitedly.

"It *is* her!" a small boy cried.

She ran up to Gil and he said, "You got to be cool, baby. Everybody knows the ballplayers are here. You have to know how to act."

"Is Leota upstairs?" she asked breathlessly.

"Uh-huh," he nodded. "Why?"

"Do you think she'd help me do up my hair?"

"Let's go ask her." Gil smiled and placed his large hand on Willy's shoulder, while he pushed the button next to the elevator door.

"I can't be braiding corn rows. We'll be here all night, girl!" Leota told Willy, holding Willy's hair in a clump away from her head. "How about a French braid and two strands twisted on either side of your face?"

"Sounds good," Willy said, smiling at Leota in the looking glass. She was only an inch or so shorter than Willy and broad shouldered with arching brows, radiant eyes, and an endearing smile, made all the more so by a small space between her front teeth. She stared at Willy so
intently that her eyes seemed to cross.

Willy met Leota's eyes in the mirror and said, "I expected to have relationships with the guys on the team, but I never expected to have relationships with their wives, too. I guess, being a woman, it's only natural."

Leota gave a hearty laugh. "Ha! Relationships with other players' wives are not exactly unheard of on this team."

"You're kidding me!" Willy squealed excitedly, jumping in her chair. "Who?"

"Don't get me started, girl."

"I don't wanna be gossiping with you now. Just give me the straight facts," Willy giggled.

"The only man I'm thinkin' about is my own. I told Gil he better keep it in his pants if he knows what's good for him or I'll cut it off!" Leota punctuated her statement by slashing the air with the comb she was using. "The one I want to know about is Fortune. Is he or isn't he?"
She waved her hand with an exaggerated limp wrist.

Willy smiled with a shake of her head. "Demmy? It never occurred to me, but now that you mention it, it kind of makes sense. But he's got baseball Annies hanging on him all the time."

"Isn't that what they call camouflage?" Leota sang out shrilly.

"If he is gay, he's trying to stay in the closet," Willy said quietly, not smiling. "The media and the fans will fry him. And the players?"

"Our team will protect him because he's one of the guys," said Leota, who had been laughing, but stopped. "If he's outted, or caught in the act somewhere, it'll be nasty."

Whimsically, Willy stated, "I'm disappointed that I didn't pick up on it earlier, but, maybe, I've been trying to connect with him because he's like me in a way. We both don't fit the mold. Do you know what I mean?"

The two friends again honed on each other's eyes through the mirror. "You need to keep your eyes on the prize. Willy, you're the one. You were born to be the one. It's your destiny."

Willy heaved a sigh, but felt warm inside at the admiring tone of Leota's words. "I don't know why they chose me to be the one. You can call it destiny or fate or karma or kismet, but maybe it's just a little hard work and a lot of dumb luck."

Leota suddenly looked sternly at Willy. "I also think you've chosen to play your role and you're going to take it as far as you can."

"That sounds so cold, Leota, like I'm out to get all I can from it. I'm not."

"I didn't say you were, Willy, and I didn't say you were doing it for yourself alone." Leota deftly twisted each strand of Willy's hair purely by muscle memory as she spoke. "Just don't let it consume you. I tell Gil, if his arm goes dead tomorrow, we'll go back home to East St. Louis, Illinois, and live like happy nobodies. We'll still be Gil and Leota Douglas and we'll still have our kids. Life won't end with baseball." Willy looked questioningly at her. "Don't lose sight of the real Willy. She can go back home again. Willy B. Superstar can't."

Awhile later, a surprise call to Willy's cell phone from the team owner interrupted Willy's showering, dressing, primping, and preening. "I want to give you a quick heads up. A gay rights group is demonstrating in front of the Golden Guilds and they might try to snag you for a statement of support. Stay away from them if you can..."

"My opinions are my own, Sebastian."

"But your image is *ours*, Willy."

Willy said to Fabian, "Let's talk about this some time in person, okay?"

"Fine," the owner replied, "but be careful about what you do or say. You may be the Ace of Diamonds, but there's no Queen of Diamonds." Willy wasn't sure whether Fabian was baiting her, or testing her. Was he fishing for the truth, or trying to find out if Willy could be trusted with a teammate's secret? Then, he said, "Listen, I'm neither *homo* nor *phobic*, but the best interests of the team come first." That was the moment when Willy was convinced that Demeter Fortune was a switch-hitter by nature as well as preference. The matinee-idol good looks, the fawning groupies, the grey-haired cougars feeling up his musculature, the rainbow of fly girls always on his arm, but never the same one twice, the male-housesitter-roommate, the machismo trash talk, the egomaniacal posture, the driven quest for stud numbers, the macho jousting with his ex-best-friend Kenny Estrada of KC, and the simple fact that he was the most desirable available teammate, but never once, even in jest, made a move to which she might well be open. Thus, if Willy's persona was a continuous unveiling of her real self, Mr. Wonderful's public act was purely subterfuge. Willy was sure Cal knew, although he may have surmised the truth, rather than Demmy coming out to him. Likewise, she had no doubt that Sebastian Fabian knew, one way or the other, by way of his routine private investigation of every player on the roster. *No secrets up in here, Willy!*

    Willy was right on time, waiting in the lobby at five minutes to seven when the limo pulled up to the door. The chauffeur came around to open it for her. He had a body that looked
like it should be hung on a hook in a meat locker, an earring in his left lobe, and a ponytail flipped over his starched white collar. Willy wondered if Sebastian had yet poured the champagne, mixed banana daiquiris, or some other jet-setters' drink as he waited for her in the back seat, behind the no-see-through glass. Willy closed her eyes and let herself take a flight of fancy, imagining

that Sebastian, lacking time or inclination to do his own research, had asked one of his minions about what kind of music should be played. A good answer would be that Willy's beloved jazz was her intellectual side, but her romantic soul would be reached through the fingers of Herbie Hancock or Chick Correa on the piano keys, or maybe the sensuous voices of Alicia Keys or Roberta Flack, filling their grand carriage with sound. Then Willy's mind raced to the touch of his fingertips on her cheek, the sound of his voice, and his lips pressing softly on hers. Willy's fantasy moved into fast-forward to the deep pile of his penthouse carpeting, satin sheets, more sweet sips in the jacuzzi–apple juice this time–dual shower heads, pillows as big and fluffy as clouds, a brisk run in the fog and dew, a high-profile courtship, high-glam wedding, front-page celeb gossip, a loveless and childless marriage in the fast-lane, a fast-track divorce, *pause, rewind,* and *stop.* "I don't think it'll work, Sebastian. Believe me, I don't want to hurt you. We share the same world, but we live in two different universes. Do you understand what I'm saying?" *Okay, Willy, let's see how the evening goes and take it from there.*

    Willy lowered her head and peeked into the limo before stepping inside. She saw Kristin Tracy, Alan Blaylock, and Trisha Patterson, the office secretary. Fabian wasn't even in the car. "Where is he?" shouted Willy.

    "He's meeting us there," said Trish. "Want a drink?"

    Willy said, "Water, if you got it," as she nestled her deflated ego and libido into the soft leather upholstery. *All sopping wet and no place to go.* Willy smiled politely at her three car mates and they smiled in return, but Trish's lip curled subtly. Then Willy saw a look of drifting away in Trish's face. *Dream on, Trisha!*

Willy entered the Golden Guild Awards reception at the posh Bel-Air Astoria with the owner of the Diamonds on her arm. Fabian appeared just in time for the photo-op. The paparazzi aimed and fired their cameras. Willy met actors who played players in the movies– Roy Hobbes, Dottie Henson, Joe Hardy, and Bingo Long. The next morning, when she read the photo caption online, *"Hollywood All-Stars Meet Willy B. Superstar,"* Willy realized that she was the only real ballplayer there, and she, not the movie stars, was the center of attraction. At the appointed hour, one of Fabian's lackeys told Willy it was time to go. "It's like I'm part of his entourage," she complained, disappointed that he hadn't spent any of the evening in her company. *His loss*, she told herself.

In the visiting team's clubhouse at Chavez Ravine the next day, her teammates jumped on Willy and had a good-natured ride. "If weddin' bells be ringin', ya think they'll do it at the Meadowlands?...Believe it, man. On the pitcher's mound!...Can she still pitch if she owns half the team?" One exception to the ribbing was Cal, another was Paul.

"What did happen, anyways?" the catcher asked her later.

His question gave her pause. "Does it matter? Why do you care, Paul?"

"We're friends, aren't we?"

Willy reached for Paul's hand. "We weren't even alone, partner. I was in bed at midnight," she said, adding with a wink. "All by myself!"

A week after accompanying Sebastian Fabian to the Golden Guild Awards, Willy saw the two of them, arm-in-arm, on the cover of *Lifetime* magazine. The bold white type read: *"The Ace of Diamonds and King of Diamonds – A Match Made in Hollywood?"* She almost bought a copy, worried about what the article suggested, until it struck her that the Ace and King of Diamonds was a private joke between the pitcher and the owner. If Fabian was the source of the article, it was just meaningless publicity fluff. However, Cal commented that the magazine seemed to imply that there was something to the appearance of a hook-up between them, at least in Fabian's mind. "Listen, Willy, this is more than a game. There are games within games. Don't get burned and forget who you're dealing with when you flutter those pretty eyes at the owner."

Willy responded indignantly. "I'm doing no such thing. Damn you, Calvin Bonham!"

Cal and Willy shouted at each other, but then laughed together. "Maybe not, but first and foremost, he sees you as a product, a piece of merchandise," said Cal. "Keep your head in the game, Willy."

Willy was awakened by the ring of the phone in her hotel room early that morning. "This is USTV News in Los Angeles. Hold for Roberta Waters..."

"Yeah, right," Willy snarled into the mouthpiece of her cell phone, thinking it was a crank call.

"Willy Beal?" said a voice. "This is Roberta Waters. We'd like to interview you for *'In Focus'* while you're in LA..."

"You're kidding me, right? Who is this–Sam, Michelle, Leota?"

"I assure you, it's really me, Miss Beal." Willy pricked up her ears at the voice that had scolded a President of the United States and solicited self-disclosure of deeply held secrets from politicians, celebrities, and billionaires in thousands of televised interviews. "What does your schedule look like today? We'd like to do a twenty-minute piece for Thursday night's program."

"Ballgame at eight," replied Willy. "I'm free 'til then."

"We'll send a car for you within the hour."

Willy sat upon the bed, holding her phone in disbelief, long after the call ended. Two nights later, after the D's game with LA, Willy coaxed Paul, Cal, and Zinger to watch *"In Focus"* with her on the clubhouse TV. The program began with a scene showing Willy, mobbed by people, strolling with Roberta Waters past the corner of Hollywood and Vine.

"I've walked down the streets of Manhattan and Los Angeles with movie stars–the biggest names from Hollywood's golden age, legendary entertainers, professional athletes, superstars one and all...but I have never, ever witnessed a reaction to anyone quite like this." On the screen, cackling boys and girls, adoring women, awestruck younger men, and still a bit dumbfounded older men swarmed around Willy. She was scribbling autographs against the willingly offered backpack of a ten-year-old. Roberta Waters's canned voice continued to narrate: "Willy Beal: Everyone wants to see her, to touch her. There's emotional electricity in the air when these fans gather round her, but she's not like politicians who work the crowd or entertainers who posture for the cameras...She stands in the middle of it and breathes it all in...She finds it difficult to tear herself away from autograph-seekers. Her teammates say she lets herself be trapped in crowds like this...This is not adulation of a hero or idol. She's no demigod with feet of clay. *She's real!* Her fans want to see and touch her because it's like touching a dream...and she's enjoying every minute of it. She's magic, and if they touch her, then maybe some of it will rub off."

"You said that, not me," Willy's voice came laughing from the television as the scene shifted to a studio living-room set; she and Roberta were seated on a couch. She asked Willy about her grandfather, Rube Henry.

Media maven Roberta Waters spoke: "Do realize what a beautiful story it is that you tell? The old-timer and his granddaughter playing baseball together from your early childhood, where he imparts a lifetime of knowledge of his craft to you...Millions of men cried like babies when they saw the film, *Field of Dreams*, where the father and son played catch in the end. You've brought that metaphor of love to girls and women as well. In a way, Rube Henry was the pioneer that paved the way for women to break through the glass ceiling in Big League Baseball."

Willy disagreed with studied composure. "I don't think he ever dreamed that a woman would play in the bigs, or that I would be the first."

Willy had already grabbed Cal's and Paul's hands. "Here it comes," she whispered.

On screen, Willy was silent as Roberta continued. "Don't you think he knew? He must have known all along what he was doing and what you were capable of.

The only way he knew to help you was to teach you and hope you'd find your own way to work with the results. He always knew. He just didn't live to see it, but these are the dreams that we have for our children and grandchildren. Willy, *you* were his dream."

Willy opened her mouth to speak, but no words came. Instead, she sobbed and covered her face, crying.

"We'll be back after these messages," Roberta's voice said.

"Aw, they cut it," moaned Willy. "Right then, Roberta said to me, 'Don't feel badly. I try to make everybody cry. It shows that they're human. I just didn't think it would be so easy with you!'..."

CHAPTER 9

Willy's celebrity status blossomed overnight and there was no escaping it–on the field, on the street, during the day, at night, and it even followed her home.

"The USTV Nightly News with Tom Rakow..." The TV blared in her squeaky-clean and totally naked townhouse condominium. "Unless you've been living in a cave or a biosphere without access to radio, television, or newspapers, you're already aware that the biggest story of this baseball season is a girl named Willy...Let's go to Dave Warren at the Meadowlands in East Rutherford, New Jersey..."

"I'm here with a woman from Westport, Connecticut," said the sportscaster, comfortably astride a railing, dangling a microphone in front of an excited looking woman with fashionably short, blonde hair under a New York D's cap, framing a "nice-teeth" smile. "What do you think of Willy Beal?"

"Willy's great. She's fabulous. It's like she's *me* out there pitching for the Diamonds. I always dreamed of being a pitcher, of winning the Series, but I never thought a woman would actually get to do it. Now there she is...Willy B.'s good. She is *so* good!"

Warren reached across the aisle and turned to a fellow wearing wrap-around silver sunglasses, a green, black, and red bandana, shoulder-length braids, multicolor tattoos, and glittering golden earrings. "Willy B.'s bad! She is *so* bad. She's the diva of the Diamonds," said the man. "Let me tell you. It's like–my New York D's, man–they got some pitchers...Let me think. If you take some real old-school oldtimers from back in the day, like Bob Gibson, Fergie Jenkins, Catfish Hunter, and Whitey Ford. Then put 'em all on the same team and what you got is the baddest front four there ever was. My man Fabe's holdin' a poker hand with four aces. Listen to me, like the Three Musketeers and D'Artagnon. Yeah, Willy B.'s D'Artagnon. You know what I'm sayin'? You do read books, don't you?"

Warren dead-panned: "Back to you, Tom!"

"The phenomenon of Willy B. Superstar is not confined to the home turf of the New York–New Jersey Diamonds," said the evening news anchor. "Here's Rob DaSilva, somewhere in the stands in Pittsburgh..." DaSilva, who once said he would rather interview a fan than an athlete, wore the face of one doomed to have his wish fulfilled as a sickness unto death. Rob had his arm around the shoulder of a chubby and nervous young woman, his chosen face in the crowd. "Thank you, Tom. I'm here with Laverne Peckham from Mount Lebanon, Pennsylvania."

With other kids' arms and legs trying to push into her space, the teenager waved and fluttered a piece of paper. "You gonna let me do my thing?" she asked.

"Take it away, Laverne," said Rob, and he put the microphone under her nose.

She peered down at it, her eyes widening from apprehension to sheer terror, as if the mic were a rattlesnake, coiled and hissing. Laverne said, "Okay, I'm ready." Then she coughed, *"ah-hem, ah-hem, hmm-hmm-hmm,"* and read: "She float like a butterfly and sting like a bee. Look out, y'all. Here come Willy B.!"

"All right!" someone shouted, followed by yells of *"Wil-lee, Wil-lee!"*

Rob gazed into the live camera as he shouted for all within earshot, "Who's your favorite team?"

The answer came as a chant of *"Let's go Dees! Hoo! Hoo! Hoo!"* with raised fists twirling.

"I'm Rob DaSilva, for USTV News, in Pittsburgh...By the way, Willy Beal and the Diamonds are not even playing here tonight! Tom?"

Rakow's face smiled his characteristic half-grin. "For Willy Beal, each accomplishment on the playing field brings accolades prefaced by 'the first woman ever,' et cetera, et cetera...and unavoidably so. This week, Willy Mae Beal was named Big League Baseball's player of the week by *Sportsworld* magazine and BLB's pitcher of the week by *The Baseball News*...the first woman ever to be so honored!"

Back home at the Meadowlands, Jack Finigan's crew was umpiring the Atlanta series and Big Jack himself would be behind the plate for the first night's game. Willy put on her best smile, juggled the game ball with her fingers, and strutted past him on her way to the mound. Willy set down the first seven Atlanta Bees in order until the lightweight catcher, Esteban Reyes, pulled a long fly ball over the left field fence, barely missing the fair-foul pole.

"About six inches to the left and it would've been strike one," said Cam. "Instead, Atlanta leads, one-nothing."

Paul hung his head as he stood at the mound, taking an old-fashioned tongue lashing. "You said he was a chump. You called for all fastballs. He hasn't hit any homers all year in his home park..."

"The house that Aaron built!" Paul said, trying to be cute to elicit a laugh.

"Shush, Paul!" He shushed. "Then he comes up here...*to my house!*...and takes me long." She huffed, shrilled, and shouted, "Oh!" Then she kicked dirt onto Paul's feet.

He shrugged. "The guy's a catcher. What can I tell ya? They'll do it to ya every time."

Willy rolled her eyes and glared at Paul. She was grinding her teeth so hard that he could see the pulsating inside her cheeks. He nudged some mound dirt toward her with his toe. She looked down at their feet and booted a mother lode of red clay dust and chunks all over Paul's trousers, shin guards, knee pads, and shoes.

"Feel better, babe?" he asked.

Willy tilted her head and smiled. "Yeah, lots!"

"Back to work!" he said.

Felix Montoya was the first baseman for the Atlantans. Felix was a catcher in the minors but, according to Paul, he was "too good looking and too dumb to be one of us." While snacking on carrot sticks and peanuts on the homeward-bound flight from the City of Angels, Paul and Willy planned to work the righty slugger with curveballs, the same way they "murdered," in Paul's words, lefties like Tatum and Ortega with sliders. Felix clocked Willy's third ripple for an opposite-field homer.

Said Paul, "In theory, it should've worked. He got lucky."

"In theory, it's two to nothing," replied Willy with ill humor.

As her loyal legions cheered, Willy punched out the next batter and retired the side with two more quick and easy outs. Next inning, Willy served up back-to-back singles and a nicely laid bunt put runners in scoring position. Tonight's crowd reportedly tallied at 76,500, although one would be hard-pressed to locate 400 empty seats. Heretofore somewhat subdued, the loyalists made their presence known. As the chanting *"Wil- lee! Wil-lee!"* rolled like a wave through the crisp night air, Willy gave her now familiar gesture, imitating the immortal Satchel Paige–"You might as well sit down!"–to the baserunners on second and third. She raised two fingers to the sky before the second out popped up to Cal and three fingers before the third out lined softly to Keith.

Cal, who singled and was caught stealing in the first, led off the sixth frame with another base hit and swiped second by beating Reyes's throw. After Demmy and Andy flew out to left and right, respectively, Roy singled, Thor tripled, Dino singled, Atlanta changed pitchers, and Keith doubled. *"Let's go Dees!"*

When Paul was retired on a fly ball for the third out, Willy and the Diamonds led, 3-2. The score remained the same until she threw her first pitch of the seventh inning to Montoya. His second home run of the evening was Burtonesque, denting an anonymous patron's car roof in the parking lot.

"Ya seem to have more trouble with righties than lefties," said Paul. "I think it's 'cause your curve don't work the same way against righties as the slider does against lefties."

"Is that so?" Willy quipped impatiently.

"You're mad at me, aren't ya? Ya think it's my fault." She nodded, keeping her head down as she drew lazy circles in the dirt with the toe of her shoe. "So does Tom," sighed Paul. "Nobody's up in the bullpen. There would be if he thought it was 'cause of you."

She raised her head to say, "Is it your turn to kick some dirt?"

"No, I'm good. Thanks anyway, babe."

Atlanta's three homers made the Meadowlands seem like a long-ball hitter's paradise, and so the Georgia Peaches played some "little ball." The inning's second batter tried to bunt his way to first, but failed due to Paul's quick snag in front of the plate and his shortstop-like throw to Thor. The next batter worked Willy for her only free pass of the night and Reyes bunted the walking man over to second. A pinch batter for the pitcher waved at a down-and-in slider, but Paul fumbled it in the dirt and the runner hot-footed it from second to third. Paul bobbled one or two pitches per game, but rarely did so with people on base. The booing crescendoed as the scoreboard indicated "PB."

"That's a passed ball for the sure-handed Cello," Jeff broadcasted. "It's only the second such miscue by number eighteen on the year, but both have come with Willy B. on the hill."

Paul simply signaled Willy for the next pitch, but she knew he was enraged at himself and she ached for him. The pitch that followed was hit between Keith and Demmy for an RBI-single, and the Diamonds trailed, 4-3. Larry Brooks loosened up in the pen, even though the game wasn't in a save situation. Lately, Tom had been giving Larry the ball, bypassing Zinger and Tim, to keep him pitching without long stretches of idleness. Willy ended the inning with her fifth strikeout, certain that she would go the distance unless the D's regained the lead. The ninth spot was to bat first in the bottom half of the seventh. Willy sprinted from the field and patted Paul's buttocks as their paths crossed. In front of the bat rack, she received a similar touching from Joe Manlius as he selected his tool to hit in her stead. Willy's eyes sought Tom's, but his back was turned as he drew a line through Joe's name on his lineup card, thumb-tacked on the dugout wall.

Willy felt calm acceptance as she sat next to Andy, who smiled and said to her, "You did your job."

"I'm not tired. I felt good out there, but we're still gonna lose it, Andy." Then her anger took hold. Willy took a deep breath to compose herself as Joe went down on strikes and Tom stood before her.

"I'm sending Larry in to pitch, whether we score some runs or not." Tom frowned at Willy and spoke loudly enough for all to hear. "If you four starters keep turning them in like this, the relief pitchers won't get much work otherwise. Good job, Willy!"

Willy showered and dressed while the Diamonds' closer surrendered three hits and a run. Montoya, naturally, batted in the insurance run with a sacrifice fly for his third RBI.

Afterward, Tom Vallery entertained the scribes in his office. "It's not a one-woman show. Willy's won one and lost three, but the way she's pitched, she could've won four or five...She's turned in all quality starts. She's consistent. She's strong. Her arm's almost tireless. She's smart as a whip...She'll be all right." Willy deliberately evaded wags' questions after the 5-3 loss, literally sitting between Paul and Cal in the clubhouse, but figuratively hiding behind them while they jawed with the reporters.

"I remember last season," said Paul, "when Gil and Sandy Lee lost five or six in a row at different times, but those guys had the long-term track record of luckin' out and winnin' when they pitched bad...to balance things out."

"We gotta help Willy hang in there and not let the law of averages get her down," said Cal. The shoe-in for all-star selection at second base was giving voice to a statistical anomaly that was being treated in the press as somehow psychological: the Diamonds were averaging eight runs a game when Danielson and Douglas pitched, but less than five runs a game when Jake and Willy pitched. Cal excepted, the position players bristled at the phrase "lack of run support." Roy especially, who had homered twice in games pitched by Willy, felt the wags were trying to instigate dissension. For Willy, her teammates' words of support sufficed.

Shortly, Willy dressed at her locker with Sam Khoury sitting on a stool behind her. "Are you my shadow or what?"

"Well, you could say you're my permanent special assignment," said Sam. "Can't I be your pal, too?"

"Um-hmm," said Willy. "You're that already, Sammy."

"So, why do you wear plain white granny panties?"

"There's enough controversy in this locker room as it is without me dressing like a girl from the Vickie's Closet catalogue."

"You have this wide-eyed innocence about you," Sam told Willy. "Like, John Updyke wrote about baseball being the first part of the adult world that a boy comes to know and can master before the onset of manhood." Willy was a bit tetchy with the line of inquiry. "It's as if you're denying or deferring your womanhood while you're playing baseball," Sam said.

"Sam, I truly believe people should stay in touch with the child inside." Willy turned, standing with folded arms, now more interested than annoyed. "I'm still the same little girl I was when I was three. So are you."

"Okay, but there's that spartan chastity or puritan celibacy or secrecy of yours, even though you could have your pick of men." Sam snapped her fingers for effect. "Line 'em up!"

"Oh, yeah, right," scoffed Willy, wagging her head.

Sam leaned closer and whispered hoarsely, "Willy, there are guys in this very locker room who'd dump their little wifies in a minute to have you."

With the swiftness of Jake's fastball, Willy snapped, "And I'd never be with anyone who would do that."

"Excellent!" Sam smiled with satisfaction. "That tells me what you're all about, right there." One of Willy's teammates dangled by, en route to the showers. Sam didn't react. Instead she said, "I wish I were you. Everybody wants to be you, Willy, except maybe the twenty-five guys on the thirty-two big league teams. You're living the fantasy the rest of us dream about."

"Like I said before," Willy told her, "I'm nothing special...I'm twenty-eight, and the average age in the bigs is twenty-eight. I'm six-foot-two, and the average big leaguer is six-foot-two. I'm average!"

"Oh, yes, you are special. They threw away the cookie cutter when they stamped you out, for sure. You're all of us, but, at the same time, you're like totally unique. You're a fully grown miracle baby, the twenty-first century woman-child, Willy B. Superwoman, showing us the way of the future."

"That's an awful lot to be putting on me," Willy said seriously.

"For sure," said Sam. "It's the same old song, Willy. The woman has to be twice as good, twice as smart. What's so cool is that *you are*."

"I don't know about that, Sam."

Sam sat with arms crossed and her legs spread apart. "Willy, do you want to know what my next piece is on?"

"Let me take a guess, Ms Khoury. Could it be about *me* by any chance?"

"I'm writing that you're Shirley Temple, Tina Turner, Lucy, and Aretha, all rolled into one. You speak–and you sing–in suburban white bread, a heartland twang, a back country drawl, urban Ebonics, Spanglish, and Brooklynese. You come from Hollywood, Mudville, Motown, and Cooperstown..." Sam paused to study Willy's reaction. The pitcher simply listened. "It's your persona, not your pitching. All of us–I mean my esteemed colleagues in the media..."

"Y'all wags!" Willy playfully jabbed.

"That's right!" Sam slapped her knee and snapped her fingers with a wink. "We wags are waiting for the real you to play peek-a-boo. But we don't get it, do we, Willy? The act is you and you are the act...You've created your public personality and you go into your act–and it's a good one, too–but..." Sam reached and pulled Willy by the arms and stood before her to say, "It has to be exhilarating and exhausting, full speed ahead, twenty-four seven."

Willy nodded slowly and confided in a small voice, "It's hard, really hard, and it just doesn't quit." She placed a soft kiss on Sam's brow as she opened for her pal's embrace.

Tom Vallery's comment about his four starters turning in quality appearances proved double-edged, as Sandy Lee's performance against Atlanta on Saturday was remarkably similar to Willy's a day earlier. The man who would be pitcher of the year was 10-2, whereas the woman who would be rookie of the year was 1-3. Montoya hit another four-bagger off the Reb and Reyes

had a poor man's perfect game at the plate: one-for-one on a walk, double, and walk.
The Diamonds' bowed, 4-1, being stung twice by the Bees in time for the Sunday editions to run "June Swoon" headline banners.

Paul talked excitedly about "my girls" being at Saturday's game. "Maybe we can all go out together somewheres later," he suggested to Willy.

In the wives' room before the game, Willy saw Paul's middle daughter, Ashley, up close for the first time. She had a short, thick mop of blonde hair and brilliant blue eyes. "She's absolutely gorgeous," Willy told Michelle. The little lady sucked the first two fingers of her left hand, while staring speechlessly at Willy. The grown-up lady, who played baseball with the daddies, leaned over to ask, "What flavor are they?"

Ashley unplugged the fingers from her mouth, giggled, and said, "Chocolate and peanut butter!"

Lorraine Cello appeared with Megan and baby Jessica, freshly diapered and gurgling. Lorraine was shorter than Michelle, barely five feet tall and looked like an adult version of her three daughters. She greeted Michelle, gazed right through Willy, and whisked away her brood, saying she had to go to the bathroom before the game started. "I don't suppose Paul's had a chance to mention me to Lorrie," Willy said flippantly. Michelle shrugged in exactly the same noncommittal manner as her hubby is wont to do.

At game's end, Lorraine met Paul at the clubhouse door. She held the infant high on her shoulder with one arm and clung to Ashley's hand with the other. Paul simultaneously kissed his wife and took her hand-off of the tiny one. All the while, the elder little girl, Megan, reached for her father with outstretched arms, jiggling feet, and desperate eyes. Paul knelt down for the hug and kiss she anxiously waited to give. Willy watched Paul wrapped in the warmth of his nest and thought for an instant that she could feel their touch. The feeling was ephemeral. A cold breeze entered her body through her eyes. She swallowed it. The dull hollowness in her stomach became a deeper, wrenching pang. As Mama always says, "Don't waste your time thinking about things that aren't going to happen, Willy Mae." As the Cellos exited the clubhouse, Paul turned his head to where Willy was standing. He flipped a small wave goodbye. "You can introduce me to the wife and kiddies some other time, baby," she muttered softly as they disappeared from her view.

      Willy stood alone in the bustling room, her heart racing, pulse throbbing, breath gasping, unable to keep her footing. She sliced through the crowd to the ladies' lav. It was thankfully vacant. She filled a basin with cold water and plunged her now-world-famous face into it to wash away her tears. After bubbling, surfacing, and backwashing, Willy found her own reddened eyes in the mirror. *You're hopeless for him, aren't you? He's not even all that cute. But you love him, Willy!* Next Willy had an imaginary chat with her absent pal. "What did you say about me having my pick of men? Just look at me now. If you only knew, Sam."

CHAPTER 10

Big Gil turned back Atlanta's crackerjack bats with a fifteen-strikeout, 5-0 win on Sunday, keeping the D's teetering in first place. The most significant event of the weekend, however, was Sandy Lee's departure from the stadium by ambulance, after having pitched brilliantly on Saturday, due to excruciating pain of unknown origin, as Larry pitched the eighth and ninth innings, saving Gil's eighth victory of the campaign. The Rebel's lower back pain was so severe that he had to be carried away by stretcher. He went on the fifteen-day disabled list and Jay Phillips received the hurry-up call from the AAA Jewels.

After Sunday's game, Paul asserted, "Hey, babe, if ya can go out with Fabe, ya can go out with me. I'll pick ya up at your place tonight."

"Where are we going? If you don't mind my asking, Paul!"

"The Italian-American Hall of Fame banquet at the Midtown Athletic Club," he said with due pride.

"Won't I kind of stand out like a black-eyed pea swimming in the tomato sauce?"

"Are ya kiddin'? Franco Harris and Roy Campanella were charter members."

"Who's getting inducted, me or you?"

"I'm not good enough and you're not quite ready yet."

"Can I ask you something, Paul?"

"Sure. Shoot, babe."

"Do you call all the pitchers babe and baby?"

"Yeah, except Jake the Snake. Him and me haven't quite got the synergy thing goin' yet. Why do ya ask?"

"No reason," she answered in a clipped voice. *Please, Paul, don't ever stop. I* am *your baby!*

"You'll feel right at home," he told her cheerily. "Ya said your grandfather's Italian buddies made him an honorary *paisan'* when he played semi-pro ball on the coast durin' the Depression. Didn't he drink his dago red wine and smoke them guinea shit-stinker cigars?" Willy slapped his arm playfully. "What was his real name? Ruben Henry? Enrico Rubino?"

"Where's Lorraine gonna be?" she asked, pretending suspicion.

"Home, switch-hittin' the baby," he replied, tapping his hand on one side of his chest and then the other.

Willy wagged her finger at him. "You talk that way to your mama or your sister?" He shook his head penitently. "Then don't talk like that to me!"

He smiled at her. "You *are* my sister. Be ready to go at 6:30. I don't wanna be late."

Willy didn't have a dress to her name, since she returned the little number with the celestial price tag she picked up in LA. She wore a black pants suit and white silk blouse. She had enough time to corn row her hair and twist a braid from in back around the top of her head like a crown.

"Wow! Ya look great, babe," Paul said when he arrived at her crib. He gently reached up to touch the bare spots of scalp between the tightly braided rows. "Looks hard to do!"

"It just takes patience and time," she sang gaily as she opened the front door. "Like learning to pitch."

Before leaving together, Paul crooked his right elbow toward his battery mate. "To Oz?" he beckoned.

"To Oz!" Willy clutched his arm with two hands. "Hey, partner, how did you know I like to pretend to be Dorothy?"

"Ya told Zinger ya seen it like a hundred times," he snorted as he laughed. "But which Dorothy are ya? Diana Ross or Judy Garland?"

"Both of them," she answered, her voice lilting with carefree joy. *That's right, Paul. Keep me laughing. It helps.*

There were luminaries of every stripe in attendance, former governors and mayors included, not limited by any means to those with vowels suffixed to their names. An appetizer of ziti was served. "That's a traditional Italian thing," explained Paul, her intercultural guide. "And, ya know, lasagna is supposed to be a second course, not the main dish."

"Aw, the sauce has meat in it," complained Willy.

Paul called one of the servers. "Can we get another side dish of pasta with meatless gravy?"

"Gravy, sir?" the server perplexed.

"Yeah, gravy," Paul said animatedly. "Tomato sauce! *Ragu* means gravy in Italian."

"Plain pasta would do fine." Willy spoke more quietly than Paul, letting her hand rest on his arm as they resumed conversation with a former pro football player who made a mint selling frozen pizza in supermarkets. When the servers came to pour the wine as the toastmaster told stale jokes from a podium at the head table, Paul covered Willy's glass and told the young woman holding the bottle, "Don't even think it. I'll have a double, though." When the meal was served, Paul slurped his chianti and asked, "Can we have two vegetarian plates here?"

"Are you afraid I'm gonna barf all over you if I watch you pig out on all that flesh and blood?"

"Naw," he laughed. "You're too cool to puke in public." As Paul related it, "the low point of the evenin'" was when Willy met one of baseball's oldest and greatest living idols, seated in a place of honor at the head table. "So, what do ya think happens? This eighty-eight-year-old hero is practically jumpin' over a table to meet *her*. Then Willy and this *legend* put their heads on each other's shoulders and whisper in each other's ears for like half an hour. What's that all about?"

"He's the most charming old gentleman in the world." Willy swooned upon her return to Paul's side. "I was afraid to meet him. I didn't know what he might say to me."

"What were ya talkin' about?" Paul demanded.

"He knew Papp in the old days...He just told me a little story I never heard before. That's all. No big thing, really!"

"No? How come you're all goofy-eyed?"

Before answering, Willy clasped hands with the catcher and sighed. "I feel like I linked hands with the past, present, and future...Forever, eternity, and infinity...The wheel of life...The great chain of being!"

"You're certifiably crazy. Ya know that?"

"Hush up, please!" A mixture of laughter and sobbing thickened her voice. She threw her arms around his neck.

"For crissakes, Willy! Quit cryin', will ya?"

"I can't," a little girl's voice came meekly. "Just sit here quiet like for a minute, okay?"

"Sure," Paul said softly and covered her face with his hands. Willy took a deep breath and closed her eyes.

This wasn't a fairy tale night, however. Long before the stroke of midnight, Willy stretched out on the bed for her evening's meditation in darkness, with lights off and blinds closed, except for the red dot on the stereo console. She took her measured breaths and started her relaxation from the toes. After her customary twenty minutes, she quickly showered and was ready for bed. She snuggled under the covers, for comfort more than warmth, wearing an old tee shirt and undies and switched from FM to AM to catch Rob DaSilva's *"Sports Talk"* radio show.

Rob's voice sounded truer and more natural over the radio: "...The issue of a woman in the majors is closed. It's a footnote in the record books. It's been over and done with, since Willy Beal made her first appearance in a game. That was only the beginning of what's going on now...The question is how good a pitcher she is and just how much better she might become someday." *Click!* Willy depressed the off-button and set the clock-radio's alarm for 5:00 a.m. She scrunched up her pillow, hugged it, and closed her eyes. "Hey, Papp, thanks for the gift you gave me. I promise you, I won't waste it."

The pace of Willy's public life quickened in the weeks to come. At six o'clock, after speeding from one appearance to the next during the prior ten hours, Willy found herself waiting to do her fifteen-minute segment of a prerecorded late-night talk show before flying off to the Meadowlands for a game at eight. She sat in the "green room" and watched the opening of the show being taped in front of a live audience.

"The Goodnight Show...with Jayson Leonard..." A production assistant told Willy she was on in sixty seconds. She entered the stage set wearing a pink and mauve floral print blouse, purple slacks, a pink replica New York D's cap, and white canvas sandals. The convivial host started ribbing her straight away.

"Success hasn't spoiled you, has it? No-o-o! Look at those pants. They're spray-painted on!"

"They are not," she giggled nervously. "Why are you picking on me, Jayson?"

"The lipstick, nail polish, earrings!" Jayson continued. "What happened to the old Willy we all fell in love with?"

"I'm still underneath all this...My pants are not spray-painted on!" Willy's eyes moved from the audience, to Jayson, to the camera, and the in-studio crew. Willy's hands were so sweaty that she felt like they were covered in chicken grease. The thought made her nauseous.

Jayson said, "I've never been a very good athlete. I was real klutzy as a kid." He waved his clasped hands as if swinging an imaginary bat. Willy hoped the attention was fully directed away from her hands, but Jayson pointed at them and yelped, "My God! Your hands!" Willy was mortified. *What is this chump doing to me?* The host reached over his desk, right into Willy's lap. Your fingers are so incredible. They're beautiful. They're humungous. Jimi Hendrix had fingers like that."

Willy diverted her eyes with her hands still tightly wrapped by the jovial host. She took a deep breath, exhaled, nodded, and said, "Jimi was like Charlie Parker and Sergei Rachmaninoff. All three artists made innovations in their music because of the physical range of their hands."

"You do the same thing with a baseball," said Jayson.

"I wouldn't say that," said Willy. "They're just tools to work with..."

Jayson Leonard, the jolly host, panned for the cameras. "Willy Beal, her fingers, and her orchestra will return after these messages, folks."

Later next day, the best team in the American Circuit came to the Meadowlands to play an interleague series with the Diamonds and brought an extra added attraction. Willy was shooting the breeze in the clubhouse with Paul, Tim, and Larry when Cal exclaimed, "KC's in town and the Crawfords are with them, the father and the son!" Youngblood Crawford was one of baseball's hottest young stars and his father, Armstrong Crawford, was recently selected for induction into the Hall of the Immortals at Cooperstown.

"Let's go over and meet him," said Paul, impulsively reaching for Willy's hand. She took hold and squeezed with such intensity that he halted in his footsteps. "Ya almost broke my fingers, babe" he said with a silly giggle, being falsely playful to mask his embarrassment. He teased her and she teased him back. Paul was as deeply mired in secretly star-crossed love as Willy was.

"I'm excited about seeing Army Crawford," Willy told Paul.

"Half the guys here don't even know who he is," Cal said regretfully.

Tim piped up, "They think Cy Young is the name of the company that sponsors the pitcher of the year award."

Armstrong Crawford was holding court in the visitors' locker room, surrounded by a passle of wags, with Youngblood at his side and baby grandson in his lap. Army Crawford was one of the most gifted and exciting players ever to take the field. He had 3,000 hits and a lifetime batting average of .309. He would have won multiple hitting crowns if he hadn't played in the same era as Pete Rose and Rod Carew. He would have been an MVP if his finest season had been with a pennant-winner. If he had played twenty years with one team, instead of nineteen with seven different teams, he would have been lionized in his twilight as a "franchise player." *If* is the operative word to describe Army's life in baseball. If he hadn't binged with a bottle a hundred times per season, stultified his inner demons with drugs, and feuded endlessly with teammates and managers, he might have been the greatest ballplayer in history. Recovery
followed the end of his career and Army Crawford devoted much of his time to helping other pro athletes overcome alcoholism and drug addiction. Finally, after waiting for more years than he played, he was voted into the shrine.

Crawford's heavily lined face smiled proudly as he bounced the gurgling and drooling toddler. "Crawford the Third!" Army proclaimed, "the next in line of the dynasty." Anxious to meet the legend, Willy thus was surprised by the way he greeted her. "I'm very happy to meet you, dear." He said, "I knew your grandfather years ago. I was just a young buck then. I know how proud he'd be to see you now." Willy thanked him with a murmur, as Army shifted his gaze to Larry. "How're *you* doin'?" he asked with great seriousness. Larry simply bobbed his head. "Are you sure?" Army asked, his eyes probing.

"I'm doin' okay," Larry answered, somewhat darkly. All the Diamonds knew the ace closer's status was tenuous, hinging on his conduct off the field, meaning staying "on the wagon."

"May I hold the baby?" asked Willy. Without hesitation, Army passed the little boy from his arms to Willy's. The child stared in silent fright for a second, then burped, called her "ma-ma-mum," grabbed a pigtail in each tiny hand, and yanked with all his strength. The cherub let go when Willy tickled his belly and cooed, "Can I take you home?" She asked the baby's grandfather, "What's his name?"

"Youngblood Armstrong, what else?" He decreed, "Y'all can call him King Crawford the Third." Then, he called out, "Young-Blood!" Army said his son's name as if it were two words. "Take this here child and put on a show for the people. Change his diaper or somethin'. I want to talk a spell with this young woman."

"Sure, Pop! C'mon, little dude," said Youngblood, as he picked up the crown prince and led the crowd of players and wags to the trainer's table. "Let's show off the family jewels."

"All-star wipes the baby's booty!" someone crowed.

"I was no kind of father to that boy," Army disclosed to Willy with astonishing intimacy. "I was a kid myself. I didn't grow up 'til I was an old man of forty...Bless his mother! She had to stop helpin' me and throw me out in order to save me. I have a new bride now. She's got the man my first wife deserved. I've found the Lord, too...It wasn't the booze alone. I suffered from depression. So, I got myself high with drugs and came down with liquor. I was a lost soul." With a sad smile, he said, "I worry every day about that boy of mine. Keep him on the straight and narrow. Baseball talent isn't the only thing that runs in families." Army held hands with Willy, whose look suggested more than empathy. "Do you wanna tell me somethin', dear?" he asked.

Willy's eyes scanned Army's rugged face and she opened her mouth to speak, but said no. She felt her father's ghost pass through the room.

Even with an all-time great gracing Kansas City's locker room, the star of the show was Kenny Estrada. In the previous season, Kenny swiped 40 bases and hit 41 homers, a rare feat, despite beginning the year in a drug rehabilitation clinic and ending it in divorce court. His myriad off-the-field soap opera vignettes were widely publicized, but he continued to be an impressive force on the diamond, able to hit, hit with power, and eat up the basepaths. Kenny was considered by some scouts to have the best arm in the game from the hot corner, but unlike his ex-best-friend Demeter Fortune, Estrada's fielding reputation was based more on his good looks than good glove skills. KC's manager, Fred Teller, thus was determined to move Kelly Swifton, last year's star rookie, from the outfield to third base and shift Estrada to first base. Telly was a feisty showboat with baseball brains, cut out in the mold of bygone days. His managerial credo: "Once I change my mind, nothin' can make me change it." Estrada complained loudly and at length to teammates, reporters, the owner, anyone who would listen, but apparently not to his skipper. "Kenny hasn't said nothin' to me about it. I told him to play first and he knew right where to go," Telly told the wags, comically gesturing toward the right-hand side of the infield. "He had the right kinda glove and everythin'!"

Kenny Estrada always drew a crowd and he seemed resigned, if not subdued on this particular day. He said, "I'm still the one who makes things happen on this team, no matter where I play. I'll just concentrate on playin' my game." The new season showed that he was indeed on his way to leading the other league in home runs and runs batted in once again. However, when asked by Dale Goodwyn why his BA plunged from .303 to .234 in the process, an amused Kenny answered, "Who would you rather have, me or Demeter Fortune?"

Upon hearing the comment–second-hand, since no room was large enough to contain both egos–Demmy countered, "In a way, he's got a point. I'm not a better player because my batting average is a hundred points higher, but it does verify my theory that there's a direct correlation between BA and IQ. Don't you agree?" How the rivalry between Fortune and Estrada began and why the two players let it persist was anyone's guess. Born and bred in the suburbs of San Diego, Demmy and Kenny were teammates in youth leagues, high school, and college. The comparisons due to similar age, attributes, and hometown origins caused the two bullish personalities to clash. "I just don't like the guy," Demmy said simply, concisely, and unambiguously. Willy suspected there was more to it than that.

In their first interleague game, New Yorkers Fortune, Gilbert, and Burton matched Kansas Citians Estrada, Crawford, and Swifton, homer for homer, but the Diamonds lost, 8-5, and dropped a second game the next day, despite a pair of moonshots switch-hit by Roy. To the pundits' delight, the D's rolled over and took a third beating in as many days. The only series in which they had been swept all year was at the hands of the team that the odds-makers were picking them to meet in the postseason in October.

Willy didn't pitch in the KC series; regardless, she had work to do. The ReVerse sneaker commercial was a piece of cake for her. The production crew was cheerfully efficient and the director walked Willy through the complete scenario beforehand. The spot involved a half hour of inside shots. Willy wore delicately sexy powder blue tights with light classical piano in the background. Then she switched to sweats and sneaks with hard-driving funk. There followed two hours of shooting outside with Willy's ReVerse-shod feet sprinting across a sandlot. After five minutes of dubbing her voice for a three-line script and twenty minutes of posing for stills for collateral magazine ads, Willy watched the rushes of unedited film and was ready to go home by four o'clock.

The American Cola commercial was another story. The concept was similar, involving aerobic dancing in a specially customized Diamond look-alike uniform. There was a six-word script: "Just catch the taste of it." The ending called for Willy to snatch a can from midair, take a sip in side profile, smile, and speak the slogan. The production took thirteen hours and was nearly left unfinished for two weeks, since Willy couldn't

schedule another all-day session until after the team's next road trip. The temperamental director and Willy argued about the music. "The guitar's too heavy metal!" said she. "It's too jazzy if we do it your way!" said he. Next,
she refused to drink from the can of the caffeinated variety supplied as a prop and one of the crew members had to buy a decaff at the nearest convenience store. Then, the director kept retaking Willy's dance movements. "Hey, I got it," said Willy, stopping after a spin and a kick. "How about if I unbutton my shirt and jiggle my girls?"

The director took a moment to think it over. "I think you might have something there."

"Did you think I was serious?"

"Oh, were you being sarcastic?"

"Maybe it's time to go."

Finally, after the sixth take of the ending, Willy was exhausted and exasperated. With camera rolling, she lifted the can and poured the soda over her head, singing, "And the Diamonds win the Series. Woo!"

"Yes! We did it! Beautiful! That's a wrap, people!" The American Cola spot, improvised ending and all, aired nationwide the following week.

Yet there were a few warm interludes amid the hectic pace. One of them was dinner at the home of Thelma and Rudy Judd in Tenafly, New Jersey. There was a cocoonlike coziness that made Willy feel as if she were back in Old Saint Pete when Papp was still alive. Thelma tried to accommodate Willy's vegetarianism by preparing an array of salad, side dishes, appetizers, and desserts–everything but a main entree. On the way back to Manhattan, Willy began to feel homesick, but the

Diamonds wouldn't be in Tampa or Miami until August and there weren't enough Mondays and Thursdays off in the meantime for a visit with her mother, Alma.

    The excursion from midtown to North Jersey through bottlenecked, gridlocked, stalled, and crawling traffic was grueling, since Willy usually set out for the Meadowlands during peak drive time. As she headed westward on the FDR Drive toward the George Washington Bridge, the traffic broke and Willy tooled along to the "all-oldies, all-the-time" radio station. Levi Stubbs pleaded, *"Sugarpie, honeybunch, you know that I'm weak for you..."* and the Four Topps repeated, *"Weak for you!"* Willy happily sang out the refrain, *"I can't help myself..."* Up ahead, a sixteen-wheeler's directionals flashed. Willy swung her little XYZ car into the breakdown lane to pass the tractor-trailer on the right. Only the horn blaring and the hydraulic brakes hissing prompted Willy to realize that the big diesel had signaled to the right, not the left. She gunned her coupe past the monster's screeching tires, careened her right front wheel off a pylon demarking the exit ramp, and swerved to avoid crashing into the guardrail running between the on and off ramps. *You almost got your number retired, Willy!* She put both hands on the steering wheel, eyes front, and cruised the rest of the way at minimum speed, her pulse still throbbing in her throat and her seat damp.

    In the stadium's reserved parking lot, Willy noticed, for all the complaining about lack of privacy, there was no mistaking the ownership of the high-ticket cars, pickups, and vans by virtue of the vanity plates affixed to them: BIG GIL, REBEL, ROY HITS, FORTUNE SS.

"Clean 'sheen, Willy B!" called the attendant as he stood up in his booth and came out to hold open her door.

"Hey, bro'," she laughed, tossing him the keys. "If you can handle it, you can have it."

"Aw, no way!" he said jokingly. "Nimocos crunch up like a beer can if ya smash 'em up. I wanna have some armor around me."

"Tell me about it!"

On the first and hottest night of the summer, Willy started her fourth game at the Meadowlands and it was her fourth standing-room-only sellout. The Diamonds averaged 40,000 per game in attendance. Willy B. Superstar averaged 75,000. Art Ridzik calculated that Willy had already contributed two and a half million dollars to Fabian's profit. "The numbers will be on Wanamaker's desk, first thing Thursday morning," promised Artie.

During Willy's warm-up on the sidelines, Paul kept stopping to talk to her. "I don't feel the pop tonight, babe...Work on the action...Concentrate!...The velocity's down...Don't overthrow. You'll blow your arm out...If you press too much, you'll release the ball too high or too low...Don't push the ball. Pitch!...Good, babes!...Let's stick with curves and sliders, and slip in a fastball to fool 'em."

The loyal and true Diamonds' fans were in full voice as the most popular player in baseball dashed to the mound, jammed her toe into the rubber–once, twice, three times–and turned to make the first of five practice throws to Pigpen Pantagones. A few moments later, she watched the real catcher assume his position. She leaned forward with her gloved left hand on her knee, tucked her right hand behind her back, and twirled the ball with her fingers, awaiting Paul's flashing signals. Monty "Man-Mountain" Guilford was calling the balls and strikes behind the plate.

Willy's first pitch to Rod Weams was a hard breaking slider. "Stee-riike!" Her second was another slider, over the top, veering away from Roddy's whipping bat. "Stee-riike two!" Paul wiggled one finger on the first of three signs and Willy B., Ace of Diamonds, sidearmed a cross-seam fastball. The Cincy lead-off batter's eyes picked up the spin. In the span of five milliseconds, Roddy's brain processed the information, which told him to extend his arms and swing at the horizontal break of a slider that was not.

"Outta there!" Cam Hammersmith exclaimed over the Millennium Channel.

She warmed up cold and came out smokin', thought Paul.

Willy raised her arms and swayed her hips, dancing to the hip-hop rhythm from the stadium's sound system, arousing the wildest cheering ever to greet the Cincy Machine's number
two hitter. There followed a groundout to Demmy at short and a single on a two-and-oh overhand fastball, slapped through the left side of the infield by Chad Boswell. Willy and Paul labored through a full-count and walked Jason McAllister. The battery mates conferred. Another full-count led to another walk, drawn by Jose Roman. The pitcher and catcher conferred again, and went to three-and-two again, but, mercifully, received a third strike call from Monty and escaped the bases-loaded jam. The music played, Willy danced her way from the mound, and the Willymaniacs called her name: *"Wil- lee!*

Wil- lee! Let's go Dees!" Willy slapped hands down the line to a far-edge seat on the bench, and Paul and Rudy huddled in the dugout.

"Mixed message, Rudy," said Paul. "She's throwin' real hard and the ball's breakin' real good, but she's missin' the corners. Monty's not cheatin' her."

"And they're waitin' on her. She's gotta stay within herself and get the ball over the plate."

Willy pursed her lips and hovered over her catcher and pitching coach. "Can *she* say something here, boys?"

They looked at her with surprise. "So, talk!" Paul nodded to acquiesce.

"Paul, you've got me pitching everybody inside out and backwards, making adjustments before I've made any mistakes. Why? I have velocity and movement on the ball. Let me go back to the alternating fastball and breaking ball, inside and outside pattern."

"She's right," Rudy said to Paul. The two men concurred solemnly. "Let's go right at 'em."

Willy threw more pitches and fewer strikes than usual, but went through the next three innings touched by only a meaningless single by Weams. Oddly, she was registering more than one strikeout per inning, as the Queen City Redlegs switched from waiting to chasing. With one out in the fourth, Gilbert launched his twelfth homer of the season over the right field wall. Burton then drew a walk and Andreason followed with a single. DeSantis advanced the runners by grounding out and Paul drove them home with a two-run single. Now leading 3-0, still pitching without her good stuff, Willy threw fourteen pitches–half of them out of the strike zone– but retired the side in order, ending the fifth inning with her seventh strikeout. Willy walked the first batter in the sixth. Boswell, up next, clouted an extra-base hit between and beyond the diving Dino and the stumbling Roy, making it a 3-1 game. McAllister drew a base on balls on four pitches and Roman hit a three-and-oh fastball that sent Burton to the base of the center field scoreboard. Roy made the catch, but not in time to make a play on Boz. Holding a 3-2 lead, Willy coughed up her third walk of the inning and fifth of the game. Paul walked to the mound, expecting to find Willy either aflame with anger or in tears, but, instead, there was a bewildered,

helpless look on his dearest teammate's face. Tom came from dugout to mound in cold silence. There was no mistaking his displeasure. Willy passed Tom the ball, bowing her head to

evade his eyes. She scooted away, receiving a loud sendoff from her disappointed, but no less adoring, public.

    After the inning was over, Paul nestled his buns next to Willy's and nudged her. "C'mon, say it," he goaded. "Ya wanna say the F-word, don't ya?"

    "You know I don't say the F-word," she replied glumly.

    "Aw, c'mon. I won't tell nobody. I just wanna hear ya say it."

    "No!" Willy said, and then bubbled up some laughter, which is what Paul really wanted from her.

    Zinger blanked Cincy through the eighth, but lefty Phillips was clipped for a run in the ninth and the game went into overtime. Langevin entered the fray and pitched hitless ball until he was lifted for a pinch-hitter in the bottom of the tenth. Brooks was tagged for a three-bagger with none out in the eleventh, but bore down to retire the next nine stick-swingers in succession. The second string moved into the Diamonds' lineup as nearly half the fans evacuated the stadium. A ninth-inning double by Darnell had been the only sign of life in the home team's offense until Benny ended up on second with a long hit to open the bottom of the thirteenth. Tom let Larry bat for himself and he delivered a scratch single. Two ground balls and a walk later, Roy stepped up to bat with the bases loaded. The best hitter in Big League Baseball stroked the game-winning base hit into the outfield. The 4-3 extra-inning win raised all spirits save two: those of Tom Vallery and Willy Beal. The manager was close-mouthed and Willy wasn't keen on approaching him. Not until after the D's next game did Vallery break the chilly spell. "You have three things going for you, Willy...control, consistency, and intelligence. You had none of those things last night."

"I think it had more to do with my action on the ball than my brains, Tom," she said sharply.

"I mean concentration," he clarified himself without apology. "I'm concerned because I don't know what to expect anymore."

"I had a bad game. That's all. One bad game!"

"Yes, but why and how many more times it'll happen is what I have to know."

"He's not just concerned," Willy told Cal. "He's really pissed off at me."

"Tom's Mr. Logic," said Cal. "He's not ruled by emotions. He's ruled by rationality, strategy, and stats. He can't deal with surprises and question marks. Sandy Lee's bad back and sore arm are question marks...Jake's erratic pitching! One game's a shutout, the next one's a blowout...Can Big Gil carry the team? Will Larry stay sober? Is Tim a big league stopper? Can Zinger still cut it? Are Jay and Strick ready?...These are all iffy questions. As of this Wednesday night, you became one more iffy question."

CHAPTER 11

Every season the interleague trading deadline is preceded by a flurry of speculation in the press about likely big names changing teams mid-season and followed by reaction from around the league about the effect on the pennant race if indeed such a trade came to be. This season, the month of June witnessed an old-time blockbuster: San Francisco sent first baseman Tony Ortega and their top minor league pitcher, Luke Pinto, to the D.C. Nats for pitcher Memo Alvarez and first baseman Bobby Ray Webster.

"The deal is a classic 'challenge trade,' exchanging players of the same position, skill level, and attributes. Bodies switch uniforms with no obvious change in the makeup of either ballclub." Thus wrote Dale Goodwyn in the *Daily Mail*.

"Two big, slugging first sackers and two righty pitchers," Cal said. "Tony's older than Bobby Ray and Memo's taller than Pinto. That's about all the difference I can see."

Demmy seemed more sentient. "I'm sure Charley Novak thought he needed to move quick. Alvarez is a good pitcher, but that's not the reason. He wanted to unload Ortega."

"So, Frisco gets Webster for half Ortega's salary," said Roy.

Andy added, "And he'll play twice as long in the future, being ten years younger, right?"

"Either way it's bad public relations," said Cal. "Ortega was popular and the fans might take it out on the new guys."

Willy wasn't slated to start a game during the weekend in Houston, but, when the Diamonds were rained out in Denver on Monday, Tom skipped over her turn. Moreover, he tabbed Jay Phillips to open Thursday in St. Louis after sending him to the hill Sunday at the Texas dome. She was incensed, but her emotions leveled by Friday night, as Willy took the mound for the East's first-place team against the Central's first-place team in the thick of a pennant race.

"That's baseball!" she said, drinking in the beauty of the stadium, out to the Gateway Arch and the grand Mississippi, in a town where teams called the Stars, Browns, and Maroons once played. The sellout crowd at the brew master's stadium was more vociferously partisan than any fans Willy had yet encountered on the road. To the Missouri folk, the New York Diamonds weren't merely rivals, but the enemy, evil ones to be hated. Tonight, at any rate, they seemed to be acting more like Chicagoans. Willy was flustered at being booed unrelentingly during her five minutes of loosening on the sidelines. The jeering that greeted Willy's jaunt to the rubber for the bottom of the first was unsettling, although her ears picked up her share of applause, as usual, from these otherwise New York baiting, Diamond hating folks.

In the broadcast booth, the Millennium Channel's dynamic duo sized up the Redbirds. "The combo of Monroe and Frazier on this young St. Louis team reminds the people around these parts of Flood and Brock on that great ballclub of the 1960s," said native son Jeff. "The key is to keep them off the base paths," said Cam. "The lineup is built for speed, from top to bottom."

Leading off for the Redbirds was Curtis Monroe, the league's number two base-stealer. Willy and Paul set him up with sliders, up and in, then down and away. With a two-and-two count, Willy fanned Monroe with a sidearm fastball. The second baseman, Terry Frazier, another speedster, was considered the best bat-handler in the league. Paul and Willy reversed the routine on Tee, as friends knew him, getting strike one on an overhand fastball. A sidebar whispered in the booth: "Hey, Cam, she topped ninety-five." Came the muffled reply: "I told you, Jeff." Strikes two and three were on sliders. The scene of the statuesque woman in pigtails pulling her fist down and wailing "Yes!" brought a spontaneous scattering of cheers from the Sloobirds' fans. Kicking off the game with two kays was the kind of result for which Rudy Judd hoped to erase the memory of Willy's previous outing.

Batting fifth and playing center field for the Redbirds was the friendly face of Mercurio Mercado. Much was made of Merk's horrendous slumps, a panoply of minor and major injuries, his diminished capacity on the bases, and decreased mobility in patrolling the outfield. After having been one of the most popular players in the Windy City for a decade, the St. Looie fandom was down on him. "Rigor Mortis Mercado" the bleacher bums' banner splashed. "We can't assume there's anything wrong with his bat," observed Paul, as he and Willy reviewed the charts the night before. He was correct. Willy found pitching inside to Merk difficult and he stroked two of the four hits given up by Willy in the first five innings.

Redbird skipper Bert Casagrande devised the "Willy B. shift" to defend against her bunting safely to first base. Willy let the bat rest on her shoulder: ball four! The D's first base coach, Silvio Romero, reached out and tugged Willy's shirt sleeve before she stepped to her right to take a lead off the base. "The message from Tom is you get fined one grand if you try to steal." Willy looked uncomprehendingly at Sil. "Even if you make it and even if you don't get hurt, it's a grand. Understand?" She nodded and adjusted her plastic helmet. "Watch the signs!" Sil said.

With Cal at bat, the sacrifice was on for the first pitch only. Cal popped the ball thirty feet, between the mound and the third-base line, and was thrown out as Willy went sliding into second. She took the smallest of leads, knowing Demmy wouldn't swing at the first pitch. He didn't and she strode out farther and watched Norm Simon, coaching alongside third. As soon as Willy heard the *thwack* of bat against ball, she dug for third base, as Norm waved his arms. In six seconds flat, Willy crossed the plate upright as Demmy slid into second base. Willy felt a rush of excitation from scoring her first run and slapped sky fives with Andy at the plate, Roy on deck, the batboy, the ballgirl, and Thor at the bat rack. She didn't take a seat on the bench, standing at the foot of the dugout steps, clapping and cheering for the rally to continue. Andy drove a fly to deep right field, where Monroe made the catch and threw "on the money" to the cutoff. Roy fouled off two pitches and drove the next one for a long single. Demmy glided around third and scored on a belly slide.

Ahead by two runs, Willy gave up nondamaging singles in the sixth and seventh. All her pitches were working, especially her "bread and butter," the low-and-away sidearm slider to right-handed batters. She felt good.

"Willy Beal's hot as a pistol tonight, fans," announced Cam.

"She hasn't even broken a sweat," commented Jeff.

Willy watched the Diamonds fail to score with runners on first and third in the eighth, wasting a triple by Andy. She took the mound in the bottom of the eighth, working on a six-hit shutout. The rich, sweet taste of win number two was on her lips. Casagrande pulled his pitcher for a pinch-hitter and sent his club's newest member to start things in the inning.

Paul strolled up to Willy. "So, tell me, babe. Who the hell is Beaumont Teague?"

"Down in double-A, he hit just about everything I threw at him."

"That could be a problem," catcher Cello understated. "Let's pitch him fastballs away. Keep 'em up. He might not have the patience to take four balls for a walk. Okay?"

"Sounds good, partner!" Big Bad Beau swished at two strikes before cracking a double.

Paul sauntered to the mound as Willy entertained the local boosters with a clay-kicking, head-bobbing, pigtail-shaking tantrum. "I guess the guy owns ya." She shot him a fierce look. "Hey, it's like that sometimes."

The sparkplugs, Monroe and Frazier, were due to bat for Bert's Birds. Curtis lined a hit barely beyond Cal's grasp and Tee took ball four for Willy's first free pass of the night. The bases were loaded and third baseman Marcus Spencer stepped to the plate. Marvelous Marcus wasn't regarded as one of the bigs' better hitters, but, at present, he was the league's leading batter at .353. Willy felt her adrenaline surge as the St. Louis bullpen pitchers turned around their caps and the crowd exhorted their heroes to rally.

Paul flashed one finger. "Slinging it sidearm...fastball, strike one!" called Cam. Paul flashed one and a decoy set of multifinger signs. "Buggywhip fastball...swung on and missed, strike two!..." Paul signaled one, three, two, and another fastball came over the top. "Just missed, ball one!" On the third set of signs, Paul put three fingers down. The belt-high slider spun toward the middle of the plate and broke away, in front of Spencer's swing. "He's outta there!" Cam howled and cuffed his mic: "Ninety-six, Jeff!"

Willy raised one finger in the air, pumped her fist, held up two fingers, and pointed at the clean-up batter, Rusty Buffington. He swung and missed an overhand slider. Looking for another slider, he took strike two on a sidearm fastball. Willy's eyes bore down on home plate. She glanced first at the runner on third, then at the one on first, as if to freeze them where they stood. She trained her eyes on the plate once more and pitched from the stretch. Buffington looked for a slider, low and away. He got it and hit it. Willy spun on her heels and watched the ball travel out to left. Andy trotted back to the wall, turned, timed his jump, then dropped his arms and hung his head, not having the stomach to watch the grand slam fall into the eager hands of the fans in the first row of seats. As each happy St. Louis run-scorer stepped on home and awaited a mate to follow suit, Paul saw Willy cover her face with her glove. He ran to his pitcher to find her sobbing and gasping.

"Keep your head down and stand right there," Paul said as he put a hand on each of her shoulders. "Don't let the freakin' TV cameras catch ya cryin'. The friggin' wags'll fry ya."

Cal joined them and listened to Willy babble, "I made the right pitch...I pitched good tonight...He stung my best pitch."

The two teammates shielded the rookie pitcher while she cried. "Tom's gonna come out here in a minute," Cal said.

"No effin' way I'm gonna let him pull her out," said Paul. A moment passed, then he looked at her and shouted, "Cut it out, Willy! You're actin' like a goddamn girl!"

Willy broke into laughter, rubbing her eyes and nose. She took three deep, cleansing breaths to regain her composure, retired Merk on a grounder, and fanned the inning's final batter. She sprinted off the mound in her usual fashion and met an unexpected but wholly welcome embrace from Gil Douglas in the dugout. "I've been there, sister."

On the Millennium Channel superstation, Cam toasted Willy B.'s "excellent, quality performance." Benny, batting for Keith, lined to Frazier–one away. Paul pulled a *"bellissima"* fly ball to left, deep enough for a homer at Camden Yards–two away. Joe, pinch-hitting for the pitcher, drove one far enough to have gone out of the stadia in Cleveland, Atlanta, or Buffalo.
As Buffington let the ball drop into his glove, the Diamonds lost, 4-2, and Willy B. Superstar took her fourth loss in five decisions.

Tom and Rudy sat Willy down after the game. Tom told her, "We've tracked your pitch selection and you've been throwing the overhand fastball five or six times a game. You're velocity's up in the mid-nineties. You're a control pitcher and a damned good one, but control pitchers are prone to long hits simply because they put the ball over the plate. Such is the balance of nature in the arts of pitching and hitting. The harder and faster a ball is pitched, the farther it flies off the bat when hit. The last thing you should do is throw a high-velocity fastball over the plate. You don't need to throw a two-seamer. The action on your four-seamer is more than adequate. You can rely on your offspeed fastball and breaking stuff and hide away the heater for special occasions."

    Willy took the advice to heart, but her mood wasn't fully cheered until she accompanied Cal, Big Gil, and Larry to an all-night soul kitchen. While the guys pigged out on barbecued ribs, Willy engorged herself on sweet potato pie, greens, and cornbread. Like most nights on the road, she ended up after midnight in a hotel suite with Paul and Zinger. After Paul exhaustively talked Willy and Zinger up and down the St. Louis, Pittsburgh, and Chicago batting orders, he compared baseball with chess: All of the pieces begin in set positions, white is the home team and always moves first, just like the pitcher puts the ball in play; all moves are limited in terms of pattern and direction, and the queen is the pitcher. "The deadliest and most vulnerable piece," he explained with a wink at Willy. Each play is based on an expected series of moves and countermoves to follow, but, after it is made, the repositioning of a single piece in the configuration leads to an entirely new set of expectations, probabilities, and possibilities. As Paul spoke, Willy sat next to Zinger on the edge of the bed and let her mind wander through snapshot-like images of the catcher using his *tools of brilliance* and the uncompromising opinion of three of baseball's most gifted pitchers that no second-stringer will substitute for Paul Cello to receive their pitches.

"Oh, Paul, you're a genius!" she shouted, so agitated she seemed angry, startling her two friends. "You're the best catcher in baseball and nobody knows it!"

"No, I'm not," he said, shaking his head and frowning. Then he giggled, "Tom does."

"I can't believe Steele and Gustafson and Boswell are giving Cliff Allyn and Casey Calderone and Wayne Cahill this kind of intellectual analysis. They can't possibly be so deep, so far beyond 'get the ball over the plate,' and also be able to go out and actually do their job."

"Those guys are good, too," said Paul, smiling shyly. "I'm what they call 'a good handler of pitchers,' which means a catcher who can't hit for shit."

"That's not so either," said Willy, still excited.

"Ya know why I'm a catcher?" he asked rhetorically, and then answered his own question: "Because I can't pitch."

There was a clear-cut pecking order on the Diamonds of New York and New Jersey and more than one clique. Willy moved in the higher circle of stars and veterans; although she was still a rookie, the second-stringers weren't her peers. She shunned Darnell Greene for reasons other than snobbishness, but was privately pleased that Cal Bonham appeared to watch over him like a guardian angel, keeping Darnell's drug use at bay, in the same way as Gil helped Larry keep away from the liquor. The gossip shop classified Darnell's status as a display. A trade loomed on the near horizon and he was the bait. He played only enough for the other team's GM to take a "look-see." The word around the clubhouse was that Tom Vallery wouldn't go through the dog days of July and August with Dino DeSantis as the everyday right fielder. The only other option besides trading for a center fielder was moving Thor or Benny to the outfield and installing Joe Manlius full-time at first, which would add offense at one position and subtract defense at two. That equation wasn't the kind of outcome Tom Vallery liked. A trade was in the offing.

Willy wasn't happy with her working schedule, as dictated by Tom, who, truth be known, had reclaimed control of the pitching rotation from the owner. Willy watched as Jay, who was supposed to swing between spot starts and long relief, again take a regular turn at Pittsburgh. Jake and Gil worked on three days rest, while she sat idle for almost a week. The Diamonds were bloodied in three of four games against the St. Louis Flock. The Bucs were on a roll, sweeping Chicago's Baby Bruins that same weekend and winning two of three from the D's. Pittsburgh was within a half-game of overtaking the Redbirds for second place in the National Central. Whereas Big Gil emerged as the league's premier pitcher, bettering his won-lost mark to 12-4, Jake was bruised in St. Louis and battered in the Iron City. He followed up a "piss poor" outing in Missouri with a "pure shit" one in Pennsylvania, to borrow Paul's adjectival phrases, carrying a mediocre 5-5 record toward the season's halfway mark Sandy Lee came off the disabled list on June 29 and took the mound against Pittsburgh that evening. Tom's suspicion that the Rebel wasn't fully sound was borne out by five runs and six hits in two-thirds of an inning, the only time in his career that he failed to finish the first inning of a ballgame. So, to avoid returning the Reb to the DL, Tom confined Sandy Lee's work to three relief appearances over the next two weeks until he was ready to resume his chores as a starter. After a news conference to update the media on Sandy Lee's health, Tom covered his mouth and hissed to Rudy, "The operative word is *hope!*"

Willy met with Art Ridzik before the team's westward swing. "Wanamaker offered us five hundred and fifty thousand dollars. I told him stiffs make five hundred and fifty grand. I figure Harvey talked to Fabian and he'll go to a million or a multiyear deal for more."

"What's wrong with that, Artie?"

"Willy, you are not an average player. I'm going in asking for two-point-five million. I'll take one-point-five on a two-year deal if it goes to two mill the second year."

"I hope you know what you're doing, Uncle Artie."

"Trust me," he said. "I'll blow off Wanamaker to get to Fabian himself. He'll give us what we want if he thinks we mean business."

When the general manager reported back to the owner of the New York Diamonds, Fabian said, "Tell that moron Ridzik that I'll pay Willy a million dollars *next year* if she wins twenty games, rookie of the year, pitcher of the year, and most valuable player. I'll pay her two million if she signs a lifetime contract...and I'll give her a million dollar bonus, right here and now, if she fires his fat ass. Tell him that, Harvey!"

Upon Willy's return with the team to New York, Art Ridzik was distraught. "That bastard Fabian is suing us!"

"What for?" Willy asked in complete disbelief.

"The American Cola commercial," Artie replied. "The Diamonds have an exclusive deal with Cola King for concessions and promotions. They're suing Fabian and he's suing American Cola and you...I mean us... for violating the personal service contract. I think we can expect American Cola to countersue if they're forced to take the commercial off the air."

"Artie, shouldn't you have known about the tie-in between my personal service contract and Fabian's deal with Cola King before you signed me up to do an ad for their competitor?" Art's response was a rambling, fairly incoherent outburst about how much he had done for her and how hard he was working. "Don't you *ever* raise your voice to me like that, Arthur Ridzik!"

"I'm sorry, Willy," he said, simmering down. "This thing has me upset"

"Listen, why don't I talk to Sebastian myself? Call me later, Artie, okay?"

Willy phoned Sebastian Fabian at Fab Co.'s corporate nerve center in Manhattan and he laughed off the entire situation. "It's business, Willy. Let the attorneys fight it out. It's nothing personal between you and I...I don't want a battle between the soda jerks to hurt us on the field."

"Me, neither," said Willy, feeling assured by her boss's attitude. However, he neglected to tell his rookie star that her personal service contract was voided and her paycheck would be reduced by $1,000 a week.

By midweek, things were further unsettled for Willy. Was everything beginning to unravel without her being aware of it? She went to an ATM near the stadium to put some cash in her pocket and got an "insufficient funds" message. She called Artie, who said it was a "mix-up" at the bank. Art said he would take care of it, but she phoned the bank herself to find that she was overdrawn and her mortgage payment check bounced. She tried to call Artie again, but he had left his office and his assistant-secretary-receptionist-coffee-maker knew not how to reach him. Then Willy read a story in the *Journal* suggesting that she collected honoraria of $500 or more from community groups for personal appearances, including a demand for payment in advance from a church group for coming to its father-daughter breakfast. Willy never saw or heard of a penny from any churches or nonprofit groups. Arthur Ridzik had some explaining to do.

Willy was ready to give her best shot at home on Thursday, the series opener against the St. Louis crew. She felt a slight tug, as if someone had grabbed her shoulder and pulled it back, when she released the first of her warm-up pitches. She gave herself a quick rub and saw Paul
running to her side.

"Are ya okay, babe?" he asked, removing his mask.

"Yeah! Why?"

"When a pitcher grabs his arm like that, catchers and managers shit their pants."

Willy laughed enormously, "*Her* arm is fine, partner."

"Ya sure?" he asked. He was skeptical, nervous, and seemingly not only professionally concerned. She answered with a smile and a nod of her head, tilted a bit to one side. "Listen, babe," he said. "Tell me if you're hurtin' and we'll get ya outta here. One game's not worth it."

"I hear you, Paul." He pulled his mask over his face and returned to his station behind the batter without another word.

Twilight blanketed the stadium as the full-to-overflowing crowd cheered, stomped, ranted, raved, and chanted for their hero, Willy Mae Beal. Curtis Monroe, who had a four-for-four game one week earlier against Jake, hit a chopper for an easy first out. *"Wil- lee! Wil- lee!"* Second baseman Terry Frazier, the batter who rarely whiffs, was blown away by the Ace of Diamonds on three pitches. *"Let's go Dees!"* Marcus Spencer, the would-be batting champ, swung and missed twice. The crowd thundered Willy's name. Paul signaled for a curveball. Willy delivered the ball overhand and Marcus connected with it over the center of
the plate. The ball bounced off the left field barrier and fell back onto the field for a home run. The booing showered Marvelous Marcus as he made his slow jaunt, circling the bases with the fingers of his batting glove waving "bye-bye" from his back pocket. Two strikes later, Rusty Buffington slapped the ball to Demmy, and the would-be gold glove shortstop failed to make the play. "That's Fortune's fifth error in three weeks since his perfect-fielding streak was stopped at fifty-five games," said Millennium Channel's Jeff McCarty. One run in the hole with an unearned runner on first, Willy locked her eyes onto those of Mercurio Mercado without

a hint of friendship or affection for her winter teammate from Venezuela. She fired three sliders and three fastballs inside at his belt, finally getting a called third strike. Willy kept her head down as she ran to the dugout while Merk stood yapping at the ump, Ken Crenshaw.

Paul expected Willy to be shaken, but, instead, she was stoic and anxious to get back on the field for the second inning. Andy clocked a three-base hit, aided by Monroe's pickup and throw on what should have been Merk's play in right center. Roy reached base on a walk and– with 75,000 voices clamoring to bring the runs home–Dino weakly flew to left, ending the threat. The Redbirds added a run in the second with another round-trip blast. This homer drew a hat-and-glove-throwing reaction from Our Lady of the Meadowlands and an inspirational wave of *"Wil- lee! Wil-lee! Let's go Dees!"* She set down the next three hitters in order. Keith doubled into the gap in left center field with one out in the home team's turn at bat, but the Diamonds failed to capitalize as Paul fanned and Willy was gunned down trying to bunt her way to first. The third began with Monroe whiffing, but Willy's mastery of Frazier ended when he beat out an infield hit and he effortlessly swiped second because she went through a full wind-up to deliver a strike to the plate. Spencer's mastery of Willy continued when he lined a single to drive in the run. The scoreboard read: STL 3 NYD 0. Willy kept her concentration intact, retiring Buffington and Mercado on a fly ball and grounder, respectively.

The Diamonds got back into the game in the bottom of the third. Cal ripped a single, stole second, moved to third on Demmy's ground ball, and touched home following Andy's hard-hit single. Willy worked methodically and put away the first two batters in the fourth before being tagged by St. Looie's third long-ball shot of the evening. Explicating her anger by shrieks of cussing as she repeatedly kicked the rubber, Paul and Rudy arrived together at the mound.

"Damn!" Paul cursed. "One day a pitcher gets away with half a dozen mistakes. She lets three go out over the plate and they take her long three times. It's screwed up!"

Rudy just listened calmly and said, "You settle down, Paul." Then he turned to Willy. "How do you feel, sweetie?"

She laughed, but angrily so. "I'm pissed, but I feel okay. I don't know what's wrong. How do I look?"

"You look real good," said Rudy. "Maybe nothin's wrong with you, but you gotta keep us in the game. This is the big time, honey."

Willy gritted her teeth, played footsie with a pile of loose red dirt, and lowered her eyes. "I'll keep us in the damned game."

Willy struck out the inning's last batter and blanked the Bye-Bye-Birdies through the next two frames, allowing only a pair of singles. The Diamonds wasted a bases-loaded situation with no outs in the fifth. Cal sparked the near-rally with a one-bagger and his second stolen base, but stood stranded at third as his mates choked. The bottom of the sixth got underway on Keith's base hit up the middle. Willy knelt on deck as Paul struck out for the third straight time. Had he reached base, she would have gone to bat to sacrifice. Instead, Tom called her, shook his head, and waved her back to the dugout. The crowd was on its feet, applauding her. Willy cocked her head and tipped her helmet with a slight trace of a smile as the fans–*her fans*–booed the name of her teammate, Darnell, announced as pinch-hitter. As always, Willy watched the rest of her ballgame from the bench. She sat with her head against the concrete back wall and legs straight out, staring in silence at the action in progress. Darnell flew out to center, momentarily raising the hopes of the crowd and dashing them asunder when the ball was caught, three steps shy of the outfield wall. Next to bat, Cal delivered his third hit, putting runners at the corners and bringing Fortune to the plate. On a one-oh pitch, the .333-hitting shortstop socked a base-clearing triple. With the score 4-3, Redbird skipper Casagrande sent for his set-up reliever, Claudio Cordero, to pitch. Andy clubbed a grounder to second base and came within a half-step of beating Tee's throw to first base for out number three. Tom gave Todd Strickland the nod to pitch for the Diamonds, and the first hitter he faced was Beaumont Teague, batting in the pitcher's place. The rookie was tagged by Beau for the first of three straight singles. Monroe and Frazier hit safely, making the score 5-3. Strick settled in to get the next three outs and to put away the Cards in order in the seventh. He, too, was lifted for a pinch-hitter, following base hits by Keith and Paul. Yet, again, the big inning never happened as the New Yorkers' bats struck three consecutive infield outs. Tim Langevin handcuffed St. Louis in the ninth, while their closer, Katsua Kitsuragawa, did the same to the D's; Kit-Kat nailed down a save by fanning Thor for the final out.

    Cam's voice radiated from the broadcast booth: "The losing pitcher, Willy Beal, turned in a gritty performance, but she was victimized by the long ball, three runs scored on homers, and anemic run production by the Diamonds, who left twelve runners on base. Once again, fans, the final score, St. Louis five, New York three...Willy Beal's record drops to one win and five losses, and the Diamonds fall into a tie with the Floridians for the top spot in the National East."

Paul came to Willy with kind words and a soft touch in the clubhouse. She munched a leafy celery stalk, talking with Andy and Joe, when the catcher began to massage her neck. "Why are you being so nice to me, partner?"

Paul, gently rubbing, said loudly enough for all to hear, "Us mighty sluggers of America's Home Team can't seem to get more than two or three runs when ya pitch. Ya deserve somethin' for your efforts." Then, he lowered his voice to jab at someone. "Hell, you've lost five and Jake's lost five. If ya lose an equal number of decisions, they should pay ya twenty-five million bucks, just like him! Right?"

Andy and Joe chuckled, but Willy didn't even smile, saying, "It's not Jake's fault we were beaten tonight. It's my own fault, nobody else's."

Shortly afterward in the wives' room, Willy grabbed Leota by the arm. Willy complained about Lorraine Cello, who had spoken to her in a friendly way last night, but put up a cold shoulder when she saw her tonight. "Well, what do you expect?" was Leota's surprising response.

"Excuse me?" uttered Willy in disbelief.

Leota looked at Willy, smiled, and held her around the waist. They were the only two souls in the wives' room when she said, "Everybody's heard about the long nights you and Paul spend together *working* on the road. Don't you think Lorrie's caught wind of it?"

Willy said, "Leota, no!" Her voice was frail, wounded. "I don't know how you can say that to me. How can you think that? I thought you knew me better than that."

"Don't you know how Paul looks at you, or the way he talks about you when you're not around? Gil's noticed, Zinger's noticed, Cal's noticed, and, of course, Tom's noticed...Don't think Lorraine would be the last to know if something was going on. The wife is the *first* to know."

Will spoke bitterly, "Nothing is going on, Leota!"

"Oh, honey, I believe you, but you can't be so naive about Paul. You're too vulnerable."

Willy took a seat, too angry to look Leota in the eye. "Paul's an old-fashioned mamma-mia's boy. Real men don't cheat on their wives."

"Oh, yes, they do," taunted Leota. "Maybe old-fashioned mamma-mia's boys don't *leave* their wives, if you get my drift." Leota's comment hit Willy like a fist in the gut. "It's not sexual betrayal that threatens most women as much as it's emotional betrayal." Leota paused to catch Willy's eye before saying, "I think you two have already done that to Lorraine."

There was a look of helplessness on Willy's face. She wanted to tell Leota that she couldn't stop thinking about Paul, although she knew he would never allow anything or anyone to come between him and his family, and her own feelings toward him were easier to control as long as she thought the infatuation was one-sided. Rather, she said, "Why can't people just let me be and leave my sexuality out of it?"

"Be real, honey!" Leota howled in her full-bodied voice. "Look at yourself, batting those long eyelashes and smiling that million-dollar smile. You're the chosen one, Willy, and you can't separate being a ballplayer from being a woman...a sexy, attractive woman! The sooner you realize that, the sooner you'll be able to deal with it."

There came jolting news of a different sort in the morning. Tony Ortega was arrested in Washington, DC with a suitcase full of cocaine, valued at millions on the streets. Willy listened to the newscaster: "Ortega pleaded innocent to all charges in U.S. District Court. In addition to narcotics charges, Ortega was also cited for carrying an unregistered firearm...There are unconfirmed reports of a sting operation carried out by the DEA and the FBI. A spokesperson for the DEA has denied knowledge of any plan to ensnare Ortega, who was traded to the Washington ball team just two weeks ago. Ortega is under suspension by the league president, Sherman Long, pending the outcome of criminal proceedings and an independent investigation by the Commissioner of Big League Baseball, Inc."

"He's out on bail on the criminal charges, but Mr. Commissioner suspended him indefinitely," said Cal.

"Is that fair?" asked Demmy. "He could sit out two years waiting to go to trial."

"Why is your heart bleeding for him, Demmy?" decried Willy. "How can you defend a ballplayer who tried to deal coke? What kind of a role model is that?"

"It's not that simple, Willy," Cal pointed out. "The players' union has to support him..He still has rights."

Benny joined the debate. "Ortega's no golden boy. He grew up hard and poor. The big money doesn't always mean the good life."

"They say he ran up some big debts," said Roy. "Some business deals went sour."

"We can't just condemn him," said Andy. "We don't know the whole story. We don't know what happened or why he did it."

Cal nodded his head slowly, listening seriously. "I think he's gonna be a fall guy ... again!" the second baseman declared.

Willy furrowed her brow. "How do you mean?"

"He's being set up to be punished for bad image as much as the crime," he replied. "The thing is, his punishment by baseball could be longer than his prison term."

The clubhouse gossip shop speculated that Charley Novak and his team's front office knew Ortega was headed for "deep shit," as Paul would say, reportedly having been interviewed by FBI and DEA agents regarding Tony's activities. On the record, Novak said he was saddened by his former first baseman's misfortune. Privately, however, Charley wiped his brow and said, "Phew! We unloaded him just in time, didn't we?" From the perspective of the pennant race, Memo Alvarez and Bobby Ray Webster were alive and playing well, while the youngster Pinto slumped and Tony Ortega cooled his heels under suspension and possibly on his way to a jail cell. As Brad Lucas wrote: "San Francisco would seem to have gotten the better of the trade with the Wash-Nats, to say the least."

Despite Manhattan's logical gridwork pattern of numbered streets from east to west and avenues running north to south, the City of Greater New York was not one of civilization's better planned ideas. Moving up and down the grid and diagonally on Broadway, Willy made six separate appearances in the morning and afternoon before racing over to Jersey for a ballgame at eight o'clock. She showed up half an hour late, after being stalled in traffic. The game was already in the third inning and she expected to be slapped on the wrist.

"That's a $500 fine," said Tom. Willy apologized, but he didn't let the matter drop. "We can't function like this, Willy. I think there's too much going on with you off the field. Your head's not in the game."

"I'm not even supposed to pitch tonight, Tom!"

"Look at you! You've lost weight..."

Where is this coming from? Willy wondered. "That's got nothing to do with my pitching." She was down to about 135 pounds, but she was trying to counterbalance irregular exercise by eating less. The hubbub and hoopla had indeed wrecked her regimen.

"See to it that this never happens again," he said and turned his back to her.

Willy was shaken by the incident, but waited until after the game to ask Paul, "What's going on around here? He was too upset...too cold...just for being late to the ballpark one time."

"Willy, let me tell ya somethin'." Paul cuffed his hands on each of her shoulders and stared intently into her eyes. "Ya got maybe five or six real friends on this team. Count 'em ... me, Zinger, Cal, Gil, and Sandy Lee, and one coach ... Rudy loves ya like you're his daughter ... and that's the long list, not the short list."

"Didn't you forget to mention the owner?" she quipped.

"Remember who your friends are." He warned her, "Who ya can trust and who ya can't!"

"I think I already know that," she said, smiling, as she hooked onto his arm.

"Remember it, babe."

Meanwhile, at his office in the bowels of the stadium, Fabian said to his GM, "I think Willy is starting to believe all the Willy B. Superstar hype. America's sweetheart thinks she can write her own ticket...You know, that cretin agent of hers isn't even registered with the Commissioner's office...Harvey, I own a stable of thoroughbred racehorses. I've ridden horses myself since I was eight years old. I learned that even prize-winning horses need to feel the whip from time to time, to let them know who's riding whom. I think it's time to corral our beautiful filly." Harvey Wanamaker responded with a grunt. Unlike the big boss man, Harvey never rode a horse and couldn't remember having been eight. "Harvey," Fabian continued, "everyone...the fans, the media, every other team in the bigs...is waiting for the New York Diamonds to hit full stride and bury the rest of the league. But we aren't quite there yet. What my Meadowlands Million Dollar Babies need is a kick in the pants. A little shock therapy!"

Harvey lifted his pencil in the air like a baton to ask, "Do we flip a coin, Mr. Fabian?

CHAPTER 12

The Diamonds clung to first place by winning two of the four games with St. Louis over the Fourth of July weekend. Willy looked forward to the second half of the season. During July she would play in Wrigley Field and she anticipated the prospect with a nearly spiritual reverie. She was to pitch for the New York Diamonds on the same mound where Rube Henry had pitched against the Chicago Gummy Bears over fifty years ago.

Willy's problems with her agent worsened with the morning's mail. She had owned her townhouse for only five weeks, but was already in arrears for two mortgage payments, the car lease payment was overdue, her credit cards were charged to the limit, and her account at the bank was overdrawn. The diet cola and sneaker ads ran, but no money for them was in her hands. She was also holding two other letters to wave in Artie's face at their regular weekly sit-down: an unpaid bill from a freight company and an eviction notice from her long-vacated condo in Alexandria. Artie had arranged to move her belongings to New Jersey, but neither paid the bill nor cancelled her lease. When he failed to show up by noontime, Willy called his office in Long Island City.

"We're sorry. The number you have reached is not in service. If you need assistance..." came the word from Horizon long distance. *First, he screws up my personal service contract, then he screws up my new contract with the D's, and now he screws me!* Willy dialed up Ridzik's home phone and sang, "There ain't nobody home and you just reached a machine...*bop-bah...*" to the tune of Glenn Miller's "In the Mood" until the tone sounded, punctuating between greeting and message. "Hello, Uncle Artie, it's Willy...You know, the cash cow you've been milking?...I'll be brief. You're fired!"

A fleeting chimera of a feeling took hold of Willy. Her dream-come-true reality was unraveling. Then she took a deep breath, turned on some acoustic jazz, and cleared her head by thinking about baseball. Her life on the field was less than ideal as well. She had pitched well enough to be 5-1, but her won-lost record was 1-5. Vallery had been unhappy with her since the stinkeroo against Cincy, Fabian was mad at her, and the wags were beginning to gnaw.

"Eat something," said Zinger, when he met Willy before the game. "You'll feel better." She reached for a carrot stick, knowing that whipping the boys visiting from Chitown on Tuesday night would turn things around in a hurry. Willy checked in at the stadium by quarter to seven, more than an hour early for Monday evening's game. Halfway through putting on her uniform, Tom Vallery called Willy into his office. He walked through the doorway with his hands in his pants pockets, jingling loose change and keys, a nervous habit she had noticed before. Willy buttoned her Diamonds' jersey and followed him inside.

"The situation's deteriorated," began Tom. "You're running on empty. Thursday night, your offspeed fastball topped out at eighty-four miles an hour. To be effective, a change-of-pace needs a wide differential, but you never used your two-seamer to hit the high eighties or low nineties."

"What are you talking about, Tom?" she asked, hearing her own voice wavering. "That totally contradicts what you told me last week about not needing to throw the heater."

"Look, your concentration is shot to hell," he said, raising his voice and eyeing her directly for the first time. "There's a lot of resentment about all the attention you've been getting. You've antagonized people with your showboating. You've alienated some of your teammates with your attitude. Some of the guys just don't like you anymore..."

Willy tried to remember the last time she talked and laughed with one or another teammate besides Paul, Cal, Demmy, and the pitchers. A few guys had always been distant and nobody got along well with Jake, but she was friendly, maybe not intimate, with the entire roster. Something wasn't ringing true in Tom's words.

"It's gotten to the point where it's going to affect the team's play. You're one and five and the team's two and six in games you've started. If we were in a rebuilding mode, I could let
you lose ten, fifteen, or twenty games and chalk it up to experience. We're out to win it all," Tom droned on, "and I can't put you above the team."

Willy wanted to speak, but she was gagged with anger. She told herself to remain calm and hear Tom out before he said, "We're shipping you down to Triple-A, Willy."

The room took on a surreal atmosphere. Willy felt as if she had lifted out of her body and was watching the scene from afar. *Is Vallery talking to me or someone else?* Her pulse throbbed in her throat and her chest felt hollow and swollen. By holding her breathing in check to stay calm, she was becoming short of oxygen, making her light-headed.

"Why're you doing this to me, Tom?"

"Willy, it's not personal," he said gently. "Sandy Lee's healthy again and I've got to see if Phillips and Zanetsky can cut it in the starting rotation."

"I have the second-best earned run average on the staff. I didn't have but one bad game. I know I'm one and five, but I gave you all quality starts, Tom!"

"Willy, I understand that. Believe me, I know you can pitch," he said with a forced laugh. "I think it's been too much, too soon for you. All the outside distractions..." Tom was interrupted by a knock on his door. He swore under his breath and yelled, "What is it?" Instead of answering, Harvey Wanamaker opened the door and took a seat in the room. The GM said nothing. "I think you've got to get out of the limelight and be able to pitch your way back into top form. You can do that at Jacksonville. We should've sent you to Triple-A in the first place. It was too fast, but we didn't expect you to lose five out of six."

"Take me out of the starting rotation. I'll pitch in relief. I don't wanna be a star. I just wanna play." She bit her tongue as she realized she was pleading. "Paul says I pitched six great games and two mediocre ones," she said.

"Paul's not objective when it comes to you, Willy," Tom quickly countered.

"Give me one more shot. Let me take my next start."

"I can't send you out to pitch tomorrow night knowing it's a test, that if we get beaten, you'll be shipped out. You can't get back on track by sitting out in the bullpen and pitching an inning or two once a week. If Phillips or Zanetsky don't get the job done, you could be back here in a couple of weeks. Maybe we'll recall you in September or bring you back up next season."

"Besides," added Harvey, "Jacksonville is close to home for you, isn't it?"

Willy turned her eyes to the Diamonds' GM and hissed, "You didn't really just say that, did you?"

"Don't worry," croaked Harvey. "I'm sure Willy B. Superstar's adoring public will find you on the minor league circuit, but, for now, Mr. Fabian's affirmative action project is over." "You condescending son of a bitch!" Willy snapped.

Harvey widened his eyes and lurched in his chair. Tom winced and gave Willy a sad look, saying, "I'm sorry, Willy, but you're going to Triple-A."

I feel dizzy. If I stand up, I'll pass out. If I open my mouth to speak, I'll cry. It's like I'm in a zone without a focal point to get my concentration under control. I think I'm gonna throw up!

"Trying to renegotiate your contract didn't help any," said Harvey.

Ring went a bell in Willy's head. She said in a suppressed voice, delivering the words slowly, "Why in the world am I talking to the two of you about this?" To Tom's surprise, she shouted, "Where's Fabian?"

Tom's cool demeanor turned from ice to stone. "Whose idea do you think this is, Willy?"

She jumped to her feet, startling both men, and screamed, "Then I want him to tell me to my face!"

As Willy charged from Tom's office, Harvey looked at the Diamonds' manager and said caustically, "You insisted on being the one to tell her. You said I don't have the people skills. Nice going, Tom!"

Willy ran from the locker room to the dugout, jostling two teammates on her way out to the field, where she would hail Fabian in his luxury sky box. Harvey ran behind her, calling, "Somebody stop her!" The Diamonds and Cubbies were on the field to take batting practice, throw a few pitches, loosen up, and shoot the bull. The usual coterie of wags mingled, scribbled, and took pictures as several thousand fans had already entered the park. Willy's hysteria carried onto the field. One by one, action and conversation abated and heads turned toward the noisy commotion.

"What in God's name is going on?" Cal Bonham asked Demeter Fortune.

Rudy Judd spoke to Steve Filsinger, who howled, "You gotta be friggin' kiddin' me!"

"Willy?" rasped Gil Douglas as he took off his fielder's mitt, slammed it to the ground, and stepped in the direction of the dugout.

Harvey caught up to Willy at the dugout steps and told her, "You're not even supposed to be in uniform."

"Aah!" she shrieked, leaping from the top step and heading straight for the water cooler. She clamped her forearms around the ten-gallon plastic bottle, hoisted it from its stand, and heaved it at the GM. It hit the ground, bottom side up, spinning and spraying water in every
direction. Harvey reached for her shirt sleeve and felt the sting of Willy's fist against the side of his face without ever seeing it coming. He yelled, "Grab her!" as she fled back to the locker room. Dozens of players, coaches, wags, and team staff personnel followed in a wild chase. A chair flew as two players reached for Willy. Two more

mates were hit with a knee in the groin and a jabbing elbow in the chest.

"I didn't think she was so strong," Joe Manlius stuttered nervously.

"Is that all you can think of to say?" Benny Marquez asked him with disgust.

"Fabian's not even in town," Keith Whalen grumbled.

Chaos reigned for several minutes as Willy rampaged in the locker room. Tom expelled everyone but Diamonds, and Andy and Joe enforced his order. Half a dozen players grappled with Willy, trying to restrain her. "Maybe we better call security," said Harvey, who was standing next to Roy Burton.

"Why dontcha just let us handle it?" said Roy. "It's a family matter. The *players'* family!"

Harvey hesitated, saying, "I don't know if that's such a good idea. She's out of control."

Then, Leroi Burton, one of the best conditioned athletes in all of pro sports wrenched the arm of the man who co-signed his multimillion dollar contract and bellowed, "Which means, get your sorry ass outta here! Now!"

Willy squealed and kicked, all the while calling and cursing Sebastian Fabian's name, as two mates cornered her against a wall. "Leave her alone! Don't hurt her!" The sound of Gil
Douglas's voice rolled through the room like a clap of thunder. No one could recall Big Gil shouting with such menace, except on the playing field. The locker room was starkly quiet as he walked toward Willy. She looked up to see his face and she found herself sandwiched between Zinger and Cal. She clutched at the front of

Cal's shirt, patted Zinger's cheek, and let out a terrible moan as she buried her face against his chest to sob.

A moment later, Willy sat on a stool in her locker cubicle with her knees tucked under her chin. "I don't wanna talk!" was all she said.

"I have to get her out of here," Zinger told Cal and Gil. "It's gonna cost me at least a thousand dollar fine, but I'll run her over to my place. Michelle's home."

Gil said gently, "I'll see if I can get Leota to go to your house to stay with her."

Zinger smiled and said, "Thanks, big guy. I'd kiss you, but you're too tall."

"I never heard language like that out of a woman's mouth," ventured Thor Andreason.

"Hey, I thought I was back home in my ex-wife's kitchen, duckin' the flyin' glass, man," joked Larry Brooks.

"Maybe she was getting it on with Fabian all along and he dumped her," crowed Bruce Jacobson, whose statement was greeted by stony silence.

"You're an asshole, Jake," said Demeter Fortune and he exited the locker room.

"I'd like to be around to hear what comes out of his mouth when they give him the shaft," said Andy Gilbert.

"Cal, somebody better head off Cello when he gets here. It could be even worse."

"Yeah, Zinger, I'll take care of it." Then Cal giggled, "Unless that hot Italian temper is already up to boiling."

"I'll be back by the second inning," said Zinger, taking his windbreaker from a hook and fishing through the pockets for his car keys.

"Move it, man," laughed Tim Langevin. "Tom'll need you in relief by the third the way Jake's been pitching lately!"

Willy slept or meditated while riding in the front seat of Zinger's car. He couldn't tell which it was. The only words she spoke were, "They can't make me take my uniform off." When they arrived in New Rochelle, there was no need to fill in the details for Michelle. The incident had already been broadcast on the news and a covert video was up on the internet. She turned down the bed in Stephanie's room. Willy went under the covers without a word, still wearing her blue, gold, and pinstriped uniform. As Willy wrapped herself in darkness, the Diamonds beat Chicago, 10-6, Tim and Larry bailing out their team after a dismal performance by the flamethrower, Jacobson. The game ended shortly before midnight and Zinger was back home an hour later.

"You may have noticed that the game got underway half an hour late," he told Michelle at the door.

"Oh, no, Steve," she groaned, reading more than his words from Zinger's drawn face. "What else happened?"

"Paul got to the stadium about five minutes before eight," replied Zinger. "He'd heard about Willy on the radio, on his way back from a sausage and peppers cookout with the Sons of Sicily in Hoboken. He lost it! He came in and went freakin' ballistic, kicking the clubhouse door open, hollering, 'Vallery, you back-stabbin' bastard, where are you?' We thought he was going to kill him."

"Poor Tom," said Michelle, quickly adding, "Poor Paul!"

"It took Roy, Gil, Larry, Joe, and Andy... the strongest freakin' guys on the team, to pull him off of Tom. Old Rudy got punched in the face."

"Of all people," said Michelle. "The gentlest man!"

"Paul said, 'Why'd you let Fabian screw Willy like this? You're the biggest ass-kisser of all!' Stuff like that."

"Paul talking to Tom that way?" exclaimed Michelle. "He idolizes Tom."

"Go figure!" shrugged Zinger. "Some wild love-hate emotions cut loose tonight. Paul was hollering about loyalty and trust and honor...This is a game. It's supposed to be fun."

At breakfast the next morning, Zinger and Michelle watched the incident replayed for the hundredth time on the news. Their kids were off to a day of summer camp and their house guest hadn't stirred.

"It's not only that they're sending her down," he told her. "Fabian is suing her over the diet cola commercial for a million bucks, which she doesn't have because of that idiot agent of hers."

"She's devastated, Steve," Michelle said solemnly, lighting his cigarette, then hers.

"Fabian acts like Willy's his creation," he said, drawing in a lungful of smoke.

"Believe me, Steve, that girl created herself."

"Yeah, she sure did," chuckled Zinger, blowing out the smoke. "That's what got him so pissed. She did her own thing, he tried to rope her in, and she balked."

"How can an owner just get rid of a player for spite?" she asked, getting only a shrug in response from her husband.

"Maybe he didn't expect her to react the way she did," he said. "Harvey seemed to think she'd be a good girl and go to Jacksonville. It backfired."

"She's completely crushed. It's like they've torn her heart out."

Zinger meekly asked, "Can you kind of... you know... do whatever it is you women do for each other at times like this.

"Don't worry, hon," she told him. "I'll take care of her."

At the westernmost tip of the Empire State, Charlene Jones watched the same scene, same time, same station. "How can they buy and sell players like cattle or slaves in this day and age?"

"That's the old ballgame, Char." Peter slumped in his chair, viewing the scene. His reaction and mood were subdued and morbid.

"Nice freaking people in your chosen line of work, Peter!" Char's hubby made no response. When the dubbed-over commentator's voice described Willy's "shocking and violent display of anger," Char snickered. "Screw you, Miss Prissy! Poor Willy!"

The next day, rumors bubbled up online and bled across the sports pages of newspapers, hence transcribed and broadcast on radio and television newscasts, about Willy's "obvious" psychological problems and "possible" use of performance-enhancing drugs, including anabolic steroids and blood-doping agents. Talk radio shock jocks screamed, "Hello, this is what 'roid rage looks like, people!" The fires were fanned further when the owner of the New York Diamonds was reached for comment while vacationing in Nova Scotia. Sebastian Fabian mentioned Willy's "unacceptable behavior" and suggested that she was "emotionally unstable." At a ten a.m. press conference, Harvey Wanamaker announced that Willy Beal was suspended indefinitely, pending psychological screening, drug testing, and agreeing to report to the farm team in Jacksonville. The innuendos about drugs initially drew derisive laughter and jeers from the assembled wags, but Harvey intoned that the matter was under investigation by the Commissioner's office.

When Zinger returned from picking up the kids at camp that afternoon, he asked his wife, "Is she still asleep?"

"Um-hmm," hummed Michelle. "I looked in on her earlier and brought her some tea. I don't think she really got much rest during the night. Let's just leave her alone."

"Willy asleep at three in the afternoon!" Zinger was aghast.

"Well," Michelle said seriously, "when she does get up, we should keep her away from the TV and the papers. Look at this!" She shoved the *Daily Mail* under his nose.

"Oh, shit!" he cursed, reading the litany of unconfirmed rumors, identified as such, but dutifully reported. "Where do they get all this crap? Steroids! Blood doping! What the hell is that anyway?"

"The blogs and other stuff on the net is even worse. There's a porno video on Me Tube with a look-alike model supposed to be Willy. And they're even talking about rumors she's been injecting estrogen or testosterone, Steve."

Zinger huffed, "The lotus blossom with the killer slider isn't the woman she appears to be. What freakin' assholes!"

Paul stopped by Zinger's house early in the afternoon. Willy, still hibernating in bed, sat up when Michelle announced Paul's presence. Michelle practically pushed her way back into the room to bar Paul from swinging the door closed. "Do you mind, Michelle?" he asked with annoyance.

Willy told Michelle, "It's okay," and she stepped away. "Hi, partner!" Willy croaked, as Paul came to sit on the edge of the bed. Then she fell into his arms and cried.

After a moment, he whispered, "I always told ya to tone it down. Ya get too excited, like Shanks used to say. See what we mean?"

She laughed, wiping the tears from her cheeks. "I heard you got pretty crazy yourself, Paul. You went after Tom. Why?"

"Fabian's a maniac, Harvey's a useless old windbreaker, and Tom is the only *human being* who could've stopped them from sandbaggin' ya...All he had to do was say no, but he didn't have the balls to do it."

"You threatened to quit the team, didn't you?"

Paul chuckled, "That was after we had the fight, after the game. It was a ploy. I offered to fall on my sword. I thought it would help."

Paul's histrionics occurred behind closed doors, away from the media, but playing the game as if nothing had happened was out of the question. Paul sat it out and Pigpen went behind the plate. When Jake read Pantagones on the lineup card and saw the chunky rookie donning the catching equipment, the southpaw pointed his finger at Rudy Judd and shouted, "That airhead is not callin' my game. I'm lookin' into the dugout for you to call every goddamn pitch. You hear me, Rudy?"

"It's not Tom's fault," Willy said to Paul. "It's Fabian's doing."

"It all started because Tom had this idea that ya needed some re-education in the minors. When Tom suggested it to Fabian two or three weeks ago, he laughed him off. This time, it was Fabian's move. Tom expected ya to be back in September, or sooner, if the pennant race stays tight. Your talent isn't the question, babe."

In fact, Tom concluded that Willy B. Superstar was being distracted by the "bright lights, big city," and thought that a stint in Jacksonville would straighten her out.

"You lashed out at Tom, just like I did," Willy told Paul. "Did you say you're sorry to him?"

"Yeah," he grunted, "but I might be catchin' in Buffalo or somewheres next year."

"I have friends in Buffalo," Willy said whimsically. She and Paul were unconscious of their posture astride the rumpled bedding. Their knees touched, their hands held, their fingers locked, and their eyes homed in on each other's. The dialogue was one of friends and teammates, whereas their body language bespoke something other.

After Paul left, Zinger moved toward the room in which Willy continued to hide. "Steve, go take care of your other kids. I can hear them downstairs, tearing apart the house," Michelle said.

"What do you mean?"

Michelle laughed. "It doesn't matter whether or not you know what I mean. Willy does. That's why she's here." Zinger approached his wife and she hugged him. "You think of Willy as your teammate, playmate, best girl buddy, but you're filling a void for her...You think you're her teddy bear, but she thinks you're her pappa bear."

"Why me?"

"It's in your nature," Michelle said and kissed him. "It's who you are. Now, go be a pappa bear."

"I guess Stephanie wants her room back, huh?" Willy said to Michelle.

"No way!" she said, waving her hand. "Everybody in the world is looking for you, and you're hiding in *her room*. Can you imagine what a thrill that is for her?" Michelle sat next to Willy, who had changed into a pair of Zinger's pajamas.

"Sorry," Willy grinned sheepishly. "The nightgown you let me have just wasn't about to fit."

Michelle smiled and said, "Cal called late last night to see how you were. So did Rudy and Thelma Judd, and Roy, and Keith..."

"Roy and Keith?" Willy marveled.

"They're not two of the warmest men I've ever met, but you never can tell about people. They're *mensches*, real human beings." Michelle handed Willy a slip of paper. "Peter and
Charlene Jones left a message and their number in Buffalo."

"Peter called?" Willy asked.

"Actually, it was Charlene. She called Leota and Gil first and they thought it was all right to tell her where you were. Charlene was pretty upset. She said if there's anything you need, she and Peter will be there for you."

Willy crumpled the note, but kept it clutched tightly in her hands. "People care about you, Willy."

"I know," she whispered.

Michelle placed her hand on Willy's face as a tear fell from the corner of her eye. "We're worried about you," Michelle said.

Willy sighed loudly. "I know you're trying to help, but I'm not ready to deal with any of this just yet."

Michelle wrapped her arms around Willy and kissed her, as naturally as kissing Stephanie or Mikey. "Rest, dear. Call if you need me. There's plenty of food in the fridge if you get hungry." Willy nodded, smiled, and slid down under the covers.

Gil Douglas and Roy Burton sat together on the phony grass at the stadium a few minutes before Wednesday night's game. "They just don't understand why Willy did what she did," said Big Gil.

"Of course not," scoffed Roy. "I'm not sure I do, either."

"She was hurt and confused, and took it out on everybody."

"Gil, that's not how to act," said Roy.

"Leroi, we've been in the bigs for five or six years. She's been up here for eight weeks! You know what I'm talking about. She's probably been half scared all this time."

"Not on the mound, though," Roy remarked.

"No, not hardly," nodded Gil, "but all the other stuff! She was the bright child, the golden girl, the chosen one, smiling and play-acting for the cameras. Now, it looks to her like they want to take it all away from her and she doesn't know why. She snaps and the front office, the fans, and the wags turn on her."

"The wags, man!" Roy chuckled softly. "You know how they can be."

"It's still a hard row to hoe, Leroi," Gil told him. "Andy and the Reb are blue-collar, work-ethic guys, but we're *naturals*. Jake and Demmy are arrogant and intense, but we're moody, surly, and..."

"Bad attitude and poison in the clubhouse," Roy pronounced sarcastically.

"You know what they be sayin' about Willy, now?" Gil said with a sniff of bitterness, "You can take the girl out of the ghetto, but you can't take the ghetto out of the girl."

Sandy Lee Danielson was standing over Gil and Roy. "Is this a restricted conversation or can a big ol' redneck like me join in?"

"Cool! Set that cracker red-ass of yours down right here," said Gil, who, since Sandy Lee's injuries flared up, was finally being recognized as the team's best pitcher.

"I just feel so bad about Willy, ya know?" said Sandy Lee. "It ain't right... and there ain't nothin' we can do about it."

"That's right, Reb," said Gil. "Nothing!"

"We're all no different from her," added Roy. "We're only as good as last season's numbers."

Sandy Lee returned to the clubhouse, paid a visit to Shelly Kravitz, and took the field wearing Willy Beal's number 28 on his back, whitewashing the Windy Citians on five hits, as the D's won their fifth straight, 2-0.

Snuggled in bed together, Michelle told Zinger, "Some boy at day camp made a crack about Willy being on drugs, and Stephanie called him a liar and beat the crap out of him. A twelve-year-old boy, Steve!"

"Oh, yeah? No kidding?" he laughed, uprighted himself, then assumed a more parental tone. "I'll speak to her in the morning, hon."

As Zinger resumed laughing, Michelle said seriously, "Willy's waiting for you to say something, Steve." She sat up to explain, "Paul's going to baby her, just like he babies Lorraine. I'll fluff her pillow and treat her like a sick child. Leota or Sam Khoury might try to badger her back on her feet, but she'll just resist them. You're the only person who can get her out of that bedroom."

Zinger rapped gently on the door and awaited Willy's beckoning. He walked toward the bed, where she had been hunkered down, under the covers, despite the mid-summer weather, concealed except for her hair, forehead, and not-so-bright-as-usual eyes. She popped out, swaddled in a terrycloth robe and his own pajamas, and sat in the lotus. "What's up, Zinger?"

"Sweetheart," he said softly and warmly before shouting: "This crap's got to stop!"

"Are you guys throwing me out of your house?" Her face withered to worrisome.

"No," said Zinger, with an unvoiced "but" implied. "We love you. We love that you feel safe with us." He sighed heavily, "Willy, what would your grandfather, Rube, say to you right now?"

"Get yourself out of the bed, li'l gal, and go whip their asses!...I really have been trying to figure out what to do," Willy said.

"Oh, yeah?" teased Zinger. "All I've seen you do is sneak around like a mouse after we're in bed, so you can go pee and steal food from the fridge."

"Shush!" she said, holding onto his hand. Zinger smiled, not so much at their joining of hands as seeing the life renewed in her eyes. "I'll call Sam Khoury. She'll help me, even if it's just to get the inside story."

"Paul and me have been stonewalling her and the other wags about your whereabouts."

"Zinger?" she said, reaching her arms around his neck and laying her head on his shoulder. "I love you guys, too. I don't know what I would've done without you and Michelle."

Willy and Zinger shared a warm and tightly held embrace. He was impervious to the well muscled, healthy, mature, and thoroughly desirable woman's body that clung to him, exactly as he had felt over the past eight weeks, dressing and undressing next to her in the locker room in chaste intimacy, no different from that which he enjoyed with his young daughter.

Over the phone the next morning, Sam Khoury said, "The best approach to public image damage control is to go public. Call a press conference. It works for people who are guilty as sin. So, why not for somebody who's innocent?"

"I wanna get the results of a voluntary drug test done first. I called Mama and she said a lab could get the results in three hours if they wanted to..."

"Great! I'll help you arrange to get Doctor Greek Name to report that you're drug-free before you even go into your news conference."

"Do you think I can trust Kyrokydes?"

"He can't falsify the results. Besides, why would he?"

"I don't know where these stories are coming from. I can't trust anybody, can I?"

"It's like the vultures are circling your carcass. They want to pick at your bones."

"I'm not dead yet, Sam."

Willy called Cal, who visited her at Zinger and Michelle's within the hour along with Keith, the D's representative in the players' union.

"Can't I appeal the suspension?" she asked Keith.

"Yes," the player rep replied, "but don't expect to win your appeal. The team can do whatever it wants with you. They can demote you and keep you in the minors for three years, and then you'll only become eligible to be drafted by another team if the D's don't promote you to the forty-player roster at the end of the season. You need at least two full years in the majors to qualify for salary arbitration and five years to become a free-agent, unless the D's release you, which they won't do. You can ask to be traded, but it's the same thing. They can say no."

"What can I do?" she asked them.

Cal quipped, "Play ball, young woman. Play ball."

"I won't go back to the minors, Cal." After saying that, she pulled her knees up and wrapped her arms around them, softly repeating, "I won't."

"You're not the first player that's gone through this, you know," Cal said somewhat sharply. "Hey, Big Gil went back to Triple-A three times before he stuck with the D's. I got sent back to the minors my second year. I'll tell you something, Willy. Most guys are mad about the way they did it, but nobody's saying they didn't have the right to do it."

Keith interrupted, "That's really not the issue anymore, is it, Cal?"

The second baseman shook his head and looked at the rookie pitcher, a dearly beloved friend. He said, "Willy, your actions blew this all out of proportion. You stole the show, just like you always do, but this time you took the heat off the owner, the GM, and the manager and put it on yourself."

"Am I the only player who ever busted up the locker room?" she said, half-kiddingly.

"The first woman ever!" Keith pointed out, lightheartedly.

Willy's next phone call was to the Commissioner's office. Although Hamilton Fisher was "tied up in a meeting," his staff was unexpectedly cooperative. Her request was granted for a complete battery of tests and public disclosure of the results the same day. Shortly, there came a statement on the noontime news from Sherman Long, the league president, saying "Willy Beal's suspension by the New York Diamonds is strictly a disciplinary action on the part of the team, related to her refusal to report to the club's Triple-A minor league affiliate. She is neither suspended from the league, nor is she being investigated by this office for drug use, as recent reports have inaccurately alleged."

Willy's final phone call of the day was to Kristin Tracy in the front office. "I'm going to demand to be traded, Kristin."

"We won't do it, Willy. Listen, we routinely ask waivers on players to test their trade value. Just last week, we put your name out on the wire and twenty-four teams were interested. Of course, we revoked the waivers right away. We do it with everybody. Today, no team will touch you, either because of the incident or since they think they can get you cheaper if we're trying to unload you."

"Release me, then," Willy told her.

"Forget it! Mr. Fabian will never allow that."

"He doesn't want me anymore, but he won't let me go. Is that it?"

"Willy," the team vice-president said. "I have no control over the man, but I do know that sending you to Jacksonville was not supposed to be a permanent move, but...you burned your bridges, so to speak."

"Blew them to hell is more like it," Willy joked darkly.

"You'll be back, Willy. No one doubts that," said Kristin, "but not in a Diamonds' uniform, at least not this year."

CHAPTER 13

The charade of drug testing played out on Thursday. Willy arranged to take her blood and urine tests at the stadium. The Diamonds were traveling the road and so only a skeleton crew was on hand. She hid herself away until mid afternoon, when the results were available, to hold a press conference. Dr. Theo Kyrokydes, the medical professional charged with carrying out the examinations, dispersed the cloud unfairly cast over Willy. The clinical report on her urinalysis and blood work came out immaculate. A spokesperson for the Commish immediately announced that BLB, Inc. had no further interest in the matter.

Meanwhile, Sebastian Fabian enjoyed the hospitality of the good neighbors to the north and was "unavailable for comment." Harvey Wanamaker told the press that phone calls were running two-to-one in favor of the team's decision to demote Willy. When Dave Warren told
Harvey that a USTV survey showed public opinion to be five-to-one in support of Willy, the Diamonds' GM growled, "We don't take a poll on who's in and who's out."

When Sam Khoury announced that Willy would take the reporters' questions in the clubhouse rather than the press room, Warren whispered to Cathy, his producer, "Khoury must be Willy's media shield." Willy wore her blue sweatsuit, sneakers, and her hair pinned up under her D's cap as she sat on a stool, surrounded by wags. Her mood was decidedly low-key.

"First, I want to apologize to my manager, Tom Vallery. I disrespected him and that was wrong of me. But, more important to me, I want to apologize to my fans, especially the kids out there. I lost my temper and I behaved very badly and I embarrassed myself." Her face seemed oddly placid as she methodically folded her hands in her lap, awaiting the next wag's query.

"Will you report to Jacksonville as ordered?" asked Dale Goodwyn of the *Daily Mail*.

"I don't know. Not yet, anyway!" she said, adding, "I've asked the Diamonds to trade me or release me. If they don't want me anymore, maybe some other team does."

"Did you have any hint that this might be coming?" came the follow-up.

"No, did any of you guys?"

"You seem to be implying that the move is spiteful," began Brad Lucas of the *Journal*. "Are you pointing a finger at Vallery, the general manager, or the owner?"

"You know who runs the team," she answered.

Another baseball pundit probed: "What about Laddy Zanetsky, the pitcher called up to replace you?"

"It's not Laddy's fault. He deserves his shot. You can't get me to say anything bad about him or any of my teammates," Willy chided.

"What about the GM, Harvey Wanamaker?" a tabloid scribbler shouted.

"This is where I say I have no comment." Then, a subdued Willy flashed a go-to-hell smile in case Harvey was watching.

Willy B. Superstar, the Ace of Diamonds, was all hyperbole, media blitz, and Broadway glitz. Everyone was caught up in it, including the manufacturer, Sebastian Fabian, and the product, Willy Beal. For Willy, Andy Warhol's fifteen minutes of fame lasted eight weeks. In the *Daily Mail*, Goodwyn wrote, "In spite of her talent, athleticism, energy, and fierce competitiveness, the expectation created for Willy Beal exceeded what would have been reasonable for any rookie, much less one with only sixteen games of professional experience. She was thrown into the fray, in the heat of battle, smack dab in the middle of a pennant race. How bad is a record of 1-5? Would a record of 5-5 be a good one for Willy, but a bad one for Jake? The stats and performance mean nothing without reference to the expectation behind them. You cannot boo a player who is expected to strike out for striking out. You cannot boo a team that is expected to lose for losing. Expectations are everything!"

Lucas's column in the *New York Journal* read: "All of us–the team, the owner, the media, and the fans–put Willy Beal on center stage. Is it any wonder she rebelled when we tried to kick her off? How can she be the most gifted natural talent in a generation one day and not good enough the next? Willy is acting as if the rules do not apply to her, that she is not just another ballplayer. The truth of the matter is that is exactly what we have been telling her all along. Overnight, Willy went from being the Madonna of the Meadowlands to the Brat from the Swamplands. This is the last piece I will write about Willy Beal until she is wearing a big league uniform again."

What Willy never knew was that a confidential letter of complaint was prepared for Sebastian Fabian, protesting the way in which Harvey Wanamaker mishandled the situation. The GM wasn't fired and he didn't resign, but day-to-day operations were taken over jointly by assistant general manager Alan Blaylock and Kristin Tracy. Harvey was given the honorific title of president of baseball operations and became something of a ghost to the team as well as the public. He snapped his fingers. "I'm out of the loop. I'm nobody."

Kristin replied, "Just like Willy!" A further irony not lost on Ms. Tracy was that Alan, not she, was the given the title of "acting GM" because of his genitalia.

Strangely, the departure of Willy solidified the Diamonds as a team. Relations between Bruce Jacobson and the rest of the D's were never cordial–mutually restrained tolerance, at best. Those close to Willy resented Jake, even suspected that he had been a catalyst in Willy's demise. Yet Jake's only connection with Willy's fate was as the other option. Fabian didn't literally flip a coin, but the choice was to dump Willy or Jake. The less costly option was to get rid of Willy. Ironically, Paul Cello moved quickest to mend his fences with Jake. Fortunately, Paul's newfound rapport with Jake made developments during the next stage of the season more tolerable. Paul and Jake coalesced their talents, mostly Jake's, and brains, mostly Paul's, and simply decimated every batting order in the league, as Jake initiated a record-setting nineteen-game winning streak. For half a season, Jake became the most dominant hurler in Big League Baseball.

During the Diamonds' next homestand, Fabian abandoned his luxury digs to sit with Commissioner Hamilton Fisher in a front row box. The owner was greeted with a chorus of Bronx cheers and chants of *"Wil-lee!"* leading to a refrain of *"Bring back Willy!"*

He departed the stadium halfway through the game and decided to maintain a low profile for a while.

Willy didn't need Sam Khoury to tell her what she should do, but she did anyway. "Suck it up and go be the ace of the Jewels for a while." Willy planned to drive home to Florida, spend the weekend with Alma, and report to the Jacksonville Jewels on Monday. Apart from everything else that happened, Art Ridzik left Willy with a massive pile of unpaid bills, bank account deficits, and emotional damage due to her trust betrayed. She also had three postal sacks of unopened fan mail plus hundreds of never-read messages on both her team and personal e-mail addresses. *I'm smothering under all this baggage!*

Willy usually was sore for a day or two after pitching a game. She hadn't held a baseball for an entire week and her arm felt stiff and flabby. Even a pitcher's arm muscles begin to atrophy from lack of use. On the last night in her Manhattan townhouse, Willy went down to the basement to launder some dirty clothes and to do her throwing. The feeble and kindly caretaker had nailed an old tumbling mat to the cement wall and put a strip of tape sixty-and-a-half feet away. She could fling a hundred pitches in twenty minutes without even leaving the building. Willy stuffed a load of white things into the washer and started it. She picked up a nylon practice ball and inhaled a deep breath before beginning her pitching motion. As she drew back her arm to throw, she felt as though a pair of steel jaws had clamped onto her shoulder and pulled it back. The pain seared down to her forearm and she let the ball drop from her fingers. She clutched her throbbing shoulder and crumpled to the basement floor.

"Oh, no," she cried. "Not this! Not now! Oh, my sweet Lord, please! No!" The little girl inside lay still and sobbing, her tears sticking to her face on the cold concrete.

CHAPTER 14

Willy vacated her townhouse, packed her belongings–CD's, books, baseball cards, lap-top, and clothing plus her synch-sacked mail bags–and jumped into her little XYZ car to go home. She got on I-95 in New Jersey and got off twenty-three hours later in Saint Petersburg. She brought three gallons of fruit juice and bags of apples, bananas, and oranges for the trip. She stopped at a rest area every four hours or so to pee, to run for five minutes, and to meditate or to cat nap for twenty minutes. She kept the doors locked, the alarm turned on, and the music plugged into her ears. When she reached Alma's house, her mother barred her from the bathtub and sent her directly to bed. "You're so tired, I'm afraid you might fall asleep and drown, Willy Mae." The next morning, Willy drove her car to her friendly neighborhood Nimoco dealer to hand over the keys, the lease agreement, and a check for two months' payments to a dazed and confused salesperson. Alma would keep her coupe, since she could easily afford to pay the installments.

"I don't know what's gonna happen now, Mama."
"Papp went from team to team and town to town for thirty years."
"My shoulder, Mama..."
"Go see the sports medicine specialist in Tampa. Find out what he can do," said Alma, lovingly stroking Willy's arm. "I'll call and make an appointment for tomorrow morning."

Alma drove Willy to visit the specialist on Saturday morning. X-rays were taken right away and

Willy twiddled her thumbs, sitting atop an examining table for half an hour, waiting for the physician, Roger Crandall, to talk with her. Crandall was young, sandy-haired, and soft spoken with a cultured southern drawl, but, after a brief chat about the pennant race, he was all business, or medicine, as it were.

"What we have here is a classic sore arm, Willy. Tendinitis! Tendons are the fibrous cords that bind muscle to bone and tendinitis is an inflammation of a tendon. Pitchers are susceptible to inflammation of the four tendons in the shoulder that form the rotator cuff. Actually, you have double tendinitis; two of your shoulder tendons are inflamed. The pull or tug you felt warming up for your last game was probably a tear and it didn't help matters that you didn't work out for over a week. Light exercise is therapeutic for tendinitis. But it doesn't just hit like lightning striking. My guess is that you've been experiencing the onset of symptoms for a number of weeks, if not longer." Willy didn't speak, but she shifted her weight to show that her interest was piqued. "The mind is an amazing thing. Feeling stiff and achy after throwing a hundred or more pitches is to be expected, but, if the dull soreness lingers and you work through it, it begins to feel normal. You become accustomed to it and your mind acts as if you were free of pain." Willy surprised the physician by asking how to get to solutions. "The damage is not permanent, but it could be chronic. The act of pitching a baseball is unnatural to the human arm to start with and the force of throwing can dislocate the shoulder on a single pitch...Here," he said, pulling a short stack of paper towels from a wall-mounted dispenser, wadding them into a ball, and handing it to Willy. "Show me how you throw." She laughed lightly and went through a slow-motion wind-up from a sitting position and glided the wad toward him. "No, no!" he goaded, tossing the makeshift ball back to her. "Gun your sidearm fastball, Willy." She squeezed the wad tightly with her fingers and sailed it against the wall behind the doctor. He reached for her arm as she released the throw and said, "Your entire upper body is at work, from the base of your spine and your shoulder blades to twisting your torso by pulling the left shoulder to the right, and then back again by throwing out of your right shoulder. You use three or four different pitching delivery motions. Isn't that right?" She nodded, conveying anxious attention. "That puts additional stress on your shoulder and biceps, increasing the chances of tearing other muscles or tendons." Roger paused to pinch her right elbow between two fingers. "Any tenderness?"

"No," she said and he pinched her harder. "Some," she nervously rolled her eyes.

"Eventually, I think you'll suffer bone chips or bone spurs from the grinding action, the way you snap your elbow with each pitch. If that flares up and swells, you won't be able to pitch at all without aggressive treatment, meaning surgery."

"What can we do for now, Roger?" Willy asked.

"We can put you on anti-inflammatory medication, physical therapy with moderate exercise, ultrasound, cortisone treatment, aspirin for pain relief...If the inflammation persists or worsens, arthroscopic surgery, but the only sure cure is rest... and I don't mean a few days
between games."

"Well, that's not the way it's gonna be," she stated self-assuredly. "Willy's gotta pitch. I found out when I threw for ten or fifteen minutes this morning that I can focus my concentration away from the pain."

"You can play with *pain*, but you can't play *hurt*! You're injured, Willy," Roger said sternly.

"If I report to Jacksonville with a sore arm, I'll never get back to the majors this year and it'll be that much harder to make it back next year. There might not even be a next year! I'll be labeled damaged goods."

"What's your plan, Willy?" he asked with sincere interest.

"Ha! There is no plan, Roger." Willy paused to study Dr. Crandall's eyes. "I trust that all of this will remain confidential."

"Without question," he said. "You're my patient. I won't talk to anyone about your condition but you." Roger Crandall smiled and extended his hand to her. "Good luck, Willy."

Willy considered sitting out for a while, giving her arm a chance to heal a bit and discovering whether the image of her lonely protest vigil would bring forth a sympathetic response from the fans and wags. Alas, Willy realized she was no longer front page news. Furthermore, she lacked the wherewithal for an old-time holdout. She felt antsy by Sunday morning! She pondered her options. If the Diamonds granted her release and none of the other teams in the bigs wanted her, she could go to Mexico, Spain, Italy, Korea, or an independent minor league team. If nothing panned out, she could go to Australia or the Caribbean to play ball in the fall. Maybe if teams in the Japanese majors knew she was open to move there, they would offer to buy out her contract. Alas, "I don't even know how to call Japan," she lamented. The only alternative to playing in AAA was quitting baseball. She called Kristin Tracy on her private line Sunday evening. "I'll go to the Jewels tomorrow," Willy told Kristin. "My request to be traded or released still stands, but I'll go."

Willy heard Kristin pause, then say, "There's only one problem. You're 'designated for reassignment,' right now..."

"What does that mean?"

"It means we'll lift the suspension when you agree to come back, but you're off the D's forty-player roster and the only spot available is with Cheyenne in the Great Plains League."

"Class A? You're kidding me!" Willy shouted into her cell phone's teeny mouthpiece. "You can't do this to me."

"Yes, we can, Willy," Kristin said calmly.

"How can you justify it?"

"You've been inactive for almost two weeks. We can classify it as a rehabilitation assignment."

A rehab stint worried Willy because she wanted to avoid a physical examination at all costs, but she got up the nerve to ask, "How can you call it a rehab stint if I'm in perfect condition?"

"Okay, so it's not a rehab," said Kristin, mutely relieved Willy hadn't picked up on Harvey's "affirmative action" comment, which smelled like a lawsuit to the owner. "Anyway, the paperwork is all in place and it can't be changed 'til later in the week. Everybody's out of town for the all-star break. I'll call Alan if you want me to..."

Willy noticed the curious reference to Alan rather than Harvey. "Forget about it," she said in a hushed and low voice. "Where in the world is Cheyenne, Wyoming?"

"We'll fly you out on USA West. Just pick up your tickets at Tampa Airport in the morning."

"You're burying me," laughed Willy. "You might as well pay for my trip to the cemetery."

Willy made connections with the Cheyenne Karats in Ogden, Utah. The only experienced Karats were three players who had been demoted from AA or AAA teams. The others were nineteen-year-old, first-year minor leaguers, all raw, immature, gawky, and deathly afraid of being passed over for the Instructional League squad to play in Deerfield Beach in September. That would mark the end of their dream. Speaking of dreams, Cheyenne's manager, Red Leighton, told Willy, "You don't wanna be here and I don't want you here. It's nothin' personal. You're in exile, if you know what I mean. So, let's make the best of it. I'll give you a start every four days and you give me some good innings. Okay?"

"Okay, Red!" In the Great Plains League, Willy returned to playing catch with the catcher. A muscle-bound boy who was a high school shortstop only five weeks earlier certainly wouldn't be making pitch selections behind the plate for Willy Beal. She had no intention of studying the lineups of the Boise Spuds, Butte Bisons, and Ogden Pioneers. She would just put the ball into play, work on her pitches, her mechanics, and her conditioning. Willy made no effort to get acquainted with her teammates before going to the mound for the Karats on her first night in uniform. She expected to be rusty and yielded five hits and three runs in the second inning. After giving up a lead-off single in the fifth, she looked over at Leighton as if to say, "Well?" Another base hit, followed by a line-drive double, made the score 5-1 and Cheyenne's manager walked onto the field. Willy trotted off the mound as soon as she saw him stand up from the bench. She flipped him the ball in passing. "About time, Red!" The soreness in Willy's shoulder was dull, but constant, on the morning after, such that she was unable to keep her mind focused during her usual workout routine. She allowed herself one day of coddling and whimpering, but vowed henceforth to work her body to the limit. Willy discovered that the pain dissipated while concentrating on the other key body parts–back swiveling, foot planting, front leg kicking, fingers gripping, wrist snapping–to release a pitch. The hurt vanished completely during meditation and concentration on her focal point, the catcher's mitt, as she pitched. Placement of the ball with respect to its target was her singular purpose. She paused only to observe its result.

   After a game on Tuesday, Willy stayed up at midnight to watch the digital video recording of the all-star game on cable. The air outside was cool and dry, following a day
of mid-summer heat. So, she hit the kill-switch on the motel room's air conditioning and sprawled naked under a sheet on the bed as she watched the telecast, copped in its entirety,
except for commercials, from USTV. She kept drifting in and out of sleep during the pregame circus, which featured highlights of a home run derby, narrowly won for the Nationals by Andy Gilbert, 7-6, over the surprise

Americans' entry, Buffalo's Toby Clay. Roy Burton had refused to participate, calling the contest "undignified." The play-by-play was a mosaic of Rob DaSilva's and Zack Traynor's voices, caught in snatches between snoozing.

"There are the usual controversies about the fans voting with big-name players from big-city teams dominating the starting lineups... The New York Diamonds are the best represented club, of course, with five starters, including pitcher Gil Douglas...Donnie Ross is not having one of his better years, but he was selected by the fans, while his teammate Eric Jackson, who is having a banner year, was named to the squad as a reserve...Marcus Spencer of St. Louis, the league's leading batter, is not here at all...Kenny Estrada of Kansas City is playing first base for the Americans, despite a pulled hamstring that kept him out of action this past weekend, while Atlanta's Felix Montoya pulled himself out of the game because of a stomach virus...Talk about surprises? There are four Buffalo Wolves on hand tonight–catcher Diego Santamaria and outfielders Toby Clay, Andre Toussaint, and Peter Jones–all named by the Americans' manager, Fred Teller. All are batting over .300 and none were selected by fan voting...The starting pitcher for the Americans is Telly's ace, Jon Anthony. Absent, however, is forty-year-old Brian Robbins, on his way, it appears, to his seventh twenty-win season for the Wolves...Also overlooked is Buffalo's young lefty, Woody Naulls, currently leading the majors with six shutouts. If those aren't all-star credentials, I don't know what would be!...Designated hitter Andy Gilbert smacks a base hit to left off Anthony...Big Gil

Douglas goes the maximum three innings, allowing one hit, one walk, and no runs, striking out three...San Francisco's Greg Ruggieri pitching for the Nationals against his former teammate, Boston's Rick MacKendrick...The family connections for tonight's midsummer classic are Youngblood Crawford and Peter Jones. Both of them are sons of ex-big leaguers. Jorge Walker of Kansas City and Domingo Walker of Cleveland–the brothers are teammates for the American squad. Andre and Darryl Harris, no relation, are together for the National crew...Demeter Fortune is one-for-three in the game. He leads the league in runs and walks, is second in hits and batting...Roy Burton leads the bigs in homers and runs batted in. He's fourth in the league in batting average and unquestionably the odds-on favorite to win a Most Valuable Player award...As things stand at the halfway point, the Diamonds have opened up a six-game lead in the National East. San Francisco leads LA in the West by five. St. Louis leads Chicago by a half-game in the Central. Kansas City's lead in the American Central has been cut to a game and a half by red-hot Cleveland, Seattle and Oakland are deadlocked in the American West, and there's a three-way tie for first in the East. Toronto, Boston, and Baltimore share a half-game lead over Buffalo. That race is too close to call, as the saying goes..."

    Willy's eyelids drooped as she sleepily wrapped the bed sheet around herself, sat upright, and listened to Zack recap the game: "The Americans are trailing one-nothing in the eighth. The only run on the board came when Donnie Ross walked, stole second, and scored on Cal Bonham's RBI-double in the first inning." DaSilva's warm and comforting monotonous drone resumed: "Joey

Reynolds of Toronto batting for Kelly Swifton...Reynolds will likely stay in the game at third base for the Americans. On the mound, LA's Corky Calderone...The pitch...A fastball, swung on...That one is gone!" Reedy-voiced Zack came over the air: "There was no doubt about it as soon as the ball left the bat and we're tied at one apiece." Dave Warren earned his keep with a few words: "Reynolds has tremendous power, but only thirteen homers on the year. It's thought that he's hampered by playing in the spacious Canadian Skydome."

"Speaking of tremendous power," interrupted Rob, "pinch-hitting for the shortstop, Billy Velasco, is veteran Peter Jones of the Buffalo Wolves, making his twelfth all-star appearance ... The last time he was here representing the LA Nationals..."

Said Zack: "P.J. is currently second in the AL in home runs with twenty-three, trailing Estrada by one, and he's second in RBIs, trailing teammate Toby Clay, sixty-six to sixty-one."

Said Rob: "And the pitch to Jones from Calderone...Deep fly ball toward the gap in left center field, falling between Burton and Curtis Monroe...Monroe catches up with it, as Jones pedals around second...The throw from Monroe is a little short to Terry Frazier, playing the cutoff...and P.J. 'Home Run' Jones is in with a stand-up triple!"

Willy bounced on the bedsprings and cheered. "Go, Peter! Go, Peter! Whoo!"

The effort was wasted as knuckleballer Bruce McElroy came into the game to fan Youngblood Crawford and Domingo Walker, ending the inning with P.J. stranded at third. The National Stars bounced back with a run in the last of the eighth to win it, 2-1. Afterward, Rob DaSilva interviewed Cal Bonham, the game's outstanding player, and Peter Jones, who said, "With my not-so-blinding speed, I guess I made it exciting. One of the young horses from the Wolves, Toby or Andre, would've had an inside-the-park job..."

"I could've had one of them, too," clacked Cal, his eyes twinkling.

"Ten years ago, maybe," retorted Peter with a jab.

There was an aura of friendship around the three men, noticeably intimate in its ease. Willy recalled what Peter and Cal had said about getting along so well with the wags due to a spirit of kinship and shared appreciation for the game's history. Willy smiled at the screen, admired her two buddies, and then looked around the dank motel room. She started to cry, as she had done every night, but this time from a hurt far deeper than the pain in her rotator cuff.

Her first ten days in the Great Plains League were inauspicious. Red Leighton wasn't surprised at Willy B. Superstar's unimpressive 0-2 debut in the bushes. "It'll take you time to get your rhythm back." During off days Willy took the opportunity to think her way through the adjustments that she was making and to work out vigorously, but not to excess. One outcome, perhaps not surprisingly, was an overall improvement in "my poor shoulder."

The towns of Cheyenne, Boise, Butte, and Ogden became dumping grounds for Willy B. baseball cards, tee shirts, and other promotional gear. They spilled out of discount racks in retail stores. Willy laughed aloud at a drug store magazine stand when she read that she had slid over from *Lifetime* magazine's list of things "in" to things "out" for the summer. On the road, some yahoo in the stands would sing, "stee-roides, stee-roids," but the fans of America's heartland were too polite by nature to tolerate that sort of behavior for long. In these parts, the folks say "Shhh!" to people who talk during the National Anthem. Hecklers were given even shorter shrift. Willy couldn't be farther from New York.

Willy felt best when she chilled with fans at the ballparks. Willy was again being Willy–clowning while scrawling her name, unexpectedly kissing a boy or girl upon the head, chattering endlessly in her enchantingly melodic voice, and fielding the inevitable question: "What are you doing here?"

"How else would I get to meet you? What's your name?"

Meanwhile, righty Laddy Zanetsky and lefty Jay Phillips turned in solid performances as the Diamonds' fourth and fifth starters. As expected, two more of Willy's spring training cohorts, Maxwell Street and Psycho Bielski, became New York Diamonds when Dino DeSantis pulled a thigh muscle and Keith Whalen went on the disabled list with torn ligaments.

The interleague trading deadline tolled at midnight, August 1. The news flash came on Dave Warren's sports update from USTV: "In baseball, it's a case of the rich getting richer or them that's got shall get! Just minutes before the midnight trading deadline, the New York Diamonds acquired Mercurio Mercado from St. Louis in exchange for pitcher Todd Strickland and two outfielders, Dino DeSantis and Darnell Greene, and– yes, that's right, ladies and gents!–an additional player to be named later."

The first thought that came to Willy's mind was a tinge of regret for Strick, Dino, and Darnell being dumped by the D's. Then she wondered if Darnell had been caught with his nose in the candy. Even if such were the case, he was infinitely better off than poor Tony Ortega, who was playing on a temporary "get out of jail free" card, and Willy herself rotting away in the Great Plains League. Without access to New York's print and electronic media, Willy was thus in the dark regarding "a couple of teams in the other league" expressing interest in acquiring her services. Alan Blaylock, the acting general manager, had gone so far as to comment, "Things didn't work out for her with us, but she's a quality player. We're not going to give her away." However, Alan was in for a drubbing from the local scribes due to his victimization by a big league bait-and-switch. Before the toner ink on the Mercado trade's paperwork was dry, the Sloobirds turned it into a three-cornered deal by sending Darnell to San Francisco for a minor leaguer. The Diamonds would never have pulled the trigger on the transaction if they knew about the second phase that strengthened their two most likely playoff opponents.

On the barren playing fields of the wild, wild west, Willy followed a six-hitter versus the Spuds with a seven-hitter against the Bisons. She was 2-2 and had thrown thirty-one consecutive innings without walking anybody. She lost for the third time to the Pioneers four days later, but, in all modesty, thought she looked good, regardless of the score.

The month of August also witnessed the induction of Armstrong Crawford into Cooperstown's shrine of the immortals. Army's face radiated as he spoke to the crowd of fans, wags, and baseball luminaries there to witness his induction. "My whole family came here today," he said with an impish grin. "Except for one of my sons! I told Youngblood if he pulled himself out of the lineup in order to listen to his old man give a speech, I would've kicked his behind!" He laughed along with those listening. Army continued, "A friend of mine, a remarkable young woman named Willy Beal, said..." He paused to acknowledge the scattered applause. "...We must pay homage to the past. We all bring something with us when we come, take something while we're here, and have an obligation to give something back. The joy of the game and love for the game is what keeps us playing and cheering. It makes no difference whether it's tee-ball or Big League Baseball. When we look back on this game of joy and love, we remember playing, not whether we won or lost, or even what the score was. Yesterday's game is our history, tomorrow's game is our future, and that's how the game brings us the gift of hope. That, my friends, is what this game of ours does. It brings joy, it gives hope, and it creates love."

"What's the matter?" Charlene Jones asked her husband, Peter, as he watched Army Crawford's induction on television.

"Listen to this guy, Char. They held him up for twenty years, even though he was a lifetime .300 hitter, because he used to be a drunk. When he quit, nobody in baseball wanted anything to do with him. Now, here he is, and he's not talking about himself, what he went through, and how he put his life back together. He's talking about giving back. Beautiful..."

"Are you crying, honey?" Charlene laughed slightly as she put a hand on Peter's shoulder. P.J.'s eyes glistened as he said no. "And tough guys don't dance either. Right, Peter?"

Yet came the second week of August and the season's end was near. Even if there were to be a change of heart toward Willy on the part of the Diamonds' front office, the sports pages showed solid pitching by all five starters as the D's burned up the Eastern Division. Laddy had won six games since joining the club and Jay had eight wins, including four shutouts in July. Jake struck out eighteen batters in Miami, falling only two shy of the all-time record. Sandy Lee was back in top form, spinning a two-hitter at Philly, and Big Gil threw back-to-back shutouts at DC and the Meadowlands against the Washingtonians. Willy began to despair.

On Sportsnet's baseball wrap-up, the announcer declared: "The big story in baseball on this night is out of Buffalo, where the Wolves have fired manager Nick Dolan after the club was swept in a double-header at home by Texas."

Buffalo general manager, Eddie Paris: "We're under .500. We've lost more games than we've won, but we were only two and a half games behind, in second place. Now we're four and a half out, in fourth. We can't expect the entire division to play under .500 and finish first by default. But we feel we've got a good team, a better team than our record shows. Being this close, we feel we should try to make a run for the pennant. To do that, we had to make a change."

The Sportsnet anchor resumed: "The Wolves' GM did not discuss the specifics of dissension on the team, dissatisfaction with both Dolan and catcher Diego Santamaria on the part of the pitching staff, or the incident involving shortstop Marty Slattery...Reportedly,

Dolan removed Slattery from the game after an error in the field. A shouting match came to blows and Dolan went up to the front office to demand disciplinary action against the shortstop. He was handed his walking papers, instead." The American East standings flashed on the screen. Toronto sits in first followed by Baltimore, Boston, Buffalo, Tampa Bay, and the New Yorkers. Less than ten wins separated first from last place. "Coach Mike Staczewski is running the team tonight, but the rumor in Buffalo is that veteran outfielder Peter Jones is being considered as an interim replacement...The general manager and the club's owners are said to be discussing that possibility behind closed doors at this hour..."

Willy mocked the voice modulating from the television screen. "They aren't discussing anything, are they Peter? They're just trying to talk you into it, which shouldn't be real hard, since it's what you've wanted all along."

CHAPTER 15

At a 10:00 a.m. press conference at Pilot Field in Buffalo, the Wolves introduced their new player-manager. A wag asked why the title of "interim manager" had been dropped sometime between breakfast and the news conference.

"I guess it's just permanent," quipped Peter Jones. "We haven't talked at all about next year, whether I'd go back to playing full-time, manage full-time, or what...I know I'm not ready to hang 'em up...but our focus is entirely on this season, to give it our best shot. Like I said, we
haven't talked about anything beyond that."

A second question: "In the last fifty years, there've been only three playing managers and only one of them was a regular player for a full season. Do you plan to keep yourself in the lineup every day?"

"I'd be crazy to pull my bat out of the lineup," Peter stated without false modesty and added, "I do think it's virtually impossible...physically, I mean...to manage a big league team from right field. It makes sense for me to be the DH...Matt Zaremba has been doing that job, but he's played first base in the bigs and we can platoon him there with Harry Washington...at least for the time being."

"How do Zaremba and Washington like that idea?" quizzed Shane Hennessey of the *Buffalo Times*.

"They're both pros," Peter answered smoothly.

"What about Diego Santamaria's situation?" Shane followed up almost immediately.

"Diego's not going to catch anymore. It's that simple," said Peter. "We've recalled Gene Tyler from Wichita to be the backup catcher and Jed Guerin is number one. Jed's been behind the plate all year whenever Brian Robbins has pitched...That arrangement wasn't a problem for anybody. Brian and Jed have played together for a few years. Diego understood that...The situation just got to be ridiculous. Diego just can't communicate with the pitchers."

"Isn't there a language problem?" someone called out.

"No," Peter said dismissively. "Melendez and Jiminez couldn't work with him either...but Diego is still an important part of this team. He's a damn good hitter and we'll keep him in the batting order. He'll play left field and we'll move Andre Toussaint to right to take my place." Peter paused to smile. "See? Everything fits together neatly."

"Aren't you shaking things up pretty fast? Three lineup changes before you've managed your first game!"

Peter smiled and wagged his head. "Listen, everybody thinks about what they would do if they had the chance to manage a team...I'm not going to let my chance go down the tubes by sticking with somebody else's lineup card."

"What about the pitching?"

"We'll run an ad in *Today USA*." After waiting for the laughter to subside, Peter continued, "Jiminez is due to come off the disabled list this week, but Van Aachen has a mild case of tendinitis and he'll probably have to go on the DL. Dunlap and Melendez are ailing, too. We're sending Dunlap to Wichita to open a slot for

Tyler, but we'll recall him after the first of September. We're running out of arms!"

Hennessey jumped back into the questioning. "How about Tito Melendez? Will the Wolves cut him loose to make room for another pitcher?"

"Teet's been around a lot of years," Peter said seriously. "He's a good friend, too. This year's been a big disappointment for him and us, but..." As Peter spoke, he thought, *Teet doesn't know it's time to quit. He just can't pitch anymore, but Dolan kept him in the starting rotation. It's embarrassing!* However, P.J. said none of that. "If there's a physical problem, we'll check it out. Teet stays, regardless!" *He won't start another game, though.*

Hennessey, apparently seeking to emulate his colleagues across the state in the Big Town, kept on: "Aren't you looking for a closer? The word is that St. Louis wants to deal Kitsuragawa now that they have Todd Strickland, the youngster they got from the Diamonds."

"I don't think that's the answer. The scuttlebutt says Kit-Kat's going to Frisco anyway. We've got four guys...Phil Abruscato, Scott Bruneau, Randy Craig, and Chris Van Aachen...two lefties and two righties. That's a nice balanced mix. I like the idea of a co-op bullpen instead of the strict roles of middle relief, setup, and a closer. Chris has thirteen saves for us. That has to count for something." *He also has thirteen blown saves. A 50% failure rate for pitching with a one or two run lead in the eighth or ninth inning isn't exactly a quality number for a big league relief ace. And if he played a game of checkers with a chimp, I'd bet on the monkey.* "With Chris on the shelf for two or three weeks, Scotty and Randy have their work cut out for them. What we need is a right-hander to complement Phil, who can do long or short relief and spot starts. A swing man!"

"How do you plan to stabilize the infield? Dolan was platooning Slattery and Harmon with Kevin McDonald flip-flopping between second and short, and Alex Suarez at one time or another was the regular third baseman, shortstop, second baseman, and utility man."

P.J. sat back in his chair and responded easily. "We've had four guys rotating in three positions. None of them knew where they stood from one game to the next. Glenn Harmon, the third baseman, was benched for striking out too much, then he got back in the lineup, hit like hell, and was benched for a field error. I'll never do that to a player! Everybody contributes and everybody plays! We'll put McDonald at second and Marty at short, and confine the confusion to third. Glenn's the good bat, Alex's the good glove, and both guys will play."

Peter mentioned that his brother, James, might join the Wolves' coaching staff.

"Aren't you worried about being accused of nepotism?"

"That's a big word for an old jock like me," Peter glibly replied. "I'd call it favoritism," laughed the former college English major. "I'd like to have someone with his experience over here, especially to be our first base coach, which'll free up Stash to work full-time as our batting coach." Actually, Mike Staczewski's real value to P.J. was as a bench coach or assistant manager. *I need all the help I can get!*

"The rest of the coaching staff was hand-picked by Nick Dolan. Will everyone stay on?"

"Irv Ashmont, Dickie Leeds, and Ferdie Burgos are all good baseball people. We're not going to dump anybody just because he was one of Nick's pals."

The final question of the press confab was for the general manager. Eddie Paris was asked, "Does it really make a difference who the manager is?"

"We think so. That's why we made this change," the former pro player retorted.

Peter impressed the local and national wags with his style, wit, and confidence, but the Wolves nevertheless were a long-shot. "Let's see how the debonair Mr. Jones does on the hot seat in the dugout tonight," Shane Hennessey told his colleagues as the meeting adjourned.

Peter Jones's debut as player-manager kicked off an eight-game winning streak. Boston went into a tailspin and fell to fourth place, while the Wolves breathed down the necks of Toronto and Baltimore, holding hands at the top with a slim one-game lead. Pennant fever swept the fair city of Buffalo and the call of the howling wolf resounded throughout upstate New York. The national media called it "P.J.'s magic."

Willy listened to the radio news as she made herself a breakfast of apples, bananas, and honey. Her cell phone rang. Since her exile in Cheyenne, Willy spoke with Sam Khoury once or twice a week, exchanged letters with Michelle and Leota, and spoke daily by phone with Alma. Yet Willy had no contact with any of the New York D's. She missed Zinger, Cal, Gil, Sandy Lee, and especially Paul. Still she shielded her shame in silent anger.

"Yeah!" she sang into the phone.

"Willy? It's Peter."

Willy closed her eyes, tilted her head upward, cupped a hand over the receiver, and whispered, "I beseech the benevolence of heaven." She cleared her throat and said, "How're you doing, Peter?"

"Listen," he said without pleasantries. "Our GM's on the horn with the Diamonds' front office. We're tryin' to pull off a trade."

Restraint be damned! Willy tossed the phone to the floor, leaped high in the air, raised her fist to the ceiling, and shouted "Yesss!" before landing on her toes in a three-point stance.

"Willy, are you still there?"

"Mm-hmmm," she said sweetly. "Am I gonna be the swing man you talked about on the TV?"

"That's it," chuckled Peter. "But don't get too worked up yet. Somebody else is in the hunt."

"Who's that?"

"We're not sure. It could be Chicago. We're offering the Diamonds a minor league prospect or a player to be named later. The competition might be willing to deal a live body."

"I'll call New York and tell them I won't go to Chitown. I wanna play for you in Buffalo, Peter. It feels like fate."

"But be cool about it, Willy. I'm not even supposed to be talking to you. It's called tampering. The thing is, our GM is dealing with the new guy, Blaylock, but he's not really calling his own shots. Fabian is."

"I think I can work my way through the D's front office. Tell your GM to sit tight. Call me back?"

"Talk to you in an hour! Bye, Willy!"

Willy called Kristin Tracy at the stadium office in New Jersey. She said, "Even if we make the trade with

Buffalo, you have to clear waivers before its finalized. Chicago can claim you or block the trade."

"Couldn't you just revoke waivers on me?" Willy asked.

"Why bother? We'd just do the deal with Chicago in that case. Besides, Fabian doesn't care where you go as long as we get a player or the $30,000 cash price."

"Kristin, I want you to tell the people in Chicago that I won't play for them."

"I don't know if it'll work," she replied, although Willy sensed Kristin was genuinely sympathetic.

"Please, Kristin! Another time, another place, another life, I'd put on a pair of white socks and die happy, but that's not my karma."

"I'll call you back, Willy." Fifteen minutes passed and Kristin told Willy, "They're offering to trade us an everyday player and...Fabian will kill me if he found out, but Chicago's GM wants me to transmit their offer to you for a contract extension through next season for one-point-two million dollars."

"This isn't about money, Kristin," Willy said with a note of anguish. "Tell Chicago...and Fabian...there won't be any trade because I'll quit."

Kristin thought a moment. "Let me see if I can talk Alan into doing the Buffalo deal for future considerations. The Wolves and Diamonds have never made a trade before, since the owners can't stand each other. If Fabian agrees, we'll pull back if Chicago claims you, but they'll probably waive you if they know they can't have you anyway."

"Why would Fabian do that?"

Kristin laughed. "It's just business. He doesn't hate you, Willy. It's time to divorce Willy and the Diamonds and get on with our lives."

Willy giggled and said, "Kristin? Thanks!"

"Don't mention it."

By two o'clock on Tuesday, Willy's name cleared waivers after the twenty-four-hour waiting period and she was on her way to Buffalo, New York in exchange for baseball's most traded commodity, a player to be named later. When Willy called the Buffalo business office to make travel arrangements, she was put on hold for a minute and, instead of canned elevator or supermarket music, they piped in play-by-play audio from Wolves' games. "That's how it ought to be!" She winged out of Cheyenne, en route to hooking up with the Wolves on Wednesday in Boston for a day-night double-header, the first game scheduled for four o'clock. Willy's connecting flight landed at Logan Airport two hours late and Willy hustled from the baggage claim area to the car rental desk with less than half an hour to game time.

"How do I get from here to Fenway Park?" she asked the rent-a-heap clerk.

"Take the Mass Pike to Kenmore Square and go down Comm Ave 'til you see the 'sit-go' sign. You're right there. Don't worry. You can't miss it."

After forty minutes of being passed on the right by cars speeding in the breakdown lane, Willy came within sight of the large, pyramidal shaped, neon oil company logo. She laughed, "Oh, yeah, *sit-go sign*! Can't miss it!" The block around Fenway was mobbed with pedestrians. She couldn't even drive in front of the ballpark, much less get to the players' parking lot. She went up and down Commonwealth Avenue three times; all the fast food lots and gas stations with "PARK $25" signs were full. Finally, she ducked into a side street and saw a man waving a red flag in front of an underground garage. One thug collected cash while a second thug directed Willy to follow the line of cars through the garage and out into a fenced-in yard, where several more thugs with windmilling arms were shouting and badgering parkers into tightly packed rows and columns. "Come on! Plenty of room! Back up!" *Clunk!* "Hold it!" Willy, more concerned than the people walking to the park that the game had begun, trotted and skipped around groups of people as she headed for Yawkey Way. When she turned the corner onto Lansdowne Street, also known as Ted Williams Way, she smelled roasting sausages, hot dogs, and big, doughy pretzels with mustard. The aromas from the sidewalk vendors cast a momentary euphoric haze. *You've been here before, Willy! You're on your journey home.*

With the Bay State Beaneaters fading out of the pennant chase, Willy expected this twin bill to be a ho-hum affair, but the old park was full to overflowing and the Old Towne's faithful reveled in the deflation of Buffalo's winning streak as the Fenway Wall Bangers scored five in the first and three more in the second. Willy made her way through the service gate, into the visitors' clubhouse to pick up her number 28 road jersey and assorted paraphernalia, and found the locker room to suit up, before joining her new team in the dugout. A bases-loaded double made the score 11-0. The New Englanders were still on their feet and cheering. Voices rang out: "Go for twenty!" Willy nervously apologized for being late to Peter, who was seated on the top dugout step, bat in hand, with his back to the field.

"As long as you're ready for the second game," Peter stated coyly.

"I'm going tonight?" she shrieked, gazing out to left field and the fabled Green Wall, less than three hundred feet down the line. "Here? You can't do that to me."

Sitting on the bench, Phil Abruscato, a one-time math major, declared, "One bad pitch and your ERA's a google."

Peter nudged Willy to sit with Irv Ashmont, formerly a short and wiry player, now a short and stocky pitching coach. "You gotta be a great pitcher to be a good pitcher in this ballpark." "If Cy Young had to pitch in Fenway, they'd have to call it the Walter Johnson award," she said and plopped next to him.

Jed Guerin joined Willy and Irv on the bench after Toby Clay's three-run homer made it a 15-3 ballgame in the sixth. "Let's go over the hitters for the second game," he said. Gene Tyler, who was behind the plate in the first game, gave his "gal pal" from last winter a peck on the forehead. Jed, like Paul Cello, was at once rough-edged, warm, and funny, but the two catchers contrasted as well. Paul worked a fast game, calculated each pitch, and analyzed every batter. Nobody ever accused Jed of working too fast. His strategy was simpler than Paul's chess game of moves and countermoves. "Get two strikes with good pitches. Then get the out with a bad pitch. The trick is not being afraid to pitch inside," he believed. With Paul backstopping, if a pitcher wasn't concentrating, look out! Jed, by contrast, never chewed out a pitcher. He simply asked, "What's the sitch? What do you wanna do? Are you awake or what?" Jed Guerin was a master of his trade, a veteran of twenty big league seasons, who signed with the Wolves for half Diego Santamaria's salary, but had now taken away his job.

Peter's management philosophy was in evidence. "Everybody talk. Willy, go to dinner with Brian and Woody after the second game. Talk pitching."

"We gotta catch a midnight flight to Buffalo, P.J.," Woody Naulls pointed out.

"Eat at the airport," Peter shrugged before strolling out to the on-deck circle in the eighth inning. A few minutes hence, P.J. hit a "Fenway pop-up" into the seats atop the Green Wall in left center field, cutting Boston's lead over Buffalo to 15-4.

Brian Robbins, the Wolves' resident legend, winked at Willy and called to Peter, "Right, P.J.! We'll grab some steaks and brews. We'll make a man out of her!"

The atmosphere in the Buffalo Wolves' locker room and clubhouse was boisterous, convivial, and totally involved with the game just concluded. There was also a free exchange of critique and kudos for one another's play on the field, quite different from the New York Diamonds' aura of individual self-importance. Jed and coach Mike Staczewski huddled together under a cloud of cigarette smoke. Woody Naulls quietly buttoned his shirt and listened to fellow pitcher Randy Craig sing slightly off-key to the mellow love ballad playing on Scott Bruneau's disc player in the locker next door. Shortstop Marty Slattery watched second baseman Kevin McDonald brushing his sleek black curls and said, "I betcha Willy don't spend as much time on her 'do as you." Kevin smirked without looking away from his pocket-sized mirror. Randy yelled over, "The bro's got so much creme in his hair, it'll explode if ya light a match near his head."

Willy had just begun to get acquainted with Sergio Jiminez, the well traveled pitcher who was having his best season ever with the Wolves at age thirty-nine, when Peter asked her into the visiting manager's cubbyhole of an office. "Twenty-four different guys have been in my office in the last week to cry on my shoulder about one thing or another. I was sort of the father confessor on this team anyway, but now it's like I'll have to start making appointments." Willy expected to hear some form of the standard orientation lecture: "This is the way we do things on our club." Instead, Peter looked tired and beleaguered as he leaned back in the swivel chair. "I talked to Harry Washington before the game. I've been pussyfooting around about platooning him and Matt Zaremba at first base. I told him that Matt would play both ends of the double-header and he'd keep playing every day unless he got hurt or stopped hitting." Willy listened as Peter sighed again. "And Harry let me know, as far as he was concerned, I was stabbing him in the back. 'Ain't it always the way? Your own kind turns on you!' I told him that was bull, but he just kept saying, 'Eleven years and this is how you do me!' What's he expect me to do? Their numbers are pretty close; they're both batting about .250, but Harry's an old war horse, going through the motions, and Matt's a young stallion who comes to the park to play...You know what Santamaria said to me when I told him, an all-star catcher, that he wasn't going to work behind the plate anymore? Diego said, 'Okay, P.J.! You're the boss?'

Do you believe it? He's the guy that should be pissed off, not Harry!"

Willy walked over to her friend and put her hands on his shoulders. "It comes with the territory, doesn't it? You wanted the job. Now you got it."

Peter craned his neck to look up at Willy, smiled, and nodded. Then he said to her, "I'm glad that damn winning streak is over with." Willy recalled the great sense of relief shown by Demeter Fortune when his hitting and errorless streaks ended, but she resisted the impulse to talk about her former team, thereby sounding like the typical new hire, who inappropriately compares his or her experiences at a former place of employment. Then she whispered into Peter's ear, "Thanks for giving me a break…Again!"

P.J. laughed, "Hey, you were the best pitcher available."

"Well, thanks anyway," she said, still speaking softly. "I like it here already."

"It wasn't a tough sell with Barry and Dana, the owners. A couple of rich, yuppy, air-heads, but they're all right…more like cheerleaders with a checkbook than owners. No power trip at all!"

Dana Hawthorne and Barry Kaplan, husband and wife co-owners, were émigrés from the concrete colossus of Gotham City, who epitomized Buffalo's *nouveau riches* and symbolized
its metamorphosis from the moribund, decaying urbs of the 1950s and '60s to the smaller, more vibrant, and quite livable city it downsized to become. Dana and Barry also owned D.B. Gumshoes, the best nightspot in town, where upstairs the food was always as good and hot as the music downstairs. Gumshoes was the place to go for out-

of-towners and Buffalo's new urban gentry to mingle with pro football, hockey, soccer, and baseball players within walking distance of the city's cozy, downtown park.

"When Eddie and I met with Dana and Barry to tell them we wanted to pick you up, Dana started clapping and jumping up and down in her chair like a teenager. 'We're gonna bring Willy to the Wolves? Oh, this is so great! Willy can take us all the way.' They never hesitated. They'll present you with a nice salary package when we get back home."

"Home?" laughed Willy. "I've changed addresses five times since February. Where am I gonna live?"

"Sadie owns a duplex in Orchard Park," replied Peter. Sergio Jiminez was nicknamed "Sadie" by his teammates.

"Sadie's a funny dude. He had me laughing and I only met him for like a minute."

Peter rolled his eyes, pointing to his forehead. "The lights are on, but nobody's home, if you know what I mean. He's been a mule for us, though. He gave us a scare with his arm trouble, but he bounced back pretty well." Peter's eyes then dimmed, showing the burden of his new job. "I don't know what to do about Teet."

For most of his fifteen seasons in the majors, Tito Melendez was one of the best pitchers in baseball, like his compatriot Brian Robbins, a perennial 20-game winner. Injuries and age began to take their cruel toll and Tito continued to toil respectably as his grip loosened on his youthful gifts. The Buffalo Wolves took a chance and signed Tito on P.J.'s recommendation. Despite some marginal success, the former Cy award winner and future Hall member was largely ineffective.

Said Willy, "I'm taking his place, aren't I?"
Peter shrugged, "I guess so."
"I hate that."

Later Willy met Stash for the first time, the former batting champion who was the Wolves' batting coach. She also met Ferdie Burgos, the bullpen coach, whose key functions were to answer the bullpen telephone and make sure that there were enough paper towels in the clubhouse washroom.

In Willy's American East debut, she gave up two runs on three hits in five innings against the Red Stockings. With the score tied 2-2 in the third, she fanned Rick MacKendrick with runners on second and third to end the inning. She came back in the fourth to strike out the side on nine pitches, bringing the crowd of 35,000 to its feet. Ernie Arnett, the radio and TV voice of the Buffalo Wolves, told the faithful watching back home, "That's four in a row. Man, oh, man! Make no mistake about it...Willy B. is back. Eat your heart out, New York!"

Woody Naulls broke his quiet shyness as Willy took a seat in the dugout with the fickled Fenway fans still clamoring for her. "Why don't they boo you? These people hate everybody. I mean, they think the Pilgrims and Indians wore red socks!"

"They're super fans, though," said Willy.

Toby Clay smiled and wondered whether she heard the catcalls of "steer-roids" mixed with "witch," "ho," and "dyke" from the bleacher bums, flaming arrows aimed at Willy that stung his ears while standing in center field.

Willy left the game with the score still tied. As Phil Abruscato warmed up for the sixth inning, Peter said to her. "You did pretty well. You kept us in the game, cuz. That's all you have to do." Willy was satisfied with herself and her new surroundings. She wasn't expected to throw a shutout in each game pitched. She was to be a role-player with the Wolves and that suited her just fine. Willy noted the Bay State Beaneaters laying off her up-and-away, letter-high offerings, which led to three bases on balls and four full-counts to the eighteen batters to whom she pitched. She resigned herself to throwing more pitches and serving more walks in the weeks to come. She wasn't the same pitcher she had been with the Diamonds. She was physically impaired, but stronger and smarter. She knew the limits of her job as well as her sore shoulder and she would live within them.

Phil gave up a run and the Wolves trailed the Bostonians, 3-2. In the seventh, the Wolves loaded the bases for Toby Clay at the plate. Harry Washington sat in funereal gloom throughout the game until Toby pulled what seemed to be a routine fly ball to left. Mario Guerra, Boston's regular left fielder, wasn't in the game. Harry saw the rookie substitute's feet step to his left, then freeze in place. "He ain't got a clue!" exclaimed Harry, as he jumped from the bench and shouted frantically at P.J. "Send the runners. It's gonna drop in!"

"Go! Go! Go!" yelled Peter, as the Wolves' coaches at first and third waved the runners around the horn. The ball caromed off the legendary wall and zig-zagged in the coffin corner in front of the hapless sub as Toby's base-clearing triple put the Wolves ahead, 5-3. Harry climbed back into his shell, speaking not one more word, as Phil got the win and Scotty nailed down the save.

Willy refused all requests from the Boston and Buffalo media corps for interviews, declaring that she could be found in her team's clubhouse and would be happy to talk to the wags about anything other than herself from pop music to world peace. Afterward, Willy chatted with Stash, Irv, and Peter, who was still mildly incredulous at the Diamonds' acquisition of old friend Mercurio Mercado. "Why does a team in the same league give them a guy like Merk?"

"Merk's finished," said Stash. "He was hittin' only about .238 for St. Louis, wasn't he?"

"Some guys age faster than others," agreed Irv.

"Sure, but he's been playing hurt all year," said Peter. "He might not be able to run or play center field the way he used to, but he can still hit. The Diamonds know that. Last season, he had his worst year ever, but you don't just roll off the edge of a cliff. Statistical and physical decline is gradual. If Merk can bounce back, the D's have the best outfield in baseball."

"To go along with the best pitching, the best infield, the best hitting...," Stash lamented.

"We've got our own league to worry about," said Peter. "We've got two weeks of interdivisional and interleague games and then we play against American East teams the rest of the way."

Willy effortlessly renewed her friendship with winter league playmates Scotty, Glenn, Gene, and Phil; new chums, Randy and Kevin, drove her to the duplex in suburban Orchard Park via Tim Russert Highway the next day. She met Sadie's plump and brassy spouse, Yolanda, and the numerous Jiminez children, too frenetically active for an accurate head count. She sat down later with Peter and Eddie Paris to talk business.

The GM said, "We're giving you a contract extension instead of a new contract. Do you know what that means?"

"I'm not sure what the difference is," she replied self-consciously.

"We're increasing your salary from the minimum to one and a quarter million and it's not prorated for the rest of the season. The increase is payable over the next nine months 'til the end of spring training next season. Is that all right?"

Willy laughed boisterously. "A year ago I was making a hundred and fifty dollars a week and living with my mother. I think this will be satisfactory, if you know what I mean." Alone with Peter, he asked about Art Ridzik. "He burned up all my money and left me with bad debts in three states. He didn't rip me off, really. He just spent money we didn't have yet. I can sue him, I guess, but he's broke, too."

"What you need is my address book, phone numbers," said Peter. "My agent, my lawyer, and my accountant…I'll call Michael Avery. He's the accountant. He's in town doing some work for me. Let him look over your finances. He'll take care of everything for you."

"I did that once before," snorted Willy, "with Artie!"

"Michael's no thief. He's a real good guy," assured Peter. "The perfect bean-counter, kind of quiet, he doesn't know or care much about sports. Turn all your problems over to him and just come to the park to play ball."

"I love Pilot Field," crooned Willy. The home of the Wolves was deliberately designed to be an intimate, traditional ballpark–not a multifunctional colossus. It was an athlete's workplace. The park was neat and clean, but the Wolves were a rough and motley crew to be sure. The bullpen trio–Randy Craig, Scotty Bruneau, and Chris Van Aachen–looked exactly like the type of people they would be if defrocked of a ballplayer's uniform: a gangsta from the 'hood, a heavy metal biker, and a tattooed and pierced gothic punk. Phil Abruscato and Sean Dunlap were much tamer in appearance and manner. Randy, Scotty, and Chris were less experienced and more immature, but far more confident on the pitcher's mound than Phil. All four relief pitchers were brooders, prone to whining as well. Likewise did Sadie and Woody often brood, but never did they whine. Alas, Brian, living legend that he was, never whined or brooded, and neither did Tito, who was quick to smile and inclined toward acts of friendship and camaraderie, as was Jed, who nonetheless bitched, moaned, kvetched, whined, swore, and spat from batting practice through extra innings. Yet Jed was generous of heart. To Willy, he was the cuddliest of teddybears and one hell of a good catcher, although a bit old, creaky, and dented. Like Paul Cello of the Diamonds, Jed Guerin of the Wolves never shaved on game day. Being a regular catcher once again, every day was game day. As the winning Wolves became more glamorous, their catcher grew more grizzled. "Good stubble scrapes your fingers," he said with due pride.

    Once Willy settled herself into the half-duplex, a circle of players began to gravitate toward her when the team was at home in Buffalo. Randy, Scotty, Chris, and Kevin McDonald would come by to visit, usually unannounced, putting a crimp in Willy's habit of lounging around in her undies or naked before bedtime. With Sadie and Yolanda's tribe on the other side of the house, Willy was rarely alone, except to sleep, although her invitations for moonlight runs were always rejected. The little group, mostly made up of unmarried players, was called the Wolves' single club and formed a cluster of friends on the road as well.

    Willy pitched twice in relief during the weekend homestand, working two hitless innings in a win and one in a loss. She made her second start for the Wolf Pack on Tuesday, again going five innings, giving up three runs on three hits, but no walks and three strikeouts. She left the game with a two-run lead and fretted as Phil, Randy, and Scotty put runners on base in each successive inning. For a moment, she returned to the Diamonds, where her first win was difficult to grasp and her second never came. By the eighth inning, the crowd was howling *"Ah-ah-ahoo!"* as Jed sputtered around the bases after his three-run home run put the pride of Buffalo out in front, 8-3. Willy had her first victory and returned to the bullpen the following night.

CHAPTER 16

Peter's dilemma about Tito Melendez came to a head the following week. Chris Van Aachen was due to come off the disabled list six days shy of September 1, when clubs could expand their rosters from twenty-five to forty players. A spot had to be opened for Chris, but Peter wouldn't dump Tito. He argued with Eddie Paris, who loosened his tongue in front of the wags, "off the record," that the Wolves would give Tito his unconditional release. When the irate pitcher read the reports of his demise in the newspaper, he told the wags at Pilot Field, "I don't believe they did this thing without tellin' me face to face, like a man!"

"Will you quit baseball, Teet?"

"The way I'm feelin' now," he said with his voice cracking, "I'm goin' home!"

Peter was incensed on the phone with Eddie Paris. He shouted at his boss, "I *never* told you to release him. That's exactly what I *didn't* want to do. You were supposed to come up with something...a coaching job, a scouting job, anything!" Most of the players who arrived at the park early listened through the thin walls to Peter's concluding words. "Now, all we do is wait for Teet to cool off, promise that he'll stay, and cut some other guy so we can reactivate Van Aachen." The solution was to send Sean Dunlap down, figuratively, to the Class-A Niagara Falls Rapids, keeping him nearby, where he could pitch two or three games and return to the Wolves after the minor league season ended to take over Willy's role as the "swing" pitcher and she would become the Wolves' closer, the ace relief pitcher.

The quality performances of the Buffalo Wolf Pack's starting rotation were thoroughly unexpected. The old and grey comebackers, Robbins and Jiminez, were tied with Kansas City's Jon Anthony for the most wins in the league, while Woody Naulls was right behind them, heading for a possible 20-win season. The bullpen cohort was quite another story. Thus, the closer, the stopper, the firefighter, the bullpen terminator was Willy. She finished three consecutive games on the road in the week that followed, two of them at Jacobs Field. She relieved Randy, who had pitched well since the fifth, with two on, two outs, and a 4-2 Wolves' lead in the eighth. She promptly served a hanging curveball to the man she struck out at will in the winter league title game in San Juan, Domingo Walker. The league's leading batsman drove the ball into the gap in right center, clearing the bases and tying the game. However, the Wolves came back with a run in the ninth. Angry and aided by the bottom of Cleveland's batting order coming up, Willy struck out the side, with two walks between the kays, to get credit for the win on a blown save. Such is the nature of the official scoring rules. She came into the next game with one on, no outs, and a 5-4 Wolves' lead. Who else but Domingo should come to the plate? This time he beat out an infield hit, moved to second on a force play, and scored one step behind the tying run from third, both runners tagging up on a sacrifice fly. Andre Toussaint in right field seemed to have taken pause to contemplate the nature of the universe between catching the fly ball at the warning track and throwing it back to Kevin, playing the cutoff in the infield. The Buckeye fans happily went home with a 6-5 win for the Lake Erie Tribe at the expense of Willy's first loss as a Wolf. She was angered, but her mood was more simmering, inwardly directed. Peter noted, "Only a halfwit would be in the girl's face, talking to her tonight." Presently, Scotty lived up to that role, tailing Willy around the clubhouse, locker room, and later at the hotel, urging her to "talk it out and forget about it." She sulked the entire evening. The weekend arrived and the Wolves opened a three-game set against the Green Machine in Oakland. As things turned out, Scotty went to the hill with a "safe" four-run lead in the seventh, surrendered five hits and five runs in two-thirds of an inning, himself blowing a save and taking a loss. P.J. sent Willy in to "get us the hell back to the hotel for a good night's sleep." She fanned the Oaks' big, bad slugger, Daniel Chu, on three straight sliders. Willy's only save was earned by pitching the last four innings of a combined shutout with Brian against the A-Team on Saturday afternoon, a much better note on which to approach Peter.

"This idea isn't working out too well, Peter."

"We'll see," came her friend's now predictable, stonewalling reply.

The Wolves may have been a dark horse in the pennant race, but their hitting was explosive, especially in the friendly confines of Pilot Field. Toby and Peter were second and third in the league in homers, respectively. Toby, Peter, and Diego were already nearing the 100 RBI mark, and big Matt Zaremba was crunching the numbers right behind them. Diego, Andre, and Kevin were hitting over .300 and Andre was likely to reach the gold standard of 200 hits on the season.

Toby Clay, a mere 24 years of age, was introspective, intellectual, and quietly poising himself for the mantle of stardom. Indeed, the rap on Toby was similar to what was said of Andy Gilbert, that he somehow lacked the fortitude of heart necessary for greatness. For Toby no less than Andy, Willy knew the notion was bunk.

Samantha Khoury visited Willy in the Wolves' locker room. She came up close to Willy and said, "Smell my hair, pal."

"Are you crazy or what, girlfriend?" Willy howled and backed away animatedly.

"Come on, Willy. Sniff!" Sam insisted. Willy sniffed. Sam placed two fingers in front of her lips, pretended to blow smoke, and then pantomimed wiping her hands. "Three weeks," she said pridefully. "I haven't put on any weight, either. Smoking made me thirstier and hungrier."

Out of Willy's sight a moment later, Sam pushed Stash into a corner and clawed at his chest. "Give me a friggin' cigarette, Big Mike. Before I die!" Stash produced a crush-proof box of Greensboros from his back pocket. Stash chuckled quietly behind his walrus-like moustache as he held a match for Sam and she sucked in three drags without exhaling. "Oh, God, I needed that," she sighed, puffing several more times before stamping out the butt on the concrete floor. As she walked away with a dreamy expression, Big Stash held out another. "One for the road?" She snatched it from his hand.

Willy always threw a hundred pitches for twenty minutes before each game, regardless of whether she expected to pitch. Willy felt stiffness and twinges of pain in her shoulder intensifying after an outing of pitching. More throwing seemed to have a numbing effect, perhaps wholly psychologically. The more she used her arm, the more the act of defocusing from the pain became her normal state of mind. She was simultaneously strengthening and injuring her pitching arm. Dr. Roger Crandall was right on target when he told Willy that sharp acute pain comes and goes, but dull chronic pain begins to feel normal. The ache was so constant, she forgot it was there. She fully knew she was paying for short-term relief with long-term damage, but she could taste the sweet reward: the Buffalo Wolves were tied for first place in their division and October was coming.

Notwithstanding Willy's unspectacular performance as a closer, she had been in a Wolves' brown, yellow, and orange uniform for two and a half weeks, appeared in half of the team's games, and garnered two wins, erasing her frustration with the Diamonds earlier in

the season. "You know something?" said P.J. to the sage and venerable sportscaster, Ernie Arnett. "Willy seems to have grown from a raw, green rook to a seasoned veteran in just one season."

Ernie, whose salary was paid by a brewery, bent his elbow to sip cream soda. "That circus Fabian put on in the Big Apple was her wildest dream-come-true, then it turned into her worst nightmare. It's like anything else in life. She lived through it, got past it, and learned from it."

Meanwhile, by snatching tidbits from the news, Willy tried to keep up with happenings in the other big league, where the Diamonds opened up a 29-game lead, set to clinch first place on Labor Day, and challenged the all-time record for wins in the regular season. Although Tom Vallery was being attacked in the media for playing "bully ball" by running up double-digit scores, the New

York D's were not only winning, but appeared to be outclassing baseball's best division and the entire league.

In the meantime, mathematical elimination began to knock off all but four of BLB's thirty-two teams in each three-division league. There were no more turning points, just make-or-break series, which, in turn, became make-or-break games. One by one, New York, San Francisco, St. Louis, Florida, LA-Anaheim, Cleveland, and Kansas City clinched playoff brackets. The final championship contenders battled it out for the American East title in the tightest four-way race of the century.

Peter Jones carried a "three-and-and-a-half-pitcher" starting rotation into the season's final month. P.J. worked Brian, Sadie, and Woody every third game on three days' rest. When there was no off-day on Monday or Thursday, which was commonplace due to squeezing in make-ups for rainouts, Willy stepped in as the fourth starter, sometimes pitching with only a one-day respite between relief appearances.

"We gotta watch out for burnout," Irv Ashmont fretted.

"We'll count pitches and watch them all closely from inning to inning," responded Peter. "But no pitcher is going to blow out his...*or her*...arm in two or three weeks. There's no time left to be cautious or patient, Irv!"

"Willy was the missing piece of the puzzle, you know," Irv cackled.

"I still think she's the perfect closer," insisted Peter. "Power, concentration, control, and absolutely tireless!"

"We've won all four games she started," Irv countered.

"Either way, Irv, we've got all the pieces together now, like you said. We *can* do it."

"We *will* do it," said Irv.

Willy got together with Michael Avery, Peter's accountant, Saturday evening. Michael was a bit staid and dressed reservedly in a sport coat and tie, but he proved not to be a nerdy number-cruncher as P.J. portrayed him. In fact, Willy thought he was cute, especially his kindly eyes, easy smile, and baritone voice. "First, I'll get in touch with your creditors and set up a payment schedule for the bad debts Ridzik left you with," Michael said. "You should be able to cover your expenses with your paycheck, but you should clear away the outstanding bills before you do anything else. You're still in a hole as far as money is concerned, but it's not too deep."

"Oh, so, I can see the top instead of just the bottom of the hole, right?" She was trying to jog his sense of humor.

He smiled slightly, eyeing Willy for a moment, and then returned to the paperwork in front of them. "Are these all your bills?"

"Well," giggled Willy. "I toss out a lot of stuff that comes in the mail."

"That's not a good idea, Willy." He was amused, but not surprised.

"Do you like baseball?"

"Sure," Michael replied easily. "But it's a little slow for my taste, though. Football's a lot more exciting, I think."

"Say what?" Willy, the game's reigning diva, was mortified.

Michael listened to the preface of what promised to be a lengthy tirade on the virtues of the Grand Old Game, smiled, and said politely, "Can we get back to your finances?"

"Certainly," replied Willy, folding her hands in her lap. "Do you like music?" she asked, after the briefest of intervals. He answered by wordlessly nodding in the affirmative. "I love music," sang Willy. "New age and modern jazz, classic swing and the big bands...Lately, I've been listening to a lot of blues."

"Blues and modern jazz?" Michael asked, astonished. "You mean like Ella Fitzgerald, Billie Holiday, and Bessie Smith? Ha, that's old! My grandparents used to listen to that stuff."

Willy kept on pushing. "I like to listen and dance to rap, hip-hop, and pop, too."

"All that 'yo, boy, yo' stuff?" the aghast accountant asked her.

"Rap isn't anything different from street-corner symphony and beat poetry of the '50s. There's a lot more to it than trashy street talk."

"Oh, I see," came Michael's words accompanied by a vacant expression.

Willy forced a smile, and said, "Mister Avery, we must have something in common." *But I'll be damned if I can figure out what.* "Would you like something to drink?"

"A beer?" he responded cheerily.

"Forget about it, Michael," she said sour-faced. "I've got all kinds of fruit juice... tomato, apple, cranberry, papaya, guava, pineapple, grapefruit..."

Michael wrinkled his brow. "Any soda pop?"

"Believe it!" chirped Willy. "I'm the American Cola girl, right? One caffeine-free, diet cola coming right up, sir!"

"No, thanks," he said unhappily. "I don't care for the diet stuff. It tastes like cough medicine! I like the classic cola."

Willy propped her chin on her hands and mumbled, "We're just two peas in a pod, aren't we?"

"Are you really a Buddhist?" he asked shortly afterward.

Willy responded with a sigh. "I study the way of Tao and practice Zen and yoga as mental and spiritual disciplines, but I've never really been able to reconcile it with my religious upbringing." She was being unexpectedly honest, surprising herself. "In the back of my mind, every time I chant my mantra with my prayer beads, I'm afraid I'll get struck by lightning or something."

"Do you want to know what I think?" asked Michael, pushing aside his hand-held Blueberry, which he had been using as a calculator. "I think the decline of the churches has caused the deterioration of the family and traditional values, especially in the inner city, where the role of socialization is being assumed by street gangs...Sure, drugs and guns are poison, but kids need a moral foundation. That's what religion provides. It doesn't matter whether it's Buddhist or Christian or Muslim or Jewish or Hindu or what kind of religion it is."

Willy looked at Michael with undisguised surprise. "Do you like children?"

"Kids are what makes us human." Even he didn't know why he answered so simply and profoundly.

Willy's eyes radiated. "I'm a believer in prefigurative culture; that's when adults and children learn from each other and we continue to learn and grow all through our lives."

Michael spoke in a soft whisper. "That's interesting. I'd really like to talk to you some more about that." He didn't smile, but his eyes twinkled as he said, "We should set a date to sit down again soon. It'll take more than one night to work out a comprehensive financial plan for you."

"How about tomorrow night?" she suggested, then quipped, "Should I go casual or wear my going-out shoes?"

"Excuse me?" Michael looked genuinely shocked.

"I'm kidding," she laughed loudly. "You know, *date*? I was just making a joke, sorry."

"Can we get some work done, Willy?" He sounded serious, but his eyes still twinkled.

"Certainly, Mr. Avery," Willy said in reply.

CHAPTER 17

The baseball season undergoes a time-frame compression as September approaches. Early in the season, slumps and losses are taken in stride by players and teams. There is a long summer season in which to get on track and bounce back from a slow start. A slump in the month of June is a "swoon," where a club can recover to get back in the race or play out the string. A stagger in the heat of August becomes a "fold." In the cooling of September, it is a "choke." Between the first and last weeks of August, the pennant race assumes its final form. Veteran and marginal players are bought and sold on speculation. There is a flurry of trading before the bell. Teams still in the hunt must bring aboard their new additions before midnight on the last day of August for them to be eligible for the postseason playoffs.

Kansas City asked waivers on left-hand-hitting shortstop Ted Balin, a nine-year vet who lost his regular job to Billy Velasco in the spring. "They can't use a guy like Balin? Let's grab him," said Peter Jones.

"He has to clear waivers, or else we eat his full salary. If we wait twenty-four hours, KC buys him out and we sign him for a song," said Eddie Paris, adding, "We also save the thirty-kay purchase price."

"Nice work, Eddie," said the player-manager to his GM.

Nice work indeed! The signing of a player before clearing waivers caused the Commissioner to cancel the transaction. Balin would have to clear waivers again, less than twenty-four hours before the clock struck midnight, tolling the postseason eligibility deadline.

"I can't believe a guy who's been working in the front office for ten years doesn't know how to handle the goddamn paperwork," an exasperated P.J. complained to his coaches, Irv and Stash. Peter spat, "What the hell does Eddie do in his office all day long?"

"He's never missed a lunch date with Dana and Barry," mused Irv.

"I believe that," groused Peter. "It's quarter to twelve. There's no way we can get the paperwork to Manhattan in time. This is great... just great!"

"Can't we file the papers by e-mail?" Stash wondered.

"The Commish doesn't trust BLB's computer net and the player's union won't approve using electronic signatures." Peter propped his legs on his desk, folded his hands behind his head, and mumbled a variety of profanities as the clubhouse fax machine clicked away.

"Willy's fan scans," said Stash. "They take selfies and scan them and then she signs them and sends them back. They come in for her anytime of the day or night."

Peter's face froze. "Fax machine!" he hooted. "A fax transmission is a legal document, stamped with the date and time and a facsimile signature." P.J. rang up the GM. Eddie, who hadn't run since he grounded into a double-play in his last big league game a decade ago, scurried about his ballpark office to fax a signed copy of Teddy Balin's contract to Hamilton Fisher's office. Eddie called Peter a minute before midnight. "Done?"

"Done!"

"Hey, P.J.?" asked Stash. "What happens to Marty?"

"Marty's my regular shortstop. I'm not going to mess with him. Teddy can play third base, left field, and pinch-hit. It doesn't matter to him or to me. We've got him. That's the important thing."

The player who had the most to lose by the arrival of Teddy Balin was Glenn Harmon, the yeomanlike third baseman, whose overall unspectacular adequacy paled next to Balin's superior glove work and proven ability to come through in the clutch. When asked his thoughts by Shane Hennessey, Glenn said, "Listen, we're out to win a pennant. If a game's on the line and P.J. sends Teddy up to hit for me, do you think I'm gonna squawk? Heck, no! I'll even let him use my bat." Willy thought: *This is definitely a different team from the Diamonds of New York.*

Teddy's debut with the Wolves was nothing less than fabulous. The KC castaway played third, batted in the number-two spot, and cracked a homer in his first ups at Pilot Field. He came within inches of homering again in the third inning, settling for a two-run double off the right field wall. Balin went five-for-five with six RBIs in the Wolves' 9-3 win over the Lonesome Strangers from Texas.

"Was it disappointing for you to wind up here instead of the team you've been with for so long?" Willy asked him.

Teddy narrowed his eyes, saying with a bittersweet tone, "The way I look at it, they let me down and the Wolves are givin' me a big chance and I'm gonna pay 'em back with interest." Harry Washington's performance in the same game was less inspiring than Balin's. "O wise and tired one," as Kevin and Marty called him behind his back, went oh-for-five, striking out all five times at bat. Eddie put out feelers for a substitute outfielder, first baseman, and designated hitter, which would allow the Wolves to drop poor old Harry from the postseason roster, although the GM was annoyed that P.J. preferred a "rent-a-player" to promoting a minor leaguer from the AAA Wichita Arrows. The first two names bandied about were Ortega and Teague, which prompted the player-manager to gag. Then, P.J. told Willy "the perfect candidate" was none other than Omar "Lassie" Lazzaro, another winter league alumnus, who clobbered twenty-three homers for Dos Laredos of the AA Tex-Mex League. Alas, Peter's best laid plans went awry owing to another paperwork snafu by the "Big Cheesehead," Eddie Paris. Peter raged about the GM's incompetence. "A technicality!" he growled. "Why didn't Eddie figure that out before the fact? What else does the front office have to do? We're the ones out there trying to win ballgames." Hence, still more of P.J.'s schemes were foiled. Sean Dunlap's eagerly awaited return from the Niagara Falls Rapids was doomed by a fractured wrist in the Class-A farm club's first playoff game. "I've got to use you where I need you, not where I want you," he told Willy. Without Dunlap, Peter had to continue her in the swing role of spot starter and long reliever.

"I don't think I'm cut out to be a closer anyhow," she argued.

"You're the only guy, excuse the expression, with, shall we say, the testicular fortitude to do the job."

Peter's arrogance angered Willy. "This isn't only about you and me, Peter."

"Willy, lighten up, please," he said, straining to smile.

Willy's expression softened as she moved in close and spoke to Peter, barely louder than a whisper. "The wise leader understands the wisdom of the feminine, the paradox of the *yin*..." Willy, pressing a finger on the tip of his nose, her eyes dreamy, recited: "By yielding I endure. The empty space is filled. When I give of myself, I become more. When I feel most destroyed, I am about to grow. When I desire nothing, a great deal comes to me." P.J. waited for Willy to finish and issued a subdued thank-you as she went out through his office door.

    Peter Jones, the youngest manager in the bigs, also one of the oldest position players on the team, whose family roots ran deep in the "blackball" tradition of the shadow major leagues, where speed and power were employed to win games one run at a time, locked the Wolves into standard Junior Circuit "slowball" by closing off their running game, such as it was. The Wolf Pack's best baserunners were McDonald, Toussaint, and Clay, all of whom collectively had been thrown out more frequently than they swiped, thus making base-stealing an unaffordable luxury in the closely contested divisional warfare that was raging. The team's inability to shut down opponents' running game was likewise a concern. At an afternoon practice at Pilot Field, P.J. sent Ted, Marty, Doug, Alex, and Glenn to work with the pitchers on a second base pick-off move. Nick Dolan had no such play, entirely relying on Diego Santamaria's arm to check opposition base-stealers. With Jed and Gene behind the plate, teams were running wild on the Wolves. Teddy went over Fred Teller's play from Kansas City, where the shortstop signals the pitcher, both count to five, and the pitcher turns and throws as the middle infielder arrives at second base to catch the ball and tag the runner. "It can work," said Teddy, "but everything happens within the base runner's line of sight. Smart and fast guys can just beat the shortstop to the bag." Then he laughed. "If the shortstop is scratching an itch..."

"Marty always be scratchin' hisself," Kevin wisecracked.

"...It can get embarrassing. The shortstop waits and no ball's thrown or a pitcher throws and there's no shortstop. Instead, we'll go to the second baseman, who can move out of sight behind the runner. Plus, it's always the pitcher's call. Signal, count to five, and throw to the second base bag." In running through the play, Brian and Willy, "the geezer and the girl," as dubbed by Alex, were the quickest and most accurate. Both made the pickoff throw with pure heat, on which neither dared rely when pitching to a batter. Yet Willy always paused or hesitated when pivoting with her right foot planted at the pitcher's rubber. She overcame the hitch in her move after several repetitions, but feared it would reappear in live action.

After the practice session, Willy and Teddy sat side by side on the grass. He said, "You know, we're the lucky ones. We get to go out and do it, but other people share the game with us by selling the beer, the hot dogs, the peanuts, or watching in the stadium, or watching on television, or looking at their baseball cards, or playing softball, or coaching little kids..."

"Or becoming a multimillionaire and buying a team," Willy snickered.

"Uh-huh, like Kermit and Miss Piggy," Kevin McDonald approached, speaking derisively of the husband-and-wife partners.

"Oh, come on now, Kev. Be nice," implored Willy.

"They're clueless. They bow at P.J.'s feet like he's the savior of the Buffalo Wolves, like he's a one-man gang or somethin'." The second baseman obviously needed to vent some hostility. "One minute he's actin' like the big brother and the next minute he turns into a freakin' dictator. He can't make up his mind. Is he a player or the boss man?"

Willy bit her tongue to keep from defending Peter, thereby alienating her teammates. *Hush up, Willy. Listen and learn. I can't!* Out she blurted: "Peter loves you, Kev."

"Oh, sister, please," Kevin groaned.

"I'm serious here." Willy reached for and clung to Kevin's hands. "He's your mentor and mine, too."

"I hear ya, Willy." Kevin continued thoughtfully. "It seems like P.J. became the manager instead of the manager becomin' P.J. Understand what I'm sayin'?"

Marty Slattery lamented, "We lost somethin' when Nick Dolan got fired. We lost our leader on the field, in the batting order, and in the clubhouse. Not the boss, the leader...He was our big brother, like Kevin says, and a best friend to any guy with problems, even personal stuff. We lost Peter Jones!"

In a fortunate quirk of scheduling, the Diamonds were to play the Skyliners in Queens and the Wolves went against the Legends Turned Cellar Dwellers in the Bronx over the Labor Day weekend. Willy gambled that an inbound call would go through to the visiting team's clubhouse at Flushing Meadow and key-padded the number on her cell phone. The D's game ended a half hour after the Wolves'. She tittered her foot and gnawed a fingernail as she sat on the hotel room's bed and waited for Paul Cello to come on the line. When he did, she just said, "I've been thinking about you." All she heard was a sigh. "I need to talk to you, Paul."

Paul said, "I wanna see ya. I miss ya, babe."

"Sure," Willy said, shutting her eyes tightly and biting her lip as she suddenly felt at once frightened and excited. "We're stayin' at the Halladay Inn on Eastchester Road, near Fordham."

Fifteen minutes passed and Paul was at her door. "You guys beat up on the Spankees real good tonight," he said cheerfully.

"You guys have clinched already," said Willy. "A month early!"

"Who would've thought at the start of the season that the D's and Buffalo would both be in first place?"

"We're nowhere near to winning it yet," she replied.

"Or that we'd be on different teams?" he said softly, unsmilingly.

"That doesn't hurt anymore," said Willy, tilting her head to one side and beaming happily.

Paul became animated, almost as if they were exchanging a series of emotions, each sending and receiving in turn. "You've got it together, babe. How do ya like doin' both startin' and relief?"

"It's okay, I guess." Her voice was now quieter, her smile more faint, and her head bowed, but her wide eyes stayed fixed on Paul's all the while. "Don't you need to get home?"

"I stay in town when we play the Amazin's. Who needs to drive all the way to Jersey this late at night?"

For a moment, Paul felt nervous as Willy looked at him so intently before saying, "The invisible wall that we both put up between us is about to come down. That line we never crossed..."

"Are ya sure ya wanna cross it?" he asked, scarcely above a whisper.

With her eyes closed, she answered, "I'm thinking about it." She raised her palms and held them open to him as if pressing against something. "How about we talk through the wall?"

Paul pressed his hand to hers. "We can always do that," he replied with a sad, half smile.

"And we always did," she said.

"I prefer chain-link fences, like on a ballfield," said Paul, and he locked his fingers between hers.

"Yeah," Willy laughed gently. "Me, too!" Still not looking away, she told him, "Thank you for harnessing my energy without breaking my spirit. You taught me more than how to pitch to batters...but you already knew that."

Paul, suddenly teary eyed, shook his head from side to side. "With me and Lorraine, it's..."

Willy loosened her grip on his hand and reached to cover his mouth. "Don't you dare mention her name."

"Sorry," he hissed, his expression pained.

"No, Paul, you don't understand what I mean," she said firmly. "For her sake, not mine! We're talking about you and me. If it's got nothin' to do with her, then she doesn't deserve to be humiliated. Does she?"

He shook his head solemnly, but then turned playful. "Ya got somethin' to say to me or what?"

"You know." She spoke with chilling certainty.

Paul averted his eyes, choked back a sob, and said, "Willy, I love you, too."

Willy raised her finger to the corner of Paul's eye and gently touched a tear. She brought it to her lips and said hoarsely, "What more can you give me than this?" Willy cupped Paul's face in her hands, kissed his cheek, savoring the salty wetness from his tears, and whispered in his ear. The most sensuous and alluring voice he ever heard said, "Now, how are Lorraine and the girls?"

"I thought ya said not to..."

"That's the way it is...in this life, anyway. Nothing's gonna change it." He pushed away, but she pulled him back. "See, I love them, too. They're part of you." She hesitated, barely able to keep her surging emotions at bay. "But so am I, Paul."

He winced, simultaneously laughing and crying. "Ya got more to tell me, don't ya?" he asked knowingly.

She smiled, her eyes once more closed, and replied, "Yes, I have lots to tell you, Paul."

Willy had been sitting in the lotus with Paul astride the side of the bed. He moved to a kneeling position. Then, absolutely instinctively and unpremeditatedly, she wrapped her long legs around his waist and they talked long into the night.

With their fingers, legs, and eyes locked, Willy looked at Paul and spoke, "I've met somebody." Willy observed as Paul blinked, averted his eyes, and tried not to react. "Look at me, Paul." Willy shook their entwined hands and yanked. She said, "Don't let go and don't take your eyes off me." He returned his eyes to meet hers. Then she sang her melodic laughter. "I zapped you in the gut, didn't I? I felt it from here." As his adorably shy smile crossed his face, she told him, "It's the same thing that happened when you thought I was hooking up with Fabian. Am I right?"

Paul raised his chin and frowned, then said in jest, "You bet I was jealous of Fabe. Was he good?"

"Nope, but he's so-o-o rich!" After the former teammates laughed raucously, Willy pressed onward. "Think how I feel, partner, knowing..." She paused to smash through an emotional wall. "I've never loved anybody so much...but I know I can't have you without hurting a big part of you, maybe even destroying you."

The most gifted catcher in pro ball told the most gifted pitcher, "I thought it would be easier when you were gone." Willy melted at the sight of his glistening, reddened eyes as he said breathlessly, "It was worse. Ten times worse..."

When he stopped short, Willy loosened one hand, raised it to his cheek, and told him, "Paul, I really, truly believe that you and me are soul mates. We've come together before and we will again, but it's not our karma to be joined in this life, here and now." Paul's lips parted to speak, but hesitated. Willy smiled and whispered, "It's okay, sugar. You can touch me."

Paul's free hand gently went around Willy's neck and shoulder. His incidental tracing of her skin with a fingertip jolted Willy with the erotic force of lightning.

"We'll just have to make one night last a lifetime, babe."

Next day at the Mammoth Stadium that replaced the "House That Colonel Ruppert Built" in the Bronx, Willy abruptly detoured on her patented jaunt from the pen to the pitcher's mound. Midway across the outfield, she knelt to scoop handfuls of dirt and let it fly off her fingers with her lips kissing a baby's breath of wind. She raised her eyes heavenward and invoked the names, "Joe D., Mick, Rog, and the Scooter." Then she intoned the spirits of the Lincoln Giants, Black Yanks, and Newark Eagles, teams that also played in the hallowed cathedral. When she reached the mound, as the game ball passed from Sadie to P.J. to her own hand, the booming voice of a classic rock DJ moonlighting in daytime as stadium announcer resounded: "Look out, the lady is back in town!" Aretha's "R-E-S-P-E-C-T" was her theme song. For five full minutes, waves of *"Macha! Macha!"* from the cheap seats contended with the higher priced spread of *"Wil-lee! Wil-lee!"* before blending into one clamoring standing ovation. Not one Pinstriper reached base from her entry with one out in the sixth to her exit with two outs in the ninth, the point at which P.J. judged it safe to bring in Chris Van Aachen. The young closer, his hair dyed yellow and orange today, stood wordlessly in awe as the fans who mercilessly booed and jeered the Wolves gave their second standing-O to the She-Wolf.

While the Wolves were in the Big Apple, Willy ventured into Manhattan for a lunch date with USTV's Rob DaSilva, who promised to heed her ban on sound bites and photo ops. "Just a couple of salads," he said. The kindred spirits met and they talked, drank, and ate baseball. When Rob told Willy that he saw her as a linchpin between baseball's past and its future, she shared her overwhelming sense that her career was somehow larger than herself.

"If you promise not to laugh at me, or use it on the air, Rob, I'll tell you a little secret."

"Absolutely," he agreed easily in his natural, off-the-air voice.

"Ever since my first game in the winter league, I felt like my Papp was right here." Willy patted herself on the shoulder. "Then, after spring training, I didn't feel him at my back anymore."

"Maybe Rube knew you were ready to fly solo," Rob observed with surprising sincerity.

"Don't you think I'm crazy?" she said with amusement.

Rob shook his head to say, "No, Willy, you're not crazy, but you're definitely obsessed."

Willy wiggled her fingers like tentacles reaching for Rob's face. "I'm not *ob*-sessed, I'm *po*-sessed," she snarled comically. "The ghosts of Jackie Mitchell and Toni Stone done jumped inside my body and said, 'Look out, y'all, we're back!'"

"I retract what I said before. You *are* crazy," he grinned and they shared a laugh.

Still playful, saying goodbye outside the restaurant near the confluence of Broadway and Fifth Avenue, Willy asked Rob, "Friends?"

"Friends!" he answered, wondering why she asked.

Willy smiled expansively and tapped two fingers on her lips. "Then give me a kiss," she commanded and he did.

CHAPTER 18

When Willy arrived at the stadium, late for the second time in as many days, Kevin confronted her in the visitors' locker room. "Where ya been? People been lookin' for ya!"

"What's it to you?" Willy asked with annoyance.

Hurt, Kevin squinted his eyes. "It don't mean nothin' to me."

As he turned from her, Willy took hold of his shoulder. "Hey, I'm sorry, Kev. I just need some space sometimes."

"Forget it," he said coldly with a forced smile.

The Wolves' brain trust took shape when Jimmy Mack Jones was added to the coaching staff. James was immediately pulled into a meeting with his brother, Stash, and Irv to review the lineup and schedule for the duration of the season. "I hate to say it," Stash said, "but Balin should be the everyday third baseman. Harmon's the kind of competent nice guy who clogs up a batting order. You hate to dump him because he puts out, but Balin can hit more and field the position better."

P.J. disagreed with a shake of his head. "Yeah, but...and it's a big but...if we go to the wire, the pennant on the line, I want Glenn with his glove, chasing the ball. He'll go head first, through the wall, and up into the stands. He'll kill himself to win. He's a throwback."

"All of your infielders are old school," said James. "They're all throwbacks."

"McDonald's got a little dog in him," laughed Peter. "Maybe we won't win it all, but we won't throw it away either, not with these guys."

James put in his first appearance in Buffalo after a brief visit with his family outside of Toronto. He offered Willy a big, warm embrace, calling her name with his sing-song voice and mile-wide smile. She brought herself close to him, raised her long-fingered hands to his face, and pinched both of his cheeks. She snarled, "You jive sucker! I heard you called me a *witch* down in Venezuela. Is that true, huh?"

"Hey, Willy Mae, let go my face!" She did, but stayed on her tippy-toes with her jaw jutting and her mouth turned down in half-mocking anger. "I never said ya *were* a witch. I said some guys *thought* ya were," James explained nervously.

"Yeah? So, you did say it!"

"Hell, ya were the best pitcher down there last winter. Ya know ya scare guys!"

"Do I scare you?"

"Yeah," he replied with conviction. Then he laughed, "Of course, all females scare me, even Katie and Amy."

"How're they doing?" she asked for his wife and eldest daughter, reaching to clasp his two hands and hold them between hers. "And Jimmy, Jeremy, and the baby?"

"Caitlin," James proudly pronounced his youngest child's name. "Good, real good!"

During Wolves' homestands, Willy rode mass transit to Pilot Field, talking and clowning with fans also en route to the game. Willy's rides became part of the local *zeitgeist*, although they occurred a mere twenty times over the course of six weeks. She never sat, always riding the railway as a strap-hanger, often wearing her brown, yellow, and orange Wolves' cap and warm-up jacket, usually given away by Willy as memorabilia to a teenager or younger child. She drove the Wolves' equipment manager to lunacy, resupplying Willy with hats and jackets. The Buffalo Wolves drew close to a million fans in the last two months of the season, selling out twenty-two consecutive home games and eclipsing their modest season's goal of 2,000,000 fans by 600,000 plus. Meanwhile, Willy and the Howlin' Wolves swept Milwaukee in the first of two sets of interleague games. She pitched three perfect innings of relief against the Brew Crew after beating them 2-1 as the starter the night before. Seven days later, after immolating the Rattlers of Phoenix, she pitched a nine-inning two-hitter against Detroit at Pilot Field, striking out eight and leaving the game tied 1-1. The Wolves went on to win it by Harry Washington's pinch homer in the eleventh inning, their second straight extra-inning victory over the faltering Music City Cats. Another win the next night would put the Wolves in first place by a half-game margin. Leading 3-2 in the eighth, Randy, pitching in relief of Sadie, gave up two hits in a row with none out. Peter sent Phil in to face a single left-handed batter and he walked him to load the bases. In the bullpen, with Chris standing ready to take over the mound, Willy and Scotty began clapping and stomping and wailed: *"We will...We will...Rock you..."* Amid their playfulness, Ferdie answered the bullpen phone after Chris got one out on an infield pop-up and nearly scuttled the game by hanging a curveball that would have gone for extra bases and plated two or three runs were it not for Marty's desperation grab and "Hail Mary" throw to Jed for a head-on collision and putout at home. With a lefty swinger due to bat, Willy expected the southpaw, Scotty, to get the hurry-up call, but, instead, Ferdie said P.J. was playing a hunch and giving the woman the nod. Quite relaxed from having loosened up earlier and stiff from throwing a hundred pitches the previous night, Willy lobbed half a dozen muffinlike throws to Jed. She didn't need to read a note card on the Motor City's clean-up hitter, Shigeo Yoshitani, a portly DH who hit thirty homers even in a bad year. Willy sidearmed two down-and-in sliders at his knees for swinging misses and slid the third strike overhand by the back door. Yoshitani watched the oblique angle cross the edge of the plate and let the bat fall from his hands as Willy leaped off the mound to the rolling thunder of *"Wil-lee! Wil-lee! Ah-ah-ahoo!"* The game was Scotty's to lose or save in the ninth frame. The free-swinging Motown Revue turned rabbit and put runners on base and in scoring position by bunting and stealing. With two away, P.J. called for an intentional walk to load the bases with a runner on first and prepared to bring an outfielder into the infield to prevent a run from scoring on a ground ball.

"Can't tempt fate in extra innin's again!" James warned with a shrug.

"How else can we play this sitch, skipper?" Stash asked rhetorically.

"Yo, Peter!" Willy leaned forward on the bench and tugged P.J.'s belt loop from behind. "The Grey Ghost!" was all she said.

Peter paused to think for a moment, then got it! "Tris Speaker played center field like a short fielder in slow-pitch softball. He barely played on the grass and threw guys out at first and turned double-plays from the outfield." Hence, five coaches and a dozen players in Buffalo's

dugout waved like traffic cops and Toby moved right behind second base. As the game climaxed, the hole created between left center and right center enticed the batter to pole the
ball out to the meadow, where the plodding Diego easily plopped the final out into his rawhide glove. The Wolves thus led the pack in the American East.

Upon morning's dawning, Scotty and Chris showed up on Willy's doorstep in a state of inebriated oblivion at 5:00 a.m. "You're lucky. If I'd been sleeping late, I'd be mad. Where've you been anyway?"

"We was at Gumshoes," slurred Chris. Willy confiscated their car keys, put the stupefied pitchers to bed on the sofa and in the spare bedroom, respectively, and headed out for her morning five-miler. Later the same day, after Willy cooked and fed breakfast to the hung-over pitchers, Kevin and Alex dropped in, as did Randall Craig. After an hour of watching the tube together, Sam Khoury–the brightest star in *Sportsworld* except the swimsuit issue–stopped by. "Off duty! No questions! No stories!" Kevin McDonald was definitely steamed at hanging with a wag during his chill time and Willy tried to defuse a tense situation as the playful peacemaker. Rather, as Willy soon observed, the trick may have been turned by Sam's hand on Kev's knee, her deep-eyed stare whenever he looked her way, her husky whispering as they spoke, and who-knows-where she groped when they were alone in the kitchen. Be that as it may, Kevin and Sam flew away together "to grab a bite to eat," they said, before that night's game–through which the second sacker seemed to glide with a smile on his face and a certain serenity despite an "oh-fer" evening.

Willy enjoyed her teammates, but she felt a sense of loss when most of the wives stopped traveling with the team as the end of the baseball season is concurrent with the beginning of the traditional school year. She especially missed Charlene Jones, Suzanne Clay, and Maggie Robbins, a warm and fun-loving woman in contrast to her aloof hubby. Willy and Charlene were nurturing a fond friendship, apart from their relationships with Peter, but Char, being a psychotherapist, had apparently decided Willy was emotionally "needy" and kept trying to draw her out. The more she did so, the more closed Willy became. Charlene was working per-diem as a therapist at an Erie County clinic, unsure about what sort of permanent position she should take. Strangely, Suzanne was the only other Wolf spouse with an active professional career. "She's got a law degree and runs her own real estate and insurance agency. "Maggie's a teacher," said Willy, sparking Char to huff, "She works part-time at a preschool. I mean, really! That's babysitting!" Charlene also found Dana Hawthorne's cute and perky attitude hard to take. "Just because you wear fancy dress-up clothes, it doesn't make you a grown-up."

    Of an afternoon, Willy neither spoke nor paused for more than a deep breath between practice pitches. She had been throwing for twenty uninterrupted minutes to Gene. She barely acknowledged his need to vent his frustration at "carrying Jed's jockstrap," and he spoke no more. Willy was methodical in each incremental step of her motion, delivery, and follow through, including bending deeply at the waist with her legs closed and straight as she picked up each new ball out of the bucket beside her right foot. No one had a clue that she was struggling to block out the constant pain in her inflamed shoulder. Randy, lacking the energy to throw hard, much less engage in a serious workout, had volunteered to download some Stevie Wonder and Smokey Robinson tunes from Willy's Running Mate to his e-Pod and go home later to burn a CD for Alma. Kevin stopped by the duplex to visit Sadie and Yolanda, then wandered out back, and sat next to Randy on the lawn.

"Watchin' the fly girl, bro'?"

"Best believe it," drawled Randy.

"She looks like she's dancin' ballet or somethin'. Understand what I'm sayin'?"

"I hear ya, man."

On this particular day, the two young Wolves took a needed break from the incipient pressure swelling around them and turned their attention to Willy's almost hypnotic concentration.

"She's somethin' else," Kevin murmured.

"That she is. Maybe as good as Old Folks," said Randy, referring to Brian. "Sure enough better than me!"

I ain't talkin' 'bout pitchin', Randall."

"Oh, I gotcha," Randy said slowly. "People be whisperin' lately. They say there's a mystery man on the scene."

"She ain't told me that," Kevin snapped behind narrowed eyes.

"Why should she tell you?" Randy sang out and laughed on a high note.

Kevin McDonald mumbled, "I could tell if there was somebody gettin' next to her. I know women. A lady in love gets crazy, starts actin' stupid."

"Y'all just wishin' it was *you*, brother man," Randy told him with a wink of his eye.

"Still, I'm tellin' ya. I'd know." Kevin pointed his forefinger at Willy in motion, her eyes riveted on her target as she delivered a rippling sidearm fastball. "Fallin' in love means losin' control. And that lady, my man, is seriously in control."

CHAPTER 19

As the month of September waned, Brian notched his nineteenth win and tenth shutout, but the Wolves lost two of their next three games. Boston refused to play dead, keeping Buffalo on top by knocking off the Birds in Baltimore. Then, the Birds of Toronto swooped into town and swept the Wolves out of first place by beating them at Pilot Field on Monday and Tuesday. The Wolf Pack came back with a nail-biting 6-5 victory the following night, bolstered by three perfect innings of long relief pitched by Willy B. and took their last day off of the season only two games behind the front-running O-Birds.

Willy gaily chattered with Ernie Arnett, the Wolves' crusty play-by-play curmudgeon, during his postgame wrap-up. Ernie was the last of a breed, one of the grand old baseball voices whose kind was fast fading into obsolescence and extinction. Ernie took his cue, looked into the camera's eye, held up two fingers, and announced: "Make the victory sign..."

"They used to call it the peace sign!"

"...and ask the man for Valentine."

"Or woman!"

"Victory *is* peace, Willy."

"No, *peace* is victory." Willy took off her cap, put it on Ernie's scantily haired head, wrapped her arms around his neck, and pressed her cheeks against his crinkled, grinning face.

"I'm Ernie Arnett for Buffalo Wolves baseball. This is a copyrighted telecast of Big League Baseball, Inc. and Buffalo-Niagara Broadcasting Company...We'll be back on Friday night, friends, when Brian Robbins takes the mound against the Mighty O's of Baltimore." When the cameras shut down, Ernie said, "I wouldn't let any other player goof around like that with me on the air." Willy took back her cap and planted a kiss on his forehead. "Not that either," he croaked. "You just did a beer commercial, you know. Doesn't it bother you?"

"Not really," she cocked her head and replied pleasantly. "Beer has been a part of the game since the get-go. Baseball, hot dogs, apple pie, and card games in the clubhouse, right?"

The four-way race in the American East was the only divisional or wild-card contest left going into the final ten days of the regular season. The media trained on Buffalo versus Baltimore. Dave Warren gathered taped footage for USTV: "Brian Robbins! Imagine that story...forty-one years old and about to be a twenty-game winner again." Old Folks chewed gum and smiled. "Thank God for the split-fingered fastball!" Dave declared, "It'll make a great made-for-TV movie, but first the Wolves have to get by the Birdies in a crucial series this weekend." The overused word, "crucial," would be used over and over again tonight.

More than 42,000 people packed into Buffalo's mini amphitheater to see Brian, the idol of greying baby-boomers, rack up number twenty and start off a three-day thrashing of the mismatched Chesapeake Canaries that would put their beloved Big Bad Wolves on top of the heap. Few doubted the result, but it wasn't to be. Brian was knocked out in the third inning and charged with a 7-1 defeat. The heavy hand of fate weighed down on Sergio Jiminez the next afternoon as Baltimore again trimmed the wild and wooly Wolf Pack, 8-5. The

Wolves tumbled into fourth place, three games off the pace, with eight games to play.

"P.J.'s magic is done gone," someone quipped.

"The Wolves are dead," quipped someone else.

"The toast of the town is just plain toast!"

Peter Jones gathered his downcast troops in the locker room after Saturday's game. "Here's where we stand," he said. "Baltimore's magic number is six, which means all we have to do is win eight in a row, if they lose eight in a row, we clinch on the next-to-last game of the season." Everyone laughed. "If...If..." Peter shouted and pointed demonstratively. "If Toronto and Boston split their remaining games! Otherwise, if the Balt-O-Birds win four and we lose two, or they win three and we lose three, we go into a tie-breaker a week from Monday. Don't even ask what happens if it ends up in a three-way tie." P.J. let his crew quiet down before he said, "We had a helluva year and gave it a helluva run. We've got nothing to be ashamed of...No hanging head, understand? So, let's go out tomorrow, play some ball, have some fun, and hope for a bleeping miracle."

Six days later, the Wolves rode a six-game winning streak into first place, on the brink of wrapping up the divisional championship, needing to win one of the two games left to go. Willy moved into the starting rotation for the stretch run, beginning the Wolf Pack's incredible roll by shutting out Baltimore in the last home game of the season on Sunday, going the distance, striking out six, and walking five. The Pack traveled to Tampa and harpooned the Sunfish by taking three straight. Only Monday's game was close. Brian tired and left the game at 4-4 in the seventh and Randy was credited with the win on Teddy Balin's ninth-inning home run, his fifth since becoming a Wolf. Sadie, with the aid of homers by Peter and Diego, and lots of relief help from Scotty and Chris, got his nineteenth win, 9-5, on Tuesday. Everybody was hitting. P.J. homered again the next night, number thirty-nine, putting him one up on Toby in their personal contest. Marty and Glenn, typically light-hitting infielders, dinged two homers apiece during Miracle Week. The workhorses of the staff throughout the season had been Robbins and Jiminez, but Woody Naulls emerged as the money pitcher, winning his twentieth game for the Wolves on Wednesday evening, eliminating the Beantown Super Sox in the process. Toronto's J-Birds had tasted blood by putting Baltimore's O-Birds on the ropes, whipping them twice in three days earlier in the week. Next came time for the Toronto Terminators to chomp on Wolf meat, but Willy knocked the Sky-Jays out of contention with her second consecutive shutout, a sparkling three-hitter. Twenty-four hours later at Skydome, Brian carried a five-run lead into the fifth inning in his third try for win number twenty. After two were out in the inning, he gave up four hits and two walks, and the Wolves' lead was cut to one run. Phil Abruscato came on to blank the Yardbirds the rest of the way for the victory. Sadie went to the mound on Saturday, in quest of his twentieth win in the one hundred sixty-first game of the year. The atmosphere was supercharged as P.J.'s Cinderellas took the field. If Baltimore obliges by losing in the Bronx, a win by Buffalo cinches the American East flag. Alas, the Toronto Eliminators led 4-0 and Sadie was in the showers. Phil again was on the mound to get the third out, but, by the time he left the game in the fourth, it was 7-0. Out in the bullpen, Willy listened to Ferdie argue with Irv about sending Phil into the game after working four innings only twelve hours before, but Peter called the tune. Randy leaned toward Willy's ear and cupped his mouth, saying, "P.J. should've sent *you* in, but he's thinkin' playoffs already. He wants ya rested. Bad mistake!" Shane Hennessey would publish and Dave Warren would print similar critiques of P.J., wondering if he had gone off the deep end with such bizarre overuse of his pitching staff. As Toronto's fourth run of the inning crossed home plate, Ferdie called, "Teet!" The one-time flamethrower was as surprised as anyone, having pitched only once since P.J. took over the reigns. Tito Melendez grabbed his glove and headed out of the pen. "Hey!" yelled Ferdie. "You ain't even warmed up yet."

"Screw the warm-up!" Tito yelled in reply, then turned around and walked back to where the other pitchers sat. "This is gonna be the last one for me, amigos." He stood in front of Willy. "Wish me luck, Macha."

Willy rose to give Tito a big squeeze and a kiss. "Next stop, Cooperstown, Teet!"

With a hearty laugh, he hollered, "I'm not gonna crap out today. Watch!"

On the field, Peter didn't speak to Phil when he held out his hand for the ball. The Wolves, like the Diamonds, disdained the fashionable passing of the game ball from pitcher to pitcher. P.J. didn't so much as look at Phil back in the dugout and the young pitcher was shattered. Peter Jones thus displayed both sides of his nature by giving Melendez the ball for his last hurrah and turning his back on Phil. (*Dear Mr. Abruscato, Welcome to the player-manager's doghouse. Please go in and don't come out until we call you. - P.J.*) To even the most *simpatico* observer's amazement, Señor Melendez shut down Toronto through the seventh while the Wolves came back for three in the fifth and two more in the sixth, making it a 7-5 ballgame. Randy gave up an insurance run in the eighth and Toronto iced the game when Buffalo's last-minute two-run rally fell short. The final score was 8-7. The team's collective depression evaporated in the clubhouse when the scoreboard showed the Balt-O's losing 4-0 in the Bronx, clinching at least a tie for first place for the Wolf Pack.

In the locker room, Peter tapped Willy on the shoulder, both literally and figuratively. "I'm giving you the ball tomorrow, cuz."

"On two day's rest?" Willy asked, surprised but happy.

"It's not like you haven't done it before. I'm going with the player who has the hot hand, as the old saying goes."

"Why not Woody?" she asked. "It's his regular turn."

Peter smiled sheepishly, nearly apologetically saying, "If we wind up tied with Baltimore, we go to a one-game playoff on Monday. Woody's the man I want out there."

Her ego slightly bruised, Willy chirped cheerfully, "As a certain someone I know likes to say, we'll see!"

Willy had Sunday morning breakfast with Alex, Chris, Scotty, and Randy. She munched on fresh fruit, crispy rice cereal, and organic tomato juice, while they gulped down huge quantities of muffins, pastries, donuts, pancakes, waffles, eggs, home fries, beans, and Canadian bacon. Then she shocked her companions by taking a bite of Alex's prune danish and licking a dab of the frosting. Each of the players had carried along a Sunday paper to read about their baseball universe through leisurely eating. Willy checked the sports section in *Today USA*. "Hey, if Jake wins today, he'll break Rube Marquard's single-season record and could carry over to next season for a chance to break Carl Hubbell's record of twenty-four in a row. Wow, good going, Jake." Clearly, Jake's individual goal led Tom to start his ace in the otherwise meaningless final game of the regular season, which coincidentally allowed the manager to kick off the playoffs with Big Gil Douglas, who posted a 20-5 mark. The Diamonds wilted in the previous few weeks, losing 14 of their last 28. If they maintained their July and August .800 winning percentage, they had a shot at the all-time high of 116 wins, but had to settle for breaking the 1930 Bronx Legends run production record, the D's becoming the first team ever to plate 1,100 runs in a season.

An hour before Willy was scheduled to start the one hundred sixty-second game of the season, she called to pitching coach Irv Ashmont, "Irv, would you catch my warm-ups?"

"What's wrong with Ferdie or one of the catchers?" he asked.

"You're the pitching coach. I need you to see if I need to make any adjustments."

Thoroughly flattered, Irv grabbed a fielder's glove. Of course, being a lefty, he couldn't use a standard catcher's mitt. He said, "Remember, I'm a little guy. Don't knock me over."

"I won't," chimed Willy. "Let's just do a quick five or ten minutes."

Willy's arm was enveloped in dull soreness, but she had no acute spasms from her tendinitis for several days. She started with a four-seam fastball, then switched to a two-seamer,
Papp's heater, straight overhand.

"Ow! Hot damn, Willy! That stung. Don't air it out like that warmin' up."

"Sorry, Irv," she said, as she stepped into her third practice pitch. She threw three sliders–overhand, buggywhip, and sidearm–and three curves, three ways before a sequence of cross-seam fastballs. Again she tossed fastballs, fingering the top seams for the overhand motion and the bottom seams for the other two deliveries.

"Ow!...Okay!...Okay!" Irv responded. Then she ran through the fastball sequence again. With each successive pitch, she twisted her back, kicked out her left leg, and swiveled her hips a little further to add speed to the overhand heater. She projected the image of Sandy Koufax's fulcrum, where the pitcher's entire body balances on her back heel and expels her full volume of force through her fingertips. "Aw, man! Stop it, Willy. What're ya tryin' to do? I know ya got a kick in your high, hard one, but you're gonna blow out your arm. You're not a fireballer. Stay within yourself, girl." Willy acted the repentant pupil and confined her remaining throws to offspeed and breaking pitches. When she finished, Irv beckoned. "Ya know whatcha doin', dontcha?"

After pitching more than three hundred innings in less than twelve months, Willy was ready to throw Papp's heater the way it was meant to be thrown. "Tell Peter I'm ready to push the envelope, Irv."

Sportsnet was cablecasting the game nationwide and Ernie Arnett would call the action for fans in western New York: "Willy B. is making her twenty-first appearance for the Wolves, her seventh start. She has a record of five wins and one loss overall, and she's a perfect four and zero as a starter. Your Buffalo Wolves have won all six games she's started...On the mound for the Jays, Len Freedcoyne. Known as 'Moondoggie,' he's quite a fan favorite here in Toronto. The native southern Californian has been known to take a surfboard out on Lake Ontario every now and then, but this afternoon he'll be trying to hold back the tide of the Wolf Pack to the American East title."

In the first inning with two outs, Toby Clay knocked a 2-1 pitch over the left field wall. He was greeted at the plate by Peter Jones, who said, "The kid's feeling his oats today!"

"Don't make me do it all myself, old man!"

"Watch me!" Peter winked before grounding out to end the inning. Quitting halfway to first, the player-manager pulled off his plastic helmet and saw Toby's shoulders heaving up and down with laughter. "Next time, that is." The home run hit by Toby loosened up the Wolves and staked Willy to a one-run lead as she went to work in the bottom of the first. A double and a single scored a run for the Bluebirds and the game remained tied one-all until the Wolves broke it wide open with four runs in the fourth. Toronto's skipper, Barney Ginsberg, was forced to remove Moondoggie from the mound without retiring a batter in the inning. Diego Santamaria homered and Toby hit his second long-ball shot of the game, making for a 6-1 Wolves' advantage in the fifth. P.J. benched Zaremba and Harmon to put Omar Lazzaro and Teddy Balin at first and third base for more punch from the left side. When left-hander Dean Clark came on to pitch for the Jaybirds, Peter sent Harry Washington to play first. Omar left the game after going hitless; his dull, frustrating, and short career with Peter and the Wolves was over. Willy allowed only four hits and four walks through the seventh. With one out in the eighth, Kevin McDonald muffed Mitch Reed's pop-up. Mitch got around on a heater just shy of 100 MPH on the radar gun, but he swung a fraction of a second late. Kevin tried to catch the ball with a one-armed, back-handed stab. It dangled in the webbing of his glove and slipped through his fingers as he struggled to hold onto it. Mitch then took a brazen, long-stridden lead off base.

"Willy B. pitches well from the stretch position," called Ernie. "But holding runners on is known to be one of her few weaknesses."

Willy and Jed worried that Grant Summer, the Snowbirds' first baseman, batting clean-up, would pull any pitch thrown out over the plate. So, she threw him a sidearm fastball in tight, and another low at the knees, hoping that he would go after one or the other to make contact to try to move Reed into scoring position. Instead, she fell behind, two-and-nothing. Willy hit the strike zone with a slider, but missed with two more breaking balls. Summer wasn't taking Willy's bait, opting for the free pass to first. She saw bodies moving around the Wolves' bullpen. "Shit!" she swore. Jed signaled three fingers, the slider, but she shook him off. "No more breaking balls!" Jed put one finger straight down and Willy stretched, swiveled, pumped, and fired the heater over the top to Joey Reynolds. A blue-sleeved right arm went up: oh and one. Again, Jed flashed one finger on the second set of hand signals. Once more, Willy came over the top, and Reynolds swung and missed: oh and two. This time the Toro-Jay's third baseman would be expecting the heat and Old Ironsides flashed three fingers on the third sign. Willy delivered the slider from the buggywhip. It broke low and Joey checked his swing. Jed just sat back in his crouch, waiting. There was no need to signal as Willy stretched and threw at ninety-five-plus velocity into the perfect stride and widening eyes of Joey Reynolds. The ball sailed up and in and exploded off his bat. As Willy twisted her neck upward, she held her glove to shield her face so that, amid the cacophony of the crowd, no one would read her lips or hear her shrieking the four-letter word Paul Cello couldn't coax her to say. The ball flew its inexorable course, but seemed to hang in midair for the briefest of instants. It was an unseasonably sunny October day in Toronto, and Skydome's roof was open, allowing a breeze to ripple from right field to left. "Ah, the wind, a divine wind–*kamikaze*!" Willy turned her gaze eastward. "Are you burning incense at the altar for me, Hideki? Thanks!" Diego, the catcher by trade forced to labor in the outfield, turned to play the carom off the wall. His strong-armed throw winged past Marty, the shortstop positioned to take the cutoff, to Teddy, standing on the turf alongside the mound. The third baseman relayed back to Kevin at second, holding Joey to a double. Both runners scored with ease. *Phew, you just dodged a bullet, Willy!* Scott Morrow, the right fielder, stepped in to bat. He had already drawn two walks from Willy. Peter was standing, arms folded, on the dugout steps. Randy and Scotty were throwing in the pen. "Stay right where you're at, Peter Jones," Willy said aloud. Jed flashed one on the first sign. She shook it off, unintentionally letting out an audible "No!" Willy paused long enough for Joey to take three long and two short steps beyond the bag at second. She held the ball in her glove behind her back and clenched her fist, dangling at her side. *He got it*, she thought, as Jed Guerin positioned himself. *Be there, Kev!* As she counted to five, she rolled her eyes without moving her head to see that there was no suspicion from Maurice Duquesne, coaching at first, and Chick Montague, the advisor at third. Willy's adrenaline surged. She kicked her left leg skyward and dug a snowball-sized clump of red clay out of the mound with her spikes as she guided a windmilled bullet halfway through a spinning pirouette into Mr. McDonald's sweeping glove to slip the tag on Joey's outstretched fingers.

Ernie Arnett heralded, "She got him! Man, oh, man! I've never seen a quicker or deadlier pick-off move to second base in thirty years of baseball." The television screen showed Willy leaping for joy, laughing, running, and trying to evade the slaps of her fellow Wolves on the head, shoulders, back, and backside. "At the end of eight innings of play, it's Buffalo six, Toronto three...How about that?"

"Look at old Maury," said Marty as he hugged Willy and pushed her toward her mates brimming over the top of the dugout steps. Maury Duquesne peered at the female phenom through his spectacles, mouth hanging open, but smiling, in unabashed disbelief.

Willy called to the Jay's coach, "Miss the sign or what, Maury?" He held out his hands, gesturing helplessness, shrugged, tipped his cap to her, and walked away.

Today USA's headline for tomorrow's editions was already being transmitted via satellite to its regional sites throughout the United States: "BUFFALO BALLET BULLET NAILS JOEY, THE JAYS, AND FLAG." At that very same moment, Barry Kaplan, Wolves' co-owner, was on the phone, making sure all was in readiness for playoff tickets to go on sale in Buffalo at 9:00 sharp, Monday morning. The team's web site's allotment would be depleted in less than half an hour.

The Wolves added two runs in the top of the ninth. In the dugout, Matt Zaremba pointed to the scoreboard, which showed: BAL 5 NYY 4 FINAL. Willy also saw that NYD lost as well, thus no record winning streak for Jake to carry into next season. She felt neither malice nor glee. "This is it, guys! The O's won," said Peter. "We have to hang on here, or else we have to go down to Camden Yards tomorrow."

"Are you bringing in Chris to close?" asked Willy.

"It's all yours, Willy B.," Peter replied.

Three minutes later, she was one out away from setting down the side in order in the ninth. With Skybird center fielder Kyle Ingram coming to bat, the still full house gave the visiting pitcher a standing ovation and the catcher in the rye signaled for the pitch. She threw a sidearm fastball for strike one, a buggywhip low-and-away slider for strike two, and hyper-velocity heat for strike three.

"What a performance!" Ernie Arnett trumpeted. "Six strikeouts and a five-hitter for Willy B. She joined this team in the middle of August, won six, worked in just about half their games, pitched two shutouts and three complete games in the final stretch...and the Wolves are the division champs! As the Old Professor, Casey Stengel, used to say, 'Who woulda thunk it?'..."

P.J., the guiding hand of the Wolves, was breathless and his voice rasped while speaking to the cameras. "Last winter in Venezuela, I said I might have to hit a home run and Willy would pitch a shutout for our team to win. Today, Toby hit two and Willy gave up three runs and I popped it up a lot, but we did it, and it took all twenty-five guys to do the job. I've never played with a tighter...*and looser*...bunch of guys. They don't quit. They just come to play."

Willy was sweaty, grimy, and giggling like a loon when the Commissioner approached and took her hand. Hamilton Fisher said, "Willy, I've been waiting to see you face-to-face since the goings-on in July to apologize for any embarrassment my office may have caused you. You're a remarkable woman, Willy Beal."

"Oh, well, thank you." She wasn't sure what he expected her response would be. She smiled self-consciously, although feeling pleased, and they parted.

For close to two hours after game's end, the visitor's locker room and clubhouse in Canada's Skydome swarmed with wags. Eventually, Peter and Eddie Paris interrupted the jabbering gibberish of uncountable concurrent interviews to announce that Dana and Barry had
rented a hospitality suite at the hotel for a "clinch" party before catching the plane for their short hop home to Buffalo at midnight. Needless to say, for all but the nondrinkers–Willy, Glenn, and Teddy–the celebration was well underway behind the screen in the clubhouse,

out of cameras' view, and continued in the air from takeoff to touchdown. Peter nursed a low-alcohol beer, hoping for some semblance of alertness at the pitchers', hitters', and fielders' meetings, called for tomorrow afternoon.

The divisional playoff would start on Tuesday night, followed by the second game on Wednesday afternoon. The Buffalo-Cleveland match-up was being billed as "The Mistake on the Lake vs. the Mistake on the Other Side of the Lake" by the snobbery of the New York City and Hollywood dominated media elite.

Willy spent a lazy morning after her triumphant performance for the Wolves. Scotty, Chris, and Randy, hung over but in good spirits, came to visit Willy at her half-duplex, which felt more like home each time she returned to it. She took the time to look through the months-long backlog of fan mail, accumulated and forwarded via Manhattan, New Jersey, Cheyenne, Alexandria, and St. Petersburg as well as Buffalo. She could only read a small portion of the cards, letters, and faxes, and would never be able to reply to more than a few unless she hired an assistant. Thus, she cherry-picked those which caught her eye. There was a letter from Old Saint Pete with a very familiar name. She tore it open as if it were a longed-for gift from a loved one. She read:

Dear Ms Beal,

I wrote three letters to you but I guess they got lost or you did not have time to read them cause you get lots of mail. The whole world calls you Willy so I hope you don't mind if I do too. How are you? I am fine. Last spring I was the starting catcher for the softball team. I hit 10 home runs. The team had a good season. We were runnerups in the states. I want to pitch next year if they let me. Tanya pitched a few games then she had to sit out cause she got pregnant again and is going to have another baby. I plan to help her with day care and stuff so we can play together next spring. We want to go play in college together then we want to be the first female pitcher and catcher battery in Big League Baseball. Everybody in St. Pete use to love the Diamonds. Now we hate them. We love the Wolves now. I tell people I know you and they don't believe me. Thats okay cause I think you will remember who I am if I see you again someday.

    Your friend,
Jennifer Smith

    Randy saw Willy's trembling chin and tears spilling from her eyes as she sat amongst her mounds of mail. "Why are ya cryin'?" he asked.

    "Cute girls with big hair always make me cry." Jennifer, Tanya, and who knows how many other young women were informing Willy's unvoiced answer to Foster Castle of *Newsline* four months ago: "I am *not* one in a million. I am the tip of the iceberg. We are legion!" Willy went to her lap-top, retrieved Jennifer's e-mail address from Wahoo, and sent a message to her and Tanya, promising a block of playoff tickets.

    Willy experienced a brief spell of guilt as she locked herself in the bathroom to treat her aching shoulder with alternating hot and cold cloths out of sight from her visiting bullpen buddies. Her 6-1 won-lost mark and her 2.34 ERA were the best on her team's pitching staff, although she didn't have enough games or innings pitched to qualify for official recognition as one of the league's top pitchers. Her team was a perfect seven-for-seven in games she started and her combined lifetime record was 7-6. *Willy, you can sit on your butt and retire with a winning record.* Her conscience told her to let Peter Jones know that she had a sore arm. The team's physician should check her. If she needed surgery, she ought to go on the disabled list and be replaced on the postseason roster rather than risking a flare-up or producing at less than full effectiveness, thus hurting her team. Willy looked at herself in the bathroom mirror and shook her head, wiggling the most famous set of pigtails in pro sports. "No way!"

CHAPTER 20

The day after the Buffalo Wolves won the American East was overcast and intermittently rainy, well matched to Peter Jones's mood. The decisions on the final twenty-five-player roster had to be made and the options weren't what he anticipated. There was no choice but that Harry Washington would be on the list, having no other legitimate reserve to pinch-hit and sub in the outfield. The once-forgone conclusion of keeping Tito Melendez off the list was negated by Sean Dunlop's untimely injury. As a result, Peter retained a thirty-nine-year-old pitcher to whom he wouldn't give the ball even once if he could help it.

Now that the Wolves wore the Eastern Division's crown, the media coterie expanded from local to national. Due to Willy B.'s presence in the spotlight, the sports wags on hand at Jacobs Field covering the Buffalo-Cleveland series were joined by feature writers from all sorts of publications and TV programmers of the news-magazine variety, playing the "woman's angle." Sam Khoury cackled gleefully to Willy, "Everybody's sucking up to me because they think I have your ear. I love it!"

Willy and Rob DaSilva met for a "quickie" interview on the field an hour before the divisional playoff's opener. "Do you expect to start in this series?" Rob asked.

"Nope!" she answered.
"Why?"
"Because!"
"Because?"

Willy giggled and counted one, two, three on her fingers. She said, "Because of Robbins, Jiminez, and Naulls." Then she elaborated, "Peter's used a three-pitcher rotation since August and I'm the swinger, spot starter, and first *guy* out of the pen."

"Any thoughts or predictions about how the series will go?" he prompted.

"Rob, the Wolves will win if we do all the things a winner needs to do." She stopped talking and smiled for the camera. "Which is to take it one game at a time, stay within ourselves, put the ball in play, see the ball, play our game...I'm sure you've heard all this before, haven't you, Rob?"

"Indeed, I have."

Baseball's time compression folds once again, as the twenty-six-week season breaks down to a five-game miniseries for the lucky ones, the final eight teams. The other seventy-five percent of Big League Baseball's population has gone home.

"This is a short series. Best three out of five! If we start out flat, it can turn around real fast. It'll be a long, cold, lonely winter," said Peter. "Your job, Willy, is to be ready to come out of the bullpen to go long, medium, or short whenever I need you."

"What if you don't need me in relief?" she asked him.

"If we're up two to one, you'll start game four," explained P.J. "If we're down two to one, I'll have to go back to Woody." Superstition inhibited him from considering that there might not be a fourth game if his team swept the first three.

In game one against the Clevelanders, Woody Naulls nursed a six-run lead into the eighth inning, buoyed by homers from Peter and Matt Zaremba. When the hometowners came back for three tallies, Peter sent Willy in to K.O. one batter, Domingo Walker, before yielding to closer-saver Chris Van Aachen. Shane Hennessey wrote in the *Buffalo Times*: "P.J. pulled his starter too soon." Given the confounded scheduling of day-following-night games to accommodate network TV and cable viewers in four time zones, the Wolves were off the field after midnight and right back on it the next day at noon. Sergio Jiminez took a five-run lead and turned it over to P.J.'s Kiddie Korps–Scotty, Randy, and Chris–who transposed it into a three-run deficit. After Toby's two-RBI long ball capped an eight-run eighth inning, Willy came on to hold a 13-8 advantage. She gave up hits to Domingo and catcher Allie Ponte, but notched the save with a bell-ringing, game-ending strikeout. Shane wrote: "P.J. left his starter in too long." Regardless, Buffalo's Wolf Pack was two-thirds of the way to the pennant series.

During the seventh-inning stretch, Peter was amused and amazed. "Char's been watching me at work for fifteen years and she never does anything except put her hands together once in a while." He pointed to the front row of seats behind the road team's dugout, the area reserved for family, friends, and VIPs. "You go, girl. You go, girl. Oh, yeah! Oh, yeah!" *Clap! Kick! Snap! Sway!* The Wolf Mates and their pups, led by Charlene, Maggie, Yolanda, Suzanne, and Dana Hawthorne, the ball club's baroness herself, were dancing and singing, bumping and grinding, for their hero on the hill, one of their own.

Back home at Pilot Field after a day of rest, Brian Robbins took the ball to the mound and drew a standing ovation before serving his first pitch. A few minutes later, Willy's eyes clouded when Peter stepped up to bat in the bottom of the first inning. *"Batting fourth, for your Buffalo Wolves, the designated hitter, number fifty-five...the Leader of the Pack!"* The crowd, 42,000 strong, exploded: *"Pee-Jay! Pee-Jay! Wolf! Wolf! Ah-ah-ahoo!"* P.J. took a bow, grounded out, and took another bow. Brian the Bold curved, knuckled, and split-fingered the Buckeyes through four perfect innings until he inexplicably "lost it," coughing up two straight walks and a three-run home run to batting champ Domingo. Homers by Jed and Mattie Z. put the Pack back on top, 4-3, but after handing Allie Ponte a base on balls with one down in the fifth, Old Folks called to the Wolf's den: "I'm done, skipper."

    Flabbergasted, P.J. watched Brian drop the ball to the ground like a rosin bag and depart even before the playing manager emerged from the dugout steps. Since it was too early in the game to set up or save, Willy had been perched at the far left corner of the bench, spitting sunflower seeds with her comrades in arms. With an angry shirk of his arm, Peter yelled, "Get the hell out here, cuz. Let's go!" Without benefit of a proper warm-up, Willy fired three fireballs in the mid-to-high nineties to notch her first of seven strikeouts before the afternoon was done. Toby's homer with two aboard in the fifth put Buffalo up, 8-4. The Lake Erie Tribe collected four hits and four walks off Willy's alternating heat and sliders, one run plating when a fly ball by Hit Man Walker was misjudged by Andre the Wolf in shallow right field. With an 8-5 victory, Willy and the Wolves won a weekend of free time–the first one in six months for any of them–and advanced to the next round for the American Circuit pennant.

Willy couldn't depart the field for ninety minutes after the game ended. Live minicam-eyed interviews with Buffalo-Niagara Broadcasting, Sportsnet, USTV Sports, and USTV News blended into a continuous stream as Willy gradually came down from her adrenaline-induced euphoria. "The first woman ever to post a playoff win...The outstanding pitcher in this playoff series...Willy, you got a win, a hold, and a save in three games...You notched eleven kays over seven innings...How does it feel, Willy Beal?" *I feel fine, thanks! How are you?* Peter Jones refused to answer questions about what happened to Brian Robbins. Jimmy Mack Jones told Ernie Arnett: "Willy was huge out there for us. Toby Clay rocks. The Wolf Pack rules. The Buffalo Wolves are for real and P.J's magic is for real. Next on the menu is chicken fried steak in Kansas City, Mo.!"

Usually at this time of year, in another place, in another life, Willy finds herself channel-surfing and flipping through the daily rags to keep up with the postseason pairings. This season, rapt in group self-absorption with her Wolves, Willy's info about baseball's final acts was sketchy, tardy, and of secondary import. KC and the Sunshine Band, featuring Crawford, Estrada, Velasco, and Jorge Walker, put the torch to the Anaheim Halos' championship hopes, but not until the tenth inning of the third game did the flame die. The Angelinos battled to their last at-bat as fully half of their broken-hearted fans exited the Orange County stadium by the seventh inning to beat the rush hour traffic on the freeway. On the National side of Big League Baseball's coin, San Francisco's Goliaths toyed with St. Louie's Chicken Wings. Cliff Allyn, Bruce McElroy, and good friend Memo Alvarez threw the wins, as Kitsuragawa and Ruggieri wrestled the saves. *"Fe-fi-fo-fum!" Swat! Thud! Splat!* Meanwhile, the Diamonds of the Meadow quickly turned the wild card "Miami Miracle" into the "Florida Flounder." Big Gil and Jake pitched back-to-back shutouts at the Mammouthlands as 74,900 voices chanted: *"Squish the fish!"* The all-whitewash clean sweep was completed at Joe Robbie Field, where Roy Burton performed a "hat trick" with three home runs. Willy was one of an estimated 20,000,000 television, cable, and satellite watchers on "Thank Goodness It's Prime Time," Friday night. Unlike Cam Hammersmith and Jeff McCarty, the talking heads simulcasting on USTV and the Millennium Channel, Willy wondered about Tom Vallery's pitching deployment. Sandy Lee sat down after completing five innings. "He's reached his pitch count quota," said Cam. *Is his back flaring up again?* Then, Tom wheeled out Laddy, Jay, Zinger, Tim, and Larry faster than skate-hockey line changes on the fly. "The D's skipper, who literally *wrote* the book, is playing it *by* the book, using his relievers for three or four batters and switching on cue..." said Jeff. *Am I crazy or is Tom using a playoff game to let all the pitchers get in some work, like a tune-up in spring training?*

  Unquestionably, the Wolves went into the championship series as the underdogs. Five teams in the league won more games than the Wolf Pack, who had a losing record against the club they needed to beat to win the pennant. Also, four of the seven games were to be played in Kansas City and Buffalo's won-lost record on the road was the poorest in the majors. Only in the third, fourth, and fifth games would the Wolves have the home-field advantage. Nationwide sentiment was on the side of the Cinderella team with its three best known and most appealing personalities, Jones, Robbins, and Willy B. Superstar. However, the best conventional wisdom in favor of the Wolves was that they went into the league championship hot from a fresh killing spree and KC–not unlike the New York D's in the rival circuit–handily won their division as well as their first playoff and was thus fat, lazy, and stale. The Wolves fought hammer and tong and came out on top only by virtue of two winning streaks, separated in time by more than two months. Yet, historically, teams that clinch early and win by a large margin do better in postseason play. Fans and pundits live for momentum, but, as Peter Jones well knew, the easy winners of the regular season win championships simply because they are better teams.

  Willy Mae would again await P.J.'s call in the Wolves' bullpen. The October Classic isn't necessarily the best show of the season. The greater emotion, desire, and intensity are often vested in the pennant series. As if to set the stage with just the right mood, KC's glamour boy and home run king, Kenny Estrada, opened his mouth. Kenny was in fine form for the media waggery on the day of rest prior to the series opener, giving his mates Crawford, Swifton, and Walker vague praise before polishing his own apple. "Buffalo thinks they've got some guys who can play. Ha! Except for maybe Robbins and Santamaria and Jones and Clay, there's nobody over there who can carry my jockstrap."

  "What about Willy Beal?" a wag inquired.

  "We're gonna kick her cute little ass all over the ballpark."

The Wolves gathered at Pilot Field for an hour-long workout on Monday before an afternoon of meetings to pore over the scouting reports on the Kansas Citians. Only Toby, Teddy, Brian, and Willy engaged in serious exercise as their mates mostly lollygagged. In the meantime, P.J. met with his brain trust–catcher Jed Guerin and coaches, James, Stash, and Irv–to size up the opposition.

"Teller is going with Anthony, the righty, in game one and Vera, the southpaw, in game two," said Peter. "We'll counter with Brian and Sadie and Woody should be able to start the third game at home." Stash and James both grimaced when Irv informed them that Woody had awakened with a mild case of tendinitis in his left bicep and was being dosed with cortisone.

"Our goose is cooked if he's goin' on the shelf, li'l bro'," James said sardonically.

Peter's response was to arch his eyebrows and resume his impressions of the KC team. "Jon Anthony had a monster year, twenty-two wins, but Nino Vera is still the ace of their staff. It looks like Telly is going to start Tucker in game three and use Guy Lavoissier out of the bullpen. He could be real tough. I'm more afraid of him than Bud Levy, their closer."

The guys on the team were nearly as interested in the broadcasting lineup as they were about the other club. Peter recited: "I can't tell whether big boss Arnie Rutledge is still running the USTV network or not. Rob DaSilva and Ernie Arnett will call the American series with Dave Warren doing the pregame and postgame shows. Zack Traynor, McCarty, and Hammersmith are doing the National."

"How did both Cam and Jeff get in there?" wondered Willy.

"I suspicion the hand of Mister Fabian," exclaimed James. Shoot, he can buy and sell all three networks. I'm sure his opinion...spelled capital O with a dollar sign...carries some weight."

"If the D's get into the series, it'll be Rob, Jeff, and Cam, not Zack, doing the games," said Peter. "In the Series, Warren will do the pregame, postgame, and face-in-the-crowd stuff. DaSilva is working on a special series preview."

"What about Ernie?" Willy asked.

"The only spot open for Ernie is to be Zack's second banana on the radio...if we make it in. It's because they say he's a *homer*, a cheerleader for the home team."

After the westward flight and hastily checking into their travel lodge on Harry Truman Boulevard in Independence, the trio of pals–Willy, Charlene, and Maggie Robbins–went to the hotel's third-floor fitness center, where several players, wives, and kiddies splashed in or around the pool.

"Do you swim, Willy?" Charlene asked.

"Nope!" Willy came back, using a let-me-be nuance.

"I believe everyone should learn how to swim. What if you fell off a boat?" Charlene challenged Willy.

"I won't go on a boat," she muttered defensively.

At pool side, Kevin, wearing a florescent "banana hammock," was the center of attention for a flock of giggly, acne-faced young womanhood. "I feel like pushing them into the pool to cool them off," declared Char. Woody's mate, Kim, turned heads and surely got a rise out of one or two sets of bathing trunks previously in relaxed repose as she slithered by in a black mesh French-cut swimsuit. She not only looked like a model, she was one by profession. "I'd love to shove *her* into the pool," said Maggie, caustically, but with a smile. Charlene loosened the tie on her robe and looked down upon her own sensible one-piece ensemble with a frilly skirt. "It's not fair. We straighten our hair, color it, fry it, and curl it again, shave our legs and armpits, tweeze and pluck our eyebrows. Then we squeeze zits and paint our faces. Now we have to shave and wax our pubic hair just to wear a bathing suit!"

"Don't be such a slave to fashion, Char," said Willy.

"Why do we women do that to ourselves? It's not fair," she concluded.

After eating breakfast, Willy arrived late for aerobics at the hotel with the Wolf Mates. Donna, Marty's wife, hooted loudly, "The wives are all here and Willy the Queen Bee stumbles in halfway through."

"Sorry, girls," said Willy, out of breath from hurrying.

Willy scoped out the room to find Charlene and Maggie, who called to her, "Willy, don't come and kick up your heels next to us heavy girls with that stick figure of yours."

"Speak for yourself, Maggie!" Charlene shouted heartily.

"I never lost the extra tonnage from my last pregnancy." Maggie pinched her middle. "It's only baby fat. Ha!"

As the music sounded throughout the room and the dance-exercise workout resumed, Charlene whispered to Maggie, "I think you really hurt her feelings. She started to come over to us, but she stopped dead in her tracks. Willy's very sensitive and she really needs to be with us. She's with the guys all the time."

"She's tougher than you think she is, Char."

"And she's more vulnerable than *you* think she is, Maggie." Charlene added, "She's carrying a lot of emotional baggage inside." She directed her gaze to Willy's effortlessly graceful kicking and jumping. "Look at her sad, puppy dog eyes, Maggie. The bounce is gone out of her step."

"Okay, Charlene! If you're trying to make me feel like shit, then I feel like shit." Maggie skipped over to Willy and yanked her by the arm over to where she and Charlene were working out. A mismatched threesome that seemingly clustered together by cultural necessity comprised Yolanda Jiminez, Marcelina Melendez, and Inez Santamaria. Sadie's wife was short, plump, and gregarious with an adorably happy face. Charlene left the group after aerobics to take some laps in the pool. Willy stayed to chat in a circle formed by Maggie, Suzanne Clay, Inez, Yolanda, Marcelina, and Donna. Kim Naulls was nowhere to be found, which was fine as far as all were concerned. Jed's spouse, Maureen, and Esther Washington joined the women. Esther, not coincidentally, came when Charlene wasn't with the group due to the bad feelings between P.J. and Harry. There was talk of the children, the ball playing husbands, and the fans on the road, punctuated by a fair measure of male-bashing.

"I don't believe some of the stuff we've had to put up with. All over the league! When the Wolves were losers, nobody cared. Now, they throw things at us."

"They call Toby *Dopey*...He really hates that."

"I got drenched with beer."

"The kids and women are worse than the men. The filthy mouths—'eff the Wolves' and 'Buffalo sucks' and 'Buffalo sucks and Willy swallows'! It's really awful."

"It's downright scary."

Charlene rejoined the cloister of womenfolk after about fifteen minutes, smelling of chlorine and looking flushed and happy from her dip in the pool. She squatted next to Willy, who greeted her by wrinkling her nose. "You snuck a cigarette, didn't you?" Esther abruptly excused herself and separated from the group. When they walked together into the changing room, Willy chose impulse over restraint and entwined her arm with Charlene's. She responded by gently clasping Willy's fingers.

"You know something?" said Willy. "There were some really beautiful people in New York—Michelle Filsinger, Leota Douglas, and Thelma Judd—but I can't even imagine the Diamonds' wives sitting around and talking like we just did."

"Different ambience, I guess," said Charlene, easily clinging to Willy's hand. Charlene patted herself dry with a towel and pulled a sweatshirt and pants over her swimsuit, saying that she would go up to her room to shower. Willy had already peeled off her body stocking and stepped into a pair of denim slacks.

"Am I embarrassing you, Char?" Willy asked, as she put on her bra backwards, hooked the eyelet at her tummy, twisted it, and pulled it up.

Charlene said, "No, not a bit. You seem happy, Willy."

Willy bubbled, "I'm very happy."

Willy had craved intimacy with Peter's wife since last winter and it was being attained at the price of her probing. "You've seen Paul recently, haven't you?"

Willy said yes and nothing more, deliberately frustrating her friend.

While the better part of North America's households ate supper, the Wolves arrived at Ewing Kauffman Stadium to practice and prepared for a long autumn night's work. On the sidelines, Willy initiated a workout of synchronized pitching, face-to-face with Phil and Scotty and side-by-side with Randy, Chris, Tito, and Sadie. The object was to imitate one another's motion simultaneously, concentrating on the mechanics of throwing rather than the act and its result.

"We breath in synch, wind up in synch, and throw in synch," said Willy. "The stop becomes a bridge between windup and stretch."

Sadie Jiminez said, "I watch Macha. She's me in a mirror."

Willy hailed loudly, "*Mira?*"

Sadie cackled, "Same thing! *Mira, mira*! Look at the mirror!"

There were a few familiar faces in the blue team's dugout. In addition to Youngblood Crawford, Jorge Walker, and Billy Velasco, there was KC's veteran catcher, Mike Jacklin. Teddy Balin, full of talk about revenge against the team that cast him off, was true to his real nature by inviting Fred Teller and family to dinner. Teddy also went out of his way to offer words of encouragement to rookie Ryan Sanchez, the young infielder KC called up to take his place. With less than two minutes to clear the playing field for the pregame ceremonies, Willy's eye caught Youngblood Crawford's approach.

"What's up, Blood?"

"How're you doin', Willy?" They shook hands rather formally. "Listen, I just wanna say good luck to you." She smiled. He acknowledged with a quick nod, then said laughingly, "I gotta tell you somethin', though. You, lady, have caused divided loyalty in my very own family. My pop said to me, 'Play your best, son, but I got some real mixed feelin's.' He's got a soft spot for you, Willy."

Willy beamed fondly. "Armstrong Crawford is quite a guy, Blood. Send him my love, please."

"I"ll do that, thanks. And, again, good luck, Willy!"

Not without argument and reluctance, P.J. agreed to allow two TV sets in the dugout
and bullpen for players to watch, but the sound had to be off. The player-manager lectured: "The tunnel vision of baseball on the tube gives the viewer one actor at a time, either a full head or body shot of pitcher or batter. Baseball has always been too fast and too complex for the medium of television."

With Peter on the field to exchange lineup cards with Fred Teller, Willy asked Ferdie to turn up the volume on the portable TV near his feet. Rob DaSilva's voice came through: "The seamless web of baseball history is very much a part of the series. We're in Kansas City, home of the modern-day franchise and the Monarchs and Blues of another era. There are family ties as well. Youngblood Crawford isn't the only second-generation major leaguer on hand for this championship series. Amos Jones, father of Buffalo Wolves' player-

manager Peter Jones and coach Jimmy Mack Jones, and Rube Henry, grandfather of Wolves' pitcher Willy Beal, played
together on the Kansas City Monarchs in the 1940s and '50s. Nostalgia aside, Amos and Rube never played on a world champion. Maybe that missing piece of those two families' legacies comes to an end as this series, and perhaps the next one, unfolds."

    As the Wolves in the starting lineup took turns being introduced and booed by the partisan crowd, Dave Warren announced, "Looking at this Kansas City team, they put together a banner-winning season by making some controversial changes in their defense alignment. Estrada moved from third base to first base, Swifton moved from right field to third, and Crawford moved from center field to right. Dion Lovelace took over in center, Jorge Walker went into left field, and Velasco replaced Balin at shortstop. Each move strengthened the club in the field, and only Velasco represented a sacrifice of offense for defense."

    Rob DaSilva stated for the benefit of the audience, "Bear in mind that the Wolves lost all six games played against this team this season."

    "Shut that goddamn thing off!" P.J. ordered.

    A member of baseball's exclusive 300-win club, Brian Robbins waited twenty years for a championship ring. He suffered a heart-breaking defeat in game one, losing to KC's Jon Anthony by 1-0, although allowing only two hits. The lone run counted after a hotly disputed call made by umpire Jack Finigan in the eighth inning. In the first seven innings, only two KC runners reached base. Catcher Mike Jacklin drew a walk on a three-and-one pitch to open the inning. Jorge Walker bunted and sacrificed Jacklin to second, bringing up Billy Velasco. P.J., a life-long hater of the intentional walk, waved to issue Billy a free pass to pitch to Lovelace, the number nine hitter. Willy looked into the TV screen in the Wolves bullpen and saw Brian put down his fist, calling for a pickoff play on Jacklin at second, the same routine used by Willy in Toronto eight days earlier. The pitcher whirled and threw to the second baseman, who swooped from behind to cover the bag. Kevin had the ball in his glove and tagged Jacklin on the arm as he slid hands-first into the base, but the ump called him safe. P.J.'s cries of "No, no, no!" set off a vehement, nearly violent, argument. Twice, James and Stash pulled the son of Amos away from Finigan and the umpiring crew chief, Ken Crenshaw, only to have P.J. break free to go at it a little more. On the air, the USTV cameras showed from three angles and in slow-motion that the play was perfect and McDonald made the tag before Jacklin slid back. However, the safe call stood. Lovelace then flew out to Andre in right field. Youngblood Crawford came to bat with Jacklin still on second and Velasco on first. Blood lined the ball over the glove of Glenn Harmon at third base, driving in the game's only run with a single. Robbins deserved to win, but Anthony pitched the best game of his career, allowing the Wolves only four hits. With two outs in the ninth, Diego hit a grounder that should have been the easiest kind of play for shortstop Billy Velasco, but he threw high over Estrada's head for a two-base error.

 In the broadcast booth, Rob DaSilva called the action: "The Wolves are threatening in the ninth with a runner on second and Harmon up. Anthony is in a bad spot, but the situation doesn't seem to affect him." Ernie

Arnett said, "Telly has had the left-hander, Lavoissier, warming up in the bullpen, but he isn't ready to make a move." Anthony fanned Glenn on three curveballs, ending the game. "No pennant playoff has had a more impressive start," declared Rob. "Kansas City defeats Buffalo, one-nothing, with twenty-two game-winner Anthony pitching a four-hitter and nineteen game-winner Robbins pitching a two-hitter. It's only the third time in postseason history that a pitcher has lost a two-hit game." Ernie added the comment, "This evening also witnessed the first serious dispute of this year's postseason, as umpire Jack Finigan called Mike Jacklin safe on a pickoff play at second base, when our video-tape replays showed the runner clearly to be out, providing the break enabling Kansas City to win."

The game ended just shy of midnight and the two teams met for their second *tete-a-tete* at two o'clock the next afternoon so as not to conflict with the Diamonds' game from San Francisco that night. The players were more numb due to the boob-tube-stroking scheduling than stunned because of their opening game defeat.

"It'll be the sinkerballer versus the screwballer," said Rob, as he introduced game two on USTV. "After the superlative pitching of Anthony and Robbins last night, we're looking for more of the same today. Sergio Jiminez...known as Sadie...who has not pitched a complete game since mid-July...is on the mound for the Buffalo Wolves. Fred Teller's choice is veteran ace, Antonino Vera." The duel failed to develop as Vera was relieved in the fifth, trailing 3-1. Nino simply wasn't at his best. KC punched eight hits and drew three walks off Sadie. The Royal Blues had plenty of chances to score, but each time opportunity beckoned the team's weakest hitters, Velasco and Lovelace, came to bat and failed to help. As Rob told the USTV audience, "KC might have chased Sadie out of the game in the very first inning, when they scored their only run. With one out, Glenn fumbled second baseman Gordon Trapello's grounder. Kelly Swifton then singled, sending Trapello to third, and Estrada tagged a base hit to left, scoring Trapello and putting Swifton on second base."

Ernie warbled, "There's action in the Wolf's pen. Two righties are up to throw, Randy Craig and...as you can hear by the mixed reaction of the Kansas City fans in the right field seats...Ms Willy Beal." As he spoke, the Wolves' second base pickoff play struck again. "This time the runner is out. No question about it," said Rob. "Taking a look at the replay, Kevin McDonald has the ball in hand as he leaps to block the runner, Swifton, off the bag." That was the second out and Sadie got rid of the side by whiffing the journeyman designated hitter, Wesley Middleton. Telly brought Guy Lavoissier into the game and he gave KC two and two-thirds scoreless innings. KC's closer, Bud Levy, pitched the ninth with his team behind, 3-1. Velasco messed up Jed's grounder, and the Wolves' catcher took second on Marty's ground out. Andre then hit a ground ball that should have been the third out, moving Jed to third. Teddy Balin, the vengeance seeker, came to bat. Ernie Arnett intoned, "Balin replaced Harmon at third. That makes three third baseman for the Wolves in two games, the other one being Alex Suarez. It looks like Peter Jones is determined that everybody plays!" Teddy singled for the only hit off Levy, bringing Jed home to score an unearned run and making the final tally Buffalo 4 Kansas City 1. The Wolves thus evened the series at one win apiece and looked homeward for a weekend at Pilot Field.

By the time the Wolves and KC were ready to get game three underway, Cliff Allyn had outdueled Jake, 3-1, on Wednesday night and Big Gil brought the Diamonds back with a 4-2 victory the next evening in the other league's championship series. After a day of leisurely rest and relaxation, Willy went to the park at seven o'clock Friday night, feeling calm and pleased with her teammates' performance. Peter welcomed her at the clubhouse with what was becoming his customarily gruff scowl. "Goddamn! Woody's arm tightened up on him. He can't even grip a flipping ball," said Peter. "You're on, Willy!" Willy yelped with joy, felt jittery and weepy-eyed as she put on her uniform, panicked about the KC batting order, warmed up with Jed twice, and took a cold shower before game time.

USTV's coverage of game three began with a video essay on Willy, narrated by Rob DaSilva. "Willy Beal joined the Wolves in the middle of August, posted a six and one record, starting seven games and relieving in fourteen others. She threw two shutouts in the last week of the season, beat Toronto in the final clincher, and pitched an opening round win over Cleveland last week. Tonight, Willy B. Superstar is starting in place of twenty-game winner Woody Naulls, scratched with a sore arm..." Then Ernie provided the counterpoint: "On the mound for Kansas City is Adrian Tucker, who came over from Philly in a mid-year trade..."

Willy stood at the mound to make her practice throws when Jed, wearing his gate-keeper's armor, walked directly to her instead of waiting for Gene Tyler to finish warming her up. She looked at the old, salty catcher expectantly. "See this here?" he asked, pulling a small, square-cut piece of sponge from inside his oversized mitt, which he needed because of Sadie's knuckler, Woody's sinker, and his own arthritic reflexes. "You stung my palm good five or six times against Cleveland with that heat you brought," he said. The woman smiled at Jed. In the cozy confines of Buffalo's home-sweet-home field with more than 40,000 howling maniacs turning the cool and breezy nighttime air to warm and toasty with their frenzy, Willy handcuffed KC's Blue Monarchs by using her sidearm, buggywhip, and over-the-top deliveries, her breakaway and backdoor slider, her hopping offspeed fastball, and the pure-heat fastball. The other star of the game was Marty Slattery, the pint-sized shortstop, who knocked two of the Wolves' five hits, a single and a double, and scored a run. Willy pitched to only thirty batters, threw less than a hundred pitches, and didn't walk anyone. She punched out four, spread five hits over five innings, and received flawless support in the field. Tucker was nicked for four hits in three and two-thirds innings. Tuck walked Diego, the lead-off batter in the fourth, and struck out Glenn, but Mattie Z. singled to left, moving Diego to second. Then Jed singled to center, scoring Diego. Willy chuckled at the elder present catcher driving in the younger former catcher. "They only hit when it counts," as Paul used to say. Next, Marty drilled a base hit to left, but fast fielding by Walker held Matt at third. Telly came onto the field to pull out Tuck. In came Lavoissier: Andre popped up, Kevin grounded out, and the inning ended with three Wolves stranded on base. The home team's offense went completely dead after Lavoissier stepped onto the mound. Only one runner reached first base and that was Kevin, who singled when two were out in the seventh. After Willy fanned Middleton to end the top of the eighth, Telly called on Levy to pitch the bottom half of the inning–three up, three down.

In the top of the final stanza, DaSilva called the play by play: "Youngblood Crawford at the plate, oh-for-three tonight and one-for-eleven in the series...He had an RBI-single in game one off Robbins...Crawford swings at the first pitch, right at third baseman Teddy Balin. There's one away in the ninth."

"Buffalo leads by two runs," Ernie said.

"And take a look at the lady on the mound!" Rob said.

Willy called time, amid chants of *"Wil-lee! Wil-lee!"* She waved her arms high above her head. She held a finger to her lips, pumped a one, two, one-two-three beat with her clenched fist, and leaned to one side. With a hand on her hip, she cupped her ear with the other hand, then raised it to wave three times in a circular motion.

"Listen...She's getting her fans to change their tune." As *"Wolf! Wolf! Ah-ah-ahoo!"* resounded 40,000 strong, USTV's Russ Heyman directed camera number one to take a full
head shot of Willy as she returned to her stand at the mound and resumed her game face. The awestruck director whispered, "A second ago, she was clowning and playing off the crowd. Now look! The eyes of fury are burning holes in the batter's head."

Willy scorched a supersonic fastball past Trapello's textbook level swing, once, twice, and thrice. Rob: "Strike three...and we picked up readings of ninety-five, ninety-six, and ninety-nine miles an hour on those three pitches."

Ernie: "This postseason is witnessing the transformation of Willy Beal into a power pitcher, friends and neighbors."

As left-hand hitting Jorge Walker swung under a ninety-five mile per hour hopper for strike one, rival pitcher Jon Anthony uttered, "Wow!" Willy threw an overhand slider, one-one, a sidearm offspeed fastball, one-two, a sidearm slider, two-two, and another offspeed fastball from the buggywhip. "Ball three!" Rob prepared to deliver: "And the three-two pitch...Checked swing on an overhand slider...Strike three called! It's over."

Ernie wrapped up: "Willy Beal, substitute starter of game three, shuts out Kansas City, scattering five hits, posting a two-to-nothing win, and putting Buffalo up two games to one in the championship series..."

As her jubilant mates slapped high fives, low fives, and sky fives, Willy stood with Marty on camera to share the "player of the game" award and split the gift to charity between a battered women's shelter and a halfway house for runaways, both in Buffalo. Willy tried to evade the media gnats by exiting the ballpark immediately after her postgame sound bite with Dave Warren, bypassing the locker room and clubhouse, but she was blitzed by a mob of wags blocking access to the runway that led to the service gate. The *impromptu* pool interview became too chaotic with the sweating hoard of men and women, wielding pens, notepads, tape recorders, video cameras, and photo cameras, surrounding Willy, pushing each other, redundantly repeating one another's questions, and complaining that they couldn't hear her answers. The gathering herd moved *en masse* to Pilot Field's press room. It was much smaller than the wags' war room at the Meadowlands, but the Wolves, unlike the Diamonds, didn't make the reporters pay for sandwiches and soft drinks. On stage again, a question came from a male wag that Willy hadn't seen before.

"On a personal note," he began.

"Oh, no, here we go again!" she sang comically, rolling her eyes, and bobbing her head.

"Isn't it true that your well known principles against the use of drugs and alcohol stem from the fact that your father was an alcoholic and a drug addict?"

"What?" she articulated slowly and softly, a look of disbelief blanketing her beautiful face as her eyes widened and her stomach churned in pain.

"Wasn't he a military vet, who exhibited symptoms of mental illness and experienced a number of psychotic episodes, ultimately leading to his death by suicide?"

There was a dreamy look in her eyes, seemingly confused and disoriented when she spoke, "Excuse me, but I don't know your name."

"Vann Hartshorn of the *Inquiring Eye*," he said politely. Every professional class has its own caste strata and the Brahmin elite of sportswriters, sportscasters, and the lesser intelligentsia of feature reporters had encountered an Untouchable, an Outcaste in their midst. Snorkling, coughing, and throat clearing sounded and expletives voiced by serpentine hisses. "Didn't your father commit suicide?" Hartshorn was being adamant.

Willy's expression was blank. She looked for Sam Khoury and fixed her eyes as if speaking only to her to say, "His name was Eddy, not Edward...Eddy, like the tides and currents of the sea! He said that's why he joined the navy." She let out a tiny laugh, but quickly stopped, her face again expressionless. The room was starkly quiet but for nervous fiddling of implements and scuffing of soles on the floor. Her body language suggested that she would say something more after a drawing of breath, but she grimaced, covered her face with her hands, and fled the room. Only Sam pursued Willy. She found her in the lavatory down the hall, leaning over a sink and crying. Willy grabbed hold of Sam when she saw her, hugging her friend tightly and gasping frightfully. Sam rubbed Willy's teary, wet face.

"Why'd he have to do that to me, Sam? Why didn't he just call me and ask me about my father. I would've talked about Eddy, especially since the guy knew all the worst stuff anyway."

"He's a slimeball, working for a scummy scandal rag."

"It just hurt." Willy sobbed on Sam's shoulder for a moment, closed her eyes, and stroked her pal's hair as though she were the one consoling rather than being consoled.

"You know," said Sam. "You kind of like set yourself up for something like this sooner or later."

"How come?" croaked Willy, still clinging.

"You never talk about your father being an alcoholic. Just because you don't come out and say it, it doesn't make it go away."

Willy allowed herself to smile, saying, "Charlene says I don't deal with my issues. She says I submerge all my emotions in baseball, as if that's gonna resolve everything."

"She's right, pal."

Willy didn't respond. She let go of Sam and wiped her eyes and nose with an embarrassed laugh.

Then she told her, "He's been dead eighteen years, since I was ten. He came home from overseas all gung-ho and patriotic. He also came home hooked on pills, booze, and dope, but nobody knew that until later on. He tried to hide it. He even lied and said he got a touch of malaria overseas. And Mama, poor Mama–a nurse–and she didn't have a clue for the longest time. He was gonna get a good job and go to school at night on the GI bill, but things didn't work out...He just couldn't cope."

"He was an uncounted casualty of war," Sam said.

Quite calm and composed, Willy agreed. "But Papp said he was a victim, that he let himself be a victim...Did you ever hear the old saying? 'Life is a bear. Either you eat the bear or the bear eats you.' That's what Papp used to say. We weren't gonna be victims like my daddy was." Then Willy announced, "I gotta pee. Do you mind?"

"Go for it, pal." Sam heard Willy let out a groan of pleasurable relief. Sam said above the sound of Willy"s tinkling waters, "Most of the reporters out there respect you too much to use what came out today, or they'll report it in a sympathetic light. I heard Hennessey call Hartshorn an effin' asshole to his face."

"That was sweet. Remind me to thank Shane, will you Sam?"

CHAPTER 21

Willy sneaked into the park at noon on Saturday, four hours early, by flagging a ride with Pandit Bharat, the Wolves' trainer. He was on hand to assess the game-worthiness of Woody's arm. A like scenario was being played out 400 miles to the east at the Meadowlands as Sandy Lee Danielson underwent physiokinetic damage control with Ted Kyrokydes calling the shots. As Peter wrung his hands, Pandit and Doctor Stu Lacy pronounced Woody fit to pitch game four. With Jon Anthony starting for Kansas City, Telly felt sure that his "Diamonds of the Heartland" would square the series at two victories each. Likewise, Peter believed KC could do it, especially since Woody wasn't at 100 percent, while Anthony had a full three-day respite.

"They say that if you hope to beat Anthony, you have to do it in the early innings," analyzed Rob DaSilva, as Buffalo counted only five hits, but four of them came in the first three innings along with two runs. One single was all the Wolves could manage for the remainder of the game. Also, for the second time in the series, Anthony pitched without walking a batter. The KC crew got seven hits, but they couldn't get them when they were vital. The Missourians would have been shut out for the second straight game were it not for a home run hit by Wes Middleton, their veteran DH. The first run off Jon was scored by Andre, who crossed the plate following Toby's extra-base hit in the first inning. Toby, trying to stretch a double into a triple, was called out on a close play after a relay throw from Crawford to Kelly Swifton, playing third base. The umpire stationed to make the call was

Big Jack Finigan, the same basepath traffic cop who called Jacklin safe on the pickoff play in the eighth inning of game one. The crowd of 42,000 thousand, which already gave Finigan a tremendous booing at the start of the game, now really cut loose while skipper Peter Jones danced in front of the man in blue, wildly waving his arms and shouting. Peter's appeal to Crenshaw was rejected and the crew chief finally restored order.

"A manager who also bats clean-up for his team can't let himself be ejected from a postseason game," DaSilva remarked. "And this time," added Arnett, "Big Jack's call is on the money," as the video-taped instant replay showed that Toby was out and the ump was correct. However, the booing continued throughout the game. Second baseman McDonald came to bat in the third inning with two away, hitting Anthony's curveball high over the right field fence for the first homer of the pennant series. The Wolves' 2-0 lead held until the seventh, when Middleton pounded the ball out of the park for KC's only run of the day off Woody.

"The American Circuit's two winningest pitchers paired off..." pronounced DaSilva, "...and Woody Naulls sends Jon Anthony down to defeat, two to one, and the Buffalo Wolves lead the league championship by three games to one."

After eating dinner in town with Stash, Irv, and James, Willy spent a quiet evening at her half-duplex. Only by switching her stereo console from disc player to FM radio did she learn of the Saturday Night Massacre in New Jersey.

Charley Novak's team blasted Sandy Lee out of the game in the first inning and buried the Diamonds, 12-

3, backed by the less than artful serves of Bruce McElroy and Memo Alvarez,
who somehow combined for the win despite passing out eight bases on balls. The big story, however, was not that San Francisco beat New York, but rather it was what Demeter Fortune said *after* the game. The National Circuit's game three on prime time drew a record number of network viewers and the Diamonds were the feature attraction. When they lost and went behind two to one in their series, the wags hounded the D's in the locker room and clubhouse.

"What went wrong?" was asked for the hundredth time as a score of microphones and hand-carried video cams trained on Demmy. The hitless narcissuperstar turned, aimed, and fired back: "It's only a fucking game!" *Beep! Screech! Whirr! Squeal! Bleep!*

"Incredible!" exclaimed a woman on the street, a man at the bar, and a face in the crowd. "Get a load of that guy! How many millions does he make? And he doesn't care? Well, *bleep* him, if you ask me." Thus, 'twas not the unspeakable adjective that ignited the furor, but the attitude that the shortstop expressed. The Diamonds' front office spin-doctors moved to damp the flames, bright and early next morning. Acting GM Alan Blaylock interpreted, "He meant to say, 'It's only *one* game'..." Field manager Tom Vallery excused, "We went through a nine-inning horror show. Nerves were raw." The owner of the team made light of it: "You know what they say. Ask a silly question!" Demmy himself apologized for losing his cool and misspeaking, but every newscast's sports segment worth its salt ditched Mr. Wonderful's morning-after apologia in favor of the carefully bleeped replay of his unedited original. Late

Sunday afternoon, as the Diamonds took their bows for the Meadowlands' home-team boosters, "Batting third..." *Boo!* "...and playing shortstop..." *Booo!* "...number eleven..." *Boooo!* "...Demeter Fortune." The Bronx cheers and Brooklyn raspberries blanketed the stadium longer, louder, and deeper than the throng's hissing how-do-you-do to the hated San Franciscans. The Meadowlanders reclaimed their good cheer as the D's beat the G's, 7-5, but Fortune remained emotionally orphaned by the fandom.

The Nationals were done with their game when KC and the Wolves suited up for their fifth–and possibly final–matchup, set for nine o'clock at Pilot Field, chilled by a blast of Arctic air from the north. Willy went shopping to purchase three sets of thermal underwear to insulate against the autumn on Lake Erie's shore. The longies did her no good at the ballpark and she jumped and shivered in the Wolves' bullpen during the pregame workout. "Aah! It is bitter cold," she sang to Gene Tyler as she bounced on her toes.

Dickie Leeds came over to Willy and Gene to talk about the Senior Circuit's fifth game, which Willy hadn't viewed. "One of your old buddies was the hero, Willy," said Dickie.

"Who's that?" she wondered.

"Bielski," answered the third base coach. Adam "Psycho" Bielski was Willy's ex-teammate from the Alexandria Dukes. "He swung at strike three, but the pitch hit him. He should've been out, but he goes up in the ump's face, kickin' dirt, gettin' crazy...Then," Leeds continued, animating his recounting with rapid arm gestures, "Vallery appeals to the crew chief and he rules it a hit-by-pitch on a checked swing."

"Who were the umps?" Willy wished to know. "Derk Morfitt and Monty Guilford," Leeds replied.

"Ha-haa!" Willy was holding her stomach, bent over with laughter. "Psycho Bielski, Derk the Jerk, and Mount Monty...Moe, Larry, and Curly!"

"So, then," he said, losing his breath, trying not to laugh. "Whack job Novak goes nuts. He gets kicked out of the game, but he don't leave. The fans get into it, throwin' shit on the field..."

"I heart New York!" crooned Gene.

"Naturally, Bielski ends up scoring the run that tied the game," said Dickie with a wave of his hand.

The twenty-fifth consecutive sellout crowd to take in a ballgame at Buffalo's Pilot Field jammed the park, expecting to watch the ageless wonder, Brian Robbins, wrap up the pennant for the Wolves. Up to this game, the championship playoff was a pitchers' series, but the hitters suddenly and unexpectedly took it away from them. The Kansas City Outlaws started the slugfest in the first inning. Youngblood Crawford had but one hit in the four games played, a game-winning single off Brian in the opener. Blood got his second hit of the series, another single, on the first pitch of the game. Trapello, the second baseman batting second, scratched an infield hit to third baseman Harmon. "An infielder needs soft hands, not sticky fingers," observed Rob DaSilva. Swifton lined to Andre Toussaint in right field and Kenny Estrada stepped in to bat with one out.

Ernie Arnett: "The man at the plate led his league in home runs for the second year in a row, hitting forty-two."

DaSilva: "He seems to be immune to the spacious dimensions of the stadium in Kansas City. He hit forty-one last year."

Arnett: "There's the split-finger...one-and-oh, the count... Kenny is two-for-fourteen in this series with only one run batted in..."

DaSilva: "He batted .263 on the year with 121 RBI's and thirty-three stolen bases..."

Arnett: "Kenny stole thirty-three bases, but was caught stealing fifteen times."

DaSilva: "Here's the pitch from Robbins..."

Kenny Estrada, dubbed the "bust" of the series, whacked a slow curve into the overflow crowd in right field. That should have been the tip-off on Brian. For a right-handed hitter to pull the ball to the opposite field off a master of finesse indicated that Brian the Old had very little "stuff." Thus, the Wolves came to bat trailing by three runs. Antonino Vera pitched a strike to Andre, leading off in the bottom of the first, and Toussaint hit the next pitch for a home run. The score was Kansas City 3 Buffalo 1. Estrada came to bat for the second time after two were out in the third inning. This time, to show his versatility, he belted the ball into the left field stands, and KC again led by three runs. In the next inning, the Wolf Pack's attack began rolling. Peter Jones opened with a single, Diego Santamaria walked, Glenn singled, and P.J. scored. Zaremba popped out and golden oldster Jed Guerin hit a three-run homer into the seats.

DaSilva: "Four runs score in the inning, putting Buffalo ahead by one run...and that's all for Vera. The one-time pitcher of the year surrenders five hits and five runs in three and a third innings."

When Telly motioned for the other lefty, Lavoissier, Peter was actually relieved. He worried that Telly would have started Guy in game six and Jon Anthony in game seven back
in Kansas City. "I don't like those odds."

In the sixth, catcher Mike Jacklin hit KC's third homer off Brian, tying the score at five-all. Ernie crowed: "It's a brand new ballgame, as they say." The top of Missouri Mules' batting order was up in the seventh. Youngblood led off with his second single, Trapello sacrificed him to second, and Swifton singled to center field, scoring Blood and putting the Mules one run in front, 6-5. The wisdom of groupthink in the Wolves' bullpen was that P.J.'s sentimentality led him to leave Old Folks in the game too long, but the hit by Swifton eliminated Brian and Peter called upon Scott Bruneau. Rob duly noted: "Here in game five, this will be the first pitch thrown by a Buffalo relief pitcher, fans." Scotty walked Estrada. Then, when Middleton singled to right center, Andre made a wild throw to Glenn at third. Two runs scored and KC led 8-5. Then Scotty walked Jacklin, putting runners at the corners on first and third, and P.J. changed pitchers again. In came the titular ace reliever, Chris Van Aachen. The near-sighted wild boar of the bullpen pitched to two batters, Jorge Walker and Billy Velasco. Both singled and two more runs scored. KC now led 10-5.

The manager's nightmare revisited: The starter falters too early; the setup reliever fails to hold; the closer comes in too soon and gets bombed. Then the manager starts working backward through the bullpen. "The sluggers feast tonight," chortled Ferdie as he yanked his thumb at Randy, Phil, and Tito, calling out, "Next!"

However, when the phone rang and Peter walked onto the field for the third time in the inning, Willy was the one who got the call. After having been stunned mute by the traveling team's barrage, the Wolves' fans thundered for America's sweetheart as she trotted across the grass toward the mound. P.J. received her sneer with the words: "Don't give me any shit, okay?"

"What's wrong with Randy or Phil?" she asked regardless.

P.J. flipped her the ball and said, "Just get us the hell out of this inning, please." Then he stalked away.

From KC's dugout, Fred Teller put on the double-steal sign. Willy's Buffalo ballet bullet and two out of three successful pickoffs at second base by the Wolves' pitchers in the championship set shut down KC's running game. Indeed, if the call had gone the other way for Brian in game one, Telly and his Blue Mules would be home for a long winter's nap. Now, however, KC had a big lead and they were ready to run. Jed put his fist down for a pitchout. Willy wanted to get the ball high and fast into Jed so that he could get off a quick throw. She did and he muffed it. Before the backstop could retrieve the ball from the dirt and take a stab at one of the baserunners, ump-in-chief Crenshaw, behind the plate, called a balk and waved them to second and third. Willy stepped toward first base before delivering the pitch, which is a "no-no." She kicked up a spadeful of dirt with her right toe and shrieked to Jorge on third, "You're going nowhere!"

Dion Lovelace, swinging at a sidearm fastball, flew out to Toby in short center, but, after running toward the infield for a hat-flying-off basket catch, he made a marshmallow throw home and Jorge scored the sixth run

of the inning. Willy's storming anger raged once more and Jed
came to her. He listened as she vented against herself and the other team, then asked coarsely, "You done, kid?" She nodded, unable to resist smiling at his bristled face. "So, let's get back to it," he commanded, thrusting the ball at her ribs. Blood, batting again, grounded out to end the inning of agony. Willy descended into a dugout full of silliness and frivolity, such is the self-protective third step in the response to a blowout, following pain and numbness.

"I guess we go home and pack our bags for Kansas City," joked the player-manager.

Willy's work was done. Randy Craig pitched the last two frames for the Wolves and there was no more scoring for Kenny and the KC Kings. There was no more scoring for the Wolves either, after Lavoissier took over in the fourth inning. His performance–seven strikeouts, one walk, and one hit in five and two-thirds innings pitched–was the best relief pitching of the series. In the ninth, down 11-5, P.J. reached to the farthest corners of the bench and Harry, pinch-hitting for Marty, became the red-bearded Guy's seventh and last fanning victim and the game was thankfully over.

Ernie Arnett began the recap: "The pennant playoff turns into a donnybrook of slugging as Kansas City routs Buffalo, eleven to five. Standing by is Rob DaSilva..."

Rob's postgame interview wasn't with the hero, but the goat. Brian Robbins said, "I didn't have enough stuff to strike out my twelve-year-old kid." That was a fair assessment of his pitching. The split-fingered fastball wasn't fast and his curveball didn't curve. Hard luck and a bad call lost game one for Brian. He richly deserved to lose game five.

Willy and Randy shut off the run-scoring hemorrhage, thereby diverting P.J.'s ire from the bullpen's ineptitude. Now festering in his brain was Andre's poor excuse for a throw, well over the head of shortstop Marty, playing the cut-off, and far out of the reach of Glenn,
covering the hot corner. Peter was also caught by the television camera and twenty million lip-readers as he threw up his hands and exclaimed, "I don't *fogging* believe it!" Of the 11-5 debacle, Peter said to Jimmy Mack Jones, "Things are coming unraveled, James."

Laying his hands squarely upon Peter's shoulders, James told him, "Keep your eyes on the brass ring. You got a team that wants it so bad they can't even tell how hard they're workin'. Look at how the lady walked in cold, got you the two outs and sat back down like it was nothin'! You got Willy and Woody and..."

"I have no bullpen, James."

"You got one, but you got no confidence in 'em," James admonished, biting his pipe stem before lighting it to smoke.

"Which means I have no bullpen!"

For game six, the starters would be Jiminez and Tucker. Prior to the game, under a full court press by the media wags, Peter was asked whether Willy or Woody would get the nod for the seventh game showdown. "We'll see," he smiled.

"Does 'we'll see' mean the lefty or the righty? The female or the male?"

"It means we'll see who wins tonight."

The series nearly was over before the Wolves knew what happened. As the series entered its second week, however, some players became ornery and resented the way KC was being credited with having regained the momentum. "How come we're one game ahead and it feels like we're losin'?" Marty complained. The Wolves arrived in Cattle Town, Missouri grimly determined to prove themselves worthy as they were greeted by "Buffalo Chokes" and "Croak the Wolves" banners at Kauffman on Tuesday night. Adrian Tucker took the mound for KC against the Wolves. Tuck pitched well, allowing only one earned run in game three, and he started off looking like a winner, good enough to send the pennant series to a seventh and deciding game. The first break for the Raging Wolves came in the third inning. Andre, whom P.J. shifted to left field after his fifth game throwing error, led off with a double. Kevin flew out and it was Toby's turn to bat. The KC pitchers kept the ball outside to Toby throughout the series, but he twice burned the American Central champs with slap-shot doubles down the right field line. Yet, Youngblood Crawford was playing straight-away and deep. Toby's heart said to pull the ball into the seats, but his mind told him to slug it inside the white stripe, up the line past first base. Toby's hit would have been an easy putout had Blood been playing on the line, but racing inward and to his left, the ball slipped from his grasp for another two-base hit and Andre trotted home for the game's first run. Meanwhile, Sadie was getting by, but not without difficulty. Two double-plays–one started by Toby in center field–saved his bacon. In the fourth, two walks and two singles gave KC a run, tying the score. The Wolves reclaimed the lead in the sixth. P.J. started off the inning by blasting a home run. After Diego popped out, third baseman of the day Alex Suarez walked on four pitches. Mattie Z. singled, Alex scampered around second to third, and Jed hit a sharp grounder to Swifton. The third baseman whipped the ball to Trapello, forcing Matt, and the second baseman turned to throw to Estrada, covering the bag at first base. Trapello's throw beat the plodding goal-keeper by several feet, but the superstar Estrada dropped the ball. Jed was safe and Alex scored. That was the second lucky break for the Wolves. Tuck finished the seventh inning and Lavoissier, who pitched brilliantly Sunday night, came into the game. *Le lancer* from Quebec received the cheers from the Cow Town fans. Eight Wolf pitchers sitting in a row groaned as one in the bullpen. "The stopper cometh!" intoned Rob DaSilva for the viewers at home. Consecutive singles by Diego, Alex, and Matt netted the Wolves a run and KC went to bat in the bottom half of the eighth, trailing 4-1. A pall cast over the home team's faithful. Sadie was still on the mound and up came the top of the order. Crawford singled, Trapello lined out, and Swifton doubled, but a good, hard throw from Diego, the former catcher playing in right field for the first time ever, held the fleet-of-foot Blood at third. The bullpen phone rang. "Randy, Chris, sit down," Ferdie croaked. The bullpen coach grabbed a catcher's mitt and nodded to Phil as Gene put on his and slapped Willy's shoulder. Sadie walked Estrada on four pitches and P.J. called for time, took out the starting pitcher, and motioned for the right-hander.

  Up in the broadcast booth, Ernie Arnett explained, "Peter Jones is gambling, using Willy Beal in relief. She's the probable starter for the seventh game, if a seventh game becomes necessary, but he's choosing to shoot the works here."

At the mound, Willy showed Peter a fearsome look. "You're not gonna let me pitch the seventh game! Why not?"

Peter tossed Willy the ball and said, "There's not going to *be* a seventh game if you punch their lights out for me and get us a day off." After turning to head back for the dugout, he added, "I'd have to go with Woody tomorrow, anyway." Then he was gone.

The situation was a classic jam, a rally ready to happen. The bases were filled and there was one out. Willy felt her blood pumping as she fixed her eyes on the plate. Telly sent the veteran Wes Middleton to bat. Willy threw a buggywhip fastball and he hit a long fly ball to Diego. Blood tagged third and scored after the catch–Buffalo 4 Kansas City 2. Jacklin fouled off a screwball, then drove an offspeed fastball to deep left field. The ball would have landed twenty feet beyond the fence for a homer at Pilot Field, but KC's catcher had to settle for a double, which scored Swifton and moved Estrada to third–Buffalo 4 Kansas City 3.

"Jacklin is safe at second with a stand-up double. Two runs clatter across the plate and Buffalo's lead is cut to one. The tying run is at third, the go-ahead run is at second, and Jorge Walker is at the plate," dean of play-by-play Arnett's voice crescendoed, then peaked. "And Willy Beal is blowing off some steam on the mound."

Jed Wolfe observed calmly as Willy kicked, stomped, and spat on the ground. Then Old Shin Pads bellowed, "You gonna pitch or you gonna cry?"

"Pitch," she said with a ladylike curtsy.

"Do it!" Jed grunted and left.

There were two on and two outs as Willy delivered an overhand slider to Jorge. A base hit meant the ball game. Domingo's brother hit the ball toward the hole at shortstop, but Willy took two strides to her right, brought her left arm across her chest, and grabbed Jorge's hot smash to end the danger. She held the ball up, pumped her fist, and yelled, "All right!" As she trotted to the sidelines, still holding the ball aloft for the edification of the crowd, Marty came alongside her, wrapping his arm over her shoulder.

"Yo, Willy, listen up! You're the pitcher," the shortstop said. "That's your job. If a ball comes straight back at you, you put your glove up to protect yourself. That's it! Don't go after it. If you bobbled it, deflected it, or threw wild to first, we would've lost the game and maybe the series. Just put the ball in play and let the fielders go after it. That's our job."

"I hear you," Willy said, somewhat deflated.

"Nifty catch, though," Marty added and smacked her buttocks.

Leading 4-3, three Wolves faced Lavoissier in the ninth and all–Jed, Marty, and Teddy– struck out. Once again, the fates frowned on the blue team as the bottom third of KC's order came to bat against Willy in the ninth. Willy tried to go "up the ladder" on Billy Velasco, using fastball at the knees, thigh, and belt, but he held up on the bat and stayed alive with one ball and two strikes. She fed him a curve, a screwball, and another curve, and Hilario took a walk to first. Telly then put in rookie Ryan Sanchez to run for him and Dion Lovelace went up to bat. Youngblood Crawford waited on deck, the dragon-slayer with sword unsheathed, ready to bring the fray to a bloody end. The sacrifice was on, as the KC throng smelled another last-chance threat brewing. Dion squared to bunt as Willy buggywhipped an offspeed fastball into his extended bat. He popped high in the air, directly in front of home. Jed danced like an ancient rain-maker as he did a quick two-step, kicked out with his toe, and pounded his mitt, waiting for the ball to descend. It dropped into Jed's padded handmaiden and he fired a dead-eye shot to first base, nailing Sanchez on the double-play that pulled a circuit-breaker on the crowd's hopes.

Willy allowed herself a moment of sadness for Lovelace, who would surely take the heat for botching the sacrifice bunt, as would Velasco, whose four errors in the series set the stage for the shortstop's job he took from Teddy Balin being surrendered to young Sanchez come next spring. Youngblood at bat envisioned tying the game with one swing. Willy had fanned him in game three with a sidearm fastball and this time he saw an overhand screamer that was ten miles per hour faster–strike one. Ready for another, he swung at a hard breaking bal–strike two. He picked up the flat rotation of the next pitch and recognized the cut fastball, thrown with her fingers across the seams. Crawford checked his swing and took ball one. Willy and Blood locked eyes. The only break in concentration came as Willy's ears picked up a chant of *"Wil-lee, Wil-lee!"* rippling among KC's broken-hearted boosters. She stepped off the rubber, touched the brim of her cap with a nod, swallowed the lump in her throat, and expressed the final pitch to Blood with a scream of *"Ye-ahhh!"*

Rob DaSilva: "There's a ground ball to third..."

Ernie Arnett: "The great American city of Buffalo, New York has been waiting for its first big league pennant since 1879..."

Rob: "Harmon scoops it, throws to first..."

Ernie: "...and they've got it!"

Jed dogged Blood's tracks up the line, flapping his arms like a great winged bird, as Willy bounded toward first base. She leaped into Jed's arms as Mattie Z. gathered the ball for the final out. Willy, Jed, and Matt danced in a circle. Willy and Marty did a face-to-face shuffle with their arms raised to the sky. *Bump! Bump!* Clowning for the cameras, Willy reached for Kevin, threw one leg outward, and fell into his arms. Amid spasms of laughter, Kevin kissed Willy loudly and wetly on the lips. "Oooh," she murmured as she straightened herself, then said, "What're you doing later on tonight, sugar?"

CHAPTER 22

Peter Jones and Toby Clay stood side by side, being interviewed by two different broadcasting crews. P.J. pointed in Toby's face, saying, "These young guys..." Toby wrapped a headlock on P.J., saying, "This old man here..." Photographers armed with digital and video cameras jumped like flying squirrels to take shots of the pennant-winning Wolves as they squeezed through the corridor to the visitor's clubhouse. On their way into the room, where the league president and co-owners waited, Randy Craig tickled Willy's ribs and Scott Bruneau slapped her shoulder.

"Ow!" she jumped, gasping involuntarily. The dull soreness in her muscles and tendons became an acute throbbing, seeming to inflame the instant she released the final pitch to Blood.

"Hey, ya hurtin'?" asked Scotty. There was concern in his voice.

"No," she said, but he noticed her eyes glistening. "It just tightens up after a game. Doesn't yours?"

"Ya sure that's all?" Scotty asked warily.

"Yeah, honey, I'm okay," she said, linking arms with him and smiling.

As the players' moms, dads, girlfriends, wives, and kids flooded the clubhouse, league president Ian Lowe stood with someone representing the sponsor, another person representing the network, Barry and Dana, Eddie Paris, and Peter Jones. Everyone congratulated each other as the first player-manager to win a pennant in more than half a century was doused by a spraying bottle of champaign, secreted from behind the partition that blanked the team's celebration from the cameras.

Lowe announced, "On behalf of the USTV network and the Nippon Motor Company, I am pleased to present the award for the outstanding player in the championship series..."

Willy waved and gave the thumbs-up sign to Kevin McDonald, who paced the team with flashy glove work and a .318 batting average. Kevin smiled and winked at the lady.

"...to Willy Beal."

Willy's knees buckled, her legs wobbled, she covered her face with her hands, and screamed, "You're shittin'me!" Her exclamation [*bleep!*] rang throughout the continental United States, Canada, Central and South America, the Caribbean, and via satellite to Japan, the Pacific Rim, and the world at large.

"Get on up there, kid!" Jed exhorted as a band of Wolves pushed and pulled Willy to the front. She was still shaky, unconsciously rocking on her heels, as the league president said something while she smacked kisses on the cheeks of Barry, Dana, Eddie, and Peter. Willy didn't catch a word the man said. She beheld the trophy and turned to thank Ian Lowe. She paused for half a second, smiled, and squeezed the statuette to her chest. Then she hoisted it above her head and howled, "It's on to the October classic. Woo-hoo!"

To celebrate winning the flag, Dana and Barry closed D.B. Gumshoes on Wednesday night at 7:00 p.m. and reopened an hour later for a private party. It was a day lost in postgame celebration, clearing out of the hotel, and a plane ride home. At the Buffalo airport, thousands of fans braved the chilly wee hours to give their victorious heroes a wild welcome. Luckily, the final series was to start Saturday night in either New York or San Francisco, allowing the partied out and hung over Wolves two whole days to revive. Willy showered and dressed to go party at Gumshoes. She resolved to have a good time and she did. In the ladies' room, she screwed on a pair of earrings.

"Are those diamond studs?" asked Maggie.

"I can't be wearing *diamonds*," laughed Willy. "See the setting? Little wolf paws!"

A handful of civilians were invited, including Rob DaSilva, who tried to reach Willy for the better part of the afternoon. "Why didn't you answer my text and voice messages?"

"I was unavailable for comment," she replied with batting eyelashes.

"Can I get you to do a pregame interview Saturday afternoon?"

"Sure, Robbie. Are you leaving? The party's just starting."

Rob nodded bashfully, flattered by Willy's disappointed frown. "I'm off to Frisco. Didn't you hear? The Diamonds blew it. It's all up to Big Gil in game seven tomorrow."

"See you Saturday, then," Willy said shyly.

"Yeah, see you later." Rob smiled at the way she made no effort to move away from him.

"Forget something?" she said, moving closer, tapping her lips with a finger, and he kissed her goodbye.

Willy also had a chat with Michael Avery, the accountant. "Good evening, Mr. Avery," she greeted him with playful propriety. "You're here as a business obligation for one of your clients, I presume."

Michael smiled easily. "I was in town doing some work for Mr. Jones. So, he and Mrs. Jones invited me to come along."

"And how are *my* business affairs, Mr. Avery?"

"Very well, Ms. Beal. I trust you're satisfied with the work I've been doing," he said confidently.

"Definitely," Willy told him, tilting her head and swaying slightly.

"May I ask why you want to buy an extra 500 Series tickets above your complimentary allotment and give them away to school children?"

"Because I don't like all the games being at night. Back in the day, people used to listen to the radio or watch the Series on the TV in the daytime at work or at school. Today the kids have to stay up 'til midnight. I think the weekend games should be played in the afternoon. At least a few local kids will get to see a game live and in person."

"What about your friends and family?"

"Yeah, I'm bringing up the kids on the baseball, softball, and track teams from Old Saint Pete. That's sixty kids. But Mama said she wants no part of all the celebrity foolishness, she calls it." Then Willy offered, "Take one of my freebies for yourself, Michael...If it's not too boring for you, that is."

"Thanks, I'm sure it won't be, Ms. Beal."

"That Michael's a hunk," Maggie whispered in Willy's ear.

Willy shrugged and wrinkled her nose. "Just a pretty face."

"I saw you kissing Rob DaSilva over in the corner," teased Donna Slattery. "It'll break the guys' hearts if you were getting it on with a wag."

"Willy's gonna wind up with a ballplayer," said Suzanne Clay. "I know it."

The hard driving music pulsated the bistro. "Oh, I wanna dance with somebody..." sang Willy, grabbing Kevin by the hand, then Randy, Scotty, Andre, and Alex, who was by far the most energetic of her partners. Willy moved with the beat and felt the heat on the dance floor, enjoying the pure release.

"Hmm, love me down, Willy," murmured Kevin as he took a chair next to Peter and Michael and joined them for shots and beers.

"Now, keep it clean, McDonald," chided Peter.

Kevin propped his chin on his hands and admired Willy once more. "Ya can tell a lot about a woman by the way she dances, if ya know what I mean." Peter and Michael just smiled politely without comment.

The morning after the blowout at Gumshoes, Willy nonetheless rose early to run, meditate, do some yoga, and tune to Sportsnet to catch bits and pieces of the daily sports roundup. She heard: *"The Watanabe Sailors are the new champions of Japanese baseball, defeating the Zaibatsu Cobras in a four-game sweep of the Yakyu Series. The winning pitcher was a rookie, Hideki Saito, who shut out the Cobras on four hits in game four at the Tokyo Dome. An American player, Beaumont Teague...who joined Watanabe in the last month of the season...belted a grand slam home run in the 7-1 victory."* Willy shouted with joy, clapping and stomping her feet. "Big bad Beau! Way to go!" She watched the faraway scene as the Watanabe Sailors of Yokohama celebrated their triumph. The smiling face of her e-mail pen-pal Hideki Saito stood out in the sea of faces.

P.J. scheduled an afternoon of meetings to go over stats, scouting reports, and videotapes of both Senior Circuit finalists. Willy rode to Peter and Charlene's house with Gene and found Peter in a dark and grumbling mood. He obviously had a fight with Charlene, due wholly to the fact that he invited all the players, coaches, and their spouses to a working dinner party to watch the game from San Francisco Thursday night. Char suddenly had to feed and entertain fifty people. "Mad? Who me? Oh, not at all?" Char chirped gaily as she held up a pretzel stick and snapped it in two as if it were her hubby's neck.

Irv, Ferdie, and all of the catchers and hurlers except Brian arrived for the planned pitchers' meeting, but instead spent the afternoon watching the game videos. In the first game, Cliff Allyn brought home the 3-1 win on a five-hitter. Jake, the best pitcher in the free world during the regular season, was knocked out by Andre Harris's run-scoring single in the sixth. The Diamonds avoided a shutout when Andy doubled and Cal drove him home with a single. S.F.'s field manager, Charley Novak, nominated Kitsuragawa to start game two the next day, but Kit-Kat failed to match Cliff's performance. Gil Douglas pitched for the Diamonds and worked his way to a 4-2 win. Next came the Saturday Night Massacre in the Meadowlands, where Diamond castaway Darnell Greene made a smashing return to his former home turf, hitting two home runs and batting in four RBI. Eric Jackson also homered for Charley's Titans and Roy Burton hit one for the D's, who lost 12-3. Sandy Lee Danielson was routed in the opening frame after Darnell's long shot and a base hit by Bobby Ray Webster, Tony Ortega's replacement, produced three runs. The Diamonds could muster only three runs in their game three debacle off the winning combo of McElroy and Alvarez, after which Demmy Fortune spoke the bleep heard round the world. Willy also noticed Pigpen Pantagones, not Paul, behind the plate and Mercurio Mercado in the lineup for the first time in the playoffs, going hitless.

Fast forward to game four, as Cameron Hammersmith told the USTV audience, "This game demonstrates the Diamonds' spirit." After the Golden Gatekeepers tallied a run off Jake in the opening inning, the New Yorkers exploded for four runs off Winston Dixon on home runs by Roy and Joe Manlius. Jake carried a 4-1 lead into the ninth with two outs, two runners on base, and a full count to Webster. Then, disaster struck the superstar southpaw. Bobby Ray drove the next pitch 450 feet, over the left field wall, to tie the score. D's manager Tom Vallery stuck with Jake, even when Darnell beat out an infield single and speed demon Donnie Ross tripled to send Golden State in front, 5-4. Half an inning hence, Psycho Bielski, pinch hitting for Jake, was hit on the arm by a pitch thrown by lefty reliever Greg Ruggieri. Monty Guilford's view was obstructed as Bielski checked his swing and the umpire maximus called strike three. The Psycho raged madly, Vallery appealed to the crew chief, and Derk Morfitt ruled a hit by pitch, causing Novak to blow his stack and a war of words ensued. The fans in the bleachers amused themselves in the interim by heaping debris and verbal abuse on the Bay Area outfielders. The dust finally settled and the Psycho was waved to first base. Subsequently, Keith Whalen capitalized on the reversed decision with a double, scoring Bielski with the tying run.

From the tape's audio, Jeff McCarty remarked, "As Demeter Fortune steps to the plate...He hit twenty-four home runs in the regular season and Gilbert hit thirty-two, but neither slugger has been able to get a hold of one in the playoffs." A moment later, Demmy crunched the ball for a two-run homer to win the game for the D's, 7-5.

"Pause the tape!" Fortune had batted right-handed against Rags Ruggieri, leading P.J. to grab his notebook and spill pages of stat tables and charts onto the floor. He thumbed through the notebook with a flurry of crinkling paper. "Let's see...Okay, Burton ... Bonham ... Gilbert ... We're dead meat!"

Game five was Big Gil's turn to start again and he gained a 1-0 victory in a magnificent duel with Cliff Allyn. Memo pitched the eighth inning, fanning two, and the San Franciscan pair combined for a two-hitter. The lone run scored after Demmy beat out a hopper to Vic Wilson at second, Roy lined a sharp single to right, and Thor Andreason popped a bloop single to short left field, just a few feet from third base, for the only run the Diamonds needed. Big Gil was the star of the game, but Thor's poke won it.

"Ain't that a bitch, man?" bemoaned Sadie. "Ol' Cliff gettin' beat on a cheap li'l hit like that!"

"No, way!" Willy shouted boisterously. "That was no accidental hit. I've seen him do it before. The infielders play in with runners on base and leave a hole in back of third base. Thor works for hours and hours on his bat control just to be able to hit the ball to that spot."

P.J. pricked up his ears. "Ferdie, hit rewind and run it back again." As Willy pointed to the screen during the replay of Thor's poke, the player-manager chortled. "That settles it. Willy, you have to sit in on all three meetings tomorrow...the pitchers', the hitters', and the fielders' meetings."

Eric Jackson, who in all respects meant to the Gigantics what Roy Burton and Toby Clay were to the Diamonds and Wolves, respectively, was out of the lineup for game five. Novak put Darnell in his stead in center field. P.J. commented on the way Novak worked the role player into the lineup and he was ready to go whenever and wherever the skipper needed him. The wheels in Peter's head turned as he said to Stash, "I should use Teddy that way."

Willy felt quiet indifference about Cal Bonham leaving the game with a sprained ankle and being sidelined for the rest of the playoff, replaced at second base by Benny Marquez. The event was completely dissociated from the friend she regarded so warmly. As the videotape rolled, Willy squatted on the floor and witnessed Memo toss a four-hitter and Sandy Lee get blown out in the third inning of game six. In this case, however, Willy bristled with uncomfortably ambivalent emotions.

"I heard the Reb bruised his hand, punchin' a wall after Vallery pulled him out of the game," quipped Irv.

"Dumb shit don't know enough to use his left hand instead of his pitchin' hand," snorted Jed.

Peter stated, "Take away his reputation and brute-force intimidation, and he's just a brain-dead heaver." Peter and Willy exchanged stares, but she bit her tongue.

All the runs in game six came by way of home runs. Gary Steele connected off Sandy Lee with a runner on base in the third. Round-trippers by Thor and Roy knotted the score at 2-2. In the home half of the seventh, with Tim Langevin on the mound in his fifth inning of extraordinarily long relief, Ross belted the game-winning homer.

After the video show was over, Willy and Scotty offered to "big boy sit" and treated Peter Jr. to a frozen yogurt sundae. Later, Willy went back to Peter and Charlene's to prepare the munchies for the evening soirée. Resourceful Char hunted down a gourmet take-out shop. "Everything's ready to zap in the microwave," she announced in triumph.

Kevin and Randy helped Willy chop veggies in the kitchen. As Kevin sought the ingredients for a dip, Willy turned and smiled with a sharp-bladed utensil in motion, chopping a stack of onion slices. Peter entered the kitchen. "Judas! Watch what you're doing, Willy. We don't need any pitchers cutting off their fingers."

"Shush! I'm being careful," Willy laughed, still wielding the slicing tool.

Charlene marched with military precision, sounding either ecstatically happy or deliriously nervous, saying, "Everything looks under control. Good!"

"Where's Brian and Maggie anyway?" Willy asked.

"They're at their place in Lake View," answered the leader of the Wolf Pack. "I guess she's been on his case to take a day off with her and the kids."

"Fancy that!" exclaimed Charlene. "A ballplayer spending time with his family? Unheard of!" She glared at Peter and strutted away.

Willy slipped out of the kitchen to find Charlene, looking lovely, but slightly awkward, in her silky black dress. The reluctant hostess hunched over her deck railing, inhaling a cigarette, scowling with every puff.

Willy came close enough to brush against her friend's arm. "How're you holding up, Char?"

Charlene's mouth smiled, but her eyebrows were still turned downward. She shook her head. "I'm okay, I guess, Willy." Charlene knew Willy wasn't referring to hosting a house party. Willy felt as though they were closing in for a shoulder cry, which wasn't exactly Charlene's style, but her eyes were glassy. "Peter's been a bear to live with. Sometimes he won't talk. He just sits and thinks about something that happened in a game. He's been short-tempered with Petie. He's been fighting with me or snapping at me. We've gone through the pressure before. He's won two rings, but with LA he was too young and it was almost too easy. Playing baseball has always been more than a job, but now it's like the Wolves are more important than me and Petie. I keep trying to get some balance, but he just pulls away. Willy, we're fighting worse than we ever used to...I can't take much more of it."

"Char, there's never gonna be another season like this one, even if Peter manages in the bigs for twenty years. His heart and soul are wrapped up in this team. It's like the fulfillment of his whole career."

"When is it going to be my turn? What about my dreams? What am I supposed to do?" There was a distinct note of pleading in Charlene's voice.

"You gotta live with the big, bad bear all winter long, no matter how this thing turns out. Give him his space for now. The Series will be over in a week or ten days. It wouldn't hurt if you cheered him on either."

"That's a pretty sexist comment for you to be making, Willy," Charlene disputed.

Instead of stiffening, Willy reached her arm around her confidante's waist. "Peter's on the threshold of his dream right now. Let it play out. Then grab hold of him and take back your life." Willy closed her eyes as Charlene listened. "If you want to follow the current of a great river and you drop a stone in, it'll sink. But if you drop a leaf in, it'll float. The leaf will ride the current to its destination. By submitting, you'll conquer."

"Go with the flow, right?" Char smiled.

"No, go with the Tao!" Willy laughed. She added, "As for sexism, I'm keeping somebody waiting right now myself."

This time Charlene grabbed onto Willy. "What? Who? Where is he?"

Just then, Peter came out to the deck. "Are you two ladies talking about me?"

Willy turned to him with a smile. "Peter, meet your wife. Charlene, this is your husband." They laughed and clasped hands and she left them alone together.

"Let the games begin!" invoked Mike Staczewski as the announcer's voice quadraphonically replicated itself on the four TV sets strategically positioned around the house: *From the City by the Bay, game seven of the league championship, brought to you by Nippon Motor Company, makers of the XYZ car, and by Braunstein Beer and Braunstein Lite...Go for the brawn!*

Jeff McCarty and Cam Hammersmith smiled from coast to coast. Said Cam: "This series between New York and San Francisco for the pennant has turned into a real barnburner, coming down to a seventh and deciding game tonight..." Said Jeff: "And it remains to be seen whether the PA system will be playing Tony Bennett singing '*I left my heart*' or Old Blue Eyes singing '*New York, New York*' when this night is over." The Goodstone blimp flew above the park, giving a panoramic view of the bay and the skyline, as Cam introduced the pregame feature. "Here's Rob DaSilva..."

"The invading army of New York Diamonds' fans descending upon this gorgeous treasure of a city for this postseason series can be seen here, there, and everywhere, wearing their D's caps, America's Home Team sweatshirts, and blue nylon team jackets. We spoke with a convenience store owner..."

The brightly turbaned storekeeper twitched his moustache and grinned. "They register about a ten on the obnoxious meter."

"How do you like San Francisco," Rob asked a trio of youngish junketeers decked out in full Diamonds' regalia. "Hey, we've come from the four corners of the metropolitan area...Jersey, Westchester, Connecticut, and Long Island...to do what we gotta do and get outta here." The three goofily smiling faces crowded in front of the minicam's eye and brayed, "Dee for demo-*li*-tion! Hoo! Hoo! Hoo!" Twirling their fists, the three trolls chanted, "Let's go Dees! Let's go Dees!"

"This is Rob DaSilva for USTV Sports."

After the introduction of the starting lineups, Cam said, "Bruce Jacobson should be starting this playoff contest, but Tom Vallery has chosen to call on the big righthander, Gil Douglas, with only two days rest. He pitched the Diamonds to two complete-game victories and he's shut out San Francisco for fifteen innings pitched. Charley Novak counters with Bruce McElroy, winning pitcher of game three. Jeff interrupted: "Eric Jackson returns to center field for San Francisco, but all-star second baseman Cal Bonham remains out of New York's lineup..." Cam resumed: "Mercurio Mercado is batting in the lead-off spot for the Diamonds, although he's hitless in nine at-bats in the playoffs. Interestingly, only the Buffalo Wolves have escaped injury to a key player in this year's postseason."

Shock waves ran from room to room at the home of the Joneses. "Aw, man!...Hex!...He jinxed us!...Oh, no, he didn't just say that!...Damn his ass!"

Big Gil Douglas rose to the occasion and completed his brilliant work in the playoffs by beating the National West champs for the third time, 5-0. The Diamond's routed McElroy after Andre Harris's error at third base paved the way for four runs in the third inning. Novak pulled strings at the bat, in the field, and on the mound–even sending Kit-Kat and Winnie Dixon to pitch in relief–but to no avail. Paul Cello wrapped up the scoring and the pennant with a home run off Ruggieri. Rags coughing up a gopher ball was received with undisguised glee by Phil, Randy, Scotty, and Chris. Gil Douglas was named the outstanding player of the championship series. On the offensive side, Leroi Burton led the league championship in everything, including three home runs and a .393 average.

"And so it comes down to this," said P.J. with a hint of irony. "The little Davids watch the two Goliaths battle to the death. No doubt about it, Gil was awesome tonight, pure power pitching ...Then, in the ninth inning, along comes Larry Brooks. And what do we have?...The same damn thing: a big right-hander throwing smoke. Show us the same pitches for nine innings and we can get in some licks off these guys."

Irv declared, "Jake and the Reb were very shaky in this series, too."

"We know we can hit some," said Andre Toussaint.

Stash laughed, "Nobody expects us to hit much outside of Pilot Field. Well, Burton, Gilbert, Fortune, Bonham, and Mercado have to fight all the wide open spaces at the Meadowlands, just like us, and our park is no banjo box either."

"Do you think they'll have Bonham back for the big show?" asked Matt.

"Are you kiddin'?" laughed Marty, "He'll play even if it's on crutches."

"You know something?" Peter asked rhetorically. "They're calling us a miracle team, the underdogs, the sentimental favorites. We won it on guts, smarts, and good luck."

"Yeah, but that's not all there is to it," James countered. "We hafta stay focused."

"Shoot, we gotta get focused," slurred Kevin after who knows how many vodka and tonics with lime. "I be blind tonight!"

Telecaster Rob DaSilva pointed to game four as the turning point, sparked by gnomelike Bielski's hit-by-pitch strikeout, while the Diamonds locked the clubhouse door and declared a media blackout. Manager Vallery's terse comment was delivered humorlessly. "This series shouldn't have gone the full seven games. We have work to do to get ready for Buffalo in forty-eight hours. Thank you!"

Peter absorbed the television image and pronounced, "Focus!"

"New York's overconfident," said Glenn.

"Oh, yeah?" P.J. retorted. "They've got a right to be. If we don't work hard and play smart, the Diamonds will cut us up like a chainsaw."

Willy felt a sinking feeling in the pit of her stomach. Her mood became dark and ominous as she came to the full realization of what lay ahead. In her gut she had been pulling for San Francisco to win, thus making it easier to harden her determination, unambivalently staring into the eyes of enemies and other strangers, save Darnell and Memo. Now, three months after the Diamonds jilted her, Willy B. Superstar was going back to the Meadowlands.

CHAPTER 23

In Friday morning's dewy haze, Willy pulled on her jogging suit with two sweatshirts and her thermal undies beneath to run in the sub-freezing air. Cars, trucks, and mobile units with network logos jammed the driveway and wags camped out on the lawn of Willy's half-duplex in Orchard Park. They greeted her with a swarming, collective hail of "Willy!" as she set out for her regular morning run.

"It's just like being back in New York," she laughed. Then she began to jog in place and shadow box–jumping, flapping her arms, pulling her sleeves down over her hands, and bouncing up and down to stay warm. Willy was asked, "What are your thoughts on the Series?...Will you start game two in New York or game three in Buffalo?...Are you out to get revenge on Fabian and the Diamonds?"

She was mute, still shadow boxing, adding some aerobic kicks to her jabs and left-right combinations and went into an eerily echolike imitation of the Champ. "We are the *greatest*! Bring on the Diamonds!...Cal Bonham, I want *you*! Demmy Fortune, I want *you*! Roy Burton, I want *you*! Andy Gilbert, I want *you*! Mercurio Mercado...you big ugly bear...I want *you*! You're goin' down!..." She shrieked fearsomely, bending, pointing, and pumping her fists, pummeling an invisible foe. "...On the ground!...Oh, yeah, the Pack is on the prowl."

"What's your prediction, champ...er, I mean, Willy?" someone called.

"Read this!" The imaginary boxer wiggled her butt, held up four fingers of one hand, and formed a circle with the other. "That spells four straight."

Willy's performance played on the airwaves all day long. She was a hit in upstate New York and a smash on the road from Portland, Maine to Portland, Oregon, but the bit didn't go over well in the Big Apple.

Roy Burton: "She should be concentratin' on her pitchin', if you ask me."

Demeter Fortune: "Real cute! Amateur night! Funny, funky home videos! [*Bleep*!]..."

Mercurio Mercado: "This is the damn Series, not a [*bleep-bleep*] comedy show."

Cal Bonham: "Willy's just being Willy. It's no big deal."

Andy Gilbert: "We just finished a tough series against a real good ball club. Buffalo pretty much breezed through their playoffs. I guess Willy and the Wolves are flyin' high right now, but we're feelin' a sort of intensity. We've got a lot left to prove."

"You and me both, Andy," Willy said as she watched him on the television screen. She turned to light two wicks of incense and knelt with eyes closed, prayer beads wrapped around her hands, feeling the heady tide of emotion, her energy rising from within, and seeking the strength to harness it for the impending battle.

Meanwhile, the manager, coaches, scouts, special assistants, and players gathered for their meetings. The pitching coach squinted and read aloud: "Willy Beal, the pitcher...Her concentration, technique, and action are the keys. She's always pitched by the book, alternating fastballs up and in and breaking balls down and away, but now she's using her fastball as an 'out' pitch. Her offspeed sidearm and buggywhip fastballs have less velocity than the overhand delivery, but she's got pinpoint control and lively action. She goes inside out, setting up with one of her offspeed fastballs, then striking guys out with the backdoor or breakaway slider. Her low-and-away slider is almost unhittable for righties and the backdoor slider is murder on lefties. The curveball is her weakest pitch, but mixin' up her delivery gives her a deceptive edge over the batter. Jed Guerin likes her to toss a cutter with two strikes, less velocity, but it jumps, and it can be effective if you're not expectin' it."

Rudy Judd turned to Lew Shankleton, who said, "She's throwin' much harder now than she did before. We always knew she could clock mid to upper nineties, but always held somethin' back. She never wanted to sacrifice the action or her control, but now her money pitch is an old-fashioned fastball. One reason Mr. Fabian dealt her to Buffalo was 'cause of Red Leighton's suspectin' she was coverin' up a sore arm. I think it's safe to say that's not the case after watchin' her pitch against Cleveland and Kansas City."

Bullpen coach Hank Froelichs entered the discussion. "I'd say you've gotta go after her first pitch and get to her early. We can let Naulls, Jiminez, and Robbins go through the order and adjust to them the second or third time around, but Willy gets stronger and keeps on coming. She just doesn't run out of gas."

The Diamonds' manager, Tom Vallery, looked at the Diamonds' catcher and spoke, "Paul, you get the last word."

"There's one thing to remember about Willy," began Paul. "She's one of the smartest pitchers I've ever worked with. You tell her somethin' about a hitter one time and it prints." Paul drew a horizontal line with a finger across his brow. "Willy watched every one of us for six weeks in spring trainin' and for eight weeks durin' the regular season. She was scoutin' us without knowin' it." Paul, who had been pacing before the group of fifteen position players, propped his foot on an empty chair, rested his arm on his knee, and smiled. "Right now, ya better believe P.J.'s got her spillin' her guts to the Wolves' pitchin' staff."

In the beautiful city on the shore of Lake Erie, Willy told her fellow pitchers, "You're not gonna get Demmy swinging and you're not gonna get Roy on a called third strike unless you fool them. You might cross them both up with breaking balls if they're batting left-handed, but you've gotta stay inside. Andy's got the wrist action to get around on inside pitches. The only one who's vulnerable to lefties is Cal..."

"Woody, Phil, Scotty, listen up!" Peter Jones interjected.

"Cal's got the bat control to spray the ball right-handed, but he can't pull it out of the park against lefties unless you lay it right over the plate. Merk is vulnerable to inside pitches, but it's tough to pitch to his weak spot the way he crowds the plate."

"I can't figure out Fortune," said Irv. "He keeps pullin' for the fences. What's he tryin' to prove."

Willy heard and felt the rumble begin: "Why's he gotta play stud muffin when he could hit .400?...*Psst, psst!*...Ya hear what Estrada said about him?...Mr. Wonderful is so special!..."   Willy didn't know how to defend Demmy–and his alleged proclivities–from her beloved, but benighted, teammates. Then P.J. spoke up. "Maybe those rumors are true," he conceded with a wry smile. "But I know what kind of guys Bonham, Danielson, Douglas, and Cello are. He's one of their crew and they'll be at his back. Look, I played four years in LA with a teammate who was gay and it's nobody's business but his own." Then Willy's already considerable fondness for her mentor multiplied exponentially as she listened to his words: "Regardless, whether he's gay or straight, the Buffalo Wolves won't go there. Not my team! I don't want to hear another word about it."

The intelligence reports from the Diamonds' camp indicated that Tom Vallery wouldn't insert Joe Manlius as the designated hitter for the games at Pilot Field. Tom would continue to platoon Joe and Thor at first base as well as Merk and Bennie in the outfield with Roy alternating between center and right. In games at Buffalo, Tom would use Andy as the DH and put Psycho Bielski or Maxwell Street in left field.

"It just goes to show what you can do when you have the right horses in your stable," Peter cryptically remarked to James and Stash. The Wolves' player-manager hadn't fiddled with his batting order in the first two rounds of the playoffs without ill effect. P.J.'s major problem involved the absence of the designated hitter rule for the first two and last two games. There was no chance P.J. would sit himself on the bench. If he went back to right field, the least damaging option was to platoon left-hand-hitting Andre with right-hand-hitting Diego in left field. To sit down either a .319 hitter or a .302 hitter would stir up some questions about the inexperienced manager's judgement and sanity, but the *coup de gras* was to move Toby to the lead-off spot. With him batting at the top of the order, the Wolves could apply first inning pressure. The wrinkle was ridiculed in the press and on the sports talk shows, but Vallery was impressed. P.J.'s opposite number and peer stated: "It's logical...I don't think it'll do him any good, but it's logical."

Shortly before dinner, Willy called New Rochelle. Zinger was out, but Michelle answered the phone. "Now what're we going to do? Willy, it's the Series..."

"It's World War Three, Michelle," joked Willy.

"Good luck, sweetie!"

"Thanks, Michelle...Give Zinger, Steph, and Mikey my love, okay? Bye!"

Willy spent a quiet evening–a snack, a five-mile run, another snack, meditation, some downtime in front of the boob tube, and early to bed before descending into the Gotham maelstrom on Saturday. In suburban Lockport, New York, Brian Robbins was basking in the afterglow of a day of home chores with Maggie, the kids, the cat, the dog, the fish, and the bird after yesterday's lazy day at the lake. Life was good. At the age of forty-one with twenty years in the bigs to his credit, Brian could have spent this season with a mediocre team, where his 300th win might have been the high point of an unremarkable body of work. Instead, his milestone was just one of nineteen on the way to a pennant. Tomorrow "Old Folks" would start the Super Series opener against the Diamonds of New York. Perhaps, a week from Sunday, Brian may finally win the championship ring that has eluded him until now. Being at home was a pleasant break from the myopia on the field and in the clubhouse. Tonight his major concern was carting the rubbish barrels out to the curbside, a backlog of trash and recycling having accumulated over three weeks of road trips, during which Maggie and Brian missed their regular pickups. He walked through the garage and failed to notice the extension cord plugged into the hedge clippers, forgotten on the concrete floor. He tripped on the cord and fell face first, unable to break the fall with his hands occupied by a plastic bin full of glass bottles. Momentarily dazed, Brian felt surreal detachment, and no pain whatsoever, as he pulled a glass fragment from his bloody right palm. Only when he raised his hand to inspect it did he notice his pinky, dangling like a loose thread from the backside of his hand. "Maggie! Oh my God, Maggie!"

Despite the terror of the moment, Maggie Robbins dialed 9-1-1, packed Brian's hand in a bag of ice from the 'fridge, mapped out a route on her GPS via secondary roads to avoid traffic and signal lights, and gave a full description of her van to the dispatcher over the cell phone so that the EMTs could switch Brian from the family minivan to an ambulance anywhere along the way. Team physician Stu Lacy performed battlefield surgery, a stop-gap repair job, awaiting the arrival of a surgeon from Rochester, Minnesota. Two hours later, the specialist took over and after another hour under the knife the medical team met the press, holding vigil. Live on local television, Peter Jones was a jumble of nervous energy, Eddie Paris seemed out of place and useless, and Dana and Barry looked like the mortician and cadaver at a funeral.

Dr. Lacy spoke first. "We saved the hand and reattached the finger. There was extensive trauma to Brian's hand, but only limited nerve damage and no permanent impairment. Brian Robbins will pitch again."

"Will he be able to pitch in the Series?" asked a wag, shouting from a far corner.

The sheer idiocy of the question escaped the senior surgeon, apparently accustomed to lay people's ignorance in the face of the obvious. He stepped in front of Dr. Stu and simply said, "It will be eight to ten weeks before Mr. Robbins can begin light exercise."

As Shane Hennessey wrote in the morning edition of the *Buffalo Times*: "Brian Robbins, his pinky, and pitching hand will survive. The Buffalo Wolves are dead on arrival."

CHAPTER 24

Willy was nervous and fretful the night before the Series opened. The loss of Brian was like a family tragedy, even apart from its effect on the Wolves' chances in the Series. Old Folks' presence on the team made them better somehow. Indeed, without Brian, the pitching match-ups for the first three games would be Jacobson versus Naulls, Douglas versus Beal, and Danielson versus Jiminez. The Las Vegas odds-makers favored the Diamonds in all three pairings, notwithstanding the fact that Sandy Lee lost two games in the pennant series and Sadie won two.

Unable to sleep for more than an hour at a time, Willy tuned in Sportsnet for a wee-hours rebroadcast of its Series preview with a blue-ribbon panel of wags, including Dale Goodwyn and Brad Lucas, presumably to pick up a few extra bucks, giving their predictions and expert analyses. Kirk Tatum, the outfielder and running back, was invited as the token player and Dave Warren hosted the show, apparently willing to take any odd jobs he could, since Jeff McCarty and Cam Hammersmith landed the "color" and play-by-play jobs with USTV for the Classic Series. "Pandering pundits punning," the host babbled. Willy's blood pressure rose as she listened to the esteemed analysts compare the D's and Wolves, position by position. With unanimity, they ranked Paul over Jed behind the plate, Thor and Joe over "Matt Who?" at first, Cal over Kevin at second, Keith over Glenn and Alex at third, Demmy over Marty at short with outbursts of not very objective laughter, Roy over Andre in right, and Andy over Diego in left. The Wolves were only given the edge with Toby over Merk in center and P.J. as the designated hitter. The sage oracles even rated Benny as a superior bench warmer to Teddy. There was more of the same when the experts discussed the pitching and further guffaws as the likes of Randy, Scotty, and Chris were compared with Zinger, Tim, and Larry. Willy was already riled up when Lucas said, "Willy Beal has been Buffalo's strongest pitcher in the postseason, and now, without Robbins, she's the Wolves' best right-hander. That means Buffalo's ace is at about the same level as the D's fourth and fifth starters, Zanetsky and Phillips, who'll be sitting in the bullpen for the Series."

Goodwyn strenuously disagreed, as did Kirk Tatum. Said Tate, "Willy B.'s in control on the mound. I'm talkin' about some serious intimidation here. She's every male hitter's nightmare...She's your mama comin' to get you." The laughter rolled. "She's your mama, your sister, your wife, your mistress–bustin' into your all-night poker game. She sits on down, deals the next hand, and cleans out all the long green on the table." There was more laughter. "Then she says, 'Get your sorry [*bleep!*] home, boy!' I'm tellin' you...She scares me!" Warren warily eyed Tate and said somberly, "Let's pause for these commercial messages."

There was no escaping the fact that the remaining days of this baseball season would be acted out by the Wolves and Diamonds in a fishbowl. The Superteam versus Cinderella Series was everywhere. ReVerse and American Cola Co. even resurrected Willy's commercial spots. Amid the pre-Series hype, the governors of New York and New Jersey got into a flap over bragging rights at a luncheon honoring the Diamonds at the Midtown Athletic Club. Just whose home team were the

Diamonds? "They play in New Jersey's Meadowlands, but the Diamonds belong to the Empire State," opined His Excellency, momentarily disinheriting the city of Buffalo in his enthusiasm to embrace the Diamonds. The Albany-Trenton tug of war rang flat and tinny upstate. "Good thing for the Guv it isn't an election year," observed Cal Bonham. "He ought to be more careful about what he says in public," thus spoke Demeter Fortune.

Willy could have spent her entire Saturday shuttling from one personal appearance to another. Instead, her only commitment was to meet Rob DaSilva to tape a joint interview with none other than Zinger. The taping was mid afternoon at the Meadowlands. For the first time in three and a half months, Willy sat in the Diamonds' dugout.

"I'm here with Willy Beal of the Buffalo Wolves and Steve Filsinger of the New York Diamonds, two pitchers, two friends, former teammates, who find themselves pitching against each other in this year's Final Series."

"Zinger used to call me *the tall girl*," said Willy, giggling as Zinger elbowed and tickled her on camera. "Like there was some *other* woman on the team who wasn't tall." Willy and Zinger sat side by side, erect from the waist up, but their legs squirmed to nudge, kick, and step on toes. "That's like me calling him a *Jewish* pitcher...which is ridiculous 'cause the Diamonds are the first pro team since the House of David with *two* Jewish pitchers." As Zinger reached over Willy's shoulder to wrap her in a headlock, her muffled voice said, "Oops, better edit that..."

"There you go with that mouth of yours..." teased Zinger, alternately tickling her in the ribs and rapping his knuckles on her head.

"People don't understand how me and Zinger get silly and..." she laughed spasmodically, losing her breath.

"Always something to say..." said Zinger while grappling with Willy, tucking her head under his arm and pinching the most ticklish part of her body, to either side of her belly button, until she squealed and begged him to stop.

Rob said with serious cadence, "The two former comrades in arms, as fate would have it, on opposing sides for the biggest games of their careers. Like enemy soldiers saluting each other from across the battlefield on the eve of the great conflagration."

Willy bent forward to lay a hand on Robby's knee. "You're sillier than we are."

Looking straight-faced into camera with giggly and wiggly Willy and Zinger alongside, the pro voice said, "For USTV Sports, I'm Rob DaSilva."

After the interview, Zinger asked, "Willy, can I talk to you a minute?"

"What's up, Zinger?" Willy puzzled at the look of anguish in his eyes.

"Let's go into the weight room," he said, as he took her by the arm. "Nobody's there."

"What's going on?" she asked warily, suspecting one of Zinger's practical jokes.

Suddenly, Zinger stood before her and cried, holding onto her hand and sending a trembling message of pain through it. "Oh, God, Willy, I don't know what I'm gonna do."

Willy felt tremors herself as tears welled up in empathy. "Zinger, honey, what is it?"

"It's little Mikey," he sobbed. "He's been getting dizziness and headaches for a couple weeks. We didn't think it was any big deal at first, but it kept on...They think it's a brain tumor."

Speaking the words between hoarse gasps for breath, Zinger fell into Willy's embrace, crying against the nape of her neck. She gently stroked the back of his head with her fingers. Then she asked, "Why're you telling *me*?"

"Who else should I tell? Can you see me blubbering this way to Cal or Paul?"

"Sure, they love you just like me," she whispered before pressing his face between her palms and kissing his cheek. "What can I do?"

"I think you're doing it," Zinger said. "I can't talk to Michelle about it. I have to be the strong one. I can't let her see me falling apart."

"Is it...malignant?" Willy was afraid to say the word "cancer."

"We don't really know yet. We have to bring him for tests." Willy and Zinger didn't go through the weight room door, but stood silently leaning against it with their hands on one another's shoulders. "How can I think about baseball? Goddamn it, there's nothing Mikey wants more than to see me pitch in the Series."

There was a dreamy quality to his voice, as Joe Manlius walked by, studied the scene, and said, "Good to see you, Willy."

"Same here, Joe," she replied softly, without letting go of Zinger.

"So, enough about me! How's by you these days, Willy?" Zinger asked humorously with a glimmer of his true self shining through his veil of despair. Willy came within a hair's breath of sharing a closely held secret with Zinger, but discretion told her that this wasn't the time.

"I know people always say this, but if there's anything I can do..." Zinger nodded to her, sighing heavily, as she raised slightly on her toes to kiss his forehead. With a parting squeeze of his hand, Willy said, "I love you, Papa Bear." Willy phoned Michelle about an hour later. The two women spent fifteen minutes bawling over the phone. There was nothing to say, but much to share.

Part of the media show prior to game one was "family hour," where players tried to look natural while parading around the artificial turf with spouses and youngsters. The Wolves were the first to promenade in this manufactured photo-op for the paparazzi and Willy deliberately lingered as the out-of-towners gradually departed and gave way to the home team, the haughty Diamonds. Willy passed Keith and Joy Whalen, receiving smiles. She exchanged hellos with Thor and Cindy Andreason, likewise Benny and Cornelia Marquez. She strolled close enough to touch Andy Gilbert's shoulder and bowed respectfully to Kwan Lin. Roy Burton was taken aback by Willy's finger pointed as if cocking a trigger, but his smile was uncharacteristically bashful. As usual, Lizann and their kids were nowhere to be found. She saw Rita and Tom Vallery with Merk and Joanna Mercado. She also saw Larry, Tim, Jay, Laddy, and Pigpen, but, not meaning to slight them, headed with quickened steps for Sandy Lee, standing next to Rudy Judd. She kissed the pitcher smack on the lips. "How've ya been, cuz?" Without a word, she wrapped her arms around the pitching coach, who whispered, "We've missed you, sweetheart."

"I've missed you guys, too," Willy said, turning to her name gently spoken by Leota Douglas, generating an almost angelic aura as she approached with Gil and their brood of two, Biko and Ashanti. Willy nestled herself between her two friends and lay her head on Leota's shoulder while clinging tightly to Big Gil's enormous hand. As children often do, the preschoolers sensed something special and tender, yet had no means of describing or understanding it. Ashanti intuitively patted the back of Willy's hand while Biko grabbed her pants leg. A few uncounted seconds passed and Willy broke the spell. "You big chump! I'm gonna whip your butt tomorrow."

Gil exploded with laughter. "Tell you what! Let's you and me pitch his-and-hers shutouts for nine innings. Then, may the best bullpen win."

"You're gunning for the all-time record, aren't you?"

"Believe it, baby!" Big Gil asserted. "I'll reach Whitey Ford's thirty-two straight scoreless innings by the eighth."

"Forget about it, bay-bee," she taunted him with a smirk. "We're gonna beat you." Willy gently touched the children's heads in turn and exchanged a kiss with Leota. Willy made a show of caressing the front of her Buffalo Wolves jersey and said, "Willy's home, Leota." Next, Willy scanned the field full of people, seeking Paul. All she wished to give him was a wink and a nod, but he wasn't to be found. "I hate this kinda shit," he would say. Then Willy saw Cal. After pecking him on the cheek, she asked him, "How's the ankle?"

"Are you scouting me or what?" He spied her impishly.

"No, Cal, I'm just asking about a friend."

"It's fine, Willy. Look out, Buffalo. I can play."

"Good," smiled Willy. "We don't need a handicap." She and Cal hugged, and then she said playfully, "If you'll excuse me, I have to go back to hating y'all now."

"Nothing personal, right?" sang Cal as they parted.

Willy took one last look in vein for the Diamonds' catcher and ducked down the steps into the empty visitors' dugout. En route to the clubhouse she focused her mind's eye on the imagery of a row of nine faceless batters in Diamond blue, gold, and pinstripes, nameless automatons to be intimidated, jammed, and struck out. *Nine bowling pins to knock down. Three times nine equals twenty-seven strikes and you're out!* Her dearly loved friends ceased to exist.

As America's Home Team meandered onto the field for pregame warm-ups and batting practice, Willy went back to the traveling team's clubhouse, bearing a makeshift "WOLF'S LAIR" sign, where a group of players and coaches gathered to catch USTV's special preview, airing an hour before game time. There was a rush of images on the screen, vintage sips of wine from Fall Series past. Rob DaSilva introduced this year's world championship as a classic matchup of powerhouse and underdog. Rob delivered a delectable piece of editorial: "In 1879, the Buffalo Bisons played in the majors. Buffalo was a big league town for seven seasons without winning a pennant. The team dropped out of the majors, but was one of the minor leagues' top venues for over a hundred years. The ill-fated Players League and Federal League briefly brought big-time baseball back to town, but those teams proved short-lived. When Pilot Field opened its doors in 1988, Buffalo became the first minor league franchise ever to draw a million fans. Buffalo has held its own as a big league sports city and now the Wolves stand ready to challenge the mighty New York Diamonds...In the fabled history of America's Pastime there have been only two brief periods of time where one could clearly name the most popular player on the most popular team in baseball...when George Herman Ruth played for the Bronx Bombers and when Jack Roosevelt Robinson played for Brooklyn's Boys of Summer...We are witnessing such a moment again because a player named Willy Mae Beal pitches for the Buffalo Wolves. With a little bit of magic, baseball's *girl of summer* just might become the game's *Ms. October*."

"Oh, Robby," Willy murmured. She turned to Stash, Kevin, and Marty, who were smiling at her. "I don't believe he said that about me."

Moments later, the theatrical introduction of players was complicated because the visiting team's manager, customarily called first onto the field, was also the right fielder and number three batter. To introduce Peter Jones third would be poor theater indeed, but this approach proved appropriate as the Meadowlander boo-crew needed time to warm up before they could do justice to one of Buffalo's best known villains. P.J. was still waving and bowing in mock appreciation for being so well booed after "Batting fourth, playing left field, number thirty-two, Diego Santamaria" was announced over the public address system. The boo-note held steady through the starting pitcher, Woody Naulls, and withered to an insulting lack of noise when "the rest of the American champion Buffalo Wolves" scampered onto the field to stand along the third base line, except for the pockets of upstate sojourners and turncoats that spontaneously sprang up on sighting the familiar long-legged woman wearing the unfamiliar flannels. Before the scattered chants of *"Wil-lee"* had a chance to take on the infectiousness of a wave, the PA boomed: "And now, ladies and gentleman, boys and girls, your National champion New York Diamonds!"

The roaring of the New York and New Jersey crowd swept the stadium like a fleet of motorcycles through a wind tunnel. Once the manager, coaches, team doctor, and trainer were out of the way, each player was summoned with a benediction: "Led the league with 212 base hits...A five-time all-star and eight-time gold glove third baseman...Led the league with 16 triples, 110 bases on balls, and was second in the league with a batting average of .330..." The accolades for Bonham, Whalen, and Fortune grew longer and the crowd grew louder, although nests of boo-birdies popped up to dump on Demmy. "Batting fourth...playing center field...led Big League Baseball with 45 home runs, 142 runs batted in, 118 runs scored, 369 total bases, a slugging percentage of .618..."

"This could go on all day," chirped Marty Slattery to Matt Zaremba.

"...and a batting average of .322..."

"Aw, gimme a break!" the Wolves' shortstop moaned.

"...number seventeen, Roy Burrr-ton!" The crowd noise rolled, thundering in the thin night air, and held its peak until the ninth batter's name was called. "Ladies and gentleman, boys and girls, please direct your attention to the sidelines..." The cheers became louder. "The pitcher..." Even louder! "Number twenty-three..." And louder still! No one at home or in the park heard the announcer say, "Bruce Jacobson."

Willy's excitement was absolute, flushed by the realization of where she was, knowing that she watched tonight and pitched tomorrow, she bounced with joyful exuberance and flitted from mate to mate, giving hugs, high fives, and handshakes. Willy was clowning as a soft-rock balladeer, grown somewhat long in the tooth since last hit tune, prepared to sing the National Anthem. Willy slung her arm around Scotty and Randy, began to sway, and belted out: *"O-oh, say, can you see..."*

"Damn, girl, the cameras are gonna find ya!" laughed James. "The whole world's gonna hear ya!" shouted Gene.

"By the dawn's ear-ly li-i-ight..."

"Yeah," whispered Kevin, who felt the powerful but sweet, melodic timbre of Willy's soprano envelop him.

"What so proudly we hailed..."

"Holy shit!" Irv exclaimed. "She sounds better than that joker at the microphone."

"What a voice!" cracked director Marc Bergeron through his headset, wired to producer Russ Heman in the stadium's media operations center. "Pipe in the audio, Marc," commanded USTV's whiz kid. Russ listened for a moment and barked, "Put Jacques's video on the monitor." Russ studied his multifunctional control panel and quipped, "What the hell!" He reached to switch off the main audio-video feed and turned on Willy. "She's the best show in town."

Peter stared with starry eyes at the pitcher he loved like his own sister. He felt tingles inside. Willy hit *"free-e-e,"* slid up an octave to high-C with quivering vibrato, and her voice sent a shudder through P.J.'s body. Andre Toussaint felt, then squelched, a tear. "She's givin' me the chills, man," Sadie said to Teet. "God, that's beautiful," Stash said to Toby.

"...and the ho-ome of the bra-ave!"

Willy opened her eyes as if waking from a reverie and was startled by her teammates breaking ranks to embrace her in appreciation. They knew she sang it especially for them– although a hundred million viewers worldwide overheard it.

The ceremonial first pitch was being thrown by some luminary, whose notoriety was secondary to having been Sebastian Fabian's prep school classmate. A moment after the honorary ball was tossed, Cameron Hammersmith, up in the broadcasting booth, announced: "The official paid attendance for game one is tallied at 76,900, the highest figure for a Series game since the 1959."

Rob DaSilva added, "There was a good deal of controversy during the regular season about give-aways and cut-rate ticket sales to boost the official attendance numbers."

Cam said, "It seems as though the sideshow gets more attention than the ballgames, but there's no question that this Diamond club comes into the finals with some impressive credentials. Joining our USTV broadcast team is my partner from the Millennium Channel, Jeff McCarty."

"Thank you, Cam," said Jeff. "As you said, the Diamonds assembled some eye-catching numbers this past season, led by the pitcher taking the mound tonight. Bruce Jacobson, shaky winner of one game in the pennant championship, was the standout performer in the second half of the regular season. Jake led BLB in winning percentage, strikeouts, and ERA...pitching's triple crown...and without a doubt, he'll be named pitcher of the year...since the sportswriters cast their ballots at the end of the season, before Gil Douglas's spectacular pitching in the playoffs."

Cam: "On the mound for Buffalo is Woody Naulls, the Wolves' winningest pitcher. He's now set to start the Series opener after the tragic injury to Brian Robbins."

Jeff: "There's no question, for the Buffalo Wolves to make a good showing in the October Classic, the key pitchers are Woody Naulls and Willy Beal. The Wolves need quality starts from both of them in these first two games."

Rob: "As the New York Diamonds take the field...Big Joe Manlius is playing first base and Max Street is in right field. Two left-handed bats, Thor Andreason and Mercurio Mercado, remain on the bench with the lefty, Naulls, pitching for Buffalo."

Cam: "Leading off for Buffalo is Toby Clay. Kevin McDonald is on deck, followed by Peter Jones..."

Rob: "The first pitch of the Series is a fastball...In there, for strike one!"

Jeff: "P.J.'s decision to move Clay to the top of the batting order has stirred up some controversy."

Rob: "Curveball on the inside corner...Clay swings and misses. Strike two!"

Cam: "It's hard to understand P.J. tinkering with his batting order when they need all the offense they can get, especially because the Diamonds' pitching staff led Big League Baseball with twenty-five shutouts by the starters and their relievers saved fifty-five out of sixty save opportunities."

Rob: "Clay fouls off a fastball from Jacobson. The count remains oh-and-two."

Jeff: "The Buffalo Wolves, on the other hand, had the worst road record in the majors and their bullpen had the highest rate of blown saves, saving only thirty-five out of fifty save opportunities, a thirty percent failure rate."

Rob: "The pitch...Lined into right field for a base hit by Clay to open the ballgame!"

Cam: "Obviously, putting Clay in the lead-off spot is a stroke of genius on the part of Peter Jones."

Jeff: [Laughing] "Obviously!"

Toby's opening hit off Jake cut the tension in the somewhat awe-struck Wolves' dugout. This was just another ballgame after all. The Wolves belted two home runs off the D's southpaw, one in the fourth by Mattie Z., the other in the fifth by Toby, following a base on balls to Marty. Leading 3-2, Woody gave up six hits and struck out eight, but the D's came to life in the eighth after Demmy walked and Roy doubled to put runners on second and third. As Chris and Scotty warmed up, P.J. called time, tapped his right forearm to indicate a righty from the bullpen, and went to the mound to relieve Woody. Chris, who always wore tinted, thick-lensed, goggles, strolled to the mound with his beady eyes dilated and unadorned by spectacles. "What the hell's going on?" Peter barked. "Did you lose your glasses?"

"Relax, skip," said Chris, who flashed a freshly tattooed *B* for Buffalo on the back of his pitching hand. "I can see. I got my contacts in. I'm just letting my personality shine through, like my idol Willy does!" Peter said something that sounded like "Judas flogging Christmas," kicked some dirt, and walked away. Sitting on the bench next to Woody, Willy touched and stroked his left arm, feeling its heat in the way she often "copped a feel" from her fellow pitchers when they left games.

"Chris Van Aachen is quite a character," Cam wittily intoned, as USTV's Russ Heman directed his number one camera jockey to get a good close-up shot of Chris's nose ring, big-gauge earlobe plugs, and peace medallion necklace. The eccentric Wolf struck out Joe Manlius, but Andy Gilbert drove a fastball deep to the warning track, allowing Demmy to tag up and score the tying run on a sacrifice fly. Chris ended the jam by fanning Paul, did likewise to Merk, pinch-hitting for Max in the ninth, and kept pitching into the tenth, yielding only one hit and striking out five. In Chris's third inning of relief, Joe and Paul singled, and Merk, hobbled by injury and coming off the poorest season of his career, went to bat with two outs.

"A long drive to deep center field..." called Rob. "And that's gone! It's over!...Mercurio Mercado raps a game-winning, three-run homer to cinch it for the Diamonds, six to three...Bruce Jacobson goes the distance and then some, all ten innings, for the win. Van Aachen takes the loss in relief for Buffalo."

The throng was jubilant, but the one-punch knockout at midnight left the pack of Wolves dazed as they exited the field. Willy felt a sense of dull shock. Afterward, P.J. was stoic. "It's tough to drop the opener, but we did a lot of things right tonight." He told the wags, "Woody outpitched Jake, inning for inning, and Chris was as good as I've ever seen him." Added Peter's brother, James: "Them's the breaks, I guess. We'll get 'em next time."

CHAPTER 25

The Sunday editions spewed forth analyses and regurgitated every at-bat and inning pitched of the opener along with pablum fluff pieces on the Wolves and Diamonds. Willy went into Manhattan to breakfast with Samantha Khoury at her ritzy midtown hotel–on *Sportsworld*'s tab, of course. "No Joisey Halladay Inn for me, pal!" said Sam. She gave Willy's nose a playful tweak. "Feeling the pressure or what?"

"You know something, Sam?" sighed Willy. "I wouldn't even be in this position if poor Brian hadn't almost cut his finger off."

Sam studied Willy's face and snickered. "After what you did in the playoffs, do you think P.J. would've kept you in the bullpen?"

"I think Peter would still want to use me as the closer," Willy said.

"Bullshit! Peter Jones *hates* modern relief pitching, Willy. He's the biggest throwback of all. He's acting out the role of an old-time manager who brings on his ace in relief to save the big game."

"Peter keyed the starting rotation around Brian, not me."

"Brian pitched *one good game* in the league championship, which he lost. He was blown out in five of his last six starts. Remember?"

Willy shook her head adamantly. "I pitched the last game of the season in Toronto so that Peter could go with Woody if there had to be a tie-breaker the next day. The only reason I started a game against KC was to give Woody an extra day's rest."

"Even if Brian were around, you'd still be P.J.'s ace. You're the stopper. Peter just doesn't want you to realize it."

"And why not?"

Sam cackled with laughter and slapped Willy's knee. "It's a guy thing. He needs to be in control. If he's in control, you kiss *his* feet. If you're in control, he kisses *your* feet."

"Excuse me! Who's kissing whose feet?" Willy sat upright with contrite propriety, thoroughly enjoying being playful with her friend.

Sam reached for Willy's shoed foot and squeezed her toe. "Nobody, human or divine, controls you but *you*, pal. Believe it!"

When Sam produced a cigarette and Flic lighter from her handbag, Willy pursed her lips. "I thought you quit, Sam."

"I did," exclaimed Sam as she dangled the unlit smoke from the corner of her mouth while rubbing the tip of her thumb against the plastic wick of the lighter. "Cold turkey is really like brutal. Give me some slack, okay?"

Willy pantomimed throwing a rope. "Here! Slack!" she quipped, half-smilingly.

Ever the showman, Sebastian Fabian pulled a rabbit out of his hat for game two. The Willy B. tee-shirts came out of mothballs, redesigned with a red circle and slash mark superimposed over Willy's face. The "Willy Busters" went for $20 on the street and $10 in the stadium. The owner himself wore one. Willy called Michael Avery, her accountant and business manager, cell phone to cell phone, inside the stadium. "Can't we stop him from using my likeness, Michael?"

"We certainly can," he replied. "But let's wait. Let him sell a million of them and we'll sue his designer pants off. It's payback time, Willy."

Next Willy ran the media blockade two hours before game time. When she went to the sidelines to warm up, the crowd's reaction was more vocal and strenuous than that for her opposite number, Gil Douglas, but decidedly of two minds. The shrieks of *"Wil-lee, Wil-lee!"* were accompanied by inharmonious boos, jeers, and calls of *"Let's go Dees!"* and *"Demo*-li-*tion!"* The undercurrent was leaden.

"Let's face it," Cam Hammersmith told the viewers tuned to the USTV network: "There was nothing less than a love affair between Willy Beal and these fans just a few short months ago."

"Willy herself has rejected the 'avenging angel' label," said Rob DaSilva, "but there's no denying the emotional backdrop for her return to the Meadowlands, wearing a Buffalo Wolves' uniform."

"As the old saying goes," added Jeff McCarty, "there's a thin line between love and hate, and we've got some 77,000 fans straddling that line tonight."

As the Wolves' starting pitcher's name was called out to the crowd a few minutes hence, Willy bowed elaborately and gracefully, then raised a clenched fist to the once adoring, now estranged, Meadowlands fans.

"And away we go!" creaked the voice of the old pro, Ernie Arnett, on the radio side. His partner, Zack Traynor cursed in disgust, off mic, at the unfurled signs reading: "BUFFALO SUCKS" and "BEAT THE BITCH."

Tom Vallery adjusted the Diamonds' lineup and batting order for game two, inserting Merk in center field and the lead-off spot, batting Cal second, and putting Thor in place of Joe at first base. However, the Wolves fielded the same setup with Glenn playing third and Diego in left, leaving left-handed hitters Teddy and Andre on the bench. Before the game was underway, Andre sat forlorn in the dugout, uncomprehending as to why Peter put Diego in his stead, but he voiced no protest, simply sitting alone and silently, and no one approached him.

After loading the bases, the Wolves had Big Gil on the ropes in the top of the first inning. Toby led off the game with a single, as he had done against Jake. Kevin reached base on an error by Keith, the D's golden gloved third baseman, and Peter smacked a single over the reach of Cal to put runners on first, second, and third base. Diego, batting in the clean-up spot, hit a hard grounder to Demmy at shortstop, who went for the double-play, allowing Toby to score, ending Gil's postseason streak at twenty-four scoreless innings. Cal's throw to Thor at first was a shade late. Diego was safe and Jed came to bat with runners on first and third. He drove a grounder to Cal and this time the Diamonds turned the twin-killing to retire the side.

Said Cam: "After half an inning of play, Buffalo leads here in game two, one-zip, with New York coming to bat and the first lady of Big League Baseball taking the mound. Willy swaggered and frolicked as flamboyantly as ever, but the stony determination on her face showed not a hint of friendship or fondness for Mercurio Mercado as he positioned his feet in the batter's box. Willy decided to go right after him with a sidearm fastball over the middle of the plate. Ailing or not, Merk's bat speed was unafflicted, as his midnight moonshot off Chris well proved. He went inside out and pulled a fly to the opposite field, high and far enough to have gone out of Pilot Field, but not the Meadowlands. Diego played straight-away and shallow. The ex-catcher lumbered several strides behind the ball as it hit the turf just before the warning track. He gracelessly fielded the bounce off the wall and turned a strong throw to Marty, the shortstop playing the cutoff. A healthy Mercado should have had the hometowners on their feet as he steamed toward the hot corner, but he scarcely beat Marty's relay to Kevin without sliding for a two-bagger.

Jed walked halfway to the mound and pulled off his mask. "Big deal!" he said to Willy. "It don't mean nothin', kid."

"I'm okay," she responded, then turned around and called to Mercado, "Get yourself a chair, Merk. You're going nowhere." His face was expressionless. Willy stood with her arms dangling at her side. *Stay loose, Willy Mae!* she told herself and took a deep breath as the PA announcer trumpeted: "Number twelve, Calvin Bonham, second base..." Cal stood alongside the batter's box and fiddled with his bat. When he settled into the box, he tried to catch Willy's attention with a wink. She saw it and returned the slightest of smiles before lowering her head. Cal looked as Willy slowly raise her head once again. As if removing one mask to reveal another, her eyes were locked in an unambiguously deathly stare directed at Jed's flashing signals. Cal said to himself: *Time to get serious. The woman has come to play.*

Willy worked a ball and two strikes to Cal on a sidearm fastball, sidearm slider, and buggywhip fastball. She would look for a third strike with a backdoor slider clipping the inside corner. He fouled it off, the count went to two-and-two, and she tried to fan him with Papp's heater, missing letter-high. When Cal saw the offspeed subsequent pitch, he swung down on it and laced a hard bouncer toward third. The carpet-skipper evaded Glenn's glove and coursed its way along the left field foul line. Diego dove to snare it and his knees hit the turf with a thud. Mercado already crossed the plate with the tying run as Diego regained his footing and fired the ball to Marty, who chased the diving Bonham back to second.

    This time Willy turned not to the Diamond on second base, but to herself for a few choice words. She shut off her self-flagellation upon seeing P.J. call time and run from right field to left after Diego knelt on a bended knee while holding his other. A hundred million prime-time viewers watched Diego grimace in agony, still clutching his cracked kneecap. Pandit the trainer and Dr. Stu Lacy came running from the Wolves' dugout and P.J. signaled for Andre to come into the game. "There goes 106 RBIs out of Buffalo's lineup..." said Jeff, as Diego hopped on one foot, propped by human crutches, Pandit and the Doc, while the Meadowlanders perfunctorily applauded the wounded adversary.

    Willy threw a sidearm slider for strike one to Demeter Fortune. She missed the strike zone with an overhand slider for ball one and came back with another sidearm fastball, high and inside, for ball two. At two-and-two, Willy hadn't thrown anything "fat" over the middle of the plate and Demmy hadn't swung at any pitch that he wasn't sure he could hit. Neither pitcher nor batter had yet fooled the other. After faking a pickoff move to second–sending Cal headlong back to the bag with a quick swivel and kick of her foot, but no throw–

Willy fired the overhand heat, waist-high, to Demmy. The call of ball three by the home plate ump, Derk Morfitt, received an angry shriek from the woman at the mound. A slider down and in, missing the inside corner, sent Mr. Wonderful walking to first base. The Diamonds' fanatics let out a roar as the best hitter on planet earth came to the plate. Roy Burton's narrowed eyes formed the only expression of emotion or thought on his face as he assumed his tight, controlled stance. The fans clapped and chanted, *"Let's go Dees! Let's go Dees!"* Willy showed him two close-in, offspeed fastballs–first sidearmed, then buggywhipped–and he fouled off both. Ahead oh-and-two, Willy shook off Jed's sign for the slider and delivered the overhand heat. The noisy crowd stilled and Willy squealed with delight as Roy rippled at strike three. The first pitch to Andy Gilbert came in high for a ball as Demmy got a good jump and bolted for second base. Cal, the decoy, had lulled the pitcher and catcher by standing pat at second until Demmy's takeoff. *Delayed double steal!* Jed's throw to Marty was high and Demmy slid safely with the stolen base. He took a big lead and Cal, at third on the front leg of the double swipe, feinted toward the plate. The Wolves' infielders were taut, ready for the squeeze play or a steal of home, as Willy pitched ball two. She baited Andy with an offspeed pitch close and a breaking ball away, but he didn't bite. With the shrill of the crowd echoing in her ears, Willy shook off four sets of signs from her battery mate, in effect, rejecting all possibilities. The salty old dog of a catcher asked the ump for time to visit his suddenly distracted pitcher.

"Settle down, will ya? We can get outta this sitch, kid!" Willy nodded her head, eyes closed, her eyelids fluttering. Then she took the first of three deep, cleansing breaths. Her head cleared, but the moment of relaxation unfocused her attention and she felt her shoulder throbbing. She stifled a groan so as not to tip off Jed, who begged, "C'mon, there's millions of people waitin' for ya."

Willy forced herself to laugh. "Get on back behind the plate, oldtimer." He patted her butt gently and resumed his station. Willy delivered ball three on a soft, slow slider. She saw Jed twist his head to look to right field, where Peter signaled Irv and Ferdie. Cam announced: "There's activity in the Buffalo bullpen." Willy sweltered on a fair and cool October night. The hair beneath her cap felt like a sopping dishrag plopped on her head. Streams of sweat trickled along her cheeks and searing pain ran from shoulder to bicep. Each arm and shoulder muscle reverberating a sickening, tingling aftershock. Again, she threw an offspeed slider, which broke inside on the quickest wrists in the majors. Andy ripped the pitch into the canyonlike depths of center field for a two-run, stand-up double.

The chant of *"Wil-lee, Wil-lee, Wil-lee,"* intermittent and scattered, now turned into a new refrain. The slow taunt *"Wiiil-leee...Wiiil-leee...Wiiil-leee..."* wafted through the multitude and enveloped it.

Jed's sad eyes met Willy's. Not long on smoothness, he said, "Just ain't your night, kid." He pricked up his ears to the sound of the derisive taunting and tried to joke. "It must be the matin' call of the Meadow Muffins." Willy didn't utter a word. Her eyes were red, her face glistened, and her chin trembled until she clamped her front teeth onto her lower lip. Jed turned from her and watched Peter's approach. Willy couldn't look at her mentor right away, but he waited patiently for her to raise her head. Peter whispered, "Listen to me, Willy," as the ball passed from her hand to his. "Walk, don't run. Hold your head up. Don't let them get to you." Willy choked back the sobs, but the tears came pouring out.

CHAPTER 26

In the broadcast booth, Cam pronounced: "This is the first time in her pro baseball career that Willy Beal has been knocked out of the box in the first inning. Willy walked slowly, straight-backed, with a hint of a strut. The voice of the masses hooted, hollered, and crowed; white hankies waved; and the USTV cameras searched for Willy Busters tee-shirts. Willy wouldn't look up at the sky box, but she knew the owner of the Diamonds was there, savoring the moment. Alex tossed her a towel as she touched the top step. She stumbled down the three-stair descent with her face hidden from the Wolves and the all-seeing USTV eye. She sat by herself in the most distant corner of the dugout, spread her legs apart, hunkered forward with her head between her knees, and buried her face in the cloth of a towel.

The D's had scored three and held a two-run lead. Randall Craig went to pitch. He gave up a single to Thor, a sac fly to Paul, driving in Andy for the fourth run, and another single to Keith. Peter Jones steamed toward the mound after motioning for the left-hander from the pen. He gave Randy an arm-waving, angrily animated sendoff and greeted Phil with what appeared to be a royal chewing out before he delivered a single pitch.

"We got the Christians and some hungry lions," said bench-rider Teddy Balin. "Time for fresh blood!"

Willy uncovered her face to see Randy entering the dugout sanctuary. He sat beside his favorite female teammate and said, "We sho' nuff ain't in Kansas no mo', Dorothy!"

She smiled weakly, then cackled, "And your little dog, too!"

Trailing 4-1, Peter felt relieved that baseball's ultimate rally-killer and strategy-squelcher would curb the rout: the pitcher was coming to bat. He took pause to mull over his first three hitters of the second inning as Phil pitched a fastball to Big Gil. The best hitting pitcher in the bigs leaned his six-foot-eight, 250-pound frame into the ball and pounded it into the light fixtures. "A three-run home run by Gil Douglas!" shouted Cam. "The Diamonds lead seven to one and their seven-run, first-inning outburst ties an all-time Series record." When the third out ended the inning at long last, Peter Jones blurted out, "The pitcher bats, my ass!"

Staked to a six-run advantage, Big Gil was tagged for a homer by P.J. in the third–some poetic justice in small measure. That made it an 8-2 ballgame, Phil having given up a run in the second. He shut down the Diamonds through the fourth when Scotty took over. He also held the D's scoreless until Keith's two-RBI double in the seventh. The score was New York 10 Buffalo 2. After pinch-hitting for his pitchers twice, Peter managed himself into a corner. With Chris laboring two and two-thirds innings the night before, only Tito Melendez was available to pitch the bottom of the eighth. The D's battered the venerable Teet for three more runs. Ahead 13-2, Big Gil carried a three-hitter into the top of the ninth when Toby took him long with a homer, Kevin singled, and P.J. walloped his second round-tripper of the evening. Alas, it ended. Rob gave the post-mortem: "Gil Douglas, following three victories for the Diamonds over San Francisco, continues his superb pitching in the postseason, beating the Wolves in game two. Big Gil has now won five postseason games in a row, but his hope for a third straight shutout was ruined in the very first inning...Tonight's losing pitcher, Willy Beal, was quickly shelled out of her first Series game...That wraps up USTV's coverage of game two, brought to you by Nimoco and the Braunstein Brewing Company. Once again, the final score, New York Diamonds 13 and Buffalo Wolves 5..."

A subdued Willy spoke to the wags after the "laugher." She said, "Nobody likes to get hit around. They came out swinging and I laid the ball right over the plate. I never got going, I guess." Peter Jones stood outside the clubhouse door to tell Dave Warren and his postgame audience, "If we could take back the first inning, it's a three-two ballgame in the eighth and a six-five game with two outs in the ninth...but we can't take it back."

"Let's just get the hell back home," said Toby, speaking for all the gang from Buffalo.

After an open date for traveling, an anachronistic relic of a bygone era, the finals resumed at Pilot Field with an overcapacity crowd of 42,000 in attendance for game three. Willy fled the wags and hid from her teammates until Tuesday night. She seemed invigorated, renewed in spirit, and not unduly distraught over her miserable Sunday night of horrors. Busloads of Diamonds' fans made the trek upstate and were seated in pockets all around the ballpark. From one group, camped on the first base side, came a fellow wearing a Willy Busters tee-shirt, who managed to climb on the roof of the Wolves' dugout, swinging an oversized broom, leading a cheer of *"Sweep! Sweep! Sweep!"* The Diamond rooters were forthwith drowned by Buffalonian boos. Cam the Hammer told the folks viewing from the warmth of home and hearth: "The gentleman is being escorted off by security..." Then Jeff McCarty interrupted, "Say, he's getting a hand from the fans." Actually, Wolf shortstop Marty Slattery had taken the broom from one of the gendarmerie and stood near the on-deck circle waving it menacingly at the Diamonds' dugout as if it were a bat. Then, hoisting it in his crotch, Marty delivered a jiggling "shove it" gesture to the New York champs. The source of the crowd's approval thus apparent, Jeff chuckled, "I thought this was a family-friendly show." To which Rob wryly observed, "The ratings for this year's Series just went from G to PG to R." An unintentional double-entendre with the term "ratings" chimed a sour note with USTV's sports czar. Arnie Rutledge saw the record-shattering viewership withering away as the Final Series died in the land of blizzards, leaving the network ankle-deep in red ink due to forever-lost advertising dollars from the Japanese car makers and Canadian braumeisters if the D's completed a four-game sweep and the fifth, sixth, and seventh games went unplayed.

    Before the game, Willy climbed the barrier into the stands, creating a predictable stir among the fans in the lower box seats, to visit Katie Jones and her kids in the players' family and friends section. This was the first time Willy laid eyes on James and Katie's newbie, Caitlin Louise. "Can I take you home?" Willy crooned to the squirmy little tike, wearing a white bow tied to a few strands of reddish-orange fuzz on her mostly hairless topknot. Caitlin's blue eyes danced with perpetual laughter and her bottom was soaked through and through. "Again?" Kate declared, exasperated. Willy giggled, "I must be a pee magnet for your kids." The boys, Jimmy and Jeremy, flagged down the vendors, hawking hot dogs, peanuts, and you-name-it. "Do you guys have your hot dog holders?" The boy siblings cringed for the lady ballplayer's anti-meat-eating lecture, which was sure to follow, but she picked up the baseball glove stuffed between their seats and daintily placed a frank and bun into it. "See? That's a big league hot dog holder."

At the same moment that Willy surveyed her protégés, Tanya and Jennifer, flirting with a pair of cute boy vendors, James escorted his father, Amos, to the front-row dignitaries' box, from which the elder Jones would make the ceremonial first toss. Amy, who had been happily chattering with her real-life hero and soul mate, saw her father and grandfather making their way from the service entrance and asked her mother if she could go to them. She ran to her grand-daddy, but, instead of a little girl expecting to be lifted and hugged, she assisted her father in guiding Amos's slow, painfully labored steps. From ten rows away, Katie burst into tears and spoke haltingly, "Oh, my God...Amy's...holding...him...up!" Without hesitation or stumbling, the seventy-five pound child was literally carrying the old man she adored on her back in a perfect act of unconditional love.

"Amos 'Teach' Jones..." his name was intoned by Hammersmith on the TV side, Traynor on the radio side, and Arnett serving as master of ceremonies on the field. "His career spanned three decades as an outfielder and first baseman for the Kansas City Monarchs, Boston Braves, and Washington Senators with a lifetime batting average of over .300..." Amos was unsteady and bent over as he received the fans' applause with a spry salute.

Standing proudly at his side were his sons, James and Peter, daughter Betty, and granddaughter Amy. The pure, unadulterated joy in the bright, owlish eyes of the octogenarian was identical to that of the girl of nine. With a smiling wisecrack that caused Jimmy Mack Jones to throw back his head and guffaw, Amos dropped the first ball into Jed Guerin's outstretched glove. As the Jones clan grabbed and hugged one another, even Big Jack Finigan, tonight's home plate judge, cracked a smile.

    Following the pregame festivities, Cam said, "It's now or never for the Buffalo Wolf Pack. Every Series game is a must-win situation, but tonight's outcome will determine whether the Wolves wake up or roll over..." The verbal handoff went to Jeff McCarty: "It's a simple fact of history that no team has ever come back to win the Series after losing the first three in a row. The Wolves have to pull one out tonight and they have to do it against the Rebel from Stone Mountain, Georgia–Sandy Lee Danielson."

    Rob DaSilva analyzed: "Both managers are adjusting their preset game plans for their use of the designated hitter, in effect for the next three games scheduled at Pilot Field. Peter Jones is his own DH tonight and veteran Harry Washington is the right fielder, since Diego Santamaria is out of action with a knee injury. Tom Vallery has put rookie Maxwell Street into left field and named Andy Gilbert as the DH. The Diamonds again have Mercado leading off and Bonham batting second, while the Wolves' lineup is juggled just a little bit–Andre Toussaint is in left, Teddy Balin is at third, and Matt Zaremba, the first baseman is batting clean-up...But the player on the spot this evening is

Buffalo's starting pitcher, the lanky Panamanian right-hander, Sergio Jiminez."

Sadie shut out the mighty D's through seven frames, giving up six hits and three walks, while striking out eight with his wild and crazy sinker. Sandy Lee, who pitched horrifically in the postseason to date, limited the Wolves to only three safeties in a scoreless tie. Marty's "up yours with a broom" routine led to a belly-flop in the batter's box on the first pitch served by Sandy Lee. The knockdown wasn't exactly unexpected. Indeed, the Wolf shortstop hit the dirt, dangling his Louisville Betsy in the air, the instant Reb released the ball. Marty laughed his way back on his feet, as did the big fellow on the mound. The Good Old Boy sailed into troubled waters in the fifth. After Andre walked, Teddy and Matt grounded out. Then Vallery ordered an intentional pass to Kevin with Andre on second. The strategy backfired when Sandy Lee also walked Harry, the ninth batter. Willy watched the unraveling of Sandy Lee Danielson with the world championship on the line. However, on the hill tonight wasn't the same athlete who had been the premier pitcher in the bigs for the past two or three years. Willy empathized with the Rebel and had the fleeting notion that he had experienced a similar empathy while watching her yesterday.

Cam called the action on the field: "Toby Clay at the plate...Danielson pitching from the stretch position with the bases loaded...The pitch is swung on...A pop fly to center field, dropping in for a base hit...Toussaint scores. Zaremba scores. Two runs batted in for Clay and the Wolves are on top, two-nothing."

In the seventh, Tom pulled Sandy Lee in favor of Larry Brooks. With one out, Larry walked Harry and

Toby wrapped up his one-man show with a towering home run, his third in three games. In the top of the eighth, Sadie showed signs of tiring and P.J. tapped Chris to finish the game. Up 4-0, Wacky Van Aachen gave the best performance of his life as he held the D's hitless, although handing out three walks. Willy watched and couldn't help but smile as Psycho Bielski was announced as the pinch-hitter for Max. The Psycho struck out to end the game.

The second head-to-head match-up between twenty-game winning southpaws, Jake and Woody, took place twenty-one hours later. Game four began in the afterglow of the Wolves' hometown win, but the rarified euphoria faded by the seventh inning. The managers continued their strategic lineup dithering. Tom put Benny in left and Max in right, while P.J. sent his floating substitute, Teddy, in to play right field and Andre remained in left field. *Does it really make any difference who's in left and who's in right?* puzzled Willy. Scoreless in the sixth, Andre lost track of a fly ball hit by Cal, allowing it to drop for a three-bagger, as if to answer the question. With the Wolves' infield drawn in for a play at the plate, Marty missed connections with Keith Whalen's grounder to shortstop for an error and Cal scored. The D's led 1-0. For the second time in the Series, Woody pitched beautifully, a little better than Jake, but the boys from New York City nicked him for another run in the seventh. Andre was again unable to find a fly ball in left field. The long hit by Keith bounced past the Haitian wonderchild and landed in the grandstand for a ground-rule double. Demmy then paddy-whacked a legitimate double into the gap in left center field and Keith scored, making it 2-0. In the bottom of the inning, P.J. tripled and stood poised to score with two outs when Diego limped to the plate to hit for Alex, the Wolf third baseman of the night, and looked at a called third strike to end the run-scoring opportunity. In less than three hours' time, the Wolves' mood went from "It's good to be home" and "They can't beat us here" to the depths of despair. In the top of the eighth, with Phil pitching in relief of Woody, Paul singled and Andy walked. Tom sent out Psycho Bielski to pinch-run and Benny cracked a single to right. One run scored, but Teddy's smooth handling of the ball and sure throw to the infield kept the Psycho from crossing the plate with another. The D's were on top, 3-0, and P.J. batted Harry for Marty to start the home half. Harry was plainly overmatched, unable to get his bat around on three high-speed fastballs. Jake returned to his split-fingered fastball with Balin up next. Teddy meekly popped out to Keith in foul territory.

Buffalo's bench and bullpen were in awe of Jake's masterful twirling with Paul Cello calling the shots. The catcher in reserve, Gene Tyler, caught Willy's eye. He leaned back, hands tucked in his pockets, and whispered to her, "I heard Paul and Jake stay up late at night together, eatin' pizza and goin' over the charts." Willy raised her head to reveal a look of hateful rage as searing and daunting as the glare any batter had seen from her eyes all season. "Oh, shit, Willy," Gene stuttered. "Hey, I'm sorry...I was just kiddin'."

She sneered, "Forget about it," and looked out onto the field.

Ferdie Burgos told Gene, "Nice goin', douchebag!"

After running hard in a vain attempt to beat Demmy's throw to Thor on a ground ball for the third out to retire the side, Andre's eyes met Peter's as the DH-manager kicked his feet against the dugout steps, bleating expletives through his teeth. Peter gave Andre no hint of encouragement. Andre's glassy eyes saw only a cold indifference in Peter's. By twice erring in the outfield, Andre had fallen from grace. The surrogate father may as well have told his progeny, "You mean nothing to me now."

The veneer of sportsmanship began to crack as the sound and the fury bubbling beneath the surface rose from deep inside. Matt and Thor bumped at first base and James stepped between them. Alex and Keith exchanged spittle-dripping words before Toby and Roy pulled away their respective mates. Teddy curled his lip and clenched his fists as he walked by Benny, who lost his smile. The two most senior members of the umpiring crew, Monty Guilford and Ken Crenshaw, conferred and girded for something to blow.

Scotty, the third Wolf pitcher of the game, did his job creditably, keeping the ball down and serving playable grounders to the infielders off the bats of the dangerous Whalen, the more dangerous Fortune, and the most dangerous Burton. The lefty reliever who hated relieving overcame his angst and set down the side in order in the top of the ninth. In the bottom half of the final frame, however, Jake and Paul continued to weave their magic. Contact hitter Kevin McDonald hit a low-and-away breaking ball to short center for the first out. Toby Clay, hitless for the night, chased an up-and-in fastball for the second out and Jake's eighth strikeout. Peter Jones, who connected with a high fastball for an extra-base hit the last time, saw nothing but breaking balls and brought the game to an end by chopping one back to the pitcher for an effortless putout.

Said Rob: "Jacobson pitches a shutout and stops Toby Clay's twelve-game postseason hitting streak...Once again, Naulls is bested by Jacobson and the D's go ahead three games to one in the Series...This Big League Baseball season could be all over on Thursday night."

CHAPTER 27

In the preceding twelve months, Willy Beal pitched more than 300 innings in winter ball, the minors, and the majors. Counting the postseason, she appeared in 58 games and her career-to-date won-lost record was 24-11. Yet, on the fourth Thursday in October, she not only bore the stress of being the pitcher to stop the nearly inevitable D's win in game five, but she also had to prove herself once more. In the morning edition of the *New York Journal,* Brad Lucas took P.J. to task for naming Willy to start the fifth game after being beaten up in the second game: "She can't beat the Diamonds, she fell apart under the pressure, and P.J. is handing Willy B. Special the game ball again...Enjoy tonight's show, fans. Get ready for foot-stomping histrionics, shrieky bravado, and theatrical tears...as Peter and the Wolves self-destruct and Captain Tom and the Diamonds walk across the water to the world championship." The words inked by Brad's poison pen whirled from the Big Apple across the country, as hundreds of dailies, including *Today USA*, reprinted or excerpted his column. The breakfast jabberwocky on *Wake Up, America!* also picked up the refrain. When Willy actually read Lucas's column, she saw more of a lambasting of P.J. than herself.

Game number five was graced by the presence of a rapper named Tin Soul Jar, a self-described ex-Diamond fan, wearing a Wolves' shirt with number 28 on the back, lured by Barry and Dana to sing the star-spangled anthem and toss out the first ball. Tinnie insisted on making the first pitch from the mound and drew a warning from Jed Guerin, the grizzled catcher.

"Watch ya don't mess up the mound with them shit kickers," Jed told him, pointing at his fancy dress shoes. "Oh, I know," the rap star responded reverently. "This is hallowed ground." Hence, Tin Soul Jar pitched a half-decent slider to the plate, walked to the on-field microphone, and reached down to his gospel roots to deliver the National Anthem in a melodic tenor's timbre. The *Masta Rapsta* spread his arms for the first standing-O of the night.

Cam Hammersmith sang his tune from the broadcasting booth: "It could be all over tonight. The New York Diamonds send Gil Douglas to the mound. He's been invincible in the postseason, winning five in a row after racking up twenty victories in the regular season. The Wolves counter with Willy Beal, who was shelled in the first inning of game two. Any thoughts about that, Jeff?"

On cue, Jeff McCarty took over: "Well, Cam, there's been a lot of controversy about Peter Jones's choice of starting pitcher and tonight he's made still more changes in his Wolf Pack's lineup, moving Clay back to lead-off, putting Balin at third and batting second, dropping McDonald to seventh in the order, while installing Harry Washington in left field and Diego Santamaria in right field..."

Rob DaSilva picked up his line: "Buffalo desperately needs Santamaria's bat, but he's playing with a hairline fracture of the patella, while Andre Toussaint, another .300 hitter, is sitting it out..."

Cam argued: "Be that as it may, Toussaint's miscues in the outfield have cost Buffalo runs throughout the playoffs and in this Series."

Jeff disagreed: "But he's a better hitter than Washington and a better outfielder than Santamaria. P.J.'s benching the guy is a punishment, pure and simple."

Cam and Jeff fumed at each other so obviously to observers in the broadcasters' pavillion that Zack Traynor and Ernie Arnett, on the other side of the soundproof partition, were chuckling about it over the radio. Ernie thus spoke on air: "Despite the brouhaha about Willy Beal and Peter Jones and the insurmountable odds against beating a team that seems unbeatable, these Pilot Field fans are not about to say die."

Willy was surrounded by the sound of *"Wil-lee! Wil-lee! Wolf! Wolf! Ah-ah-ahoo!"* She made her patented sprint to the mound, slung five quick warm-ups to Jed, and danced in a circle around the mound with her fists pumping at the D's dugout and her long braided and beaded pigtails swaying. She expressed the ballgame's first pitch to Mercurio Mercado, a ninety mile an hour heater at the belt for a strike.

"Is she tentative after being rocked her last time out?" Zack asked his radio listeners. "I think not!" Merk went down on three swinging strikes and the spillover crowd of Buffalo boosters clapped, howled, and rose to their feet.

The Wolves scored the first run of the game in the third inning on an opposite-field home run by Kevin. In the sixth, Merk led off for the D's with a single. Cal followed and sliced a looper to short left field. With his knee braced, wrapped in bandages, and shot numb with pain-killers, Diego made a swan dive for the ball. He slid on his belly, or, rather, seemed to glide upon the grass with his right hand cupped over his glove, delicately upheld in front of his cocked head, looking as if he were offering a chalice to the gods. When the recaps ran the play in slow-motion, the gentle tones of a harp's strings fit nicely. Although it seemed he would continue to glide forever, Diego jumped to his feet and uncorked a flat-footed throw to Kevin in the middle of the diamond. Merk, the base runner, was hung up after running past second and halfway to third and was nailed dead as Kevin relayed to Matt at first for the easiest and biggest DP of the season.

"Like Say Hey Willie's over-the-shoulder basket catch in 1954," said Cam. "It wasn't the catch, it was the throw...eliminating the run which would've scored with ease." More important than the double-play was the rise Diego's catch gave the Wolves on the field and in the dugout. "Hot damn!" exclaimed the normally reserved Alex Suarez. "We're gonna turn this thing around," promised Glenn Harmon.

Demmy then tagged Willy for a single that would have given the Diamonds a 2-1 lead were it not for Diego's fielding feat. The Wolves sparked a fire and smoked Big Gil with a six-run outburst in the bottom of the next inning. The power pitcher *par excellence* used his fastball exclusively, "a big right-hander throwing smoke," to quote P.J. Toby swung and stood on first. Peter swung and two were on base. Mattie Z. swung and Toby scored. Diego checked his swing and walked to first base. Jed swung, Gil departed, and Jay Phillips threw the ball. Harry swung and two more scored.

Rob's rich voice rose over the crowd's joyful drone. "Gil Douglas...whose performance was being compared to some of the greatest pitchers of all time after winning five of five so far this postseason...was bombarded for six runs tonight and a total of eleven in two games against the mighty Buffalo Wolves."

When Jed and Kevin came home to score on Harry's base hit, Willy greeted them at the plate. She latched onto their hands and held them above her head as the trio ran to the Wolves' den. The jubilation of the Buffalo fans became even more frenzied at the sight of the most popular ballplayer in the world climbing to the dugout's roof, dancing a hip-hop step, and clapping to the beat of the howling Wolf cheer. Willy jumped from the roof and flew to the mound when the side was retired. With the Wolves leading 7-0, waves of *"Wil-lee! Wil-lee!"* swirled through the ballpark and showed no sign of letting up as the Diamonds went to bat in the top of the seventh. Meanwhile, workers pushing hand trucks rolled down the corridor to the back door of the visitor's clubhouse to remove the cases of champaign stacked in anticipation of a D's victory, which seemed a sure thing a few hours ago.

Even as Willy struck out Thor with a slider on the inside corner, Jeff's bias showed when he took the Wolves' moment and stood it on its head, proposing: "The way she's pitched down the stretch, in the playoffs, and in this game, *imagine* if Willy Beal still had the Diamonds' lineup behind her." Rob shot Jeff a contemptuous look and took over the mic: "Imagine if dreams were wishes and wishes were fishes..." *You're an ass wipe!* is what he would like to have told him.

At the plate was Paul. Willy teased him with a false, toothy grin and he smiled honestly back at her. Yet she could feel him trying to read her pattern of pitches. He guessed wrong twice, oh-for-two, grounded out and popped up. This time he would wait on the first pitch.

Sorry, Paul! I'm coming inside, outside, and inside with offspeed fastballs. Then say hello to the widow-maker.

"A ball and two strikes to catcher Paul Cello," said Rob. "Strike three! She got him swinging," said Cam. "She scorched him with that one, reading ninety-four on the radar gun," said Jeff, now a reluctant believer. Five minutes later, Rob: "A two-strike count to Keith Whalen, oh-for-three on the night...a fastball...Strike three! That's strikeout number seven for Willy Beal...And listen to this partisan crowd roaring its approval." Cam: "Willymania, born in New Jersey, is alive and well on Lake Erie." Prior to breaking for a mindlessly macho Braunstein Lite commercial, the screen showed Willy remaining on the mound as the teams changed sides. She doffed her cap, gave her pigtails a shake, and raised her arms to embrace the multitude. Then she turned and signed "I love you" before scampering off the field.

"Another standing ovation for Willy B.!" pronounced Zack via AM, FM, and HD radio. "She's completely stifled the New York Diamonds through seven innings...and the score is Buffalo seven, New York nothing!"

Dave Warren greatly preferred wining and dining in the press room with a portable TV set between containers of takeout Chinese food, rather than straining to see the action from the glass-enclosed broadcasting booth, jutting out above the field from the upper deck. "Look at that!" he said, pausing to wash down a mouthful of *moo-shi* chicken and crunchy noodles with a swig of styrofoam-cupped tea. "I never noticed her buns being so plump before."

"You slimy dog, you!" laughed his protégé, Cathy, the newly promoted sports director of USTV's New York affiliate, also known as the Amazing Catherine, since her prescient flagging of Willy's fourteen-inning marathon and its antecedents in the 1930s and '60s.

"No fooling, Cathy. Take a look, will you?"

"She's gonna waste a breaking ball, then jam him with a fastball." Cathy edged closer to the screen, now showing Willy in motion, delivering her pitch. "You're right, Dave! Those pants are really snug in the tush. I think she's put on some weight, at least ten pounds," Cathy concluded, as Max Street chipped a foul ball.

"D's kiss Willy's fat butt? There's no story there," lamented Warren as he poured sweet-and-sour sauce over his partially consumed egg roll.

The mini TV buzzed: "A broken-bat bouncer to third...on a two-two fastball at the fists...no trouble at all for Balin...to Zaremba...and there's one away in the eighth." Merk, the next batter, had singled and drawn a walk after fanning to start the game. With a full count, Merk caught a piece of a sidearm fastball and again hit a single. Cal, gunning for an infield hit, dragged a bunt up the line toward first, but Matt scooped the ball and flipped it to the fastest player on the field, who sped to cover the bag. With two outs and a runner on second base, Willy pitched to Demeter Fortune. She took Demmy to a full count and he watched a backdoor slider cut the inside corner for a third strike. With a fall-away motion, Willy already began to run from the mound as the pitch left her fingers. "Uh-oh!" said Cam, as Demmy made a beeline for the pitcher and cut off her departure. The thundering hooves of Matt and Kevin came from one side and Jed from the other as Demmy's and Willy's paths intersected. She quickly wrapped her arms around his shoulders and said, "Hey, guys, it's just me and Demmy talking. It's cool!" Her teammates pulled back and Willy took stock of Demmy's crystalline blue eyes as he whispered thickly, "Why'd you have to show me up like that?" She replied, whispering as well, "I didn't think about how it would look. I'm sorry, Demmy." Demeter Fortune, who knew Willy Beal rarely did anything without thinking, set his angular jaw and said stiffly, "Okay, forget it."

Willy trained her visage on the Wolves at bat in the eighth with Zinger pitching for the Diamonds. His sinkerball struck out Jed, got Kevin to pop out, and struck out Marty. Zinger's small triumph was a hitless, scoreless inning against Willy's Wolves. For a brief moment, she pictured Mikey and Stephanie cheering for their daddy. She saw little Mikey's face in her mind, shivered, took a deep breath, grinded her teeth, and went back to her unfinished work.

In the ninth, Willy whiffed home run king Leroi on an up-and-in fastball and walked Andy. Psycho Adam Bielski entered the game as a pinch-runner and proceeded to take a hambone-dancing lead off first base. Willy spun about and fired a hypersonic throw that came within a hair's breadth of knocking a dent in his helmet. Mattie tossed the ball back to Willy and her withering glare received a smug leer from the Psycho. She kicked her left leg, swung her right arm toward him again, and sent him face-first into the dusty red clay. A stadium full of people laughed with delight as Rube Henry's granddaughter twirled the unthrown ball in her hand for all to see. The USTV camera relayed her winning smile to millions of viewers watching at home, followed by her transformation into the fierce competitor as she delivered the first of three hard sliders to fan Thor for her tenth and final strikeout of the game.

"She is one fired up lady!" declared Cam Hammersmith as Willy strutted and pranced around the mound between pitches, pounding her glove, pumping her fist in the air, exhorting her teammates, the ball, and herself to get the last out. Jeff called out, "There are 40,000 wild, ecstatic Wolf Pack maniacs ready to blow the lid off this joint." When Thor's uppercut swished through the air, Rob delivered his summation: "For almost a week, it looked like a mismatch, but now, as we head back to New York, we've got ourselves a *real* world-class Series."

Dave Warren led the charge of minicam journalists in quest of sound bites from Braunstein Beer's player of the game. USTV's underground fiber optic cables transmitted the scene from Pilot Field to earth stations, a satellite link, its worldwide distribution hub, and via another satellite relay to affiliates across the country, dedicated lines for webcasting by Horizon Online and Wahoo, cablecasting through Sportsnet and the Millennium Channel, and secondary feeders form Alaska and Canada to the tip of South America and across two oceans.

In San Pedro, California, an eighty-eight-year-old woman clapped her hands and kissed her twenty-two-year-old great granddaughter, who played three sports in college and reminded her *nona* of the beautiful and empowered athlete in all her glory on the screen.

In Mount Lebanon, Pennsylvania, Laverne Peckham posted the homemade video of the teen reciting her poem on Me-Tube and put a hard copy in an envelope addressed to Ms. Willy Mae Beal c/o Buffalo Wolves. In a high-pitched yet steady voice, she read: *"You go, girl. You go, girl. Oh, yeah. Oh yeah. / She bats like a girl and she runs like the wind. Oh, yeah. Oh, yeah / She's a diva and a sensei and a shiva and a yogi. Oh, yeah. Oh, yeah. / She's a lotus and a humming bird and a jasmine and a dove. Oh, yeah. Oh, yeah. / She's a femme and la macha and whitebread and a homegirl. Oh yeah. Oh yeah. / She's a woman. It's her pastime. Oh, yeah. Oh, yeah. / Her name is Willy. It's her ballgame. Oh, yeah. Oh, yeah."*

After Willy unleased the game-winning strike to Thor, the constantly simmering pain in her shoulder flashed with renewed intensity and seared the length of her arm, tingling and stabbing all the way to her fingertips. With the pandemonium around her, the burning and throbbing brought the water to her eyes and a moan to her throat. She was dizzy and out of breath as Dave Warren went into his spiel: "Willy Beal, who couldn't get out of the first inning in game two, comes back to win game five on a five-hit shutout, the third whitewash in as many games at Buffalo's Pilot Field...Willy, have you and the Wolves stolen the momentum from the Diamonds?"

Willy felt Kevin at her side and appealed to him hoarsely, "You have to get me out of here, Kev. Please!"

The star rookie looked at Willy's pain-ravaged face, stepped between her and the cameras, and sang out, "Sorry, no quotes tonight! We gotta go *par-tay*!" Then Kevin hustled Willy away, leaving Warren and crew talking to themselves.

During the obligatory fifteen minutes of silence before the media onslaught, the doors to the Wolves' locker room and clubhouse were locked when "the stuff done hit the fan," in the words of Jimmy Mack Jones. Willy writhed in anguish, cringing against the wall, sobbing and cursing between rapid exhalations of breath. Kevin stood by helplessly. In a rage came Peter Jones. P.J. hovered over her, shouting as she clutched her shoulder. "I don't believe this. In the middle of the mother-flaggin' Series and my two best pitchers are on the shelf." Willy, totally absorbed in her pain, didn't look up at him. "Damn you for doing this to us. I'm sending you out to pitch and your arm's hurting so bad you can't even stand up!"

Kevin reached to lay a hand on Peter's shoulder. "Hey, ease up on her, man."

"Go take a shower, McDonald!" Peter snapped angrily. The player and his manager stared tensely, not speaking.

"What're we gonna do now, P.J.?" Irv asked.

"Hell, I don't know," Peter mumbled. "We're screwed."

"Wait a minute," said Willy, her chest heaving, face swollen, and eyes reddened. "I just went out and won game five for us and you're talking about me going out there again, aren't you?"

"What the hell do you think?" P.J. spoke bitterly. "You're the *best* I've got. You're *all* I've got."

"What about Woody and Sadie?" Willy asked provocatively.

"I'll start Woody on Saturday and Sadie on Sunday. We'll be okay, but..."

"And what about me?"

"You, Willy, are the long, middle, and short man...pardon the expression...and the closer. If we don't need you to relieve Saturday, maybe you'll start Sunday instead of Sadie. Whatever we have to do! We didn't come this far to lose."

Now lucid, Willy spoke in a hushed voice, "So, just leave me alone and give me the ball."

"Willy, you have to go see the doc," P.J. implored.

"No!" she protested adamantly. "He's gonna wanna shoot me up with pain killers."

"Oh, sister, please!" Peter groaned.

"I won't have a clear head and I've gotta keep my head," she insisted softly.

"You're going to see the doc, whether you like it or not, Willy."

After Willy went into the trainer's room, Peter slammed his office door, immediately followed by pounding on the wall, the tinkling of plaster, and a chair skidding across the floor.

Said Jed to Gene, "I hope he kicked the wall, 'cause if he punched it with his hand, we declare a forfeit and go home. We can't afford to loose his bat and her arm on the same day."

Kevin said to Stash, "I can't believe how close I came to sluggin' P.J. I mean, he's *my* mentor, too."

"Family spat! Don't dwell on it, son. Relax and have fun." The coach gave the second sacker a slap on the back. "It's only a game, remember?"

Willy sat on the trainer's table and peeled off her shirt so that Pandit and Stu Lacy could take turns poking and prodding her arm and shoulder. Dr. Lacy said calmly, "When you arrived in August, you said you never had a hint of arm or shoulder pain. If we'd done an MRI, the tendinitis would've shown up." She looked down at her feet dangling over the linoleum floor. "I can't let you pitch, Willy."

"You can't stop me."

"You're jeopardizing your career."

"This *is* my career," she stated soberly.

Dr. Stu said to the trainer, "Pandit, we have to try to alleviate the pain and keep the swelling down." The doc lifted her right hand and asked her to crook each finger, one by one. When she yelped, "Ow!" he said, "It's probably just a pinched nerve or a minor muscle strain, unrelated to the tendinitis. We should take x-rays."

"No!" shouted Willy, startling both men, jostling Pandit as if she were readying to flee. "No drugs and no x-rays or MRIs!" She was vehement.

The team physician looked at Willy, first sternly, then curiously. Stu asked, "Is there anything else you haven't told me?"

"No," she fibbed. She folded her hands and twiddled her thumbs, her body language causing Stu to question her answer.

"Do you have any other hidden condition, Willy?"

"No," she repeated to the team doctor whose primary obligation was to his employers.

Willy consented to a localized injection of cortisone and Stu Lacy left her for a rubdown with Pandit. As the trainer's nimble fingers worked the tension and ache out of her muscles, he asked her, "Is this the very bad spot?"

She rolled her head, eyes closed, savoring his sensual massage, and hummed, "Mm-hmm!" Willy, seated on Pandit's table in the lotus, was unconcerned that the towel around her came unwrapped. Pandit gently kneaded her shoulder.

"Remember," said the medic from Sri Lanka. "I will get a Series bonus check, too."

"Keep on doing what you're doing, Pannie, and I'll give you my own share."

CHAPTER 28

Willy's friends found that she was again incognito until late Saturday afternoon, when she joined the players and coaches at the Meadowlands for a half-serious workout and deadly serious "head session." She loosened up with calisthenics and wind sprints and threw the ball for a few minutes. Her arm felt heavy, but unstiffened quickly, and her daily dose of cortisone brought relief if not healing to her arm and shoulder. Willy sat with Phil Abruscato in the otherwise vacant dugout, sharing a can of no-caff cola, when Eddie Paris called her aside for a chat with Barry Kaplan in the visitors' clubhouse. The co-owner said to her, "Dana and I want you to know that, win or lose, regardless of your rotator cuff injury, we want you to stay with us...You're the soul and inspiration of the Buffalo Wolves."

Willy quietly expressed thanks, but sensed this wasn't a pep talk. She wasn't surprised when Eddie withdrew a sheaf of paperwork from his briefcase and spewed forth talk of terms. "A two-year contract with a third year at the club's option...A total package of seven million, plus incentives, starting at two million for next season...We ran the numbers by your guy, Avery, and worked out the deferred monies versus base salary for..."

"No new contract! I never asked to renegotiate. You had no business talking to my agent without my say-so." Willy's anger caught both men off guard.

"Is it the arm trouble?" Barry asked. "It's not fatal! Tendinitis can be treated. You can come back next spring even if you go under the knife."

The general manager screwed up his face to ask, "What is it, Willy? Do you think you can climb through a loophole and sign with somebody else for more money?"

Instead of becoming angrier, Willy's excitement waned. She took a deep breath, her eyes cast downward, not looking at Eddie or Barry. "Just submit your offer to Michael Avery and we'll be in touch after the Series is over." She rose, still not looking at them, said "Excuse me," and walked out.

Down in the locker room, momentarily, Peter hailed, "Willy, what in the hell is up with you? I just talked to Eddie."

She marched toward him and said, "I've got something to tell you, Peter."

P.J. looked at Stash and James, wondering if they knew anything, and both coaches responded with widened eyes, foolish smiles, and shrugs. Willy and Peter retired behind closed doors.

An hour in advance of the most talked about ballgame of the season, Peter Jones met the press and was asked if he planned to bring back Willy to start the seventh game. "Plan?" he mocked jovially. "The only plan is to win tonight. We'll go with Naulls on two days rest. He's pitched two great games for us, but if I have to use Willy or Sadie for an inning or two in order to win it, that's what I'm going to do."

Shane Hennessey probed, "There's speculation about Willy Beal having a sore arm, a torn rotator cuff."

"It's just a pinched nerve in her hand," voiced Peter, as rehearsed.

Meanwhile, Barry's wife, Dana, cornered Peter's wife, Charlene, in the elevator dropping down to the lobby of the swank midtown hotel on their way to the suburban stadium. "Is something going on with Willy?" The manager's mate shrugged. The co-owner scrunched her facial muscles and siddled her mouth up to Char's ear. "She let something slip to Yolie Jiminez about a visit to a clinic before we left Buffalo...and it wasn't a charity or publicity event."

Char concluded, "The sore arm thing, I bet."

Dana Hawthorne informed Char, "Even I know they don't take *blood tests* for tendinitis." Charlene and Dana pictured an identical snapshot of an athlete on a mission, waging a holy war as if there were no tomorrow, no waiting until next year. "I'm worried, Char."

"You're scaring me, Dana."

Rob DaSilva set the stage for game six: "The dueling lefties, Woody Naulls and Bruce Jacobson go at it one more time tonight. Both pitchers working with forty-eight hours rest between starts...and Tom Vallery skipping over Sandy Lee Danielson to give Jake the nod." Toby Clay, stopped by Jake in game four, regained the upper hand with a two-out home run in the first inning. However, Woody proved unequal to the task as Cal ripped him for a double, moved to third on Keith's bunt, and scored the tying run when Roy singled in the bottom of the first. In the second, Andy, Max, and Jake hit singles, scoring a run to send the Diamonds ahead, 2-1. Still in the same inning, Woody walked Cal to load the bases and P.J. relieved his southpaw starter as Phil and Willy prepared themselves in the bullpen, but Randy emerged from the jam with the aid of questionable base running by the D's. Keith lifted a shallow fly to Diego in left. Max, running after the catch on command of third base coach, Norm Simon, was easily cut down at the plate by the Dominican shotgun for a double-play. The Wolves evened the score at 2-2 in the sixth when Matt's RBI-single plated P.J. Randy, bounced around in one-third inning in the second game, blanked the Diamonds through the fifth. Peter tried to keep the sixth-inning rally alive by pinch-hitting for Marty, but Harry grounded out. Next, Teddy batted in the pitcher's spot. Jake was on the ropes, but he didn't hit the canvas. He blew a high, hard one past Teddy for strike three and the Meadowlands faithful rose to cheer: *"Jake! Jake! Jake!"*

As Chris took the mound for the Wolves in the bottom of the sixth, today adding a pentacle necklace to his gothic bling-bling, Stash told third-base guide Dickie Leeds, "Vallery's gotta stick with Jake. You gotta go with your ace. Ours is waitin' in the wings." Chris gave up a hit and a walk while fanning eight D's over the next four innings. This was the closer's third abnormally long stint of the Series and his third superlative performance. Jake went into extra innings twice during the postseason, beating San Francisco and Buffalo in turn, but this time the left-hander's luck turned sour when Kevin shattered the deadlock with a tenth-inning homer. With two away, the fearsome twosome, Diego and Jed, thwacked back-to-back singles. Vallery removed Jake to a standing ovation and brought Larry Brooks into the game. The D's bullpen stopper was clipped for another hit by Mattie Z., whose RBI made the score 4-2 in favor of the Wolf Pack. The New Yorkers rallied in their half of the inning, scoring once on a walk to Keith and singles by Roy and Joe.

The president of USTV Sports whimpered a little prayer for Buffalo to pull the game out of the fire, drooling at the prospect of the highest ratings in television history to watch Willy B. Superstar stick it to the Diamonds in the final game for the championship of the world. Arnie Rutledge didn't give a hoot who won; he slobbered in anticipation of ad revenues escalating to infinity. Rutledge's hired hand, Rob Da Silva, pronounced: "With 77,000 fans on their feet, it's nail-biting time for the Buffalo Wolves. They lead here in the tenth, four-three, with two on and two out...One swing of the bat and the New York–New Jersey Diamonds can win it all!...Player-manager Peter Jones is calling time and making a very slow walk from right field to the mound...Chris Van Aachen, who's had another *career night* up 'til this inning, comes out of the game and..." The camera zoomed in on the Wolf's pen as the next pitcher set foot on the turf. The mixture of groans, cheers, and jeers from the bleacher creatures made her identity obvious. "Peter Jones, just as he did in the deciding game of the league playoff, calls on Willy Beal to try and save it...the only difference being that this time it's *sudden death*."

Jeff pitched in with his view: "This is a gamble by Jones, which all but rules out her starting tomorrow."

Cam piped up to defend P.J.: "But she's the best option if the D's tie the game because she can stay in the game another nine or ten innings if need be...as we all know."

Willy greeted Peter with unconcealed annoyance. "You've done it to me again. You're bringing me in now, so I can't start tomorrow. What's wrong with Phil or Scotty?"

Peter laughed matter-of-factly. "Are you finished?" Willy stabbed the rubber with her spiked soles and nodded. "Look who's up," said Peter with coy self-assuredness.

Willy knew that Paul was next in the batting order. Her first big league batterymate was gone from the on-deck circle and the PA announced: "Batting for Cello, number twenty-five, Thor Andreason!" She glanced at the potential tying run on third, Roy Burton, standing alongside the Wolf hot-cornerman, Glenn Harmon.

"You know what to do," quipped P.J. "If he tries his trick shot, we're ready for it."

Willy squinted, "What if he smells the bait and swings away?"

"Well, then, one of the outfielders will just have to catch it!" shrugged Peter. He tossed the ball into the air for Willy to snatch bare-handed and disappeared.

Jed and Willy called the four infielders to the mound and put their heads together. "Glenn, play at regular depth and back-peddle toward the outfield grass when I let the pitch go. Jed, he'll chase a high, inside, offspeed pitch. The rest of you guys, look for the forceout at home to stop the run unless the ball's caught in the air." Everyone returned to their stations and Willy nodded to Glenn, who spat reassuringly onto the turf. She paused to absorb the clamoring of the fans–*"Let's go Dees!"*– in anticipation of the kill.

Up in the broadcasting turret, astute observer Jeff McCarty bellowed: "Glenn Harmon, unbelievably, has moved behind the third base bag and positioned himself about three feet inside the line with the tying run ninety feet from home plate." Said Cam, "Maybe Buffalo has a scouting report that says Andreason might hit the ball that way." Jeff was fairly ranting and raving, as Glenn scampered in back of the base with the pitch. "No, no, Cam! You don't play at regular depth and concede the tying run in extra innings. That's just bad baseball." On the screen, Willy lobbed outside to Thor and he stroked a soft liner directly into Glenn's glove. "Sonofa...mother!" Jeff blurted before cuffing his microphone. Cam laughed: "It doesn't get any better than this fans." So did Jeff: "Shows how much I know!"

Rob summed up: "Buffalo wins it, four to three. Willy Beal retires Andreason with two on and two out to pick up the save, her third of the postseason along with three wins and one loss...Chris Van Aachen is the winner, Bruce Jacobson is the loser, two and one in this Series, and Toby Clay hits his fourth home run of the Series. The best fielding team in all of baseball committed *four errors* on this night, two by shortstop Demeter Fortune...And it's *winner take all* in game seven tomorrow night at nine o'clock."

The largest crowd to witness a baseball game this year numbered well over 80,000 souls, jammed the Meadowlands in East Rutherford, New Jersey, plus another 20,000 fans paid up to $30 to take in the action over closed-circuit TV at the Brendan Byrne Arena and 5,000 howling maniacs braved the "wind kill factor" to do the same at Pilot Field in downtown Buffalo, 400 miles to the west. In the tri-state area of New York, New Jersey, and Connecticut, the atmosphere was ambivalent. "Dee for demo-*li*-tion" intermingled with expressions of grudging respect for the Buffalo Wolves, a team that somehow matured and solidified in the course of the Series.

Cam kicked off USTV's worldwide telecast: "The Diamonds and Wolves come down to one climactic game for all the marbles. Having used Willy Beal in the game-saving role last night, player-manager Peter Jones selects Sergio Jiminez, who shut out the D's in game three, to start this final game, while Tom Vallery brings back Gil Douglas for his third Series appearance." Said Rob: "As he did with Jacobson in last night's dramatic sixth game, Vallery is using his starting pitcher on only two days rest." Said Jeff, "If not now, when? This is the show, right here and now."

    Rob commented, "Both managers continue to make adjustments. Jones again has Clay leading off, Santamaria batting clean-up, Balin starts the game at third base, and Toussaint sits. And Vallery shakes up the Diamonds' lineup. Bonham is back in his familiar leadoff spot, Mercado and Andreason will bat second and third, ahead of clean-up hitter Burton. Left fielder Gilbert bats fifth and shortstop Fortune bats sixth...Of course, once again, the designated hitter rule is not in effect...A telling statistic is that the D's big three sluggers, Burton, Gilbert, and Fortune, have yet to hit a home run in this Series."

    Sadie, the yeomanlike journeyman who gave the Wolves inning after inning of quality pitching all season, wasn't in top form. The Diamonds came out smoking, as they had in game two, with Cal ripping a base hit on the first pitch thrown and going to third on Merk's single up the middle. Thor laid down a bunt and the Wolves were caught flat-footed on the suicide squeeze. Cal streaked home and Thor was safe at first base–1-0, Diamonds. Roy hit a line-drive single to right center field, between Peter and Toby, to score Merk and put Thor on third–2-0, Diamonds. Thor jogged to the plate on Andy's grounder to Kevin at second base–3-0, Diamonds.

The gentle people of the Meadowlands kicked back and said as one: "This is more like it." P.J. signaled Ferdie in the bullpen as Sadie pitched the first of four balls to Demmy. The Wolves' pitcher comically implored home plate umpire Monty Guilford, who antagonized Sadie by rigidly adhering to the BLB standard of no reaction when calling a ball. The two lefties, Phil and Scotty, jumped to warm up for the Wolves, but, after loading the bases, the D's scored no more.

Diego walked to open the second inning. Thor, a superb first baseman, then was charged with throwing errors on two successive plays, one on a bunt by Jed and the other on a grounder by Teddy, filling up the bases. Diego scored when Matt hit into a force, Teddy being out at second as the D's tried to turn a double-play. Jed tallied on a deep sac fly by Marty and it was a 3-2 ballgame. Both Willy and Woody watched the action from the bullpen. In the second inning, every pitcher in the pen took a turn to get loose. P.J. said, "I'll use nine pitchers in nine innings to win this thing." When Merk and Thor walked back-to-back and Roy singled with one out, Peter called time in right field.

"Sergio Jiminez is finished for the night," Rob told his viewers as Jed affectionately stroked Sadie's back while they waited for the player-manager. "P.J. is signaling for the right-hander...That's right, folks! Willy Beal takes the mound for the Buffalo Wolves in game seven, her fourth Series appearance."

Willy and Peter exchanged a look before he asked her, "Anything to say?"

"You could've saved yourself a lot of aggravation by giving me the ball from the get-go."

Peter rolled his eyes at Jed and put the ball in Willy's open palm. "Just do it," he said and took his leave.

CHAPTER 29

The largest worldwide audience ever to view a sports event saw the pitcher with the fluid motion of a ballerina, the speed of a sprinter, and the endurance of a super-marathoner kick out her left leg and unleash a pitch through the invisible wall of fire in her right shoulder. She held the ball in front of her face and talked to it after getting a called first strike. She threw a fit when Monty called the second pitch a ball, and kissed the white sphere when it returned to her following strike two. She threw six pitches to the D's left fielder.

From the USTV audio, Rob: "A full count to Andy Gilbert...Swinging strike three!"

Jeff: "And that's the second time she's gotten Gilbert to chase a high-velocity fastball after setting him up with her sidearm and three-quarter-overhand offspeed pitches."

Cam: "Gilbert connected with her slider in game two and he hasn't seen that pitch since!"

Rob: "Demeter Fortune steps in. He's drawn four walks in the Series...Strike one on a hard fastball, right down the middle!"

Jeff: "That was one gutsy pitch by Willy B. She knows Fortune religiously lays off the first pitch and she really teased him with that one, dead center at the knees."

Rob: "A slider breaks low, missing the outside corner for a ball...One-and-one's the count."

Jeff: "Remember, Fortune has yet to hit the long ball in this Series."

Rob: [Laughing] "When our telecasting partner, Cam Hammersmith, made that kind of an observation in the league championship, Fortune responded with a game-winning homer off Greg Ruggieri...There's another jumping fastball. Called strike two to Fortune!"

Cam: "I'm just an old play-by-play guy. I'm not psychic. If I was, Sebastian Fabian would be paying me a whole lot more money."

Rob: "The one-two pitch from Willy Beal...Fortune rips at a down-and-in slider and he's out of there. Strike three!"

The TV video feed showed Demmy tossing his bat in one direction, his helmet in another, his mouth twitching inaudible consonants, as the digits of his left hand pulled at each finger of the batting glove on his right hand in a maddened parody of daisy petal picking. *She burned me...She burned me not...!*

Jeff's bias again showed, lamenting, "Demeter Fortune struck out only 30 times in 660 plate appearances this season, but Willy B. hung him out to dry."

Rob tilted the bias the other way, telling the viewers, "The avenger comes and quickly erases the threat...But, after two innings of play, it's New York 3 and Buffalo 2."

In the top of the fourth, the dynamic duo of Diego and Jed struck again. Diego caught a fastball from Big Gil and sent it into left field for a base hit. Oldster Jed followed with a game-tying double and scored the go-ahead run when Mattie punched a single. In the bottom of the fifth, with the Wolves up, 4-3, Paul stood on-deck and watched Willy feed an offspeed fastball to Demmy, who hit the ball on one bounce to second base for a ground out, exactly as Roy had done before him. She was going through the D's batting order for the second time and only Thor had reached base on a walk. Not a ball had been hit out of the infield.

"Oh, you're so damn good, Willy," Paul said in his mind. "Maybe you're not as blazing fast as Jake, but you're close and a whole lot smarter. Maybe you're not quite as pinpoint accurate as Sandy Lee, but you can nip the black outline on either side of the plate, drop the curve into or out of the strike zone, and break the slider down and in or low and away, and you throw the ball three different ways. You give nothing away and the batter doesn't know what's coming next. Big Gil and Larry completely overpower the batter with intimidation and speed, but you take no small measure of fear from men who've been practicing their craft all their lives. You were my best pupil, Willy. The catcher who dreamed of being a pitcher could live his dream through you. It's no wonder Jones let you go the distance Thursday, then brought you on in relief Saturday and again Sunday. P.J.'s a real managerial genius: *Willy, here's the ball. Go pitch!*"

Paul tried to register eye contact with Willy as he stood in the box, but she focused only on her target, Jed Guerin's mitt.

Paul continued to talk to Willy in his head: "Hello, Willy, it's me, Paul. I know all your little secrets and I also know your weakness, the hidden flaw. Papp's heater, your bell-ringing fastball, doesn't jump every time you throw it at full velocity. Maybe one in five times it barely rises. If a batter can foul off the lively ones, he can wait to get around on a flat one. Of all the numbers being crunched and analyzed, one stat stands out: Willy Beal hasn't been tagged for a home run since she debuted for the Wolves in August–not one! Until now, that is.

Remember what I told you about the 'best hitter in the league' and how us catchers will beat you every time? I'm not slam-bamming my way to the Hall of the Immortals. I'm one of the nameless, faceless, supporting players, but my career prospects need a little boost right about now. I love you, babe, and I always will...but this one is *mine*. I hope it doesn't hurt too much."

Cam: "Catcher Cello has fouled off three pitches this turn at bat..." Rob: "Here comes the oh-two pitch from Willy Beal. Swung on and...What a shot off the bat of Paul Cello! Toby Clay races to the 450-foot marker, stops at the wall...and you can kiss that one goodbye. The game is tied at four-four!" Jeff: "That's not only the first round-tripper off Willy B. in this Series. It's the first home run she's given up in over 100 innings pitched for Buffalo in the regular season and playoffs." Cam: "And what a time for it to happen, too!"

Paul's feet pummeled the dirt as he sped around the basepaths. He kept his head down. There was no slow trot, no upheld fist, no stopping to admire the ball's trajectory, and not a hint of a swagger. Paul avoided looking at Willy, but he could feel her smoldering gaze and his mind's eye saw her standing with arms dangling at her side, kicking the ground with her toe. Paul ignored third base coach Simon's offered hand as he rounded the corner and barely touched Keith's fingers when he crossed the plate. He never looked up or smiled until he disappeared into the dugout.

Willy and Jed stood at the mound, impervious to the calls of *"Let's go Dees!"* Willy cursed bitterly, "Of all people!" to which her catcher replied, "Who the hell else knows you better than him?" Jed patiently let her grumble and groan a moment more, then cut it off. "C'mon, the game ain't over, kid."

Willy continued to set down the Diamonds through the seventh inning. After issuing bases on balls to Thor and Demmy, causing P.J. some brief angst, Paul knocked a routine grounder to short to end the inning with the two walkers left aboard. As Willy headed for the visitors' dugout, the real announcer said over the air to the ex-jocks in the booth, "Uh-oh, I think our viewers can tell what's going to happen next." Rob DaSilva's voice rang above the din. "Say what you will about New Yorkers and Diamond fans..." The din became louder. "We've got 80,000 people on their feet..." The din grew still louder. "In spite of her single-handed destruction of the home team...It's a standing ovation for Willy Beal!"

Said Jeff: "But will she acknowledge them, after her treatment by these same fans one week ago tonight?"

Said Cam: "She's stopping in front of the Wolves' dugout..."

Willy looked up and swiveled her head to one side and then the other, whipped off her cap, gave her pigtails the familiar wiggle, and waved the hat in the air like a lariat.

Rob: "Of course, she did..."

Jeff: "No one would blame her if she didn't..."

Cam: "But she's Willy Beal–a class act all the way!"

In the top of the eighth, after a valiant effort, Gil Douglas was through for the season. "That's all for Big Gil, who was tagged for five hits and four runs in seven innings pitched against the Pack of Wolves," said Rob. "Laddy Zanetsky is in to pitch for the Diamonds," announced Jeff, while Laddy methodically worked through his warm-up pitches. Cam commented that Steve Filsinger and Larry Brooks were loosening up in the D's pen. Rob explained, "With two innings to go and a tie game, there's no way Tom Vallery can bring in Brooks, his ace reliever, but it's safe to say we won't be seeing Tim Langevin pitch 'til next year."

In the Wolves' dugout, Peter, James, Stash, and Irv stood shoulder to shoulder, like the brain trust or general staff surveying the field of battle. P.J. gloated, "This should be Langevin's situation, but he's in Tom's doghouse and not about to get out."

"Kind of like you and Phil, huh?" Irv chided, rhythmically chewing a piece of gum.

"Tom's too logical to admit he's wrong," trumpeted Peter. "Stubborn sonofagun!"

"Oh, yeah!" nodded Jimmy Mack Jones. "Stubborn seems to be the common denominator with managers in this here Series. Right, fellas?" He slapped his brother in the gut. Ready to take his stand at the first base coach's box, James left an unamused P.J. between Stash and Irv, who broke up with laughter.

With two outs, Glenn Harmon, who replaced Teddy Balin at third base, muscled an inside fastball through the hole for a hit, bringing Matt Zaremba to bat. The Wolves' first baseman walloped Laddy's first pitch ten rows deep into the crowd, just outside the foul pole.

On the TV side of the broadcasters' work area, Cam said, "Talk about a close call!"

"He threw him a curveball at the knees," commented Jeff, the retired catcher. "You never, ever throw a low, inside curve to a right-handed pull hitter. You've got a better chance of beating him with a low, outside fastball."

"The Diamonds lucked out that time," added Rob, as Matt lambasted Laddy's next pitch into the same general direction, only higher, farther, and *inside* the foul pole.

On the radio side, Zack Traynor gestured for the man sitting next to him at the desk to do the honors. With crinkled cheeks creased in glee, Ernie Arnett drawled, "And that bawl is go-ing...go-ing...gone!"

Behind the transparent plastic partition, Rob gave Zack and Ernie a thumbs-up sign and crooned, "The Wolves are up, six to four, and 'Matt Who?' joins Toby Clay, Kevin McDonald, Diego Santamaria, Peter Jones, and Willy Beal in a very crowded pantheon of Buffalo Wolf Pack heroes...And when we go to the bottom of the eighth, Buffalo will be just *six outs away* from its first world championship."

Following a teen pop nymphet caterwauling "God Bless America," there was more idiotic braying for the entertainment of the viewing audience. Jeff McCarty was popping, hissing, and shouting into his mic: "I can't believe Zanetsky threw him the same pitch to the same spot. Zaremba pulls the first curveball a mile foul and Zanetsky comes right back with it again."

While Jeff frothed at the mouth, Cam calmly informed, "The homer by Matt Zaremba is the tenth pounded out by the Wolves in the Series, compared to only three for the Diamonds."

Willy's ex-teammates challenged her in their half of the eighth inning. With one out, Joe Manlius batted for Laddy and clouted a single to right field. Tom then sent Benny Marquez to pinch-run for Joe. P.J. looked for his opposite number to play "little ball," to chip away at their two-run deficit. Said Jeff, "Willy B. has not been as overpowering tonight as she was in the game at Pilot Field, when she clicked off ten strikeouts. Here tonight she's struck out two and walked three." Willy pitched a sidearm slider to Cal. He swung and hit it on two hops to Kevin, playing halfway between first and second, who threw to Marty for the front step of the double-play, but the shortstop's relay had no chance of beating Cal's rocketlike advance to first base. "That brings Mercurio Mercado up to bat," said Rob. "He has seven hits in this Series. A very fine performance indeed!" Willy jammed Merk with a buggywhip fastball, up and in, for strike one. Then she tried to cross him up with a cutter, but he uppercut the ball and sent it bounding past the pitcher's mound and over second base. Marty, playing beyond the infield in mid center field to counter the buoyant artificial turf, swooped on the ball, gloved it, and swept toward the bag as Cal slid with spikes high to take out the fielder and break up the play. Marty leaped to evade the D's mighty gnome, but Cal hooked an ankle as he crossed the bag and sent the Wolf headlong to the plastic-over-concrete surface. Marty's left knee fractured on impact with the turf as umpire Ken Crenshaw thumbed the third out. The inning ended as Willy, her Wolves, their team doctor, and the trainer hovered over their injured shortstop writhing in agony, cursing Calvin Bonham and the anonymous inventor of artificial grass.

    Willy batted first in the top of the ninth. She gave Peter a questioning glance before picking up a bat and helmet. A strategic option was to pinch hit for Willy and send in Chris to get the save, but P.J. simply smiled at her and jerked his hand toward the field. Before planting her feet in the batter's box, she took a practice swing and turned to look at Paul, stooped in front of Monty Guilford.

"You had to be the one to hit that homer, didn't you?" Willy asked, turning eyes forward.

"Ya gotta do whatcha gotta do," Paul answered, pounding his knuckles into the pocket of his mitt.

She tilted her head and smirked. "Feel good, partner?"

"What a rush!" he cackled.

Willy smiled, planted her feet, and crouched to meet Larry's first pitch. Dickie Leeds, coaching at third base, flashed a succession of phony signs. Willy batted twice in the game so far, each time knowing her one-for-twenty .050 lifetime batting average was stenciled on video screens from coast to coast and around the world. She flew out and bunted for a sacrifice her previous times at bat. Now, the D's lay in wait for her to drag a bunt, as Thor and Keith at the corners charged the plate. Willy made full contact, sliced with her bottom hand, and pulled off her top hand, driving an outside fastball 400 feet to deep center field. Andy cut in front of Merk to make the catch. Willy returned to the dugout elated, notwithstanding having made an out. She sang her own praises: "Hey, that would've been over the fence and out of the park at home."

Stash, the one-time batting champ, smiled broadly. "I think you should stick to pitchin'."

The full house at the Meadowlands was stunned silent by Mattie Z.'s home run, a seemingly fatal blow. The crowd found its voice once more, after Buffalo failed to add on to its lead, anticipating last-minute heroics in the long season's final half inning.

Said Cam, "Listen to the dueling chants."

"Wil-lee, Wil-lee!"
"Let's go Dees!"
Said Rob, "A house divided..."
For the bottom of the ninth, Peter replaced himself in right field with Unhappy Harry and sent Alex to shortstop in place of Marty, standing on crutches in the dugout, refusing to exit the stadium by ambulance to treat his wounded knee. Willy shut her eyes tightly and took three rapid, shallow breaths before a longer, deeper one, as Jed said to her, "Okay, kiddo, let's run through it. Andreason?"
"Smoke and sliders!"
"You walked him twice."
"Not this time!"
"Burton?"
"Sliders! He can hit the smoke."
"Gilbert?"
"Smoke! He can hit the slider."
"Fortune?"
"He won't get his ups."
"Keep that thought," Jed laughed and he left Willy alone on the mound.
She took in Thor at the plate. *He's thinking fastball. He knows it's coming, but first comes the decoy.* Six-tenths of a second later, he takes a sidearm change-up: *thump!* – no balls, one strike. *Here comes the heater, Thor.* Four-tenths of a second later, he swings: *swoosh! thump! Way late!* – no balls, two strikes. *You waited too long, Thor.* One-seventeenth of a second after the overhand fastball left Willy's fingertips, Thor decided to swing again: strike three!
Jeff declared: "Willy Beal turns it up a notch in the ninth with her third strikeout of the night."

Cam took over: "Both of these clubs have had one dominant force with the bat in the Series. For Buffalo, it's been Toby Clay with ten hits, four home runs, and eight RBI. For New York, it's been this man...Roy Burton." The on-screen graphics read a .370 average for the entire postseason. "Burton was the big gun for the Diamonds in the first two playoff rounds as well...but with considerably higher power output...six home runs in ten playoff games, compared to no home runs in seven games in the Final Series."

Rob put things in perspective: "That tells you something about the quality pitching of the Buffalo Wolves."

Willy studied Roy's face, devoid of expression except for twitching brows over widened eyes. Willy shook off Jed's first sign and gave no visible response as four fingers flashed. Out of the overhand delivery, the pitch looked like a slider coming from the outside, but it came in flat. In its trip of sixty and a half feet, the most dangerous hitter in baseball paused and halted when his eyes failed to pick up the rotation of the seams as the screwball dropped.

Rob called the pitch: "Ball one...Burton showing much more patience at the plate throughout this postseason!"

Jeff hit the counterpoint: "He'll take a walk if he can get it."

As Willy spun another backdoor slider to Roy, her eyes met his and mouthed the words, "Goodnight, sweet prince!"

Said Rob, "The one-two pitch from Willy Beal..." Roy turned his right shoulder inward. His bat whipped and stopped perpendicular to his left ear. He held the bat straight up as he watched the breaking ball slide inside to nip the edge of the invisible cubic strike zone. He twisted his head to look at Monty. Rob issued the decision: "Called strike three!"

Said Cam, "Roy's shaking his head, but there's no argument." Roy glanced up at the stands as the crowd's noise grew louder with a low, frowning note. His look was visibly pained. "I think he knows the booing is directed at him," Cam needlessly added.

In the home team's dugout, Roy slammed his bat against the rack, sending several pieces of lumber onto the ground. When his own piece of milled ash failed to destruct as intended, he splintered it across the dugout steps. A few nearby players startled at the sound of wood smacking and cracking. A number of others averting their eyes, flinching, but otherwise not giving any notice. The slugger already lost the still-sealed balloting for the league's MVP award to his teammate, Cal Bonham, despite winning two of the three legs of the triple crown. As one member of the baseball writers' guild put it, "Cal's a good guy. Screw Burton!" The rarely emotional Mr. Burton looked at manager Vallery and pointed to the owner's sky box. "That miserable bastard! The winnin' pitcher's got the wrong uniform on." Roy peeled off his Diamonds' jersey, walked the runway to the clubhouse, popped open what all the Diamonds called "a Willy B. special"–a low-cal, no-caff diet cola. Joe and Benny, long since out of the action, watched the game on the tube. *Slurp!* "Less taste!" *Burp!* "More spilling!" They did to the case of Braunstein Lite what the Diamonds should have done to the Wolves. They raised their cans to the ceiling, crunched them, and sang, "Dee for demo-*li*-tion!" *Burp!* "Ahhh!"

"And so it comes down to Willy Beal and Andy Gilbert." Rob DaSilva delivered his benediction to the final act. "The true measure of a ballplayer is contained in the question: *Who do you want?* When you're going for the gold and it's down to one game, one time at bat, one play! Who do you want holding the bat or pitching the ball?...Make no mistake, *both* Tom Vallery and Peter Jones have the players they want in this spot."

"The Buffalo Wolves are one out away," said Cam. "This might not be the biggest upset in Big League Baseball history, but the woman on the mound knows *exactly* where she is and what she's about to do."

"Willy Beal could be the first player named rookie of the year and comeback of the year in the *same year*," said Jeff.

Andy stepped into the box, holding the bat straight out in front of him. He looked down at the plate, his feet, and the bat in his hands. He raised it to his shoulder. He craned his neck toward Willy, first staring blankly, then glaring, though his lips curled a little smile, as he aimed the bat right at her, looking down the barrel, like a sharpshooter ready to fire.

Willy turned her eyes to Kevin at second, Alex at short, and Glenn at third. She stepped off the rubber and walked a quick circle around the mound. The occasional fluttering in her abdomen usually passed momentarily, but this time it kicked a wallop. "Whoa," she shouted out loud, patting her belly.

"I wonder what that's all about!" chuckled Cam on the air.

"Butterflies, maybe," Jeff chipped in while the screen showed the pitcher fanning herself with her fielder's mitt.

Willy stopped and stepped back onto the rubber, both feet toeing the slab. She took a deep breath through her nose and let it out slowly between slightly parted lips. *Loosen up, Willy*, she told herself, then backed her right foot off the rubber. All the while she continued to focus on the steely blue eyes of the man who would lead the world with 56 home runs and 165 RBI *next year*.

Said Rob: "Andy Gilbert slugged thirty-two round-trippers this season. But he's struck out eleven times in the Series. One more and it's a new all-time record."

Back home in Old Saint Pete, with a toddler and an infant crawling on the carpeted floor, Tanya hugged her "best friend forever," Jennifer, and they cried, giggled, and shrieked for joy. Across town, Alma Henry Beal turned her teary eyes to her gentleman companion of long standing, saying, "That's my little girl." Then Alma gazed at the screen and purred, "I love you, sugarpie."

Willy wound up, paused to rest her right hand inside her gloved hand, already set with the top-seam grip of the heater. She held ball in glove and pumped her leg from the stretch position. *Sorry, Andy, but it's time to punch out and go home. It's over!* She let out a menacing cry as she rifled the pitch. She heard only her own scream and not the crescendo of the crowd that drowned it out. Her adrenaline high was so intense that she barely felt her arm in motion, let alone its pain. She never broke her lock onto Andy's eyes, but her mental focal point was still Jed's mitt, right down the center of the plate.

Monty, the behemoth ump, practically turned a cartwheel with his massive bulk to call the pitch. "Stee-rike!"

Russ Heman, the USTV director, switched the scene from the batter at home plate to what would be the last full head shot of Willy Beal in a big league game. Over a hundred million sets of eyes saw her eyes bearing down on the batter. Her eyelids shuttered as she recognized the sign from her catcher, nodded, and resumed her cold, hard, unflinching stare at Andy.

"We've seen some hard throwing in this championship final," said Ernie on the radio. "But nobody has thrown harder than the beautiful lady on the hill." Intoned Zack, "She knows when to finesse and when to turn on the smoke, even sneaking in a screwgie against Burton, but now it's power versus power, head-to-head."

Willy stretched, pumped, and threw: "Stee-rike twoo!" Monty bellowed with aplomb.

Willy frantically pounded her Rawhide glove with her fist. The crowd noise blanketed the stadium in the electrified night air. From their partitioned cubicles in the broadcasting center, some twenty radio, television, and cable announcers were shouting the same story in English, Spanish, Portuguese, Japanese, Korean, Chinese, and two different dialects of French. "The absolutely incredible comeback of the Buffalo Wolves...The woman from St. Petersburg, Florida, who literally came out of nowhere to the elite majors...She's one pitch away from saying *sayonara* to America's Home Team."

Tonight was Willy's ballgame. The moment when her dreams, her fantasy, her real life, and her karma converged. Still, she wasn't alone at the center of the diamond. She recalled the Tao: *"You are a fertile and powerful nucleus...If your life works...the ripple effect spreads throughout the cosmos."* She spoke to her grandfather, Rube, her grandmother, Minna, and, yes, her father, Eddy. Not only for them, but also this game was for Amy, Caitlin, Petie, Stephanie, Mikey, Tanya, Jennifer, Laverne the poet, and all the little Willys with their rainbow of eyes that see only joy in the world. Most of all, this win was for people whom Willy had never even met. It was for Zinger's heroes: ordinary people who dreamed, tried, and failed, but still had the guts to get out of bed in the morning. The invocation of names came out as a primal scream from deep in her throat and the utter bottom of her soul as she expressed a nine-inch-diameter sphere to the plate at 101 miles an hour. She watched Andy widen his eyes, lean his right shoulder downward, stride his right foot outward, twist his mouth into a snarl, shut his eyelids, and uncoil his torso to swing. His bat stopped halfway as the ball jumped across the plate over his checked swing. Not a syllable was audible as Monty kicked with his left foot, threw up his right arm, and held it one, two, three seconds before the realization of finality hit thousands of souls on hand and millions of others watching, listening, and waiting. The call of "stee-rike threee!" was heard round the world. Yet no one noticed that Willy's legs went numb and she fell to the ground.

CHAPTER 30

The earth beneath Willy's feet seemed to shake as the crowd in the stadium exploded like a clap of thunder. She collapsed after throwing the third strike to Andy, but leaped to her feet as Jed barreled toward her. He still wore his mitt, mask, and helmet as he lowered his head, wrapped his arms around her thighs, and hoisted her over his shoulder. Willy shrieked for sheer jubilance as she dangled upside down like a loosely strung puppet. From across the field and out of the dugout, all of the Wolves descended upon Willy and Jed. Thirty bodies–sweating, laughing, crying–fell into a clump at the center of the infield. *It's over*, Willy thought. *We won!* Then she heard herself call out, "Where's Peter?"

Suddenly, she was alone, sprawled on the phoney grass in front of the pitcher's mound. She lost consciousness for two or three seconds and revived when she hit the seat of her pants. The torn and aggravated tendons in her shoulder burned. She saw Jed, Andy, and Monty remain at home plate. She hallucinated during her brief fainting spell. She dreamed the scene of Yogi Berra lifting Don Larsen in the air after the perfect game in '56, conjured from the film clips shown on Rob DaSilva's special Series preview. Willy staggered to her feet. Her legs were unsteady and she felt lightheaded and nauseous, but her mind was clearing. The nighttime air never smelled so clean, the blue-green artificial sod never looked so vivid, and the mazda-lit sky never shone so brightly as Willy's teammates rushed to her, not to celebrate, but to see what happened. Just as no one noticed Willy's faint, neither did anyone–in the stands, in the booth, on the field, in the two dugouts, in the owner's sky box, or from the Goodstone blimp overhead–take note of Jed Guerin dancing madly around the plate and batter's box. One by one, the home plate umpire, the rest of the umpiring crew, Tom Vallery and Peter Jones, and Andy Gilbert heeded the fact that Jed dropped the third strike and couldn't find the ball.

    The crew chief, Ken Crenshaw was trying to call time because of the chaos ensuing on the field. Fans flocked to the railings and dripped on the field as Monty attempted to signal for play to resume. Andy, all the while clutching his bat with his hands, careened down the line–hell-bent for first base, headlong into the dancing crowd of players, coaches, wags, and fans. Meanwhile, Jed still searched for the ball. Andy lost the bat somewhere along the way, climbed, kicked, and clawed over everyone in his path. He lunged at Matt Zaremba, who, for some reason, stood fast at his position, straddling the first base line with legs spread apart. Andy clotheslined Matt with his forearm and the two gladiators tumbled onto the base together. Andy's hands gripped the bag so hard that he yanked it loose from its moorings. He fanned for the twelfth time in the Series, but he was safe at first. Andy sighted the ball, at rest thirty feet behind Jed at the base of the netted fence barricading the seats in back of home plate. The Wolves' catcher had no clue where the ball was. One umpire called "time," another yelled "play ball," and a hundred cops came on the field to get a thousand people off it. Andy–by now exhorted to go by frantic voices from the D's dugout–ran toward second base and dove the last ten feet to hug the bag as if it were his long lost mother.

Rob DaSilva took the microphone. "The Wolves, who came back after being down three games to one, appeared to have won the game...*and the Series*...with two outs in the bottom of the ninth, as Willy Beal threw strike three past slugger Andy Gilbert, but the pitch also got past the catcher, Jed Guerin."

"As Yogi used to say," began Jeff McCarty. "It ain't over..."

"Please," groaned Cam. "Can we get through a baseball game without somebody spouting that tired old cliché?"

"Sorry, Cam!" Jeff clucked.

Hundreds of reporters, photographers, and fans swarmed the players as the umpires finally managed to call a temporary halt to a game most of the world thought ended. Peter Jones mildly protested that Andy should be out on interference after tackling Matt and taking second in the midst of total confusion. The six umps huddled and answered in the negative. "The fielder obstructed the base runner. The runner is safe," Crenshaw ruled. When Peter, a bit stupefied by the turn of events, returned to the Wolves' dugout, Irv said, "Why the hell didn't Jed just fake it, make like he had the ball in his glove?"

P.J. shook his head and rolled his eyes. "Good question! Who would've known the difference? Damn!" the skipper muttered, still shaking his head.

When sanity returned, Jed stood with Willy alongside the pitcher's circle. "Oh, God, kid, I'm sorry. This is the worst thing I ever done."

"Was it a wild pitch or a passed ball?" Willy wondered, unselfconsciously touching her arm in response to its sharply penetrating pain.

"It took a helluva jump. It really sailed on me, but that don't matter. I should've stopped it anyways." The scoreboard displayed "E2," signifying an error on the catcher. "That ain't no plain old error. We had those suckers beat! It's all my fault, Willy."

Willy took a gentle swipe at Jed's forehead with her open palm and said, "Hey, are you gonna play, or are you gonna cry?" The pitcher and catcher shared a laugh and then she sighed, "Now what do we do?" Willy looked over at Andy standing on second base and Demmy stepping up to bat. Then Jed groaned, "Aw, shit, no!" He was watching Peter in the dugout. The player-manager, oft quoted as believing the intentional walk to be a fallacy, was signaling with a hand wave. "He wants us to put Fortune on, kid."

"No, Peter!" shouted Willy, noticing that the world's best hitting shortstop watched the argument unfolding, visibly amused, leaning on his bat like a cane.

In the meantime, the broadcasters tried to describe the inaction. Rob: "She's saying something to him." Jeff: "He's smiling." Cam: "She's not."

"Doesn't he think I can get him out?" moaned Willy. "That's putting the tying run on base."

"Yeah, but it's also a force play at any base," said Jed, scratching his two-day-old stubble. "Let's do it, but be careful, kid. If I bobble one, we're dead meat."

"I'll be soft as a swan, sugar."

Willy noticed Chris warming up in the bullpen as she delivered the four perfunctory lobs for her fourth base on balls in the game, the first truly free pass. As Demmy flipped his bat aside and trotted to the open spot at first base, Willy saw Peter step from the dugout and amble onto the field. She spent every drop of emotion and energy in getting the twenty-seventh out of the ballgame. There was nothing left to vent at P.J. He said, "There's no way in the world I'm going to let you stay out here and lose this game. Chris can come in to save it. That's his job, right?" Willy looked at him with saddened eyes, but made no reply. "I asked more of you than I had any right to do." He was smiling proudly at her. "And you gave me more than I asked for. Willy, nobody said you had to be the greatest pitcher who ever lived."

"I never said I was," she protested, but returned his smile.

"But for the last three weeks, and especially the last three days, you've been the best pitcher in baseball...*and everybody knows it.*" P.J. put a hand on each of Willy's shoulders. "It took twenty-five players to get us here. You did all you could do. It's up to the rest of us now. If we lose, then so be it."

Kevin sauntered over to Willy, Jed, and Peter. After exaggerated throat-clearing, "Ahem, ahem!" Kevin said, "I do believe the customary protocol is for the departin' pitcher to depart when the new pitcher comes to the mound. My man Chris is standin' here with his finger up his ass while y'all be jawin'. The whole world is waitin' on ya."

Peter laughed heartily, clapped Kevin on the back, and turned to Willy. "You know what you have to do."

"Walk don't run, right?" she quipped with a nod and a sniffle.

Peter tapped Willy's elbow for her to hand him the ball, saying, "Take your final bow, Willy B." She did, without tears, exiting with arms stiff at her sides until she reached the visitors' dugout when she raised them for a final wave to the Meadowlanders before ducking under the roof and stepping down the stairs. The players and coaches on the Wolves' bench were both tense and giddy, momentarily distracted by Willy's quick dash to the can to relieve herself, a scene which was humorous because it was so out of character in the midst of a game.

Up in the broadcast booth, the announcers killed time. Said Jeff, "I hate to keep singing the same old song..." *But we know you will*, thought Rob. *So, let's hear it.* "What we have here is the Wolves going for an infield out, but player-manager Peter Jones has painted himself into a corner by overmanaging. In this crucial situation, he has a makeshift lineup on the field."

Rob took over as play resumed. "Let's see if the Diamonds can pull off a miracle ... Gilbert on second, Fortune at first, two outs, and Chris Van Aachen on the hill for the Wolves ... Vallery makes his move. He's calling Cello back for a pinch-hitter."

The PA announcer heralded: *"Batting for Cello, number thirty-four, Adam Bielski."* Cam: "Paul Cello's hit a couple of homers, one in the playoffs, the other here tonight, but the D's have no more outs to spend. Bielski's the guy Vallery wants up there. He's aggressive at the plate and on the bases."

Jeff: "Remember game four of the pennant playoff? He'll beat out a bunt, get hit by a pitch, or do *anything* he can to get on base."

Rob: "And, if he does, he represents not just the game-winning run, but the world championship...Here's the pitch from Van Aachen...Bielski squares to bunt, but *takes* for ball one."

Cam: "He just *showed* bunt to draw the Wolves' infielders in and keep them off-balance."

Rob: "The pitch...He *is* bunting! A dribbler down the third base side...Gilbert's easily into third...Bielski tears up the line...Van Aachen comes off the mound to field the ball..."

Jeff: "Which is rolling..."

Cam: "Whoa, Jed Guerin shoves his pitcher to the ground to let the ball go..."

Jeff: "...foul!"

Rob laughed as he explained, "Guerin is helping Van Aachen back up, somewhat surprised by it all..."

Said Cam: "Luckily for Peter Jones and his Wolves, their old catcher may be slow-moving, but not slow-thinking."

Rob: "The infield's in, the outfielders are playing straight-away...The pitch...Fastball, high! Two and one's the count...Van Aachen looks in to catcher Guerin, working from the stretch, and the pitch...Bielski flicks it off, two and two."

Jeff: "All four Buffalo infielders are charging in on each pitch. Whoever fields a grounder will throw home, surrendering first base and stopping Gilbert from getting past third and scoring."

Rob: "Bielski hacks at *another* fastball."

Jeff: "That's the only pitch Buffalo's bullpen ace throws, isn't it?"

Cam: "Fouling it off his foot..."

Rob: "Psycho doing a little ooch-ouch dance..."

Jeff: "The guy will *not* be struck out."

Cam: "He'll keep fouling 'em off all night."

Rob: "And the third two-two pitch...A hard ground ball deep in the hole at short...A tough play for Suarez. He backhands it, turns, looks to third..."

Cam: "Coach Norm Simon holds up Gilbert at third..."

Rob: "...Suarez looks to first, looks home, and holds onto the ball."

Jeff: "You can bet that isn't the play Peter Jones called for, but, right now, *no play is the right play*."

Cam: "A good throw to first wins the Series, Jeff!"

Jeff: "But a bad throw to first brings in two runs and puts the winning run into scoring position, while a throw home gets Buffalo nothing."

In the dugout, Peter loudly disagreed for all to hear. "Alex choked on us!" Willy rose from her spot on the bench between Irv and Stash on the bench. She said, "I played with Psycho and I know, even on a good throw, he'd go flying into first to push Matt off the bag or pull the ball out of his glove." Peter grumbled and awaited Vallery's next move as James motioned to reposition the Wolves afield with the bases loaded. The PA announced: "Batting for Whalen, number thirty-six, Maxwell Street."

Rob: "Coming out on deck is Pigpen Pantagones. The backup catcher will bat in the pitcher's spot. If we go into extra innings, Bielski goes to third and Pantagones goes behind the plate."

Cam: "Moves, countermoves, and counter-countermoves..."

Said Peter Jones, "This game's a bitch. It just won't end!" Then, unexpectedly, Buffalo's first baseman called time. Matt Zaremba staggered and fell into the arms of Silvio Romero, the Diamonds' coach stationed on his left. As it turned out, the collision with Andy fractured Matt's collar bone and cracked three ribs, but he said nothing and gritted it out until he could no longer withstand the pain. "All guts and no brains!" Peter sputtered. The sole position player on the bench was Andre Toussaint, since Gene Tyler had pinch hit earlier. "Go play first," Peter barked at Andre, who loped to the stairs with his five-fingered fielder's glove. "Get the right glove, dammit!"

"Can I use Mattie's?" A few unproductive moments passed as the dugout-bound players fruitlessly sought Zaremba's first baseman's mitt, which he kept tucked under his armpit while being stretchered to an ambulance. The brief distraction was sufficient for Peter to think more clearly.

"Wait a minute! What am I doing?" P.J. exclaimed, then told Andre to go to right field and moved Harry over to play first. Peter winced at the field positions, dictated by a series of flukes. His stomach churned, full of bile. He saw Harry at first, Andre in the outfield, and Marty on the shelf. *If I move Santamaria behind the plate, the Wolves will morph back into Nick Dolan's team,* P.J. mused. "Damn!"

Unflinching after a brushback dusted his chin, Max swung on a fastball from Chris. The off-key thwack of a broken bat, splitting vertically in the batter's hands, sent the proverbial "frozen rope" into right field, where Andre stepped forward, then backward, and ended up on the same spot of turf, his arms dangling idly in front of him.

Peter Jones threw up his hands and cried, "I don't freakin' believe it. We're friggin' toast." James "Jimmy Mack" Jones saw his brother's face cross the threshold from prime time to middle age. All eyes watched Andre stride to his right, reach the ball on one bounce, and turn the most important throw of his career. Andy flew home to score in three seconds flat. Then, in the dumbest base running move of the century, Psycho Adam Bielski blew through Norm Simon's "stop" sign and passed second base at full tilt.

An invisible, imaginary clock ticked off the final ten seconds of the ball game. Fortune and Bielski slid together into third base. Street came to a dead stop halfway between first and second. Andre's throw skidded two feet in front of home plate. Jed grabbed it and stepped on the plate. Monty frantically waved his arms. "No force out!" Jed looked at the two Diamonds on third with his arm cocked. A throw on the mark would allow Glenn to tag out either base runner, but a throw off the mark would let both base runners score. Peter Jones called out, "Don't throw!" Street retreated to first, Bielski back-peddled to second, and Fortune froze at third. Tom Vallery called out, "Go! Go! Go!" Then Street turned and broke toward second, Jed set his feet to throw, and both managers wailed, "No! No! No!"

The instant the ball flew from Jed's hand, Bielski spun on his heels and Fortune bolted for the plate. Kevin speared Jed's throw with his bare hand in midflight as he leaped over the second base bag to evade the sliding Max, easily safe. Two runners and Kevin's perfect return throw converged on the plate. Demmy hooked a slide to Jed's left as Psycho bowled the catcher end over end. The Psycho buried his head in the pillow of Jed's chest protector and wrenched the ball from the catcher's mitt as the goalkeeper desperately flailed to slap the tag on the skidding spikes of Demeter Fortune.

CHAPTER 31

Rob DaSilva and Cameron Hammersmith cringed with professional embarrassment as Jeff McCarty crowed, "The Diamonds win the Series. What a comeback! The Diamonds win the Series. Unbelievable!" The unfortunates watching USTV only knew *what* happened after the videotape replayed and the announcers coolly recounted *how* it happened minutes later.

All thirty players and coaches of the new world champions were pulled as if by a magnet to home plate, where Fortune and Bielski had blown past 200 pounds of scrap iron to win the gold. The losers quickly escaped to join their comrades in the visitors' dugout. The television camera panned the losers' hideaway, showing players seated in stark silence. Each frame sent a snapshot for worldwide view. Toby's glassy-eyed stare, Diego's trembling chin, Andre plaintively raising his eyes skyward, Kevin compulsively shaking his head, and Willy holding and caressing Chris Van Aachen's face as he sobbed against her breast. The camera fixed, sans announcer's explanation, for none was needed, as Tom Vallery stood beside the dugout with his hands on Peter Jones's shoulders, their heads bowed, talking quietly.

Hundreds of reporters and thousands of fans flooded the field as the joyous celebration of a victory nearly lost began to move one or two players at a time to the clubhouse sanctuary. Shrill voiced and breathless, the winning manager was pinned by the sheer magnitude of wags, technicians, cameras, and microphones, and he succumbed to an unwanted pool interview. "I don't know how my guys pulled off those base running moves, but it was the longest ten seconds of my life."

Players on the two teams kept their distance, the intensity of their present emotions being so utterly different. Willy resolved that whenever she met Andy in later years she wouldn't speak of the last strikeout. One day, Sandy Lee would tell her that Andy said, "I could've dug in and swung a hundred times and never hit what she was throwing." Her own emotions drained, Willy felt herself connect with Jed even before he, like Chris, found her shoulder. She kissed the old pro's head as he clung tightly to her, buried his face, and wept like a child.

Rob DaSilva's voice was coarse with anger, due to an exchange of messages among the broadcasters, Arnie Rutledge, Hamilton Fisher, and a couple of thin-lipped vice presidents from Braunstein and Nimoco. Rob told the viewers, "We're holding off on our announcement of the Series' outstanding player award...There's a question about whether a player from the losing team should be given the award, or whether two players could share it. The broadcasting team...that's myself, Jeff, and Cam...selects the outstanding player, but the sponsors of the award have raised an objection to our choice. The Commissioner is reviewing the situation and it seems that he'll be the one to decide...That's really all we can say at the moment."

In the narrow corridor between the dugout and clubhouse, the first few players, coaches, batboys, ballgirls, and various sundry persons scurried to evade the made-for-TV presentation of the world championship trophy. The members of America's Home Team wanted to go behind the screen and get to the real celebration, off-camera. The Commissioner, the manager, and the owner exchanged blathering kudos until an anonymous looking young woman reminded the Commish that it was time to announce the name of the Series' outstanding player. Ham Fisher led the media corps *en masse* to the losers' clubhouse.

As Mr. Commissioner gushed a stream of words about fighting spirit, a fantastic effort, and seven fabulous ballgames, Willy received sisterly kisses from Toby, Woody, and Kevin, the quartet of top contenders. Fisher said, "It gives me great pleasure to present the outstanding player award to..." Willy shut her eyes and inhaled deeply. "Toby Clay!"

Willy's eyelids opened and she hissed under her breath, "You're kidding me!" Her silent outrage and disappointment subsided when she saw Toby's happy jaunt to the podium with his pretty woman, Suzanne, in hand. After all, the award meant more to him than it did to her, which is precisely what Fisher reasoned when he made the decision.

The game ended less than five minutes ago, but the phrase "when Jed Guerin dropped the third strike" was already becoming part of the game's folkore. The catcher's error would submerge his twenty years in the bigs, follow him to the grave, and headline his obit fifty years from now. A moment after Toby took hold of the award, Peter found Willy whispering to a very sullen Jimmy Mack Jones. Then his brother smiled and kissed the lady ballplayer's cheek.

"Willy," said P.J. "I think you better do what you have to do. It's getting late."

"Let me talk to Dana and Barry first," replied Willy. "Give me ten minutes. Can you find Sam Khoury? She said she'd set it up."

"I'll take care of it," said Peter and Willy hurried away.

After midnight Dave Warren stood before his network's cameras to say, "We will be breaking to our affiliates for the local late-night news shortly, but our Series coverage will continue...We've just received word that Willy Beal has called a press conference." Dave demonstratively checked his watch. "It's due to start in about ten minutes." He looked into the camera, raised his eyebrows and chirped, "Stay tuned, ladies and gents."

Willy entered the stadium's press room still wearing her uniform and brown Wolves' cap. She nodded to Sam, who called, "Ready to go!" to several wags malingering in the corridors. "Willy's press agent!" someone snickered as Sam accompanied Willy to the front of the room with a cluster of microphones and cameras in place. Willy and Peter positioned themselves before the assembled media corps, one of whom whispered, "I don't know what she's up to, but, whatever it is, she's upstaged the whole damned Series."

A few of Willy's teammates were off to one side, near the locker room doorway. Randy Craig and Scott Bruneau stood next to Kevin McDonald, whose face was angrily contorted. "Can't you tell what's goin' on here? She's gonna quit!"

"Aw, nah," scoffed Chris as he joined them. "Why would she do that?"

Stash, standing with Irv and James, caught Kevin's eye and sadly shook his head. Kevin bit down on his lower lip and rasped, "I gotta go. I can't watch this."

"Hey, my man, maybe not..." Randy called after the second baseman as he vanished into the locker room.

Willy let out a nervous laugh, fanned herself with her palms, and spoke: "The last time I did a news conference after midnight was in June. I'd just pitched fourteen innings and lost. All I wanted to do was get into the bed and sleep, but y'all wouldn't let me. So, I guess, we're even." She hesitated, her voice wavering slightly. "I won't be back next year." Willy couldn't bring herself to use the words "quit" or "retire." There were groans of protest and disbelief from around the room as Willy struggled to steady the trembling throughout her body. Amid shouts of "Why?" she explained. "I've been pitching with untreated tendinitis in my rotator cuff since July...I know I've aggravated my condition by continuing to pitch and..." Willy was being interrupted by questions hurled from every direction. She had clearly upset a roomful of people. She didn't expect such an emotional reaction from a gang of wags. "I'm not saying I did all there is to do in baseball," she continued, "but...talk about a career year!...I had a career *in* a year!"

"Tendinitis is treatable!" came a faceless voice.

"Of course, it is," she said with a forced laugh. "But if my shoulder doesn't respond to therapy, I'll need to go in for arthroscopic surgery, which can't happen until June or July of next year..." She left a pregnant pause, then smiled as her redoubtably full voice boomed for the world to hear. "Because I'm gonna have a baby!" A few whistles came from the audience, as Willy bounced happily on her toes. She responded to shouts of "How?" by shrugging her shoulders, shaking her head, and lolling her tongue. "Now, listen to me, before my Mama jumps on the next plane to come right up here and whip my behind, I want you to know...I'm married."

She pointed at Brad Lucas, Dale Goodwyn, and Shane Hennessey, in turn, taunting, "All season long! All the prying! All the personal questions! The biggest secret of the season and all y'all missed it. Ha-ha, gotcha!" As the questions, "When? Where? Who?" flew by, Peter and Sam each grabbed an arm. Willy sang, "I'd like to introduce my husband...Michael Avery!"

"Who the hell is *he*?" a female reporter wondered aloud to another wag.

"I'll be damned!" chuckled Cathy Stafford to Dave Warren. "Willy B. Superstar, married to an accountant?"

After shepherding Michael to Willy B.'s side, where they exchanged a chaste kiss for the cameras, Peter stuck his face between them and announced, "I want everyone to know that I brought these two kids together. I guess I'm personally responsible for this marriage." Then, Peter whispered off-mic, into Willy's ear, "And *you* are personally responsible for saving mine. I don't know what you said to Charlene that night, but..." His voice choked before he finished with "thank you." The words weren't necessary.

Dale Goodwyn looked at Michael, obviously unaccustomed to being on stage, and said, "The poor guy!"

"Yeah," laughed Shane Hennessey. "He's not real comfortable up there."

"That's not what I mean, Shane," said Dale. "He's gonna have his hands full, as they say."

"That's true," said Shane, adding, "Would you trade places with him, Dale?"

"In a minute! ... Lucky bastard!"

"How did you keep it a secret?" a wag wanted to know.

"That's the beauty of a big league schedule," she laughed. "You can be on the road for three or four days...long enough to wait for a blood test, get a marriage license, and do it...and still be home in the same state. We did it in New York City on Labor Day weekend."

"How far along is your pregnancy?"

"I'm just in my second month," she replied, laughing again. "Our honeymoon was a one-night stand. So far, our *marriage* has been a one-night stand."

As most of the audience gawked at the couple, Michael showed a pained expression, "Do I need to keep standing here?" Willy suggested he go back to the hotel, telling him to stop at her locker to get her keys, wallet, and carry-all. The "honey do" list drew more than a few chuckles from the wags as Michael gratefully departed.

Brad Lucas shouted, almost bitterly, "Are you telling us that Willy Beal is going to stay home, have babies, and bake bread?"

"Well, I'm having at least *one* baby and I've baked bread before, but, like millions of women in this world, if you ask whether they work or stay home and take care of their families, the answer is *both*."

"But why quit?" Lucas barked sharply.

"I would be putting the Buffalo Wolves organization in an awkward position," she answered, completely composed. "My baby's due in June. Come next summer, I still won't be in playing condition, even if I rehabilitate my shoulder without surgery. If I do need to have surgery, I'll have to sit out next season. I'll be thirty by the time I come back to play and there are still no guarantees. Remember what happened the last time a team tried to send me down to the minors?"

As the expected laughter rolled through the room, Sam shouted to Willy, "There's a call being piped through on speakerphone."

Willy bubbled with excitement. "Is it the White House?"

"No, it's Sebastian Fabian," came the voice from on high and Willy theatrically arched her eyebrows.

"Willy, listen...I'm not sure whether the Buffalo Wolves were sent from heaven or hell to make us prove we were the best, but they never quit. There were no losers out on that field tonight, regardless of the final score...You gave a virtuoso performance. The outcome doesn't change that." Willy had no idea what to say. She simply smiled and whimsically played with the braided end of a pigtail, but there came a wave of memories and emotions inside her. Fabian said, "Samantha Khoury was right. There's never been a pitcher like Willy Beal before." *Click, click, buzz!*

Willy cast her eyes toward the ceiling in an entertainingly comic gesture, and said tentatively, "Bye, Sebastian!" with a fluttering of fingers. "Can you believe that?" she joked and then went on in a more serious tone. "No one will ever know what it was like, playing these seven games...Believe me, I wanted us to win this Series more than anything, but there are some people over there who I love a lot...and not just the players...people like Leota Douglas and Michelle Filsinger...I can't mention everybody..." She paused and took a deep breath to regain control. "More than anything, I want to thank the fans, all the beautiful people that made me feel like I was doing something important in their lives, creating something larger than myself...I always said I'm nothing special. They are!"

Peter Jones stood at the front of the room, studying Willy nimbly fielding the wags' questions, and let his mind carry him elsewhere. The Buffalo Wolves were a former fifth place team that improved itself to win the pennant. Baseball's iron law of averages predicted that the Wolves would naturally tend to revert to fifth place rather than to repeat as league champions, regardless of whether his two best pitchers, the female phenom and the senior citizen, returned or not. P.J. wanted to do double-duty as player-manager one more year. Then he planned to devote himself exclusively to running the team–unless the law of averages brings the team back to reality too dramatically for Dana and Barry's preference after glimpsing the mountain top, whereupon his managerial failure would put a simultaneous end to his playing days. Such is the natural law of rising expectations.

Even as Willy said goodbye, Brad Lucas was writing his Monday morning column: *"The idea is older than the Series, older than Big League Baseball. Do you sacrifice yourself to win one game today or save something for tomorrow? Do you sacrifice to win a championship now instead of contending for more titles in years to come? Willy Beal and Peter Jones made their choice. Baseball's greatest female star, and she was always more than its first female player, has no second thoughts. Willy the performer took center stage and brought the entire audience with her to feel the joy. Willy's personal victory is one which we all can share."* Brad declared, "This is the schmaltziest column I ever wrote," as he fingered his laptop keyboard for the final punctuation mark.

From the rear of the room, someone queried, "Where are you going to live?" That was Willy's exit cue, unrehearsed, but perfectly timed. Softly, she said, "Well, I grew up in Florida and I've lived in Virginia, New York, New Jersey, and Wyoming just this year. Michael lives and works in LA. So, we've got some choices." Willy took a deep breath and projected from deep in her diaphragm as if to sing: "Where do you think I'm gonna live? The number one sports town in the USA–Buffalo, New York! I spent the *best* time of my life there and I'll spend the *rest* of my life there." Then she signed with arms across her chest, two fingers raised, and clenched fist. "Love, peace, and power! Thank you all. I love you."

As Willy strode quickly to exit the conference room, Dave Warren rushed to her. "Who gets the live exclusive?"

Willy reached for his hand and told him, "Sorry, it's nothing against you, Dave, but I promised Robbie he could come behind the screen with me...Kindred spirits, if you know what I mean."

Willy sat on a stool next to Rob DaSilva in her locker cubicle as they waited to go live. She asked him, "Get that sweatshirt off the shelf for me, Rob," never imagining that the famous TV sports personality might be offended and, most definitely, he wasn't. She took the sweatshirt from him and pulled it over her black sports bra. "I have to protect my wholesome image," she laughed. "I can't blow it *now*."

"Never happen, Willy," said Rob, barely taking a breath before changing his voice to an on-the-air baritone, beating out the introduction and his first question for Willy. She didn't notice anyone standing behind her until Rob gestured with uplifted chin. Willy raised her head with a jolt. "Paul?" she said, turning quickly back to Rob, "I didn't see him there!" then to Paul again, "I didn't know you were there," and to Rob, a look of surprise on her face, completing the triple-take. Paul was neat, clean, shaved, and showered, and dressed in a dark blue suit and tie. Had she ever even seen him wear a tie except for the Italian-American Sports Hall of Fame dinner? "What're you doing here, partner?" she asked him, standing to lay her hands on his chest and receive a peck on her cheek.

"Zinger and I decided before the Series started, no matter how it came out, we'd come over here and find ya and tell ya...Willy, you're the best. We love ya."

"Oh, Paul, honey," she murmured, squeezing hard as they hugged. "So, where's Zinger?"

"Him and Michelle are leavin' at six in the mornin' to go up to Children's Hospital in Boston," said Paul. "They're startin' treatment right away on Mikey...I guess it looks good. They're doin' okay."

Willy stretched her neck downward to hide her face against his tie and lapel. "Shoot, I'm crying and drooling all over you."

Rob, wholly unlike his normally composed demeanor, threw his hand-held mic at his camera jockey. "Turn that damn thing off, for chrissakes."

"Aren't we on live, Robbie?" Willy asked, turning away from Paul.

Rob laughed, "We switched off for a two-minute break. You can relax."

"What about Cal?" asked Willy, returning her attention to Paul.

"He felt kinda awkward about comin' into your locker room like this," whispered Paul. "Especially after breakin' Slattery's kneecap! He said he'd give ya a call later, though."

"We're on the air in three seconds, two, one..."

"I hafta tell ya, Willy," Paul spoke carefully, knowing he was being recorded. "If anybody was gonna beat us, it should've been you guys. I'm so damned proud of ya, babe."

Paul left shortly. Only Rob, not the camera, caught the secretive intimacy of a wink as the pitcher and catcher parted. Willy wiped her eyes, rubbed her nose, drew both palms slowly down the sides of her face, and rejoined Rob. No question or prompt was needed. "I still can't believe that happened," sighed Willy. "For him to come in here like he did?...In a way, I grew up with them over there...That was really something. What a nice thing for him to do!...Sorry, Rob, I just don't have anything else to say."

When Rob asked Willy, "What have you learned from your one-year-long career in Big League Baseball?" she laughed uproariously.

"A lot of things! Let me tell you," she clapped her hands and held up a finger as if to count. "First, *there's no such thing as a natural.* I've watched hitters like Toby Clay and Roy Burton and pitchers like Brian Robbins and Gil Douglas and nobody works harder than they do...Second, *winning doesn't always come down to which team wants it badly enough.* Who didn't want to win this Series, the Diamonds or the Wolves? We both did! Next...what am I up to, a third thing?...*It isn't always about winning or losing*...and it isn't all about *money* either."

Rob DaSilva returned to his on-air voice and on-screen face to say, "I think something very special and very unusual has happened here tonight. Or, maybe, this is the way it's always been and most of us never realized it. This is not 'only a game,' as Demeter Fortune said. Neither is it a game where 'winning is the *only* thing.' One thing is certain, though. This baseball season will be remembered as the year of Willy Beal. Things won't be quite the same anymore for two reasons: because she was here and because she'll be gone."

CHAPTER 32

Willy awoke, covered in sweat and panting, in the pitch darkness of the hotel room. The clock face read 4:55. For the first time in her adulthood, after badgering by Michael and Dr. Stu Lacy, she consented to take medication: a pain killer and sedative, but nothing that would affect the baby. Yet she didn't sleep beyond her normal predawn rising. The effect of the medication, its artificially induced relaxation, no less than her physical and psychological let-down, was confusion and a dreamlike stupor. Hallucination blended daydream with nightmare and she had no idea which was real, whether the Wolves had won or lost the Series. Had she fantasized everything. Her first clear thought was to take her full bladder to the bathroom and pee. That proved a clue to reality. "I am definitely still pregnant."

Michael, cloaked in a sheet, teetered on the far side of the bed, the spot to which he retreated after Willy's sprawling seizure of territory throughout the night. He lay asleep with the pillow covering his face. Willy patted his leg. "Sleep on! The next hundred years with me are gonna be busy. You're gonna need your rest."

The Wolves took a short night flight to Buffalo, deplaning at two o'clock in the morning, when a couple thousand banner-waving, horn-blowing fans welcomed them home. The Wolf Pack's close-knit troupe already was fracturing as the time came to divvy up the postseason loot. Willy was unanimously voted a full $150,000 share, although she had been a Wolf for only a third of the season, but part-timers, including Teddy Balin, Omar Lazzaro, Glenn Dunlap, Gene Tyler, and coach Jimmy Mack Jones, were given half shares. Quarter shares were doled out to the ex-manager, team physician, and trainer. The batboys, ballgirls, groundskeepers, and clubhouse staff got zilch, except for the Christmas and Chanukah cards to come from Dana and Barry with bonus checks inside.

    Willy and Michael remained in the city to wrap up some unfinished business related to her fouled-up relationship with Art Ridzik. Two hours hence, Michael brought Willy to JFK Airport to see her off to Buffalo on a noontime flight. He had to stay another day in the Big Apple taking care of other business affairs before crisscrossing the continent to close his LA office. Willy was to begin the rest of her life alone for a week before Michael joined her on a visit with Alma in Florida, after which they would permanently plant their feet in Erie County, New York.

    Willy wore a scarf around her head, dark sunglasses, and a long cloth coat. She was beyond simple exhaustion, walking in zombielike silence and dozing off whenever she sat still for but a moment. Even "dressed up like old peasant woman," as she playfully described the day's fashion statement, several people approached her. "Willy who? Me? No, I'm some other too-tall pregnant girl with pigtails going home to Buffalo." By the time Michael pushed and dragged her to the gate, the real Willy stirred within and started to talk again. "I can't do all of that boosters and fan club banquet stuff Dana and Barry want me to do. It'll get worse when the season starts. Can you see me waddling like a duck with my big belly, throwing out the first pitch on opening day? I'll be fat."

"Don't worry about any of that now, Willy. Why don't you take a nap on the plane?"

"I'm sleepy because I'm weak from being exhausted, but I'm...too...tired," she said, flopping her head onto his shoulder.

Michael stroked Willy's cheek with his fingers, saying, "Just do what you need to do and go home."

"Home? Ha!" she scowled. "You're gonna be in LA all week long, while I'm supposed to go buy a house in Buffalo."

"It's just for a week, Willy. It takes a month to close on a house. I'll be with you soon."

"Peter did the same thing to poor Charlene last winter," sang Willy. "He said, 'Go find us a house, Char.'...'Go find us a house, Willy.' Sure, no problem, guys! Speaking of Peter, I still haven't forgiven you for telling him we were married. I could've died when I went into his office to tell him about us and he says, 'Yeah, I know. Michael told me!' I don't believe you did that to me."

"You told Sam and Paul," Michael objected softly but firmly.

"That's different," Willy said, rapping a finger on the top button of her coat. "Telling Peter could've wrecked everything. If Barry and Dana knew I was pregnant, they might not have let me pitch in the Series. Then what?" Her voice was cracking. Michael's expression was blank. Willy smiled at him, then lowered her voice, and patted his hand. "From now on, you don't talk to anybody about anything unless I say it's okay. Got that, honey?"

"Yes, ma'am," Michael replied with a mix of amusement and affection. He was relieved to put Willy aboard the airplane, but missed her terribly as soon as they parted. She was a full-time job and he had work to do. Michael hadn't told Willy that one of the pieces of business on the calendar for his trip to Los Angeles was a meeting with an attorney to review the undated, unsigned contract given to him by Mr. Kaplan and Ms. Hawthorne, $10 million a year for five years plus a million dollar bonus, effective any time Willy chose to sign it. Barry put his money on "same time next year," meaning August, while Dana guessed Willy would make her comeback after two children or two years, whichever came first.

    Samantha Khoury took a midday flight to the city on the shore of Lake Erie after Willy e-mailed her to say she was going to Pilot Field to clear out her belongings. She wanted to catch Willy there to set up dates for working on a profile and a series of articles for next year. The ideas were easy to sell to *Sportsworld*'s editors: "Willy's Life After Baseball"; "At Home with Willy, Michael, and Baby"; "First Big Leaguer to Give Birth"; and "Baby Throws First Pitch." Sam Khoury could make a career out of Willy Beal and she was sounding out the idea of ghost writing an autobiography. Sam would make sure that Willy knew she was the best friend she could ever have and would be on Willy's doorstep to visit and have some "sappy girl talk" over root tea (*Ugh!*) and croissants. Sam would carry along a jar of coffee and a coffee maker, unless Michael could get one into their new home. *Good luck, Michael!* Sam couldn't help wondering if Willy ever let him get on top. She had her doubts.

    Sam caught up with Willy in the Wolves' locker room, painfully examining every item of stuff that she packed. "Something's been bugging me, pal." Sam asked, "Why is it that all your closest friendships in baseball–Peter, James, Paul, Zinger, Cal–are all part of the over-thirty crowd?"

"I don't think age has anything to do with it," shrugged Willy. "But we come from the same subculture. We all grew up speaking the same language."

"How so?" Sam didn't follow.

"Baseball," hummed Willy. "If its lingo isn't a language, then tell me what it is. If its values, rules, and systems aren't a culture, then what are they?"

Sam sat upon Willy's three-legged stool and started to scribble notes. "So, did you start a true revolution in the baseball universe? Let's see how many more women show up on major and minor league rosters and how soon."

"I made it through the door, but there's still a long way to go. It's not only about players on the field. Bart Giamatti was ready to hire the first woman as an umpire more than twenty years ago, but, after he died, she got screwed. We've got to get people talking about recruiting female umps. We need to see Cathy Stafford doing play-by-play and Kristin Tracy working with full power as a general manager. That's when I'll know I've made a difference."

"How does that trickle down to the grass roots, to everyday people?"

"We'll see more and more girls growing up to be the women coaching their daughters...*and their sons!*"

"Speaking of which...you've picked out names, haven't you?" asked Sam, quickly changing subjects. "Jasmine if it's a girl, right?"

"Listen," Willy said impatiently, although she enjoyed Sam's company and cherished her friendship. "Why don't you call me after New Year's? Come to La Maze classes with us or something."

"You got it," promised Sam. "But do me a favor. After you do the deed, don't tell me about all the blood and guts. Okay, pal? I *hate* childbirth horror stories."

Willy chuckled and threw a punch in jest at Sam's chin, then turned the tables, posing a question of her. "Why is it that you're the *only* one–including my over-the-hill baseball peeps–who doesn't think I'm just a little bit crazy?"

"Ha! I'm a wag, remember?" Sam shifted her weight and reached for Willy's hand. "You're not crazy just because you talk to a few ghosts and have an occasional cosmic revelation or epiphany out on the pitcher's mound. Let me clue you in to the dirty little secret about people who write for a living. Writers are by nature people who hear voices in their heads."

Sam hurried away to her next assignment, leaving no pretense that her stopover in Buffalo was anything other than shoring up her professional contact and personal bond with Willy. Alone once more, Willy looked around and felt a surge of energy at the realization that this indeed wasn't the last time she would set foot in a big league locker room. Willy looked into the full-length mirror inside her cagelike locker, pulled up her shirt, and slipped her hand under the waistband of her sweatpants. Her belly button stretched and would soon disappear, her middle thickened, and the bulge in her abdomen was visible beneath her clothing. Willy closed her eyes and caressed her tummy, swirling her hands, cooing sweetly. "That's right, Jasmine, my little hummingbird. Just like your mommy, they'll say your body's not built to fly, but they're wrong." Willy walked from the locker room to the dugout and took in the view of the forever sunlit field of play. "It's in your genes, baby girl. Your mommy was the first, but she won't be the last. *We'll be back!*"

Made in the USA
Middletown, DE
06 June 2018